PRAISE FOR

D0000489

"If you want to know how the American colossus looks to the rest of the world, *Rogue Nation*, by Clyde Prestowitz, is your book. . . . The forbidding details of international commerce . . . are explained with welcome clarity, and without a trace of antiglobalist cant."
—*The New York Times Book Review*

"Prestowitz writes crisply, with chapters that are clear, digestible primers to America's problems around the world."
—*Chicago Tribune*

"A conservative's sober warning of the dangers of unilateralism and the temptations of empire."
—Joseph Nye, author of *The Paradox of American Power*

"This is a brave book that should be read by all who care about America's success. A man of impeccable conservative credentials, Clyde Prestowitz directly challenges a new orthodoxy on the right—that the U.S. should aggressively pursue its own interests regardless of what others may think. No one writes with more authority and love of country."
—David Gergen, Director of the Center for Public Leadership, Harvard University, former White House advisor to Presidents Nixon, Ford, Reagan, and Clinton.

"[Prestowitz] has a talent for making the most complex questions intelligible and fascinating."
—*The New York Review of Books*

"Clyde Prestowitz, in *Rogue Nation*, not only dares to ask timely questions that most do not dare to ask, but, more daring still, he even answers them."
—Zbigniew Brzezinski

"Prestowitz makes an authoritative contribution to the debate about the United States' role in the international system, and a passionate defense of its legacy of fostering international institutions. *Rogue Nation* is an indispensable contribution to the present debate."
—Etienne Davignon, Vice-Chairman, Belgian General Society, former Vice-President of the European Commission

"Mr. Prestowitz's book deserves to be read even by those who utterly reject his thesis for its courage, its clarity and its attempts to see the United States as all too many others see it."
—*The Economist*

"*Rogue Nation* provides a compelling analysis of the current geopolitical situation and America's role in the world. With insight gained from years of living and working abroad, Prestowitz explains how many across the globe feel disappointed and betrayed by an America that seems to be turning from the international standards it has done so much to help create over the past fifty years."
—George Soros

"Clyde Prestowitz lucidly addresses a crucial issue: Will the United States succumb to the temptation of changing roles from sole superpower working with partners to the world's imperial power in search of followers?"
—Gunther Burghardt, European Union Ambassador to the United States

"In *Rogue Nation*, Prestowitz says what Latin America has been feeling for so long: the United States needs to pay more attention to the global ramifications of its actions."
—Rubens Antonio Barbosa, Brazilian Ambassador to the United States

"Mr. Prestowitz says that 'we need to rethink American exceptionalism,' recognizing that other people's problems 'are our problems too and that we don't have all the answers.' This is not a popular message in Washington today, but that's where it needs to be heard."
—*The New York Times*

"Prestowitz's theme could not be more topical or more important: how does the world's only superpower see its role in the modern world? He throws a personal light on why so many of America's greatest admirers—among whom I count myself—have been concerned about the answer."
—Chris Patten, EU Commissioner for External Relations

"What Clyde Prestowitz has said so constructively needs saying and should be factored in to deliberations of our nation's top leaders."
—Admiral Joseph W. Prueher, former Ambassador to China

"If you want to find out how the U.S. lost the once ample reserves of political goodwill it held around the world, Clyde Prestowitz' persuasive and well-documented *Rogue Nation* is the book for you."
—*Business Week*

"I am so inspired by [*Rogue Nation*]. This is a courageous and thoughtful book, and it begins the debate about America that Americans must engage as this war [in Iraq] reaches its ultimate stages."
—Stephen Cohen, President, Institute for Middle East Peace and Development

ALSO BY CLYDE PRESTOWITZ

Trading Places: How We Are Giving
Our Future to Japan and How to Reclaim It

Asia: After the "Miracle" (co-edited with Selig S. Harrison)

Powernomics: Economics and Strategy
After the Cold War (with Ronald A. Morse and Alan Tonelson)

ROGUE NATION

American Unilateralism
and the
Failure of Good Intentions

CLYDE PRESTOWITZ

A Member of the Perseus Books Group
NEW YORK

Hardcover edition first published in 2003 by Basic Books
A Member of the Perseus Books Group
Paperback edition first published in 2004 by Basic Books

Books published by Basic Books are available at special discounts for bulk purchases in
the United States by corporations, institutions, and other organizations. For more information, please contact the Special Markets Department at the Perseus Books Group,
11 Cambridge Center, Cambridge MA 02142, or call (617) 252-5298, (800) 255-
1514 or e-mail special.markets@perseusbooks.com.

Designed by Brent Wilcox

The Library of Congress has cataloged the hardcover edition as follows:
Prestowitz, Clyde V., 1941–
    Rogue nation : American unilaterism and the failure of good intentions /
Clyde Prestowitz.
      p. cm.
    Includes bibliographical references (p.) and index.
    ISBN 0–465–06279–2 (hc)
    1. United States—Foreign relations—2001–   2. United States—
Foreign relations—1993–2001.   3. Unilateral acts (International law) .
4. United States—Foreign relations—Philosophy.   I. Title.
E902.P74   2003
327.73—dc21
ISBN 0-465-06280-6 (pbk.)

                                                            2003004508

04 05 06 / 10 9 8 7 6 5 4 3 2 1

For my kids
ANNE, CHUMMY, and BRIAN

"We are willing to become citizens of the world, but only if the world becomes an extension of the United States."

—James Warburg
Council on Foreign Relations

Contents

1   At Odds with the World—and Ourselves   1

2   The Unacknowledged Empire   19

3   America's Game   51

4   Running on Empty   81

5   Who Lost Kyoto?   111

6   In Arms We Trust   143

7   Peaceful People, Endless War   171

8   Wagging the Dog: Two Tales   193

9   Friends and Foes   227

10   City on a Hill   267

Epilogue   *285*
Notes   299
Recommended Reading   319
Acknowledgments   325
Index   329

1

AT ODDS WITH THE WORLD—AND OURSELVES

Rogue, adj.—No longer obedient, belonging or accepted, not controllable or answerable; deviant, having an abnormally savage or unpredictable disposition.

—Webster's Encyclopedic Unabridged Dictionary

Consider that wee shall be as a citty upon a hill, the eies of all people upon us.

—Governor John Winthrop

The title of this book is purposely provocative. So let me hasten to emphasize that I in no way mean to equate the United States with Saddam Hussein's Iraq or any other brutal, dictatorial regime. Indeed, I have always preferred to think of my country as the "citty upon a hill," if sometimes a bit more cloudy than shining. No, what troubles me, and has inspired my title, is that increasingly large numbers of people abroad, including many longtime friends of America, are beginning to see us, if not exactly like Saddam or other brutes, certainly as, in the words of Webster's dictionary, "no longer . . . belonging, not controllable or answerable, and with an unpredictable disposition." In fact, today's (Monday, February 24, 2003) *Washington Post* carries a front page story saying that many people in the world consider President

1

George W. Bush a greater threat to world peace than Saddam. Nor is this a recent development resulting from the debate over what to do about Iraq. Listen to the *Guardian* of London: "America, the 'indispensable nation,' begins to resemble the ultimate rogue state. Instead of leading the community of nations, Bush's America seems increasingly bent on confronting it. Instead of a shining city on a hill . . . comes a . . . nationalistic jingle: we do what we want . . . and if you don't like it, well, tough."[1] That was not written yesterday, but in the spring of 2001 at the time of the U.S. rejection of the Kyoto treaty to control global warming.

It was at that time that I was beginning to discover the depth and rapidly expanding extent of the foreign alienation from America in a series of trips during which I interviewed leaders around the world. In fact, I was on the last leg of one of these trips when, at 3:45 P.M. on September 10, 2001, I heard the last call for the four o'clock plane from San Francisco to Washington Dulles and quickened my pace. This was the last afternoon flight before the dreaded "red eye." I was tired and not feeling well and didn't want to miss it. So I ran and ducked into the Boeing 777 just as the door was closing. My travels had taken me to Tokyo, Singapore, Jakarta, and Honolulu for a series of conferences and interviews dealing with globalization and America's role in the world. As a sometime resident abroad and head of a foreign policy research institute, I had become uneasy with what I had been reading and hearing about widening gaps between America and its longtime friends.

The trip had not laid my concerns to rest. The picture of America as seen from abroad was increasingly ugly. In Asia, as previously in Europe and Latin America, I had heard rising criticism and even fear of a United States that was often at odds with the rest of the world as well as with its own professed ideals. Recent American moves withdrawing from the Anti-Ballistic Missile treaty, accelerating deployment of a national missile defense, and declaring China a "strategic competitor" had raised fears of a new Cold War. In addition, the gospel of economic globalization preached by the United States had, in the eyes of many Asians, been found wanting in the financial crisis of 1997–1998. Developing countries in Asia and Latin America suffered devastation while

American hedge funds and banks escaped unscathed. Some had even begun to see globalization as a new form of imperialism. I had also heard criticism of America's unilateralist tendencies, as evidenced by its rejection of both the Kyoto Treaty to control global warming and the international treaty banning use of landmines in the face of nearly universal ratification by other countries, including all of America's traditional allies and friends.

As I hurried home and brooded over these and other criticisms, momentous events with which we are now unfortunately all too familiar were in train that would dramatically escalate these questions of America's role and behavior in the world. As my plane lifted off from San Francisco International Airport, two obscure visitors to the United States, Mohammed Atta and Abdul Aziz Al-Omari, drove from the Milner Hotel in downtown Boston to a Comfort Inn in South Portland, Maine. Meanwhile, a National Security Directive calling for military and intelligence operations against one Osama bin Laden and an organization called Al Qaeda continued to sit on National Security Adviser Condoleezza Rice's desk awaiting presidential approval. I arrived at Washington's Dulles airport at about 12:30 A.M. on the morning of September 11 and drove home as Atta, Al-Omari, and their friends slept.

At about 9:15 A.M. I groped for the ringing phone, thinking it was my assistant Sonjai Harrison, calling to tell me she'd gotten me an early doctor's appointment. It was Sonjai, but she wasn't calling about the doctor. "Turn on your television," she commanded. After the initial horror, I couldn't help but think that the alienation had gone much further than I realized.

At a press conference shortly after the attacks, President George W. Bush was asked, "Why do they hate us?" The "they" in the question were the terrorists and their backers, including what were being called "rogue nations" and what Bush subsequently labeled the "Axis of Evil." The immediate answer to the question, however, came from a different, far more important and far more numerous "they" who demonstrated dramatically that, far from hating, they *loved* us. President Vladimir Putin of Russia, our longtime Cold War adversary, was the first to call the White House. He was followed quickly by President

Jiang Zemin of China, another country with a history of troubled relations with the United States. Jacques Chirac, president of France flew quickly to New York and became the first foreign leader to view Ground Zero. Others followed. Of course, these were the prescribed and perhaps even calculated courtesies of diplomacy. But there was no denying the genuineness of the expressions of sympathy that poured from common people around the globe. American embassies from London to Moscow to Singapore were buried in flowers. In Paris, the French flag flew at half-mast along the river Seine, and the journal *Le Monde* proclaimed in a banner headline *Nous sommes tous Américains,* "We Are All Americans."[2]

A similar attack in any other country would not have released such an outpouring of sentiment. It was as if the whole world felt the same loss of innocence as the Americans. For despite the criticisms I had been hearing, people around the world still saw the United States as the "citty on a hill" and all "eies" were upon it now because it had the potential, if it wished and as it had demonstrated over its history, to assure the triumph of hope over fear. It seemed as if people everywhere had desperately wanted there to be at least one place invulnerable to the monsters that prowl the rest of the globe. Thus, the world joined with Americans to mourn and to resolve that such devastation would not happen again. This was the silver lining to the cloud of September 11, 2001. It provided an opportunity for America and its friends to wipe away the carping and suspicions and hurt feelings of the past and, in the words of former President Lyndon Johnson and the Bible, to "come to reason together," to get back on the same wavelength, and to be present at the creation of a new, better world order.

It didn't happen. A year and a half later, the UN Security Council convened to consider how to handle Iraq's lack of full compliance with UN resolution 1441 calling for Iraq to prove that it had destroyed and halted development of its weapons of mass destruction. Noting that the resolution called for Iraq to show the evidence, and not for UN inspectors to chase all over the Iraqi desert looking for it, Secretary of State Colin Powell urged the Security Council to defend its credibility by issuing an ultimatum to Saddam Hussein to cooperate or face destruction of his regime.

Powell was followed by the French Foreign Minister Dominique de Villepin who called for more inspectors and more time for them to run around the desert. In a virtually unprecedented and strictly forbidden demonstration of sentiment, the gallery of observers broke into applause for de Villepin. The following weekend millions of marchers around the world demonstrated against war and the United States carrying signs calling America the "rogue nation." Thus, the opportunity for a new beginning seems to have slipped away. Instead of "reasoning together" we find ourselves increasingly alienated from, mistrusted by, and mistrusting of others—at odds with the world and ourselves.

While the immediate issue this winter of 2003 is Iraq, the roots of the alienation from America go much deeper and will remain long after Saddam is gone. My purpose in this book is to try to explain to baffled and hurt Americans why the world seems to be turning against them, and also to show foreigners how they frequently misinterpret America's good intentions. While I will be giving a sober view of America, I do not aim to bash it. I have spent much of my life in Asia, and may, for example, loathe North Korean leader Kim Jong-il even more than President Bush does. I am not a French socialist or an unreconstructed 1960s American flower child who didn't inhale. In fact, I am an unlikely person to write this book. The product of a middle class, conservative, rock-ribbed Republican, superpatriotic, born again Christian family, I attended Swarthmore College where, in reaction to the reigning liberal (some would say pinko) orthodoxy of the campus, I founded the college's conservative club. I went on to study in Japan and to become a diplomat in the foreign service. I volunteered for service in Vietnam, but was posted to the Netherlands instead. There in the U.S. embassy in The Hague, I was the officer responsible for defending U.S. Vietnam policy, and remained a supporter of the war long after many other conservatives had abandoned it. I went on to work for several multinational corporations and lived as a businessman in Brussels and Tokyo while traveling extensively throughout the world. In 1981, I joined the Reagan administration and eventually became counselor to the secretary of commerce in which post I was a lead negotiator in a number of commercial agreements with Japan, and participated in a wide variety of other international trade talks where I acquired a reputation as a "trade hawk." Subsequently, I founded a non-profit research organization, or "think tank," that focuses on analyses of global issues.

It is this international experience and analysis that has made me deeply worried about where we are going. For while I don't believe the United States is evil or a rogue as Saddam is, America can be like a "rogue wave," a large swell that, running contrary to the general direction of the waves, takes sailors by surprise and causes unexpected destruction. America is a big and unpredictable nation and has a long history of an alternately generous and uncaring approach to the rest of the world. While we think of ourselves as the "good guys," we are blinded to our own sometimes irritating behavior by the strength of our mythology and the dominance of our culture. I fear a dangerous gulf is widening between America and its friends as we Americans listen to but don't hear, and look at but don't see, the concerns and perspectives of other countries and at the same time also fail to recognize how some of our behavior flouts our own values. Right now we are attributing criticism of American policies to envy of our success and power and to chronic anti-Americanism. That is certainly some of the trouble, but not all of it. Perhaps we should also look at how we deal with some key issues and how our behavior is perceived and comports with our values.

The list of major concerns begins with American unilateralism and what the world sees as a peculiar American brand of "soft imperialism." Tied to this is the question of globalization as Americanization and whether it is to be embraced or resisted. Energy use and global warming are two major linked issues of global significance on which there are sharply differing views. Energy use and America's growing dependence on foreign oil, in particular, have implications for war and peace that may dramatically affect other countries. Also with great implications for war and peace are America's views on sovereignty, freedom of action, and military dominance. Of course, the issue of Israel and Palestine cannot be escaped, and neither can we ignore the hot spots of Iraq and Korea. And the question of whether America and China will be friends or enemies lingers. Indeed, the question of who are now our friends and who are now our enemies is increasingly being asked in other places as well. In the wake of the end of the Cold War and the start of the War on Terror, relationships seem to be in transition, with tensions increasing between old friends while old enemies discover each other's heretofore hidden charms. Finally, there is the overriding question of what America wants to be: the bully on the block, in the words of then Chairman of the Joint Chiefs of Staff Colin Powell; or, as most of us like to see the United States, the city on the hill.

I discussed these issues with foreign leaders during another tour of fourteen world capitals in Asia, Latin America, Europe, and the Middle East in the summer and fall of 2002. Everywhere I went I found a feeling that the United States was deliberately separating itself from other countries and blatantly asserting its right to supremacy. The best example was the situation with the North Atlantic Treaty Organization (NATO). Recently there has been much criticism of NATO in the United States because of the reluctance of some of its members to support the U.S. drive for regime change in Iraq. But for more than fifty years, the United States made NATO the cornerstone of its security strategy. In the wake of September 11, NATO invoked Article Five of the treaty for the first time in its history. This is the provision that compels all members to regard an attack on one as an attack on all and to support a military response if necessary. The decision (and it is important to remember this in view of current American irritation with the actions of France and Germany) was unanimous even though, technically, a terrorist action by a nongovernmental organization may not actually constitute an attack under NATO rules. Moreover, France, Belgium, Britain, and other NATO members not only offered but begged to be allowed to send troops to participate in the operations against the Taliban and Al Qaeda in Afghanistan. The Pentagon took a few British special forces, but told the others, "Thanks, but no thanks. It's simpler without allies. We'd rather do this ourselves. We'll call you when we need you." Along with the withdrawal from the ABM treaty and deployment of the national missile defense, this manifestation of American unilateralism is causing great resistance to U.S. efforts around the globe. Indeed, a top Malaysian leader told me, "The way things are going, pretty soon, it will be the United States against the world." American talk of "coalitions of the willing" and of preventive or preemptive war, coupled with a stated strategy of preventing the rise of any power equivalent to the United States, scares people and makes them think they are back in the jungle, or perhaps that they never left it. This fear of an imperial America, or of what the Chinese call American hegemonism, exacerbated by the "back us or be irrelevant" rhetoric is part of what lay behind the Security Council's reluctance to go along with Powell's compelling arguments. Indeed, there is a great irony here. The effort to remove an out-and-out rogue such as Saddam, was being undermined because fear of him was tempered by fear of the United States.

These sentiments were best expressed by a longtime European leader and firm friend of the United States, Etienne Davignon, who said to me, "After World War II, America was all-powerful and created a new world by defining its national interest broadly in a way that made it attractive for other countries to define their interests in terms of embracing America's. In particular, the United States backed the creation of global institutions, due process, and the rule of law. Now, you are again all-powerful and the world is again in need of fundamental restructuring, but without talking to anyone you appear to be turning your back on things you have championed for half a century and defining your interest narrowly and primarily in terms of military security."[3] Added another Atlanticist, co-chair of the Trilateral Commission and former World Trade Organization Director General Peter Sutherland in another conversation, "You no longer seem as committed to the multilateralism you did so much to foster." And yet another European, the former EU Ambassador to the United States Hugo Paemen, remarked that "Domestically you have the wonderful system of checks and balances, but in foreign policy you are completely unpredictable, and your pendulum can swing from one side to the other very quickly, while those of us who may be deeply affected have no opportunity even to make our voice heard, let alone to have any influence. This is really worrying because while your intentions are usually good, your actions are frequently informed by ignorance, ideology, or special interests and can have very damaging consequences for the rest of us."

Strange as it may seem to Americans, many people abroad feel that despite all our talk of democracy, human rights, and free trade America's real aim is to control the destiny of other nations in pursuit of its own short-term interests or ideological preoccupations. Examples are legion, as we are invested in some way in almost every country in the world. Take Korea. Americans tend to see it as a country that owes a lot to the

United States—for saving the Koreans from the North Korean and Chinese communists in the early 1950s at a cost of 36,000 American dead, and for providing much of the basis of the Korean economic miracle. More recently, Americans have seen themselves as defending South Korea by linking North Korea with the Axis of Evil, and by withholding promised food and electricity aid to the North until it abandons its nuclear weapons' programs.

Pleasing and logical as this picture appears to Americans, it can look very different from the other side. While Koreans acknowledge and are grateful for the American sacrifice in their defense, they note that the U.S. action was not 100-percent selfless but was part of a larger policy of containment of communism aimed at protecting American interests. Koreans also point out that after the end of the war, the United States supported a series of brutal military dictatorships that systematically abused the rights of the Korean people without visible protest from Washington. Kim Dae-jung, who has just finished his term as Korea's president, still walks with difficulty because of his years of torture and imprisonment. While it is true that U.S. troops still face North Koreans across the Demilitarized Zone, it is also true that our troops enjoy a kind of imperial status. One of the biggest U.S. military bases in the world is in downtown Seoul where it is a constant irritant. The recurring incidents of U.S. soldiers accidentally killing Koreans in traffic accidents, assaulting local women, and committing infractions of Korean laws have seldom led to an American's being thrown into a Korean jail or tried before a Korean court. The Status of Forces Agreement (SOFA) between the United States and Korea provides that only U.S. authorities are to deal with offenses by U.S. soldiers when they are on duty (in principle, Korean authorities have jurisdiction over off-duty soldiers, but in practice this too is restricted) .

As for the U.S. effort to destabilize North Korea, the South Koreans emphasize that they didn't ask for it and that it conflicts with the "sunshine" policy of the south, which has been trying to build bridges to the north in an effort to achieve gradual change. When I met last year with one of Korea's top foreign policy officials, he begged me to explain to Washington that South Korea cannot afford a sudden collapse of the Northern regime. "We are not West Germany," he said, "and we cannot afford to absorb the North as West Germany absorbed East Germany."

U.S. relations with China, a more significant subject for Asia and the world, show a similar disconnect. Although the improvement in U.S.-China ties through cooperation on combating Al Qaeda is one of the bright spots of the War on Terror, U.S. attitudes remain ambivalent. On the one hand we have promoted trade and investment with China, so much so that our largest bilateral trade deficit is no longer with Japan but with China as tens of billions of dollars of U.S. investment have poured into the country. On the other hand, with the collapse of the Soviet Union, we have tended to shift the focus of our defense establishment toward China as a potential threat because of its growing economy, its rhetoric about regaining its "rightful role" in the world, its nuclear weapons and upgrading of its military forces, and its insistence on eventually raising the Chinese flag over Taiwan, which it regards as a renegade province. It was partly as a result of these concerns, and in a state of some schizophrenia in view of the rapidly growing economic stakes that the United States moved ahead with the missile defense deployment and designated China a "strategic competitor." With regard to Taiwan, U.S. attitudes have been particularly ambivalent. Although we cut off formal diplomatic relations with Taiwan and affirmed a "one China" policy after President Nixon's opening to China in 1972, we have continued to maintain close economic ties with the island. Moreover, as it has recently emerged from dictatorship into a democracy and has talked of declaring independence from China, U.S. support of Taiwan has become even stronger, with President Bush announcing major new arms sales and emphasizing that the United States would "do whatever it takes"[4] to defend Taiwan.

In my travels in Asia, I found that these actions were causing more alarm than comfort. Few shared the view that China, with its eighteen ballistic missiles and a defense budget one tenth that of the Pentagon, has either the intent or the ability to become a strategic competitor to the United States in any meaningful period of time. Indeed, the Chinese leaders I met were continually expressing the fear that, in lieu of the Soviet Union as an enemy, America now wants to make China the bogeyman and to "keep China down." They pointed out that it is not China that has ringed the United States with bases or constantly patrols its coast with spy planes. They also pointed out that China's emphasis, with enthusiastic support from both U.S. industry and the U.S. government, has been on economic development, which could be retarded by large military expenditures. As one official in Shanghai said to me: "We want to sell to America, not attack it." Others, including a former U.S. Defense Secretary, noted the danger of self-fulfilling prophecy, pointing out that if we treat China like an enemy it may begin to think it is one. As for Taiwan, many Asians expressed shock that, after thirty years of carefully maintaining a "one China" policy, we might now endanger the stability of the region by changing a position on which our whole relationship with China is founded. Even in Taiwan, a majority does not support independence, nor is there much fear of a communist invasion. Indeed, it is the Taiwanese who are invading the mainland, where they have invested more than $60 billion. Nearly 500,000 have gone to live in Shanghai alone. Some Asians I spoke with wondered whether the United States just needs an enemy.

Many foreign leaders also mentioned another troubling aspect of U.S. unilateralism—inconsistency and neglect. Afghanistan, they pointed out hardly existed for Americans until 1979, when the Soviet Union invaded and established a puppet communist regime. The U.S. reaction was to fan an Islamist jihad reaction and to fund and arm the Mujahedin, including Osama bin Laden, to oppose the Soviets. Once the Soviets left the country, America lost interest and didn't say a word when the Taliban forced Afghan women out of the schools, out of employment, and back under the veil. Now, of course, America is again keenly interested. From this perspective, the United States can appear unreliable, selfish, and amoral.

A similar Janus face is seen with regard to globalization. America's economic power is as inescapable as its geopolitical presence; over the past fifty years, the United States has become the high priest of globalization, preaching free trade, open markets, privatization, deregulation, and interdependence. When economies like those of Indonesia, Brazil, and Malaysia have gotten into trouble, the United States and the international bodies with which it is closely associated (like the International Monetary Fund) have made emergency loans conditional on an end to subsidies and "crony capitalism." In endless negotiations with Japan, Korea, and Europe U.S. officials have insisted on an end to protection and subsidies for so-called sensitive sectors, and demanded the opening of markets for rice, beef, citrus fruit, and a host of other products. Preaching "trade not aid" the United States has emphasized free trade agreements such as the North American Free Trade Agreement (NAFTA) as the best road to development and growth.

So the world was heartily disappointed by the imposition of emergency tariffs on steel imports into the United States in 2001. Even more offensive was the rationale. Steel, said the U.S. government, is a "sensitive sector" suffering from surges of imports. Many around the world who had suffered the browbeating arrogance of U.S. trade negotiators could only laugh. More significant, however, was the U.S. farm bill that sharply raised subsidies for a whole range of American agricultural products. To mention the impact on just one country, as a result of emergency tariffs and subsidies, nearly 75 percent of crisis-ridden Brazil's exports would not be able to compete in the U.S. market. "So much for trade not aid," the Brazilians remarked. The situation of Mexico was even more egregious. Despite the NAFTA agreement, strict quotas prevented most Mexican sugar from entering the U.S. market. Meanwhile, Mexican sugar workers lost their jobs as heavily subsidized U.S. corn sweeteners replaced sugar in Mexican soft drinks.

Like trade, global warming has been the object of extensive negotiations over the past twenty years. As the world's biggest source of the greenhouse gases that contribute to the warming, the United States has been a key player in these talks. While the fact of warming is generally agreed upon, its causes, likely extent, and implications remain matters of debate. Because reduction of emissions could also reduce economic growth, the United States has expressed cautious concern but resisted quantitative targets until more is known. In 1992, the United States committed under the Treaty of Rio to make efforts to retard warming, but determinedly kept quotas or specific targets for emissions reductions out of the agreement. Then in March 2001, the Bush administration turned away from any treaty by rejecting eventual ratification of the Kyoto Agreement on Global Warming.

Popular at home, this move was widely condemned in the rest of the world, especially the argument that the world's richest nation couldn't join other countries in trying to stave off potentially severe environmental degradation by reducing emissions because there might be some economic costs.

When President Bush visited Göteborg, Sweden, on June 14, 2001, for meetings with the heads of fifteen European Union countries, he was greeted by hundreds of demonstrators, and the Swedish Prime Minister Goeran Persson spoke for the European leaders when he told the press the United States was pursuing "wrong policies that would endanger the environment."[6]

On no issue is the gulf between America and the rest of the world greater than on the Israel-Palestine question. For Americans, Israel is a close friend and ally. Millions of Americans have been to Israel as tourists and hundreds of thousands, if not millions, have lived there themselves or have friends and relatives who live there. For many Jewish and Christian Americans, Israel is the Bible's Promised Land of the Jews. American technology companies have made large investments in cutting-edge factories there. For nearly forty years, the United States has been Israel's chief weapons supplier, defender, and financial backer. Moreover, in the wake of September 11, Americans have come to see Israel's struggle with terrorist suicide bombers as like our own war against the terror of Al Qaeda, and President Bush's demands for an end to Palestinian violence and for new elections to replace the currently elected leaders of the Palestinians (i.e., Yassar Arafat) thus seem quite natural and legitimate in the United States. Abroad, however, several U.S. allies said that according to their understanding of democracy they would deal with whomever the Palestinians elect, including Yasir Arafat if need be. The rest of the world, while condemning the suicide bombings, also notes that the Palestinians have been under occupation for nearly forty years and that Israeli settlements in the occupied territory have grown inexorably over the past ten. This, say many, constitutes a kind of creeping, quiet violence. Indeed, some have likened it to the U.S. treatment of Native Americans during the settlement of the American frontier in the nineteenth and early twentieth centuries. In interviews with me in the summer of 2002, a number of foreign leaders emphasized that calling for an end to Palestinian violence without mentioning Israeli settlements is unfair and counter-productive.

This issue has gone far beyond Israel and Palestine and is seeping into a broad range of our foreign policy concerns. During a recent trip through Southeast Asia, I found that attitudes in countries like Indonesia and Malaysia are rapidly being radicalized. Strategically important and traditionally practitioners of a liberal Islam, neither nation has significant ties with the Middle East. Yet few conversations could get past the Israeli-Palestinian imbroglio. Every night on television, they see U.S. leaders holding pep rallies with Israeli leaders and Israelis using American weapons to attack Palestinian targets. The result is that many old friends of America conclude that the United States is attacking Islam itself. In Europe, the situation is not so emotional, but an official in Paris remarked to me that, in view of France's large Muslim minority, "U.S. policy in the Middle East could be seen as a security risk by my government."

Thus, on issue after issue, many of our friends and allies take a point of view almost completely contrary to our own. Are they idiots? Wimps? Corrupt? While it would be comforting to suppose so, the fact is that it is usually we who are the odd man out. As a nation, we are an outlier. We often don't realize it because of our very size, which tends to blinker our view of others, and of our power, which allows us to assume that our standard or our view is the globally dominant one, or should be. (Thus, on a parochial level, we cling to miles, inches, and Fahrenheit degrees even though the rest of the world long ago moved to the far simpler metric system.) The really perverse aspect of this phenomenon is that because of our power, the rest of the world accommodates us, thereby enabling us to remain blinkered.

While the rest of the world watches America carefully and takes its views into account, Americans are often unaware that other views even exist—or if aware, they don't care. The thing that most irritates foreigners about American unilateralism is not our conscious policy decisions but the obliviousness behind those policies.

Furthermore, as I shall discuss, our sense of mission and self-righteousness makes it hard for us to hear. On the one hand, we don't listen very well because we don't have to, and we tend, in any case, to believe that no one else has much worthwhile to tell us. On the other hand, the rest of the world avoids telling us unpleasant truths because it fears to annoy us. An indication of how blinkered we are is reflected in the results of a massive global public opinion poll done in 2002 by the Pew Research Center for the People and the Press. These results confirmed what I had been hearing in my travels and interviews: namely, that while there is still a reservoir of good will toward the United States, its water level is falling. Two findings, in particular, were significant for my discussion in this book. When asked if America considers others in its policy making, 75 percent of Americans said yes; but in nearly every other country, large majorities said no. A second question asked respondents to give their opinion, first, of Americans as people and, then, of America as a country. The answers showed more positive views of individual Americans than of the country as a whole. For example, in Jordan only 25 percent of respondents had a favorable opinion of the United States, while 53 percent said they liked Americans. Similar figures were obtained throughout the Middle East. All of which seems to confirm that people abroad like us better than they like what we do.

Thus while our intentions are usually honorable, we are capable of making atrocious mistakes. The attacks of September 11 are a perfect example. In retrospect, it wouldn't have taken a Sherlock Holmes to deduce impending danger from clues that were lying around, even on the desk of our National Security Adviser. But we couldn't hear because we didn't think we had to listen. Or think of Vietnam. The French had taken a terrible licking before us—but they were the French. Hadn't they given up as soon as they got a whiff of German lead in World War II? Besides, we weren't trying to reestablish some empire. Our motives were pure. We were fighting godless communism and trying to stop the dominoes from falling. There was just one problem: We didn't have a clue that communism had nothing to do with it. It was all about nationalism and independence, something that we of all people should have understood, but didn't because we didn't pay attention.

It was like a personal experience I had as a graduate student in Japan in the early 1960s. I had been studying Japanese for two years, and while not perfect, I wasn't bad either. One day at Tokyo's Haneda airport, I asked the information booth attendant a question in Japanese. In English she replied that she spoke only a few words of English and thus couldn't answer my question. I then turned to my Chinese wife, who did not speak Japanese, and told her what to say. When my wife repeated my question in Japanese, the attendant responded at once, also in Japanese with the desired information. My point is that the attendant *knew* foreigners can't speak Japanese, and so couldn't understand her own language when spoken by someone who did not look Japanese. In the same way we Americans often fail to understand because we project ourselves onto the situation.

It is not that we are always wrong while other countries are right. In the case of the Kyoto Treaty, for example, there are good arguments to be made for the Bush administration's position, as I'll discuss. But our tendency to pronounce rather than explain or even to acknowledge the legitimate concerns of others often undermines our case, even when we have the right argument. In the case of Kyoto, our unilateral approach may have the perverse effect of making it nearly impossible for us to sign onto a modified agreement that is now quite acceptable. More importantly, it has already greatly complicated our efforts to achieve support and cooperation on other more vital issues such as Iraq and the war on terror. In fact, it is because there will inevitably be times when we must act unilaterally that we should lean over backward to act multilaterally whenever we can in order to minimize resistance when we absolutely cannot.

Some may wonder, why we should care at all about what others think as long as they can't hurt us. But that is just the point. They can hurt us, in thousands of ways: for instance, by not cooperating on intelligence about terrorist activities, by not providing staging facilities or overflight rights for American expeditions, or by boycotting American products or promoting alternatives to them. The fact is that the world has become too small and too dangerous for America to ignore the truth of its own role in global affairs or to misunderstand that of others. It's time to wake up to the need to see ourselves as others see us and to decide whether we really want to be "no longer . . . belonging or accepted, not controllable or answerable." Or whether we want to be the people we imagine ourselves to be, John Winthrop's ideal echoed by President Reagan.

As you read the following chapters keep in mind that choice and its significance—not only for America's foreign relations, but for America itself, for what it was meant to be—the ideal that left our embassies abroad buried in flowers after September 11. Bear in mind also, the second, usually unmentioned part of Winthrop's sermon: "If we shall deal falsely with our God in this work we have undertaken and so cause him to withdraw his present help from us, we shall be made a story and a byword through the world, we shall open the mouths of enemies to speak evil of the ways of God and all professors for God's sake: we shall shame the faces of many of God's worthy servants, and cause their prayers to be turned into curses upon us till we be consumed out of the good land whither we are going."

2

THE UNACKNOWLEDGED EMPIRE

We Americans are the Peculiar Chosen People—the Israel of our time. We bear the ark of the liberties of the world.

—Herman Melville

Lying on the banks of the Potomac, where, after a wild dash through the mountains of Virginia and Maryland, the river broadens and turns for a final leisurely glide to the Atlantic, Washington, D.C., is one of America's loveliest cities. Its broad avenues, radiating from a central hub and punctuated by roundabouts and graceful monuments and plazas, give the city a slightly European air reflecting the taste of its original designer, the French urban planner Pierre L'Enfant. Its size and modesty set it apart from the capital cities of other great nations. With a population of less than 600,000, an area of just 68.25 square miles, and a legally mandated absence of skyscrapers, Washington is a relatively small city by world standards and lacks the powerful impact or awesome spread of a New York or Los Angeles, the grandeur of Paris, or the dense intricacy of Tokyo or London. The Greco-Roman style of the city's monuments as well as of many of its public buildings establishes a linkage with the glories of the classical past, specifically with great republics and republican institutions, not with empires and imperial traditions.

The city's statues and monuments commemorate those who have played key roles in U.S. history. Many are non-Americans. The Marquis de Lafayette, George Washington's great friend and inspiration from France during the dark days of the American revolutionary cause at Valley Forge, has the best view of the White House from his own park across Pennsylvania Avenue. Of course, Jefferson, Washington, and Lincoln, the great founders and saviors of the country, have special marble temples whose walls are inscribed with their speeches. Homage in Washington is directed toward the principles and ideas of statesmen and philosophers who championed liberty and the inalienable rights of all men. Here are no monuments to conquests or conquerors. Washington has no Arc de Triomphe, no Brandenburg Gate, no Buckingham Palace or Forbidden City. The most visited monument commemorates the only war America ever lost. Every day a steady stream of people somberly descend the gentle slope of the Vietnam Memorial near the Reflecting Pool to find the name of a friend, son, daughter, husband, wife, or lover etched on the black granite walls listing the roll call of the fallen. No general or admiral attracts such an endless flow of visitors. In Peking or Vienna or Rome, you cannot avoid feeling the proud imperial tradition. Washington displays a humbler, simpler mien, for it was never designed as the hub of an empire.

If you stroll from the Vietnam Memorial a few blocks up Constitution Avenue toward the Capitol, you come to the Ellipse on your left; from there you can see the rear of the White House. Though surely the best-known residence-cum-office in the world, it is not impressive as these things go. It pales in comparison to the 66,000 square foot mansion Microsoft Chairman Bill Gates built himself on the shores of Lake Washington, in Seattle. The grounds and gardens are pretty and well maintained, but insignificant compared with the Rockefeller estate in Pocantico Hills or the Emperor's moated and forested fortress in the center of Tokyo. Even more strikingly understated are the White House offices. I was surprised on my first visit to the Oval Office . . . at how small it is. Most CEOs of major corporations have a bigger working space. Other offices in the White House are downright laughable. The National Security Adviser, for example, barely has room for a coffee table and a visitor's chair, and his or her deputy has an office that barely holds a desk. The White House was clearly never intended to be a palace.

We Americans are schooled in an antiimperialist, antimilitarist tradition.

We learn that our forefathers and foremothers came to this land to escape the oppression, corruption, and power politics of Europe's monarchies and empires. It was Ralph Waldo Emerson's "embattled farmers,"[1] the Minutemen of Concord and Boston and the volunteers who took time off from planting and hunting to join George Washington at Monmouth and Yorktown, who won America's independence from the British Empire. It was plain-speaking Ben Franklin who, eschewing the fancy dress and manners of the European courts, outsmarted both the French and British crowns to enlarge the boundaries of the new United States of America and ensure the advance of liberty. For these early Americans, it was an article of faith that standing European-style armies, along with the "entangling alliances" (Jefferson) that they seemed to entail, were a danger to be avoided. The American tradition was long one of citizen armies raised to confront emergencies and disbanded once the crisis was over. *Empire* remains a word that for Americans means conquest and subjugation of foreign peoples against their will. It represents the antithesis of the ideals on which America was founded and the very essence of the old world wickedness Americans hoped would evaporate in the light of our own example.

As American power grew in the twentieth century, so also did the concept of the "reluctant superpower."[2] The historian Ernest May best articulated this concept when he said, "Some nations achieve greatness. The United States had greatness thrust upon it."[3] In this view, America doesn't seek power or territory; it asserts its power only under duress and for the noble purposes of ensuring peace and defending democracy. This belief has been articulated by American leaders from both political parties. Clinton administration Deputy Secretary of State, Strobe Talbott, said, "In a fashion and to an extent that is unique in the history of Great Powers, the United States defines its strength—indeed its very greatness—not in terms of its ability to achieve or maintain dominance over others, but in terms of its ability to work with others in the interests of the international community as a whole." Deputy Treasury Secretary Larry Summers added that the United States is the "first nonimperialist superpower."[4] Not to be outdone, then Governor of Texas George W. Bush told a California audience in the fall of 1999 that "America has never been an empire. In fact, we may be the only great power in history that had the chance, and refused—preferring greatness to power, and justice to glory."[5] On this point, Bush was surely in tune with the vast majority of his countrymen.[6]

Three years later, however, on June 1, 2002, the same George W. Bush spoke, now as president, to the graduating class of cadets from the United States Military Academy at West Point, and signaled a change of view that would turn two hundred years of American strategic doctrine upside down. He began predictably enough by saying, "America has no empire to extend or utopia to establish." "We wish for others," he asserted, "only what we wish for ourselves—safety from violence, the rewards of liberty, and the hope for a better life." Then, however, Bush emphasized that while the long-standing American defense doctrine of deterrence and containment might still apply in some cases, "new threats also require new thinking." He continued that "we must take the battle to the enemy, and confront the worst threats before they emerge. In the world we have entered, the only path to safety is the path of action."[7]

The first action came in less than two weeks, when the United States formally withdrew from the Anti-Ballistic Missile Treaty on June 13. Then on September 20, what was now billed as the new doctrine of "preemption" was more fully fleshed out in the annual National Security Strategy of the United States, a document every president is required to submit to Congress. The report began by asserting that the United States would not use its unparalleled military strength to press for unilateral advantage but rather would seek to create a balance of power that favors human freedom. It stressed that only nations committed to "protecting basic human rights and guaranteeing political and economic freedom will be able to assure their future prosperity." It went on to say that

> people everywhere want to say what they think, choose who will govern them, worship as they please, educate their children—both male and female—own property and enjoy the benefits of their labor. . . . These values of freedom are right and true for every person, in every society—and the duty of protecting these values against their enemies is the common calling of freedom loving people. The United States will use this moment of opportunity to extend the benefits of freedom across the globe. America must stand firmly for the non-negotiable demands of human dignity: the rule of law, limits on the absolute power of the state; free speech, free-

dom of worship, equal justice, respect for women, religious and ethnic tolerance, and respect for private property.[8]

Nothing unusual there, but then the paper spelled out how these goals were to be pursued. The president said the United States "will not hesitate to act alone" and, if necessary, will defend itself by "acting preemptively." Just in case there might be someone who had not gotten the message, the document closed by emphasizing that "our forces will be strong enough to dissuade potential adversaries from pursuing a military buildup in hopes of surpassing, or equaling, the power of the United States." In other words, we're on top, we deserve to be there, and we intend to stay there.

This dramatic new doctrine of supremacy and preemptive attack not only reversed years of American national security policy, it also struck at the heart of the Treaty of Westphalia, which has underpinned the modern international system of nation states for more than three hundred years. Signed in 1648 to end the Thirty Years War, this agreement acknowledged, as a fundamental principle of international relations, the sanctity of national sovereignty and noninterference by one state in the internal affairs of another. Bush's doctrine also seemed both to contravene the Charter of the United Nations, which outlaws the "threat or use of force against the territorial integrity or political independence of any state," and to contradict the conclusions of the Nuremberg trials that treated "preemptive war" as a war crime.

Although it came as a surprise to the world, the new policy had actually been under discussion for some time. After the collapse of the Soviet Union toward the end of the first Bush administration, the U.S. defense establishment suddenly faced an existential question. Without the "Evil Empire," what exactly was the rationale for maintaining America's large, far-flung forces and the budgets that supported them? Dick Cheney, then secretary of defense, asked Undersecretary of Defense Paul Wolfowitz to work with the Chairman of the Joint Chiefs of Staff, Colin Powell, to prepare guidelines for a new U.S. defense strategy. Powell hinted at the new strategy during testimony to the House Armed Services Committee in early 1992. The United States, he said, required "sufficient power" to "deter any challenger from ever dreaming of challenging us on the world stage." "I want to be the bully on the block," he added, so that "there is no future in trying to challenge the armed forces of the United States."[9] The new Defense Planning Guidelines, as leaked to the *New York Times* in March 1992, said that the first objective of U.S. defense strategy was "to prevent the re-emergence of a new rival," and that to achieve this, the United States must convince allies and enemies alike "that they need not aspire to a greater role." Preemptive force was to be an option, and the U.S. would maintain a substantial nuclear arsenal while encouraging others to downgrade or abandon theirs. Finally, the new guidelines suggested that in the future alliances would be "ad hoc assemblies, often not lasting beyond the crisis being confronted, and in many cases carrying only general agreement over the objectives to be accomplished."

The leak of the draft created a firestorm of criticism, and a Pentagon spokesman attempted to distance Cheney from the document by calling it a "low level draft" that the secretary had not yet seen. A watered-down version was eventually made public by the Pentagon in January 1993, but at that point it was little more than a farewell gesture as Bush *père* made way for the new Clinton administration, which promptly put the new guidelines on the shelf. Now, nine years later, a second Bush administration had taken them down, dusted them off, and adopted them as America's new national security strategy.

The move probably shouldn't have been surprising because an impressive group of forerunners had been marking the course to a new American empire for the preceding decade. Thus, former *Wall Street Journal* editor Max Boot called for American occupation and imposition of liberal democracy in Afghanistan and Iraq and possibly in other places, just as had occurred in Tokyo and Bonn after World War II. Richard Haass, a scholar at the Brookings Institute who later was to become State Department Director of Policy Planning, wrote a book entitled *The Reluctant Sheriff* in 1997. By the summer of 2002, he was saying that if he had to do it over again he would delete the adjective,[10] and conservative commentator Irving Kristol asserted, "One of these days, the American people are going to awaken to the fact that we have become an imperial nation, even though public opinion and all our political traditions are hostile to the idea."[11]

Perhaps the best picture of the new order was to be seen in Mexico in late October 2002 following publication of the new strategy document. The heads of the economic powers making up the Asia Pacific Economic

Cooperation forum gathered in Los Cabos for their annual confab held in conjunction with the CEO Summit of key business leaders from around the Pacific. At the concluding dinner hosted by Mexican President Vicente Fox, the presidents and prime ministers were seated on a dais at one end of a large hall with entertainers singing and dancing on a stage at the other end and the businessmen at round tables in between. This being Mexico, the event didn't get underway until 9 P.M. I glanced at the dais and knew many of the leaders were suffering. The Chinese President Jiang Zemin, seventy-six years old, had just arrived the previous day from Beijing. He was obviously jet-lagged, as was the Japanese Prime Minister Junichiro Koizumi. Others were in various stages of fatigue. President Bush, who had made the three-hour flight in Air Force One from his ranch in Crawford, Texas, earlier in the day, looked to be in good shape. He was seated at the end next to the Vietnamese prime minister. It didn't look as if they were having a very exciting conversation. In fact, they didn't seem to be talking at all. By 10 P.M., with no food having yet been served, we at the business tables were chewing the last of the pre-dinner crackers and polishing off our bottles of water. Just as I was wondering if Bush (famously early to bed) would make it through the entire dinner, he got up and walked out. He had to get in bed to be ready for the 6 A.M. jog on the beach the next morning. I am sure the Mexican officials had been alerted in advance to the president's probable departure. But the businessmen certainly had not been, and they noticed that Jiang and Koizumi and the others were sticking it out even if the president wasn't. One Mexican executive commented, "Who does Bush think he is, the emperor?"

THE SHAPE OF EMPIRE

It was a better question than the businessman knew. I am sure Bush doesn't think of himself as an emperor. Empires are something Europeans or Chinese or Japanese have, but not Americans. Nevertheless, if it looks, walks, and quacks like a duck, chances are it's a duck. Of course, America has few direct colonies or territorial possessions in the classic manner of the Britain and Japan of the past. But empires are also measured by their ability to project power, to compel or entice others to do their bidding, to set and enforce the rules, and to establish social norms. If we look at how the United States stacks up in that regard, the unmistakable visage of a duck begins to appear.

The aircraft carrier U.S.S. *Kitty Hawk*, which usually patrols the western Pacific from its home port in Yokosuka, Japan, is more like a nuclear-powered floating city than a mere ship. It is more than 1,100 feet long, as tall as a 20-story building, and carries a flight deck 250 feet across. This behemoth houses nearly 6,000 crew, pilots, and mechanics along with its 70 state-of-the-art aircraft. Wherever it goes it is accompanied by an Aegis cruiser outfitted to knock down incoming missiles, several frigates and destroyers, one or two hunter killer submarines, and supply vessels. The *Kitty Hawk* can steam at more than 30 miles per hour; to support the U.S. attack on Afghanistan, it covered the 6,000 miles from Yokosuka to the Indian Ocean in twelve days. This is a truly awesome concentration of military might.

The United States has thirteen of these carrier battle groups. No other country has even one.[12] And whether it is bombers, working ballistic missiles, strategic submarines, laser-guided smart bombs, ground-hugging cruise missiles, pilotless drones, or gun ships, American dominance is more or less the same. Moreover, these forces are scattered at more than seven hundred U.S. installations around the globe,[13] with 120,000 American troops in Europe; 92,000 in East Asia and the Pacific; 30,000 in North Africa, the Middle East, and South Asia; and 15,000 in the Western Hemisphere outside the United States.[14] The United States' share of the total defense spending of all countries in the world is at 40 percent and rising; it spends as much as the next nine countries combined.[15] In terms of sheer military dominance the world has never seen anything like this.

Economically, the United States looms nearly as large. At $10 trillion, the U.S. GDP accounts for more than 30 percent of the combined GDP of all countries in the world and is twice that of the number-two country, Japan. While the GDP of the combined European Union is about $9 trillion, including the newly joining countries, the EU is not yet a state and acts as a peer of the United States only in limited areas. Even so, the United States is bigger economically than all of Europe and is four times as big as Germany, Europe's largest economy. At market prices, China's economy is only a tenth the size of the U.S. economy and Russia's is less than half that. Even after the loss of $7 trillion of U.S. market value as a result of the collapse of the recent technology bubble, the capitalization of U.S. stock markets accounts for 36 percent of global market value.[16] More significantly, U.S. productivity growth is 50 percent more rapid than that of other developed countries. Moreover, the numbers are all moving in the United States' favor. As its share of global GDP, asset valuation, and productivity growth continues to rise, the United States economy will loom ever larger. One consequence is that it will be able to increase the already overwhelming size and power of its military forces while spending a smaller percentage of GDP on defense.

Nor can we ignore American leadership in key technologies or its intellectual and cultural dominance. U.S. research and development spending accounts for more than 40 percent of the global total, and in the area of medical and biotechnology research, the United States spends more than the rest of the world combined.[17] More than 85 percent of the world's computers run on Microsoft Windows or Unix and are powered by Intel or Motorola microprocessors. The software and systems integration businesses are dominated by U.S. companies like Microsoft, Oracle, EDS, and IBM, and the vast bulk of new drugs and medicines are developed in the United States. Close to 75 percent of all Internet communications globally pass through the United States at some point in their transmission. American films account for about 85 percent of box office revenue in Europe and more than 80 percent in the entire global market. In a recent survey of the top-ten movies in twenty-two countries, 191 of 220 possible slots were American.[18]

Dominance like this is unprecedented. At the peak of its empire, in the late nineteenth century, Great Britain's GDP per capita was less than that of the United States, and its defense spending was less than that of both Russia and France.[19] Nor did Britain dominate culturally in nearly the same proportion. The French did not dine on fish and chips or flock to British entertainment. Even the ancient Roman empire pales by comparison. Great as it was, it was strictly a regional operation. The Persian empire was a worthy competitor, and China's GDP was probably larger and its technology arguably more advanced.

Being big, strong, and influential doesn't necessarily equal imperialism, or if it does, perhaps the imperialism is a matter of seduction rather than coercion. In fact, America's power makes itself felt in at least three distinct ways: coercion, seduction, and persuasion.

Coercion is, of course, the most direct, and we have recently seen a particularly striking example of the resentment it causes. On June 13, 2002, two U.S. Army officers were moving an armored mine-clearing vehicle from the American military base in downtown Seoul to training grounds outside the city. As they rounded a blind curve at high speed—on a narrow road that was also the least desirable route to their destination—they hit two teenage girls, who had been walking on the pedestrian shoulder of the road, and crushed them under their wheels. As prescribed by the Status of Forces Agreement with Korea, the soldiers were not investigated by Korean authorities but were tried by a U.S. military court. In late November, they were both found not guilty and transferred out of Korea.

While hardly unique in the history of the American military presence in Korea, this incident was notable for its timing. The officers' acquittal occurred two weeks before South Korea's presidential election. Shortly after the decision was announced, fifty thousand protestors took to the streets in Seoul, and their anger galvanized the campaign of Roh Moo Hyun, a self-taught civil-rights lawyer who was running on a platform opposing U.S. policy toward the North and advocating revision of the unequal terms of alliance with the United States. Roh's opponent, Lee Hoi Chang, ran as a firm advocate of the traditional alliance and of the U.S. line. Nearly 60 percent of Koreans in their twenties and thirties voted for Roh, giving him the margin of victory and raising concern in Washington about Korean anti-Americanism.[20] Roh was elected in large part because Korean young people resent being a client state of the United States.

That is the key point. While most Americans think of Korea as a spunky, hard-working, independent ally, it is actually in many ways a satellite, and it is not the only one. Ninety miles across the Korean Straits lies Japan. Several years ago, one of Japan's leading politicians, Ichiro Ozawa, sparked a continuing debate with a call for Japan to become a "normal country."[21] Most Americans were surely not aware that Japan is an abnormal country. But Ozawa's point was precisely that Japan, too, is a client of the United States. Like Korea, it hosts many U.S. bases, and as in Korea, there are continual incidents—people run over with vehicles, fights between residents and American soldiers, rapes of local women, and so forth. Yet, the ability of local authorities to investigate and try U.S. military personnel is restricted. The most concrete example for me of the nature of the relationship occurred when I accompanied then Vice President Bush on a trip to Tokyo in the mid–1980s. At one point the vice presidential airplane needed a part that had to be flown in from outside Japan. Someone asked whether we needed to obtain Japanese permission for the route of flight, and the officer in charge responded instantly that authorization was unnecessary because "that's our airspace."

Japan's American-written constitution prohibits it from making war, and its "self-defense forces" operate within a highly restricted framework. Both Japan's and Korea's security treaties with the United States are one-way arrangements. The United States undertakes to come to the defense of these two countries if they are attacked, but there is no reciprocal obligation to defend the United States. Just as Korea's army is under U.S. command in the event of war, Japan's is effectively in the same position.

But this issue of sovereignty goes beyond military matters. During the 1997 Asian financial crisis, Japan tried to mount an independent rescue operation for the nations of Southeast Asia, only to be stopped by the opposition of the U.S. Treasury. Korea was forced to restructure its economy under the tutelage of the International Monetary Fund, which is heavily influenced by the U.S. Treasury. What Ozawa brought to light is that when the nations of the world sit down to play, Japan comes without a full deck of cards.

The only comfort here is that Japan is not alone. As Irving Kristol has noted, "It is now a fact, still short of overt diplomatic recognition, that no European nation can have—or really wants to have—its own foreign policy. They are dependent nations, though they have a very large measure of local autonomy."[22]

American power is also seductive—in two ways. The first has to do with excellence and entrepreneurial rewards. While there are many problems with the U.S. educational system, there is no doubt that it has the best universities in the world, and they are open to all comers regardless of country of origin. In fact, many of them recruit abroad. The result is that at any particular moment there are about 600,000 foreign students studying at U.S universities, and over the years literally millions of foreign students have graduated with American degrees.[23] Many leading graduate programs in science and engineering at elite schools like Berkeley or the Massachusetts Institute of Technology draw a majority of their students from overseas.

America is also the world's mecca for entrepreneurs. Silicon Valley is national-origin blind when it comes to funding and nurturing good ideas. In 2000, for example, more than 40 percent of the new companies established in the valley were started by Indian entrepreneurs, many of whom have subsequently started major operations in their home country.[24] This arrangement is good for the entrepreneur, good for the United States, and good for India. If your thing is not starting companies but hitting baseballs or stuffing a basketball through a hoop, America is again the place for you.

The second manner of seduction is less about excellence and more about persuasion. Take that most successful of all international companies Coca-Cola. With sales of $20 billion and two-thirds of its revenue coming from international markets, it might seem to have little to worry about. But it does worry, a lot. To keep attracting investors and talent it has to keep growing. When you are as big as Coke, that means adding billions of dollars of sales every year, and when you have already penetrated much of the world market, you begin to wonder where your growth is going to come from. Fortunately there are a lot of people in places like India or Indonesia who still drink tea or water, and while "thirst cannot be manufactured, taste can be. . . ."[25] So Coke invests some of its enormous income in advertising (often using American success images) to convince Indians and Indonesians that Coke is the cosmopolitan thing to drink. While tea is probably better for you, it doesn't have that American image of success, so people around the globe keep switching to Coke, and Coke keeps growing.

Through military might, unequal treaties, intellectual excellence, entrepreneurial reward, and friendly persuasion, America has established an unprecedented condominium over the globe. The answer to my Mexican business friend is that whatever he thinks he is, Bush is the emperor.

THE MAKING OF AN EMPIRE

Although born in revolt against empire, America harbored the seeds of its own from the beginning. Two kinds of people ventured to the New World to establish colonies in the early seventeenth century, both in search of their destinies. To Virginia with Captain John Smith went the adventurers and artisans in search of fortune. To Massachusetts with Governor John Winthrop went the pilgrims and puritans in search of paradise. Those two searches have driven American expansion ever since.

There was—to begin with—a certain duality in the minds of the country's founders. On the one hand, Washington and Jefferson warned against entangling alliances, and John Quincy Adams famously noted that "America does not go abroad in search of monsters to destroy. . . . She might become the dictatress of the world. She would no longer be the ruler of her own spirit." Yet it was Jefferson who dreamed of an "empire of liberty," who boldly doubled the country's size with his purchase of the Louisiana Territory and who imagined a time when "our multiplication will cover the whole northern if not southern continent." Adams echoed him, saying, "North America appears to be destined by Divine Providence to be peopled by one nation." Actually, the unilateralist attitude toward foreign countries and the expansionist spirit were two edges of the sword called American Exceptionalism.[26]

From the start, Americans saw themselves as an exception to the normal run of nations. Having formed the first republic since classical times, they saw it as the start of a whole new human history. As such, it was not to be contaminated by reliance on or adoption of the ways of peoples of the old history. At the same time, Americans were convinced that they were a beacon to mankind, and came to think of themselves as, in the words of the chapter epigraph, "the Peculiar Chosen People—the Israel of our time." If Americans were the chosen people, then America was the Promised Land. "Manifest Destiny" was the term for the doctrine that Americans must create one nation spanning the continent from sea to sea. By 1885, that had become a reality. Of course, it was a reality that came at the expense of Mexico, which lost half its territory in an American-instigated war, and of Native Americans who were nearly exterminated. That reality somehow went unnoticed at the time, garbed as it was in the rhetoric of what President Andrew Jackson called "extending the area of freedom."

This area was about to take a quantum leap by the end of the nineteenth century. With the materialization of its manifest destiny, America's expansionist spirit turned toward foreign shores. In fact, the United

States was no stranger abroad, having already fought overseas on more than one hundred occasions. Indeed, the U.S. Navy had been patrolling China's Yangtze River since the 1840s. But in 1898, President McKinley asked Congress to authorize use of force to protect American interests and halt Spanish oppression of Cuba. Said McKinley, "We intervene not for conquest. We intervene for humanity's sake" and to "earn the praises of every lover of freedom the world over." But when the end of the war left the formerly Spanish Philippines in American hands McKinley, after much "prayerful agonizing" (and despite a declaration of independence by the Filipinos) concluded, "There was nothing left for us to do but to take them all, and to educate the Filipinos, and uplift, and civilize, and Christianize them."[27] Thus the Philippines became an American colony after four hundred years as a Spanish one.

Woodrow Wilson, who presided over no major expansion of American controlled territory, nonetheless articulated McKinley's sense of mission in a new way with profound implications that would reverberate down to our own time. First, he waited until German submarine attacks "pushed" America into World War I, and when he led the country into the war, it was for the purpose of making the world "safe for democracy." His League of Nations failed because, it was said, of isolationists in the U.S. Senate. Actually, however, the opposing senators had been enthusiastic supporters of U.S. colonial expansion; they weren't isolationists. Rather they rejected the League because they were unilateralists. In a way, this was American exceptionalism, versus American exceptionalism, and if Wilson lost the first round, he nevertheless established the tone and framework of American foreign policy for the rest of the century.

American policy and objectives in World War II were almost totally Wilsonian. Said President Roosevelt upon declaring war: "We fight not for conquest, but for a world in which this nation and all that this nation represents will be safe for our children."[28] America, of course, emerged from the war as the overwhelmingly dominant power. Yet, it did something no such power had done before. Rejecting its old tradition of unilateralism, it laid the foundation for a new world of multilateralism. It is fascinating to speculate on how the world might look had there been no Cold War. But there was, and President Truman chose to respond in the now familiar way, saying, "If we falter in our leadership we may endanger the peace of the world and we shall surely endanger the welfare of this nation."[29]

The policy of containment, by which America and its allies outlasted communism in the Cold War, was built on several supports. First, the United States defined its national interest in terms of entangling itself in alliances and multinational institutions aimed at preventing the spread of communism and, where possible, at preserving and promoting democracy, the global rule of law, nonaggression, and due process. Second was the maintenance, apparently permanent, of a very large standing military force, which entailed the expenditure of 3 to 10 percent of GDP on defense and the creation of an enormous and powerful military-industrial complex.[30] Third was a habit of expediency. With full knowledge that such actions undermined its credibility as an advocate of freedom, the United States frequently backed dictators and authoritarian rulers as long as they professed anticommunism. (The Shah of Iran, Ferdinand Marcos in the Philippines, and a succession of military dictators in Latin America, South Korea, Pakistan, and Taiwan come readily to mind.) Finally, free trade and open markets became inextricably entwined with the promotion of democracy, the view being that free-market economic policies would lead to political liberalization. These policies were also, of course, good for U.S. commercial interests. The Cold War was thus won through the classic American quest for both fortune and paradise that I mentioned earlier.

In the sudden absence of any threat to U.S. security and with most of the world rushing to adopt democratic politics and market capitalism along with free trade, it almost seemed there was nothing left to debate. In his *The End of History*, Francis Fukuyama heralded a new era in which the adoption of the universal U.S. or, more broadly, "western" values and systems would establish global prosperity and peace. Now that American values had apparently triumphed, here was the moment when the nation could step back, dramatically reduce its military establishment, close many of its far-flung bases, revise American commitments abroad, and lead the world by example. The U.S. could stand fast as the "Citty upon a Hill," glad to have "the eies of all people upon us," as the Governor John Winthrop had envisioned centuries ago.

But while U.S. forces and spending were reduced, their presence abroad remained large, and their proportion of the world's military force and expenditure actually grew, as former Soviet and other forces melted away. The hegemony America had exercised during the Cold War began sliding toward supremacy. During the Cold War, America had been *primus inter pares*, the first among equals. It was the leader of its various alliances, but still had to consult and achieve some measure of consensus. Now it moved toward complete dominance. Driving it were the forces of inertia and habit, the interests of a large professional military, a resurgence of the do-good Wilsonian strain of American exceptionalism and unilateralism, the Gulf War of 1991, and an enhanced economic agenda.

Still, in the absence of a strong opposing power, certain contradictions began to surface. If our example was so powerful, why did we need all these soldiers and guns? The initial answer from the strategists was that a weakened Soviet Union could unleash instability and regional conflicts that only the United States could manage. U.S. forces would have to remain preeminent to ensure that the emerging order would be shaped in accord with American interests. The Gulf War strengthened this thinking. But behind it was a larger rationale: If history had ended, it had left winners and losers. At a 1997 press conference, President Clinton chided China for being on the "wrong side of history"[31]; and in a speech in Hong Kong in July 1998, he said that America had come to define "the right side of history."[32] America was now at a moment, in the words of House Speaker Newt Gingrich, Republican from Georgia, "of unmatched wealth, power, and opportunity" to direct the world's destiny, and that opportunity was not to be squandered.[33] Clinton was echoed by future National Security Adviser Condoleezza Rice, who in 1999 told the Los Angeles Foreign Affairs Council that the essential question was whether the United States would "accept responsibility for being on the right side of history."[34]

A big part of the "right side of history" is globalization, the removal of all barriers to the movement of goods, information, money, and people and the creation of one integrated worldwide system of commerce. As the *New York Times* columnist Tom Friedman said, "We want enlargement of both our values and our Pizza Huts."[35] America's role, according to President Clinton, was to be "at the center of every vital global network" that "dramatically increases our leverage to work with people for peace, for human rights, and for stability." In this context, the strategy of America's immense military machine became one of "engagement" to "shape the international environment" in ways conducive to the advance of the "right side of history."[36]

At first, the election of President Bush in 2000 suggested a new direction. During the campaign, Bush had said, "If we are an arrogant nation, they'll view us that way. But if we're a humble nation, they'll respect us." He had also advocated reducing America's many foreign commitments and warned against "nation building."[37] But early into the new administration, the terminology for China was changed from "partner" to "strategic competitor," and the need for scrapping the ABM Treaty and building a National Missile Defense was reemphasized in urgent terms. Whatever potential might have existed for new directions was definitively erased by the events of September 11. Speaking to Congress on September 20, the president said, "Freedom itself is under attack." In his West Point speech of June 2002, where he spoke of promoting our model of human progress "based on the nonnegotiable demands of human dignity, the rule of law, limits on the power of the state, respect for women and private property and free speech and equal justice and religious tolerance," he added, "we have a great opportunity to extend a just peace by replacing poverty, repression, and resentment around the world with the hope of a better day." Thus did Bush unwittingly declare himself emperor of a dominion whose "recognition," in the words of the Protestant theologian Reinhold Niebuhr, we are "frantically avoiding."[38]

THE SPIRIT OF EMPIRE

"It has been our fate as a nation not to have ideologies, but to be one."

—Richard Hofstader

America is the only country with an "ism" attached to its name. "Americanism" is a familiar word (more commonly heard in the negative, "anti-Americanism," but we never hear "anti-Japaneseism" or "anti-Germanism"). Other countries are typically birthright communities whose identity derives from a common history and heritage. But America was founded on a set of ideas, and one becomes an American by converting to those propositions in what Emerson called a "religious experience." As the English writer G. K. Chesterton noted, "America is the only nation in the world that is founded on a creed."[39] Richard Hofstadter took it a step further with his comment that serves as epigraph to this chapter.[40] The key principles of that ideology are liberty, equality, individualism, populism, and limited government.[41] Seeing themselves as a chosen people laboring in God's vineyard to create a new, perfect society, Americans find in these values their true religion. They may differ vigorously on everything from God to football, but none will question the validity or universality of these propositions.

In the wake of September 11, American flags were displayed, it seemed, in every available space. Every speech ended with the words "God Bless America." Having just returned from abroad, I knew how strange and irritating this must have been to foreigners. When Irish Republican Army terrorists had carried out attacks in Britain, or Algerian terrorists in France, or Aum terrorists in Japan, those nations were not suddenly bedecked with flags and their prime ministers didn't call for God's special blessing. Did the Americans think they were somehow more sacred than others? No—but they were certain they had a better, more sacred idea than others. President Bush expressed it perfectly when he said that "freedom itself has been attacked"—not the World Trade Towers or the Pentagon or America, but something much more important: Freedom, the creed, the true religion, the only thing that provides hope for a better world.[42]

Because Americans believe in the universality of Americanism, they don't see themselves as being better or more sacred so much as being in the vanguard. The nice thing about this religion is that it is a kind of super church that anyone can join regardless of other beliefs or associations. Indeed, the chief reason Americans are blind to their own empire is their implicit belief that every human being is a potential American, and that his or her present national or cultural affiliations are an unfortunate but reversible accident. Emerson wrote that America would be the "first nation of men"—the first nation of individuals rather than of kings or classes, but it would not be the last.[43] Americans see themselves as showing the way for others, and in their view, the rest of the world wants to follow. When American leaders promise to promote the spread of freedom globally, what they have in mind is Americanism.

This creed, is powerfully attractive in many respects—in none more than in the assertion of equality. In the American creed, equality doesn't mean equal social status or equal reward; it means equal opportunity. The earliest colonists came to the new world to get rich, and the creed has promised all its adherents the same opportunity for now and evermore. As the American historian Frederick Jackson Turner noted, "Since the days when the fleet of Columbus sailed into the waters of the New World, America has been another name for opportunity, and the people of the United States have taken their tone from the incessant expansion which has not only been open but has even been forced upon them. . . . The American energy will continually demand a wider field for its exercise."[44] For most of our history, America has been open to newcomers and has been the place where talent, entrepreneurial skills, and hard work can expect a just reward (or better), and nothing is impossible. I once wrote, in comparing Japan and the United States, that in Japan everything is prohibited unless expressly permitted, while in the United States everything is permitted unless expressly forbidden. It is that freedom, perhaps even more than political freedom, that makes America a magnet for immigrants and a source of hope for many peoples around the globe. Adding to the attraction is our tolerance and the inclusiveness of our immigrant society. As long as you hew to the Creed, you can be almost anything you want.

In particular, you are free as far as your other religion is concerned. Despite fears to the contrary, the founding insistence on the separation of church and state was a stroke of genius for ensuring the vigor and power of the churches. While established churches in Europe became entwined and synonymous with aristocracies and authoritarian governments and began gradually to die, the independent churches of America thrived. Tocqueville noted in the 1830s that Americans were the most religious of people, and that has remained true to this day. On any given weekend, more than half of all Americans will attend a place of worship, as compared with 10–20 percent in most European countries and Canada. In this regard, America is more like the Muslim societies.

The tone of religious life in the United States has always been set by the Protestant sects, which emphasize an individual and personal relationship with God and thus promote strict adherence to a moral code established directly between man and God. The result has been a strong strain of moralism running through American history and particularly through the American view of other nations.

The combination of this religiosity with the anything goes spirit of equal opportunity has produced mixed results. The most dramatic and powerful has been the flowering of talent that has produced America's great wealth and its leadership in technology, medicine, the arts, and university education. Not only does America have the highest standard of living in the world and the overwhelming majority of the world's richest people, it is also by far the leader in charitable giving. Great universities such as Stanford, Harvard and Yale owe their existence to the generosity of philanthropists. Andrew Carnegie, who proclaimed that "the man who dies rich dies disgraced," lived up to his words. Americans with a personal fortune of $10 million give away about 9 percent annually, and the average American gives to church and charity more than 2.2 percent of his or her income. Altogether, U.S. contributions make up about 1 percent of national income compared with about a half percent for Europe and less elsewhere.[45] Part of the reason for this, and for the success of equal opportunity, has been a steady improvement in social justice over the years. Although it lasted for a long time, the contradiction of a religious people dedicated to the proposition of equality, while practicing racial discrimination, ultimately could not be maintained. Not only has it been resolved by a slow cessation of discriminatory practices (a process that is still working itself to completion), but this resolution has occurred largely nonviolently, because the morality of Americans can't, in the end, accept brutality.

On the other hand, a good mythology can cover a multitude of sins. It is an interesting contradiction that a country whose religious views have circumscribed abortion makes frequent use of the death penalty. This mystery highlights other peculiar aspects of U.S. society. More than fifteen thousand people are murdered in the United States each year—far more per capita than in any other industrialized country and a rate that may or may not be related to the fact that the U.S. civilian populace is armed to the teeth.[46] American jails are also fuller than those of any other major country. Nearly one in every eight American men has been convicted of a felony, and one in twenty has been in jail (for black men the ratio is one in five).[47] With 5 percent of the world's population, the U.S. accounts for about a fourth of the world's prisoners.[48]

The economic contradictions are equally striking. The gap between rich and poor in the U.S. is very large for such a wealthy country. In 1998, for example, about one in eight Americans was living below the poverty line, and about 20 percent of them were children—in each case about double the figure found in Western Europe.[49] The lack of a national health plan means that more than 40 million Americans lack health insurance. At the same time, the rich are doing outstandingly well: The top 1 percent of American households have accumulated more wealth than the entire bottom 95 percent. In this, too, America leads the developed world. Interestingly, none of this seems to make its citizens terribly unhappy. The myth of equal opportunity is so powerful that Americans don't scheme how to bring the rich down; instead, they focus on how they can get rich, themselves.

So when American leaders speak of enlarging the realm of freedom, what does this mean for the outer reaches of the empire?

The American creed is inherently generous. To the extent that they think about it, Americans want opportunity not only for themselves but for the world. Unfortunately, Americans don't think too much about the world because they see themselves as the only world that matters. It was no accident that during the Vietnam War, soldiers would talk about going home as "going back to the world." Americans, in general, don't learn foreign languages (U.S. universities graduated nine Arabic speakers in 2002)[50] or travel abroad, and most couldn't find the "Axis of Evil" countries (Iraq, Iran, North Korea) on the map. America is where the opportunity, the new ideas, and the stars of whatever profession are, and anything outside is marginal almost by definition. An important aspect of the American empire is that because Americans don't see it as such, few look at the totality or thinking about where it is going and what it needs, and certainly no one is in charge. This inattention creates neglect and incoherent, often contradictory policy initiatives.

Indonesia, for instance, is not only the world's largest Muslim country but also one of the few Muslim countries with a secular, democratic if fledgling government. When I met with its leaders in the summer of 2002, they were desperately trying to create the basic structures of democracy—things like a constitution, town councils, nonmilitary police forces, and independent judges and magistrates. Some of the top Indonesian officials pleaded for American assistance, and U.S. Ambassador

Ralph L. Boyce did his best to respond. But since the Cold War, U.S. diplomatic representation in Indonesia had been cut by more than 50 percent, and Boyce was severely limited in what he could do.

Nor is this true only of Indonesia. The *New York Times* reported in July 2002 that U.S. diplomatic posts in countries ranging from Saudi Arabia, to China, Russia, and Pakistan are severely understaffed.[51] A few months earlier, the *Times* had reported the rapid growth in Pakistan of fundamentalist Islamic Madrassas (schools) that are filling the void left by the collapse of the government's budget. Canada, in response, was foregoing—as the U.S. was not—repayment of its loans to the Pakistani government in exchange for spending on education.[52] Another *Times* story in July 2002 reported that the United States had withheld $34 million in funds designated for the U.N Population Fund because of fear that the money might help the Chinese government implement its programs of coercive abortion.[53] Never mind that only $3 million would have been spent in China, or that its purpose was specifically to counter coercive abortion by demonstrating the effectiveness of voluntary family planning. Never mind that the U.S. Department of Health and Human Services was simultaneously announcing cooperative programs with the same Chinese Health Ministry being denied the population funds. The denial of funds to the UN still makes no sense except as political grandstanding. As the American writer Gary Wills has asked, "How can we tell other countries they can't have abortion counseling when it is legal here?"[54] We can and do because in the United States abortion is an issue freighted with religious significance, and we see all these other countries as America wannabes. Other than in that light, nobody thinks about them very much.

Unless, of course, something gets in the way of opportunity or something nasty occurs. Either one inevitably draws a focused response. In the event of a blockage of opportunity the response may be one of overwhelming pressure. In the mid–1990s, for example, massive illegal copying of Microsoft Windows software in China was killing Microsoft's business there and elsewhere. The same U.S. government that cut diplomatic representation in Indonesia in half, and didn't care a fig about the state of schools in Pakistan, pulled out all the stops and got the Chinese government to crack down hard on the pirates. I know, because I was an advisor to the U.S. government at the time. In the case of something nasty, the response may be much more deadly.

Samuel Huntington has pointed out that the American creed and identity have been largely developed in opposition to an undesirable "other," which is always defined as liberty's opponents.[55] Initially, the other was the aristocratic oppression of Britain and then, more broadly, of feudal, monarchic, imperialistic Europe. Later, the United States metamorphosed into the leader of the European-American civilization against threats to that civilization from imperial Germany, Nazism, fascism, and Japanese militarism. Afterward, the U.S. defined itself as leader of the free world against the Soviet Union and world communism. In each instance, the effect of America's religiosity has been to make the contest a moral crusade. Because Americans are expected to act in accord with their conscience, they find it difficult to support what seems an unjust war, or one fought for mundane or self-interested reasons. To endorse a war, Americans must see themselves on God's side, fighting for good against evil. And because the fight is against evil, the victory must be absolute, and surrender unconditional.

This is the response the events of September 11 have triggered. This is why President Bush says that "you are for us or against us" and "we'll get them dead or alive." And why he echoed Ronald Reagan's "Evil Empire" with his own "Axis of Evil." To be worth fighting, the enemy's villainy must also be absolute.

It is against this background that the United States is pursuing what State Department Policy Planning Director Richard Haass calls the doctrine of integration. It is aimed at integrating "other countries and organizations into arrangements that will sustain a world consistent with U.S. interests and values and thereby promote peace, prosperity, and justice." The doctrine is to be based on persuading governments and people to sign on to the "nonnegotiable demands of human dignity: rule of law, limits on the power of the state, respect for women, private property, equal justice, and religious tolerance." These values are "not narrow American values that benefit Americans only, but universal values that would benefit people everywhere."[56]

Such statements pose obvious questions, the main one being how all this is to come about. The answer seems to be through continued promotion of globalization, coupled with "coalitions of the willing," to effect changes of regimes that we deem dangerous. In this context, globalization is seen as a kind of "soft power"[57] that will induce integration within the empire by dint of others wanting voluntarily to do what we want them to do. It is believed that people will see integration as the way to prosperity, that prosperity will yield liberalization and democratization, and that these in turn will lead to permanent peace and stability. This soft power, exerted by American markets, culture, and institutions, is seen by the cognoscenti as a kind of secret, unique weapon that, in contrast to the Roman and British examples, will make the American empire a voluntary one that remains largely unacknowledged because it will be based on cooperative arrangements led by the United States and held together by the glue of American soft power. Although the experience of the past fifty years provides evidence to support this seductive scenario, there are two caveats. First, the contrast with other empires is a misreading of history. The Roman empire ruled not primarily by force but by extending its system of law, culture, and even the rights and duties of Roman citizenship to other peoples. Rome often preferred indirect rule and usually used force only as a last resort. As Montesquieu noted, "It was a slow way of conquering."[58] By the same token, the British empire was famously acquired "in a fit of absence of mind."[59] And it was the British statesman George Canning who said, "Commerce without power wherever we can, Commerce with power if we must."[60] The Romans and the Brits eventually found that hard power not only led but also seemed to follow soft power.

The second caveat follows from the first. Thomas Friedman calls globalization the international system that has replaced the Cold War. There is no doubt that globalization can create wealth and interdependence, powerfully challenge old concepts, and spread new ideas. As former French Foreign Minister Hubert Vedrine says, "America can inspire the dreams and desires of others thanks to its dominance of global images." But what kinds of dreams and desires, based on what values, and within what political and social framework? (When I recently turned on the TV in a Jakarta hotel room, the first channel I found was showing *Baywatch*.) As Hong Kong's Securities and Exchange Director Andrew Sheng told me recently, "American values can only thrive with huge resources at your beck and call. If we assume that what you have in the United States can be had by all, we're crazy. For starters, just think if everyone consumed like Americans. It would be an environmental disaster."

Globalization is driven by markets, but markets are amoral and Darwinian, and consumption is their anti-God. Michael Prowse notes that "utility maximization in which morality has no place has for many become a total philosophy of life, but it is not consistent with good social behavior."[61] The fantasy of the last decade that no two countries with McDonalds' restaurants would fight each other evaporated with the Serbian repression in Kosovo and child soldiers in Sierra Leone wearing shirts with the emblems of their favorite U.S. sports teams as they lopped off prisoners' hands. The modern democratic nation-state is a vessel of values in which the public good trumps private interests. But capitalism is inherently uninterested in nations and their values. Until now, nations have tamed capitalism by imposing certain value-based restraints. But globalization attacks and undermines the nation state and its values. Ironically, although globalization in some ways promotes interdependence and international cooperation, it also reinforces the fragmenting forces of what the writer Benjamin Barber calls "jihad." Indeed the forces of the terrorists are much more effectively globalized than those of the current integrationists, and an ironic result of the open world the United States is promoting is that it has made America less rather than more secure.

Jihad even resonates, in a peculiar but significant way, in the heartland of the empire. Home schooling has become a booming business in the United States, with 1.5 million students currently in various programs and increasing by 7 to 15 percent annually.[62] The cause of this rise is primarily the desire of religious parents to avoid having their children imbibe the materialistic values of globalization. The conundrum was framed perfectly, if unwittingly, by President Bush when he told Americans they were now at war, and it was their patriotic duty to keep the economy running by consuming more. Thomas Friedman has suggested that "the emerging global order needs an enforcer," and that this is "America's new burden."[63] But he never says what exactly America will be enforcing and how. Will the United States use force to sell *Baywatch*? Will it do so alone, or with allies?

Presumably, the answer is that it will enforce the nonnegotiable, universal demands with the help of "coalitions of the willing." But here arises the question of the true universality of those demands. Bush's demands are almost a perfect match for those of Woodrow Wilson in 1917, with one striking addition—respect for women. This new universal value Americans discovered only recently. Is the American definition of respect for women in fact a universal value whose fulfillment is nonnegotiable? Or take limits on the power of the state. Virtually every country in the world disagrees with how the United States sets these limits. They would increase the state's powers in many instances—for example, by strictly regulating guns—and make them more humane in others—for example, by abolishing the death penalty. If we are looking for coalitions of the willing, the evidence suggests that many countries don't accept the universality of our values and are becoming increasingly unwilling.

SENTIMENT IN THE EMPIRE

In the cold winter of 1948, one of the first major confrontations of the Cold War took place in West Berlin. Located in the heart of the Soviet zone of occupation, West Berlin was an enclave of freedom occupied by U.S., British, and French troops in the midst of the Soviet armies. Not wishing to attack directly but intent on taking over all of Berlin, the Soviet authorities imposed a blockade. They would not supply the enclave, nor would they allow supplies to be trucked in from the west through the territory they occupied. In a desperate improvisation, U.S. forces launched the now legendary Berlin airlift, flying thousands of tons of supplies daily into Tempelhof airport, while daring the Soviets to stop them. It worked, and West Berlin remained a beacon of freedom for forty years, until the fall of the Berlin Wall finally reunited the two halves of the city. Berliners and American presidents have always had a special relationship. It was in 1963 that President Kennedy told the city "*Ich bin ein Berliner*" (I am a Berliner) to uproarious cheers, and it was in 1987 that President Reagan heard the same cheers when he called on the Soviet leader Gorbachev to "tear down this wall." But when President Bush visited the city in May 2002 he was met with jeers, not cheers. What had happened?

To find out, the Pew Research Center for The People and The Press undertook a massive survey of global public opinion on the United States, interviewing more than 38,000 people in 44 countries during the spring and summer of 2002. For an American, the results are both positive and disquieting. On the one hand, they demonstrate a vast store of good will toward and admiration of the United States from around the globe. At the same time, they reveal that these sentiments are declining, while mistrust and dislike of the United States are rising. Perhaps most significantly, in a number of areas the views of Americans are dramatically divergent from those of virtually all other peoples, and those who know us best are showing the steepest declines in positive sentiment. In every country surveyed, except Argentina and those in the Middle East, people having an overall favorable view of the United States account for well over half of respondents. At the same time, the favorable percentage has declined virtually across the board. For example, in 1999, 78 percent of Germans said they had a favorable view, while in 2002 that percentage had declined to 61 percent. In Great Britain, the percentages were 83 favorable, falling to 75 percent. In Indonesia, it was 75 percent, falling to 61 percent; Japan, 77, falling to 72; Argentina, 50 percent, falling to 34. A few went the other way. France, interestingly, climbed from 62 to 63 percent while Russian went from 37 to 61 and Nigeria from 46 to 77. But the overall trend was down, and in countries like Turkey, Pakistan, Jordan, Egypt, and Lebanon, the United States was rated unfavorably by about 70 percent of respondents. As shown in Chapter 1, many respondents have a much more favorable rating of our people than of our country. Thus, for example, only 25 percent of Jordanians rated America favorably, but 53 percent rated Americans favorably.

America and its neighbors differ widely in their views of the world's gravest dangers. For Americans, number one is nuclear weapons. Except for, understandably, Japan, no other country has this at the top of its list. Pollution and the environment rank lowest among U.S. concerns but high everywhere else, particularly in Asia. AIDS and infectious disease are also major concerns elsewhere but not so much in the United States. Religious and ethnic hatred is the leading candidate in Europe, the Middle East, and much of Southeast Asia and Africa, but again not in the United States.

America is most admired for its technology and science, with large majorities in every country scoring a favorable impression here. With a few exceptions such as India, Bangladesh, and several Middle Eastern countries, American pop culture is also a big winner, with two-thirds of Europeans and Latin Americans and more than half of Asians saying they like it. In a seeming contradiction, however, no one seems to approve of the spread of American customs and ideas. More than half of Canadians, two-thirds of Europeans and Asians, and more than three fourths of those in the Middle East viewed these unfavorably. American ideas on democracy received a more mixed, but in some ways more disturbing reaction. In Africa and Asia outside of India, these ideas are received quite favorably, but opinion in Latin America and Europe is divided fairly evenly. In Britain, for example, 43 percent like U.S. ideas on democracy while 42 percent dislike them. In Canada it is 50–40 against.

Three key questions were: Does the United States fail to solve problems and increase the gap between rich and poor? Does the United States take the views of others into consideration when making international policies? And would the world be better off with a second superpower? On the first, the response was overwhelming that the United States does not solve problems; and that with important exceptions such as Egypt, Pakistan, and most of Africa, it increases the rich-poor gap. On the second, as noted in Chapter 1, large majorities everywhere say that America doesn't pay attention to the views of others—except in the United States, where 75 percent of respondents say that America pays significant attention to the concerns of others. This gap is in some ways to be expected, but its size and universality are telling. At the same time, large majorities in most countries say the world would be a more dangerous place if there were a second country equal to the United States in military power. While that is comforting, it should not obscure the significance of the disaffection. In particular, a final disturbing point is that those who know the United States best—the Canadians, the Brits, and other West Europeans—are often the ones who rate it most poorly or who show the biggest decline in favorable ratings.[64]

These statistics merely quantify both what the subjects in the empire are screaming at Americans and what I have heard in thousands of conversations around the world. The Bilderberg Meeting is an annual gathering of U.S. and European government, business, academic, and media leaders who discuss trans-Atlantic relations, off the record, over a long spring weekend. The 2002 meeting took place in Washington over the weekend of the president's West Point address. The Europeans at the meeting expressed emotions ranging from disbelief to anger to disappointment and a sense of betrayal and insult. As one former French representative to NATO noted, the United States was effectively saying it would "chaperon Europe" in a kind of protectorate relationship. A former European Commissioner emphasized that "if the United States sees consensus as optional, that will be deeply corrosive to the world order we have struggled to create for the past fifty years. This idea is not only antiglobalization, it is actually contrary to the American model itself." Added one of the world's richest financiers, "Optional unilateralism undermines all that the United States stands for by negating checks and balances and the rule of law. Whether consciously or not, the United States is essentially saying might is right." The Washington-based ambassador of a leading ally of the United States emphasized that the preemptive war doctrine sets a dangerous precedent. "What will you do when a nuclear armed India or Pakistan decide they too must adopt this strategy?" he asked.

Nor was this a purely European reaction. Shortly after the Bilderberg Meeting, I had dinner in New York with the ambassadors to the UN from Mexico, Brazil, France, Switzerland, the EU, Singapore, Japan, Egypt, and Nigeria. They actually arrived well past the rendezvous hour of 8 P.M. because they had all been delayed in a Security Council debate over American demands for special treatment of U.S. citizens as a condition for U.S. agreement to creation of an International Criminal Court, a body the United States had itself originally proposed. They were still seething when they reached our host's apartment on the Upper West Side. Having already agreed to what they considered elaborate safeguards against politically motivated prosecution of Americans, they found further U.S. demands for exceptional treatment insulting and unconscionable. Said one Latin American ambassador, "The United States mistrusts the whole world. It relies only on military force and has no vision of itself working with others. Everything is always only about itself." One of the European ambassadors captured the overall feeling when he said, "In the past the United States has been a beacon to the world, but more and more it seems to be acting not only without regard for others, but also without regard for the very principles that made it a beacon. This is terribly depressing and disappointing for all of us." To a man they expressed personal opposition to and even disgust with the U.S. position. Yet most admitted that their governments would probably direct them to accommodate the Americans. Why? Because the United States had many ways to make life unpleasant for these countries, and none wanted to offend the world's greatest power over any but the most critical of matters. So when the American proposal for special treatment under the treaty came up for a vote on the Security Council, they would all hold their noses and vote "aye." But they wouldn't forget the indignity.

Similar resentment is also found in broader circles. At the APEC meeting in Los Cabos, in October 2002, the CEO summit featured an instant polling system that provided a rapid visual projection of the audience response to various questions posed by the program moderator. Two such responses were of particular interest. In one instance, it was noted that 100,000 U.S. troops have been deployed in Japan, Korea, and the rest of Asia for more than fifty years. The audience was asked to say whether it expected those troops to remain for another ten, twenty-five, or fifty years. Nearly two-thirds of the respondents chose twenty-five or fifty. Later, the audience was asked to vote on the most dangerous threat to regional security, whether terrorism, the rising power of China, the remilitarization of Japan, mass movement of people across borders, water shortages, AIDS, or American hegemony. While nearly 60 percent of the audience chose terrorism, American hegemony was in second place with 30 percent, far outdistancing all other choices.[65] This wasn't a group of left-wing radicals. These were eight hundred top business leaders from around the Asia-Pacific region saying they were more afraid of American hegemony than anything else except terrorism.

What the world is longing for is what Michael Hirsh calls an American vision of "inclusive idealism,"[66] a United States that, in Thomas Friedman's words, is interested in what the real problems are and in what it is doing wrong. Instead, as one Chinese diplomat put it, "the United States imposes its way and does so without knowing what it is doing." A vivid example is the *New York Times* story of December 22, 2002, about the oil riches of Nigeria. The story notes the contrast between the richness of the homes of the Chevron/Texaco terminal managers in Ugborodo, Nigeria, and the shacks of the oil field workers on the other side of the creek who seized and occupied the rich houses as part of a peaceful protest. The situation is complex and has much to do with the corruption and ineffectiveness of the Nigerian government. But the sentiment was best expressed by Victor Omunu, a local municipal official, who said: "Yes, the Nigerian government has failed, but we know the Americans influence the policies of this government. If they have the interests of the community at heart why is it they can't draw the attention of the Nigerian government? . . . The Americans who claim to be freedom fighters, the Americans who claim to want to better mankind—for us they are the devil. Can you tell me they are not worse than Saddam Hussein or Osama bin Laden? They come, take, and leave without putting back."

A longtime State Department official and former ambassador to Saudi Arabia Chas Freeman put it a bit more diplomatically, saying that "the United States is a City on a Hill, but it is increasingly fogged in." He added, "We need a war on arrogance as well as a war on terror."

3

AMERICA'S GAME

"It doesn't seem fair that the financial markets should make Brazil pay an economic price for having a democratic election."

—Rubens Barbosa,
Brazil's ambassador to Washington, D.C.

Supachai Panitchpakdi is a pleasant, round-faced man with the academic air of the professor he once was. Having swapped the university for politics, he became Deputy Prime Minister of Thailand in the mid–1990s and is now director general of the World Trade Organization (WTO) . In October 2001, before he had taken up his position at the WTO, we shared lunch at the Shangri-la Hotel in Shanghai where we were both attending the meetings of the Asia Pacific Economic Co-operation forum. As we looked down over the bustling ship traffic passing the Bund on the Huangpoo River, we enjoyed an unexpected reminiscence. It seemed that we had both been living in the city of Rotterdam in the 1960s without, of course, having had the opportunity to meet. We tried our rusty Dutch on each other (his was better than mine) and I learned he had been sent by Thailand to study economics under the renowned Jan Tinbergen at the University of Rotterdam and had stayed on as a professor for ten years before returning to Thailand. I had been the Vice Consul at the U.S. Consulate in Rotterdam from 1966 to 1968.

Our discussion turned from the distant past to the more recent past. We switched back to speaking English, and he suddenly turned very serious and said of recent economic developments: "The impact of the Asian financial crisis was devastating to Thailand and Southeast Asia, and caused many to question whether the U.S. and the IMF had a good understanding of how globalization affected Asia's economies."

THE CRASH OF '97

Supachai was referring to events that began unfolding in Bangkok in the autumn of 1996. During the 1990s, the economic miracle that had begun in the 1960s in Japan, and spread through Korea, Taiwan, Hong Kong, Singapore, and Malaysia, finally came to Thailand. For Southeast Asia it was the best of times. With the end of the Cold War, democratic capitalism was the sole surviving economic system and master of all it surveyed. In the race to create wealth, it had simply outrun communism. "Globalization"— the integration of national economies and corporate entities through trade and cross-border investment on a worldwide basis was the new watchword. Best-selling books by authors such as Japan's Kenichi Ohmae sang the praises of the new "borderless world" in which the national frontiers marked on maps had become meaningless, and the best thing governments could do was to persuade the corporate masters of the universe to invest in their countries and then get out of the way. Among the high priests of the global economy at the U.S. Treasury, the IMF, the World Bank and the elite universities, a general view developed with regard to the path to the future that became known as the "Washington Consensus." Popularized by Tom Friedman under the rubric "the golden straitjacket," the formula called for balanced budgets; low taxes; free flows of capital, goods, and services; privatization; deregulation; protection of property rights, particularly of intellectual property rights; small government; and liberalization of interest rates. Implementation of these measures, it was argued, would bring prosperity and narrow the gap between rich and poor, which in turn would bring democratization, which in turn would bring stability and peace. Friedman further explained that a main mechanism by which all this would happen was the "Electronic Herd," that group of faceless gnomes who stare at computer screens in the hushed aeries of Wall Street, Kabuto-Cho, The City, and elsewhere, and send trillions of dollars coursing around the globe with the click of a mouse.

In the 1990s, the Electronic Herd discovered Southeast Asia and it developed a special liking for Thailand. What later came to be seen as one of history's great financial bubbles was meanwhile gathering steam in the United States. Low interest rates and a booming economy released a tidal wave of money looking for high returns. Investors from the slow-growth economies of Europe and Japan were also looking for greener pastures, and with its high growth, high interest rates, and low risk by dint of currencies pegged to the dollar, Southeast Asia looked like a gnome's nirvana. Between 1993 and 1996, European, Japanese, and American banks lent over $700 billion in the region. Short-term foreign loans to Thailand alone amounted to nearly 10 percent of GDP in each of those years.[1] Foreign direct investment (FDI) also poured in, with General Motors, Ford, Toyota, and Daimler Chrysler all announcing new auto plants in Thailand while new skyscrapers darkened the skies. In 1994 the leaders of the Asia-Pacific nations, meeting in Indonesia, embraced the globalization doctrine by announcing formation of the Asia Pacific Economic Cooperation forum and its commitment to achieving complete free trade in the region by 2020. At the conferences of the global glitterati in Singapore, Davos, and Washington, learned professors, hardened bankers, and savvy political leaders all pointed to Southeast Asia as the most dynamic part of a global economy that was leading the way to utopia.

Few noticed, in late August 1996, the collapse of the Bangkok Bank of Commerce. Some eyebrows were raised in February 1997, when Somprasong Land Company defaulted on its Euro bonds, sending the first signals that the real estate bubble might be about to burst. Later that month, Finance One, Thailand's largest finance company, suddenly began seeking a merger partner. With that the Electronic Herd began a stampede out of the corral. Foreign bankers began calling their short-term loans while hedge funds sold the Thai baht short, anticipating that the peg to the dollar could not hold and that the currency would eventually have to be devalued. Fearing the same thing, Thai companies that had borrowed heavily abroad began dumping baht for dollars. In an all-out attempt to support the exchange rate, the Thai central bank poured its dollar reserves, $26 billion in all, into a desperate buying effort.

In the wee hours of the morning of July 2, 1997, central bank officials called the Minister of Finance, Thanong Bidaya, with a somber message: There would soon be no more dollar reserves. Thailand was effectively bankrupt. Well before dawn, Bangkok's leading bankers were awakened by telephone calls from officials summoning them to an emergency meeting. At 6:30 A.M. they gathered in a low, squat building across from the ornate Bankhumprom Palace, which houses the Bank of Thailand. They were told the government was out of reserves and thus no longer had dollars with which to buy baht so as to keep its valued pegged at twenty-five to the dollar. The government had no choice but to abandon the fixed exchange rate and let the baht float—or sink—freely. At 9:00 A.M., the exchange market opened and the baht immediately fell 15 percent. It would eventually lose 60 percent of its value. By early December, the government had closed fifty-six of the country's top fifty-eight financial institutions. Former tycoons could be seen selling sandwiches on the streets of Bangkok as unemployment rose to 20 percent. Cab drivers added a new wrinkle to the standard sightseeing tour: a drive down Asoke Street, Bangkok's Wall Street, to see the dead banks. The party was over.

But hey, it was only Thailand. I remember speaking at a conference attended by leading U.S. officials and economists who emphasized that while the collapse of the Thai economy was a shame and painful for Thailand, we shouldn't forget that the whole Thai economy amounted to only $185 billion dollars, less than the city of San Diego. Clearly it was no big deal. None other than President Bill Clinton seemed to agree, for as the international community, led by Japan, struggled to put together an emergency financial package for Thailand, Clinton declined to have the United States participate, saying the whole problem was just "a few glitches in the road" to global prosperity.[2] But if it was a hiccup for Clinton, it was stomach cancer for the Thais, who remembered that when Mexico had had similar problems in 1994, Clinton had moved heaven and earth to put together a rescue package. The Thais also remembered their help for the United States in Vietnam, and that the United States had all along been pressuring them to convert to the gospel of free trade and open financial markets. As Supachai's comment to me in Shanghai suggested, the Thais would not soon forget these "glitches in the road" and the United States' lack of response to them.

And then suddenly it wasn't only Thailand. In July, shortly after the fall of the baht, Malaysia's ringgit and Indonesia's rupiah began to fall, while the IMF offered the Philippines $1.1 billion in a preemptive move. At the same time, the Korean car maker Kia sought emergency assistance. By October, the ringgit had lost 25 percent of its January value and the rupiah had lost 28 percent. Malaysian Prime Minister Mahathir stopped short sales of Malaysian stocks and imposed limited controls on money flows into and out of the country in an effort to prevent a collapse like that of Thailand. For this he was severely criticized by virtually the entire elite of international finance, including top officials in the U.S. government, who said that such a move would completely and permanently undermine international investor confidence in the Malaysian economy and condemn it to eternal slow growth. Never shy, Mahathir unleashed a diatribe against international speculators, calling financier George Soros a moron and sharply criticizing the United States and the IMF for policies that enabled speculative attacks and that undermined the ability of developing countries to catch up. Mahathir later told me that his cabinet officials and advisers wanted him to shut up because every time he opened his mouth the ringgit fell further. "But I must tell the truth," he said. At the IMF/World Bank annual meeting in Hong Kong in September, he told the world's top bankers that currency trading is immoral and should be banned. Indonesia's currency, which had been tracking the ringgit, fell in response to his comments, while unemployment rose inexorably.

Despite the turmoil in Southeast Asia, the financial leaders at the Hong Kong meetings seemed to be in tune with Clinton. Even as the Electronic Herd was heading for the hills, the IMF's leaders requested a change in the organization's charter to allow it to put more pressure on developing countries to deregulate and open their financial markets to all global players. They did put together some rescue money for Thailand and Indonesia, but nothing, of course, for bad-boy Malaysia. That there really wasn't much worry was made clear by the glowing IMF annual report on the Korean economy, which, according to the IMF authors, was doing just about as well as it is possible for an economy to do. Here, apparently, was a case of near-perfect execution.

The storm broke with full force as the masters of the universe were unpacking their bags at home after returning from Hong Kong. The Hong Kong dollar, with its firm peg to the U.S. dollar, became the target of one of history's most aggressive speculative attacks. Huge global hedge funds developed their own version of Dungeons & Dragons. They would sell Hong Kong's Hang Seng stock index short while also selling Hong Kong dollars. The dollar sale, they calculated, would force the government to raise interest rates to hold the peg to the U.S. dollar, but rising interest rates would drive stock prices down, thus making the short stock index positions profitable. In fact, they were extremely profitable. As Hong Kong reeled and Indonesia was forced to accept an IMF bailout package calling for domestic austerity that was certain to drive unemployment through the roof, Japan floated the idea of creating an Asian Monetary Fund, to be financed largely from Japan's huge reserves and used to underpin the region's sick economies. I was one of those to whom the Japanese explained the idea, but when I reported it to appropriate officials in Washington the response was strictly negative. The idea quietly died for lack of oxygen. While it was expiring, so too was that paragon of good performance, the Korean economy.

Throughout October, the Korean won had been declining. In November, a number of major Korean companies were forced to announce delays or suspensions of domestic and international investments. In 1996, the United States had championed Korea to become the newest member of the Organization for Economic Cooperation and Development, the club of developed countries. Although it was a way to have a second Asian member (after Japan) in an otherwise all-western fraternity, it also facilitated U.S. negotiators in pressuring Korea to open its financial markets. On joining, Korea was flooded with foreign money as a $13.1 billion increase in foreign bank loans came into the country. Now the foreign banks, including a number of major U.S. institutions, grew nervous and began to head for the door. It couldn't have happened at a worse time. Korea was in the midst of a presidential election and no one was watching the store. In a desperate effort to hold up the value of its currency, Korea repeated the Thai experience until, in late December 1997, its officials had to tell its president there were hardly any reserves left.

At this point, a new mood overtook Washington. Korea, after all, is no glitch in the road. It is the world's eleventh largest economy and a major strategic ally of the United States. You can't let a country like that go down the tubes. In November 1997, Hong Kong had put an end to speculative attacks by having its Monetary Authority simply buy a large portion of the outstanding shares on the Hang Seng index. This was a complex maneuver, but in effect it was not too different from Mahathir's control on money flows into and out of Malaysia. Because Hong Kong did it with an apology rather than with Mahathir's defiance, American and international officials swallowed hard but gulped it down. So the U.S. embassy in Seoul,

South Korea, and the U.S. Treasury in Washington began burning the phone lines to Wall Street with the message that Washington would really appreciate it if the U.S. banks would refrain from taking their money out of Korea, and in fact would be most grateful if the loans were rolled over. In the category of offers you can't refuse this was a beauty. Of course, it amounted to the same kind of capital controls Mahathir had imposed, but Korea had a real economy and was a real ally.

It actually worked, but not fast enough. By the spring of 1998, the hemorrhaging had been largely staunched in Asia, but Russia, which had been on the edge for some time, now defaulted on its government bonds. This sent a chill through world credit markets that virtually froze lending to countries such as Brazil and Argentina, and even financial markets in the United States were feeling the effects. One group in particular was badly squeezed—Long Term Capital Management (LTCM), a hedge fund based in Westport, Connecticut. This was one of those outfits tailored just for the very rich. It would take your money only if you agreed to put up a minimum of $10 million and keep it there for three years. In return for that commitment, the fund promised to make at least 15 to 20 percent a year by investing in very complex ways that you didn't want to know about, not because there was anything wrong with them, but just because you really wouldn't understand. If you were looking for gnomes, you couldn't have done better than these guys—a group of Wall Street high rollers leavened with two Nobel Prize-winning economists.

Actually, underneath the complexity, the basic idea was relatively simple. Over time, the interest rates on similar kinds of bonds tend to be similar. It would be surprising if things were otherwise. In the short term, however, for all kinds of extraneous reasons, such rates can diverge. So if you invest when they diverge and bet on convergence over time, you are almost sure to win. That's what LTCM was doing. There are two keys. One is leverage: The spreads or profit margins on these bond investments are extremely narrow, so to make money you have to buy a lot of them, preferably with borrowed money. The other key is probability, which is where the mathematicians come in. You need to have a pretty good idea of how long it will take for the divergences to converge, because if it is longer than you expect, you can lose a lot of money really fast. LTCM had the best mathematicians and the best computer models, and it borrowed the most money and bet it all. For a while the scheme worked as it was supposed to. In three years,

LTCM earned an average 34 percent annually for its investors while making its partners among the richest people in the world.[3]

By the spring of 1998, investors were begging to put more money into the fund and the fund doubled its bet with a total of over $1 trillion of leveraged funds. But there was a problem. The world was acting funny. All the assumptions on which the computer model was based were proving wrong. Convergence wasn't occurring on schedule and LTCM began to hemorrhage money as if from a fire hose. This was, of course, bad for LTCM and its investors, but it had some other important people worried too. One of them was Alan Greenspan, the Chairman of the U.S. Federal Reserve system and the most important central banker (some would say the most important man) in the world. A disciple of the extreme libertarian novelist Ayn Rand and high priest of the virtues of unfettered markets, Greenspan had assured the U.S. Congress in extensive testimony that there was no need to regulate hedge funds like LTCM because as professionals they knew the risks and were prepared to accept them. But now the risk staring Greenspan in the face was the collapse of the whole global financial system. LTCM had borrowed so much money and placed such risky bets that if it collapsed it threatened to take major banks and perhaps the system itself with it. Faced with that risk, Greenspan blinked and organized a bail-out of LTCM. In effect, he too imposed capital controls, and in doing so he probably saved the global financial system. He certainly saved the bacon of some major Wall Street players. In Kuala Lumpur, Mahathir could be heard laughing.

So this is one face of globalization. The IMF and many U.S. officials later admitted mistakes and inappropriate policies, but the United States escaped the worst global financial crisis since the Great Depression largely unscathed. The Indonesians, Malaysians, Thais, Hong Kong Chinese, and Koreans still bear the scars, and they still remember the unconcern, inconsistency, self-righteousness, and ignorance of the United States and the institutions of globalization.

DO AS I SAY, NOT AS I DO

On August 6, 2002, President George W. Bush signed into law the Trade Promotion Authority Act, designed to improve the ability of his administration to negotiate international free trade agreements. Said Bush, "America is back in the business of promoting open trade." He further promised that he would "use this new authority to create more jobs and higher standards of living for American families." In earlier remarks to the Council of the Americas, he had emphasized that "open trade is not just an economic opportunity; it is a moral imperative." These views were further elaborated by Secretary of State Colin Powell, who said, "The reality is that free trade and globalization promote worker and human rights over the long run, one that helps the environment and improves economic equality for greater wealth for all."[4] He added the Bush administration is determined to "pursue free trade at every opportunity for the simple reason that trade works. It gives people hope, helps them feed their children, puts roofs over their heads. They start up the ladder, and they will never go back."[5] Neither Bush nor Powell were saying anything new or unique. Free trade and open markets have been the policy and the mantra of every American president since Franklin Roosevelt.

But try to tell that to Mody Sangare of Korokoro, Mali, in West Africa. Shortly before Bush's signing ceremony, as reported in the *Wall Street Journal*, he hitched his one-blade plow to two oxen and began the first of the fourteen days it would take him to till his fifteen acres of cotton. Even as he toils at this backbreaking labor, he has little hope that it will do him much good. Prices being offered to Mali's cotton farmers this year are 10 percent below last year's record lows, and last year, after all the costs of production were paid, the Sangare family was left with less than $2000 to support two dozen people. With prices falling again and costs for imported fertilizers and pesticides rising, the family may be unable to support the education of some of its children.

The same *Journal* piece noted that, while Mody sweated and worried, on the other side of the globe, in Gunnison, Mississippi, Ken Hood stepped into his air-conditioned tractor, seated himself on his air-cushioned seat, and adjusted the global positioning satellite system to find out just how much fertilizer he needed to squirt on seedlings already pushing through the soil on his 10,000-acre spread. Despite falling world cotton prices, Hood and his family continue to buy land, and Hood, a director of the National Cotton Council, says "there are lots of reasons to be optimistic." Given the $800,000 average net worth of American cotton-farming households, it is easy to understand Hood's confidence.

But it is important to understand what lies behind that confidence and the vast gap between Mody Sangare and Ken Hood. A logical and readily acceptable explanation would be competitiveness and productivity. In another speech, President Bush emphasized that "American farmers and ranchers are the most productive in the world," a fact that could easily account for Mr. Hood's prosperity in the face of Mr. Sangare's poverty. Ten thousand acres and modern equipment going against oxen and single plows on tiny plots wouldn't seem to be much of a contest. Maybe, as Mr. Hood says, "the farmers in Africa should not raise cotton." But actually, Mississippi Delta cotton farmers are not the low-cost producers. They are the highest-cost producers in the world, spending about $600 to produce an acre of cotton. All that high-tech equipment is expensive. Delta land is irrigated, and the seed is premium priced because it is genetically modified to resist pests. Then there are the costs of expensive fertilizers and defoliants. So why all the optimism in Gunnison? Easy: subsidies. A few days before Mody Sangare roped up his oxen and Ken Hood climbed into his tractor, President Bush signed into law another piece of legislation that is expected to substantially increase last year's $3.4 billion in cotton subsidies. Of this, Ken Hood expects to get nearly $1 million.[6]

But the good fortune of Mr. Hood and the rest of America's 25,000 cotton farmers comes not only at the expense of the American tax payer. It comes also at the expense of the entire economy of countries like Mali and, perhaps eventually, at the expense of American lives and national security. Despite its high production costs, America is the world's largest exporter of cotton, competing in global markets with Mali. West Africa, as a region, is the third largest exporter. The U.S. subsidies assure American farmers that they will earn 70 cents per pound of cotton regardless of the world price (55 cents per pound as of January 2003).[7] Further, they set no limit on acreage planted. Not surprisingly, U.S. planters harvested a record crop of nearly 10 billion pounds last year, creating a huge glut on the world market that pushed prices far below the break-even mark for most farmers around the world. In short, U.S. subsidies mean that the world's highest-cost producers dump cotton on world markets and gain a greater and greater market share as they drive the low-cost producers out of business. That isn't the way capitalism is supposed to work, but that's how it looks from Mali, one of the ten least developed countries in the world and a place that can't even provide its people with basic health care and education, let alone match U.S. subsidies. A recent World Bank report calculates that annulment of U.S. subsidies would reduce U.S. production and lead to a rise in world cotton prices that would bring as much as $250 million of extra revenue to West and Central African countries—a fortune in a region where many live on less than a dollar a day.[8]

The subsidies are undermining more than the world's cotton growers. They also undermine U.S. efforts to combat global poverty as a central element in the war on terror. In an attempt to break the cycle of misery and instability that makes the developing world susceptible to hosting terrorist groups, the U.S. government has begun to emphasize development aid and open trade. In Mali, for example, the United States spends $40 million annually on education, health, and other development programs.[9] But that sum is almost totally negated by the state cotton company's loss of $30 million caused by sinking world cotton prices. The result is increasing bitterness in this predominantly Muslim country of 11 million. Says Mody Diallo, a leader of the farmer's union, "This is where America is heading. It wants to dominate the world economically and militarily." Fortunately, such sentiment has not yet boiled over into action, but the impoverished citizens of West Africa are increasingly crowding into European cities, and those who stay behind are seeing more mullahs from Pakistan and the Middle East in their mosques and Quranic schools, while there are reports of Malians and others going abroad for religious training. In West Africa, the face of American-style globalization and free trade is not the hope-inspiring one of Colin Powell, but a harsh, hypocritical one that inspires a drift to radicalism and perhaps to terrorism. The cost of dealing with that would, of course, far exceed anything spent on subsidies or aid.

One Malian, Bakary Traore, president of the state cotton company, has a creative solution. "It would be better for the United States to pay their farmers not to plant cotton," he says. He is surely correct. In fact, Delta farmers could grow corn, soybeans, or wheat much more inexpensively than they can grow cotton. With these crops they could compete in world markets without subsidies. But Ed Hester has the answer to that: "I can only run cotton through my cotton picker." And because Ed and his fellow cotton farmers have powerful friends on the agriculture committees of the U.S. Senate and House of Representatives, there is little doubt that he will be running cotton through his picker for some time to come. How much that will eventually cost the United States and the world, only time will tell.

STEEL IS FOREVER

On the other hand, the cost of the emergency tariffs President Bush imposed on imports of a wide range of steel products in March 2002 was known instantly and precisely. The impact of the 30-percent tariff would raise costs for U.S. steel users by $3 billion while cutting the sales and profits of foreign steel producers and exporters by 20 percent.[10] Coming at a time when efforts were underway to launch a new round of trade liberalization negotiations aimed at restarting the then stalling global economy, this protectionist action unleashed a firestorm of criticism from all corners of the globe. It was seen both as a violation of the very free trade principles the United States was pushing for the new trade liberalization talks and as another example of the United States rejecting the pleas of its allies and acting unilaterally in its own selfish interests. Actually, it was a case of the President doing the wrong thing for the right reasons.

As a result of often unfathomable dynamics, certain industries take on special symbolic significance. The airline industry is a good example. Airlines rarely make money, but virtually every country has one whether it makes economic sense or not. It is as if you aren't a real country if you don't have an airline. So it is with steel. Along with steam power and railroads, steel was one of the pillars of the industrial revolution. For most of the nineteenth century, Great Britain led the world in steel production and measured its industrial supremacy in terms of its lead in this vital commodity. First Germany and then the United States protected their industries to enable them to catch up to the British, and when they did, it was seen as a sign of the emergence of new powers and of British decline. Japan got into the game in the early 1900s; after World War II, the European Iron and Coal Community served as the forerunner of the formation of the European Common Market and eventually of today's European Union. During the Cold War, Soviet Prime Minister Nikita Khrushchev promised that communism would bury capitalism by, among other things, out-producing it in steel, and nearly every developing country from Korea and Malaysia to Mexico and Poland has felt it imperative to develop a steel industry as part of its industrialization strategy. It follows that the world has installed a lot of steel production capacity over the past hundred years.

Nor is it easy to close a steel mill once production has begun. At $1 to $2 billion a pop, steel mills are extremely capital intensive, with fixed costs accounting for 35 to 40 percent of the total cost of producing a ton. Because of this high fixed-cost ratio, it is economical to produce and sell steel even at a substantial loss as long as the revenue is covering at least a part of the fixed costs. Beyond this is the fact that steel mills employ a lot of people directly, and even more indirectly in the industries that supply and service the mills. It is common to speak of "steel towns" because frequently the steel mill is the life-blood of an entire city or region. Moreover, as an old industry with roots in the class warfare of the late nineteenth and early twentieth centuries, steel is everywhere strongly unionized and politically powerful. Thus, as new mills have been added in various places over the years, old mills have tended not to shut down. Instead they have struggled on, often selling at a loss and, in much of the world outside the United States, forming cartels to prop up prices while also becoming the recipients of substantial government subsidies. The result has been accumulation of production capacity far in excess of actual demand. Some analysts have estimated that nearly one-third of the world's approximately 1 billion tons of steel production capacity is in excess of demand.[11]

Over the past twenty years, most of that excess production has found its way into the U.S. market, a fact that has led to dozens of bankruptcies of U.S. steel firms, the shedding of 18 million tons of capacity, and the shrinkage of the American steel labor force from 459,000 workers in 1982 to 139,000 today.[12] Behind these painful statistics lie three major factors: the relative openness of the U.S. market, the relative lack of U.S. government assistance for the industry, and the peculiarities of the U.S. pension and health care system. Despite much criticism of U.S. protectionism, the fact is that the United States is the export market of choice because even with its idiosyncrasies it is far easier to enter than any other major market. The trade statistics demonstrate this dramatically. While imports take about 24.1 percent of the U.S. market, they account for only 19.3 percent of the EU market and a paltry 10 percent of the Japanese market.[13] One reason for this is that Europe, Japan, and other countries are dominated by cozy business arrangements aimed at controlling imports and operated through industry associations and groups of interrelated companies. Another factor is the extensive government assistance provided to many non-U.S. steel industries in the form of injections of public capital, and absorption of debts, or provision of critical infrastructure—all aimed at restoring corporate competitiveness. A final factor is the "legacy costs" of pensions and health care.

Even without the protection and the public assistance received by their foreign competitors, many U.S. steel producers have dramatically cut costs and improved productivity to remain cost-competitive for consumers in the U.S. market. (U.S. production per manhour increased from 70.5 tons in 1980 to 142.9 in 2000, compared with 67 and 127.9 in Germany and 63.2 and 134.1 in Japan.)[14] But even as they have downsized and cut staff, they have been increasingly saddled with higher and higher bills for pensions and health care, which tend to make them uncompetitive. In most steel-producing countries, health care and pensions are publicly funded. In the United States, of course, these programs are provided by employers, and in the steel industry they have been a major part of the contracts negotiated between the companies and the United Steel Workers. Under the agreements, retirees and workers who have been laid off, along with their families, continue to receive inflation-indexed pension and health care benefits for as long as they live. Often made under heavy U.S. government pressure, these agreements and their legacy costs mean that an industry of 139,000 workers has the pension and health-care bill of an industry two or three times its size. Not only are these costs a heavy burden, they also tend to inhibit moves that could make the industry more competitive. Globally, the trend has been toward mergers and the creation of very-large-scale production facilities. This has not happened so much in the United States because no company can afford to take on the legacy costs of any firm it might acquire. Thus, while a merger of U.S. Steel with Bethlehem Steel would make economic sense, it cannot occur as long as the legacy cost problem exists.

In dealing with the adjustment problems of the steel industry, the U.S. government has long had the choice of moving proactively to assume these legacy costs, as other governments do, or imposing emergency tariffs on imports that are found under U.S. trade law to be a major cause of damage to the U.S. industry. Under the law, the U.S. industry must present a recovery plan to qualify for the tariff. Historically, however, such plans have usually not worked, and the tariffs have provided only temporary relief from low-price competition. By raising costs for users like auto and machine tool companies, they help make these industries uncompetitive as well. They also cause harm to the exporting economies, and yet do nothing to make the domestic industry more efficient.

Clearly, the preferable route in March 2002 would have been for the U.S. government to assume some of the legacy costs and make the industry more competitive. In a meeting with the chairman of one of the major U.S. steel companies, I was told that that was also the route the industry would prefer, because it would allow mergers and other measures that could bring the industry up to world-class levels. I was also told by the EU Trade Commissioner, Pascal Lamy, as well as by various Japanese officials that neither Europe nor Japan would object to such a U.S. policy. The Bush administration's decision to impose anti-dumping duties instead was due to its political desire to please the steel unions, which preferred that choice, and to its market-fundamentalist economic philosophy of avoiding anything that smacks of industrial policy. While it was certainly right to react to the industry's problems, the manner of acting caused an enormous negative reaction abroad and damaged U.S. credibility. At the very moment it was calling for new trade liberalization negotiations, the United States responded to a political problem by taking the easy way out and passing its costs on to the exporting countries, in direct violation of its own free trade doctrine.[15]

THE SOURCE OF MIRACLES

There is another face of globalization, and it is one that I know intimately. I first encountered it in 1958 when I sailed from New York to Amsterdam to spend time in Europe as an exchange student. Our voyage took ten days and cost about the same as today's seven- or eight-hour flight. I remember my amazement at the thousands of bicycles parked in every imaginable spot around Amsterdam's streets and canals. I was sixteen years old and I had just acquired my first car a few months before. Yet, here, even grandmothers were riding bicycles. I boarded the train in Amsterdam for Basel, Switzerland, and as the grandson of a railroad man, was delighted to find it pulled by a steam engine, something I had never seen at home. In the small Swiss village at the foot of the Alps where I was to stay, I became accustomed to the hot water cutting off in the middle of my shower and learned to go grocery shopping every day because the refrigerator was too small to hold more than a day's supply of food. Europe in those days wasn't poor in the way of a developing country, but neither was it rich in the way of the United States.

I arrived in Japan to pursue graduate studies in 1964, at about the time Norman McRae first proclaimed the Japanese "miracle" in *The Economist*. It sure didn't look like a miracle to me. Again, transportation was mostly by bicycle rather than car. My wife and I rented what our Japanese friends termed a "luxury" flat. It had no running hot water, no bath, and no range, and heating was by kerosene stove. We slept on futons rolled out on the floor at night, went to the public bath, boiled our baby daughter's diapers in a bucket over something that resembled a Bunsen burner, and wore gauze masks to protect ourselves from Tokyo's noxious air. We never saw Mount Fuji until we were driven to it on a sightseeing tour. Our Japanese friends worked six days a week, never took a vacation, and lived in conditions that resembled what Americans would call camping. Again, Japan wasn't really poor, but it wasn't nearly as rich as Europe, let alone the United States.

Two years later I was back in the Netherlands as the Vice Consul at the U.S. Consulate in Rotterdam. Eight years had made an astonishing difference. Bicycles were out, and motorbikes and cars were in, and the trains had all been switched to diesel or electric engines. The growth industry was installing central heating in houses as northern Europe's gas fields were developed, and the quaint little grocery stores were giving way to supermarkets. I soon understood the major factor behind this rapid development of wealth. The Consul General told me my tasks would be to promote American investment in the Netherlands and Dutch exports to the United States while keeping track of developments in the port of

Rotterdam. It wasn't called globalization then. A best-selling book by the French author Jean-Jacques Servan-Schreiber called it *Le défi américain* (The American Challenge) . Regardless of what it was called, Rotterdam had already become the world's largest port as the flow of investment capital into Europe created factories that sucked in raw materials and shipped out finished goods destined for the huge U.S. market. International trade and investment were making the Dutch and other Europeans truly rich—in the way of the United States.

By 1972 I was living in Brussels, Belgium, as director of European marketing for Scott Paper Company. As I struggled to create a unified marketing plan for Scott's various national operations in Europe, I developed great empathy and admiration for the European leaders who were harnessing the power of global capitalism to shape an entirely new European economic power. In 1976 I was reassigned to Japan, where I discovered that McRae had been right about the miracle after all. Traffic was impossible; the public baths were rapidly going out of business as people installed their own *ofuros* at home; the work week was down to five and a half days; and despite former Secretary of State John Foster Dulles's comment that the Japanese couldn't make anything Americans would buy, Japan had a large and growing trade surplus with the United States. One of my friends at the U.S. embassy in Tokyo bragged that he had done a better job of promoting Japanese exports to the U.S. market than I had done in promoting Dutch exports.

By the time I became a trade negotiator in the Reagan administration, the trade deficit with Japan had grown to $15.8 billion and the overall U.S. trade deficit was running at the unprecedented level of $27 billion annually.[16] Many analysts said this deficit was unsustainable, and Secretary of Commerce Malcolm Baldrige told me it was my job to reduce it. By 1986, as the deficit with Japan hit $55 billion and the overall deficit climbed to $150 billion annually, it was clear that I had failed, and I left the administration to try my luck at writing a book about trade negotiations. I did not imagine that the U.S. trade deficit (technically the current account deficit) would be running at an annual rate of nearly $500 billion by the end of year 2002. That number has immense significance in a number of ways, but above all it is a measure of how America, working through globalization, has contributed to making much of the world rich.

This did not come about by accident. After World War II, the United

States determined to avoid the mistakes of the aftermath of World War I and adopted a policy line that might today be called "nation building." The Marshall Plan provided the equivalent in today's dollars of more than $90 billion to help rebuild Europe, and the Dodge Plan was crafted to get Japan back on its feet.[17] With the dollar as its cornerstone, the International Monetary Fund was created to assure stable international financial markets, while the World Bank was established to provide essential funding for developing countries. The United States was and remains the biggest contributor to both institutions. Perhaps most importantly, the General Agreement on Tariffs and Trade (GATT) committed America and its major allies to reduction of tariffs and to realization of free trade on a truly global basis. Beginning with the Geneva Round of trade talks in 1947 and continuing over fifty years to the Uruguay Round, which concluded in 1994, the United States led the industrialized world to reduce tariffs and formal trade barriers to insignificance. Over that time, free trade has become largely reciprocal, at least among developed countries. But in the beginning, the United States sharply reduced its tariffs without requiring reciprocity from its trading partners in Europe and Japan. Very importantly, the United States also held the value of the dollar fixed for twenty-five years, while the rapid recovery and development of its trading partners dramatically reduced the huge American productivity lead of the immediate post-war period. Finally, U.S. industry was urged by its government to assist in the development effort by investing abroad, licensing technology, and increasing imports. The former Motorola Chairman Robert Galvin tells of being urged by President Eisenhower in 1957 to try to increase imports from Japan so as to help strengthen its economy and cement its alliance with the United States.

Europe was the early export star as Volkswagen's famous "Beetle" gained an incredible 5 percent of the U.S. auto market in 1958, and any bicycle with a gearshift and skinny tires was known as an "English bike."[18] But with the help of people like Galvin, Japan caught up rapidly. It specifically adopted an export-led growth strategy; by 1964, when I showed up in Tokyo, Japanese companies already had large shares of the American consumer electronics markets and were moving quickly to dominance. Japanese autos would come later, but textile, steel, and components imports from Japan were displacing U.S. factories and causing sharp trade disputes.

The rest of the story is well known. Japan caught up to and surpassed the United States in several key industrial sectors and technologies, and today enjoys a per capita income that, depending on exchange rates, is sometimes greater than that of the United States. Korea, Taiwan, Hong Kong, Singapore, and Malaysia quickly learned to imitate Japan and then added a new twist—they courted foreign investors and lured American and other companies to take advantage of lower costs by locating factories within their borders. Soon the world was talking about the Asian "tigers" and "dragons." More recently, the North American Free Trade Agreement (NAFTA) has led to a 137 percent increase in Mexico's exports and made it America's second largest trading partner (after Canada) and a major target of U.S. investment.[19] Taking the world economy as a whole, over the past fifty years freer trade has been a major growth factor as exports and imports have increased more than one-hundred-fold while global GDP has grown 4 percent annually.[20] Moreover, the rise of China and India into the ranks of the newly industrializing economies has made a major dent in world poverty levels. Millions of people in these two most heavily populated countries have moved above the $2 per day income that defines extreme poverty. It cannot be emphasized enough that America's contribution to this is central and indispensable: The United States absorbs 25 percent of Asian and 60 percent of Latin American exports with its huge trade deficits and is the direct or indirect cause of 35 percent of total global investment in factories in developing countries.[21] Can globalization be good for non-Americans? Without question. Is it organized to maximize global welfare? Let's see.

BUT AMERICA OWNS THE SANDBOX

The foundations of today's global economic system were laid in 1944 at the Bretton Woods resort in New Hampshire, where the Allies reached agreement on the key elements of the financial structure that would be put in place upon conclusion of World War II. The objective was to avoid a repeat of the "beggar-thy-neighbor" protectionist trade policies and competitive currency devaluations that brought the economic disaster of the Great Depression and the rise of fascism. At Bretton Woods, the United States and Great Britain determined that the new international system would depend on universal rules to enforce openness and mutually agreed responses to particular difficulties. It was here that the IMF was established as arbiter of the new system, and the World Bank was created as a multilateral funding mechanism for the development of third world countries. The United States insisted upon and was granted decisive voting rights in both institutions.

A great debate raged over the nature of a new international payment system, with the great British economist John Maynard Keynes arguing for creation of a new international currency that would be backed by gold and called the Bancor. Keynes's rationale was that such a currency would place all the system's members on equal footing. The objective was to keep the system operating in equilibrium. Thus if a country began to run a trade deficit, rather than simply devalue its currency it would be forced to adopt austerity measures at home that would enable it to export its way out of difficulty. The IMF would facilitate this adjustment by making transitional loans in exchange for the austerity programs. It was also proposed that countries running trade surpluses adopt policies to stimulate their economies, and that temporary tariffs be imposed on their exports. Capital flows between countries were to be strictly regulated and controlled so that national interest rate policies could effectively adjust the domestic economies.

In the end, the United States insisted that the dollar and not the Bancor would be the international currency. It would be freely convertible into gold at a fixed rate, while every other currency would be pegged at a fixed rate to the dollar. Changes in currency rates could be made only upon agreement with the IMF, which in effect meant with the United States. The capital controls (which limited international banking opportunities) were also part of the final agreement, but the temporary tariffs on trade surplus countries were abandoned. Countries running deficits would be automatically disciplined to adjust, since they would need to finance their deficits by obtaining transitional loans from the IMF—or so it seemed at the time.

The new system worked beyond all expectation. International trade soared as tariffs fell by 73 percent between 1947 and 1961, and Europe and Japan recovered so quickly it seemed miraculous.[22] By the early 1960s, the huge American trade surpluses of the immediate postwar years had been turned into inexorably growing deficits, as the rising productivity of the European and Japanese economies made their goods increasingly competitive in the now relatively open U.S. market. America had insisted on the dollar as the international currency because this gave us the advantage of paying for whatever we wanted in our own currency. Still, the deficits exposed some unexpected difficulties. Without the temporary tariffs on surplus countries' exports proposed by Keynes, there was no pressure on them to raise the value of their currencies or reduce exports, and they began accumulating large piles of dollars in their coffers.

Because they effectively created extra reserves in the banking systems of the surplus countries, these dollars tended to enlarge money supplies and stimulate inflation. In effect, the U.S. trade deficits, as long as they were priced in dollars, were an export of inflation and an example of the United States's escaping the discipline that applied to all others in the system. But there was a remedy. The quid pro quo for acceptance of the dollar as the international unit of payment had been the U.S. promise to hold the dollar's value against gold and to make it freely convertible into gold at a fixed price. Led by France, some countries began to turn in their dollars for gold; throughout the 1960s, U.S. gold reserves shriveled. Faced with the agonizing choice of either maintaining the system by subjecting itself to the same discipline as other countries and adopting domestic austerity measures, or scrapping the system, the United States scrapped the system. Moreover, it took advantage of its great power to do so unilaterally. As the effort to pay, without a tax increase, for both the war in Vietnam and the Great Society domestic programs inevitably inflated the U.S. economy, the strain on international payments became unbearable; and on March 3, 1971, President Nixon simply suspended the convertibility of the dollar into gold. This created a de facto dollar standard in place of the gold exchange standard and made the dollar the world's fiat currency, for whose management the United States undertook no obligations to the rest of the world. Other countries' currencies would float against the dollar, and their economies would have to adjust according to the vagaries of U.S. economic policies. After all capital controls were lifted on New Year's Day 1974, the United States could truly buy whatever it wanted with its own money without consequences to itself or obligations to others. This was real freedom. As for the rest of the world, Nixon's Treasury Secretary, John Connally, perfectly captured the American view when he said: "We had a problem and we are sharing it with the rest of the world—just like we shared our prosperity. That's what friends are for."

The virtually unlimited ability to print the world's money gave America immense advantages in shaping the framework of globalization. Most importantly, it allowed America to become the world's consumer of last resort: We could forget about saving and run continuous trade deficits. Whereas other countries had to keep their trade more or less in balance over time and only consume roughly as much as they produced, the United States did not have to sell anything in order to buy. It could simply print dollars. The dollar standard also greatly facilitated overseas investment by U.S. companies and allowed the United States to run a cumulative current account deficit of nearly $6 trillion while investing cumulatively some $1.1 trillion abroad by the end of twentieth century.[23]

But the dollar was not America's only tool. The sheer size of the American market, the spread of English as the world's *lingua franca*, and immense U.S. military power have all worked along with the dollar to put America in the driver's seat of globalization. Take the movie and television broadcasting industries. If you are an American moviemaker or broadcaster, you start with a potential domestic audience of 280 million people, compared with about 60 million if you are French and 80 million if you are German. Of course, if you are Chinese or Indian you can count on billions, but your audience will be strictly domestic. As an American, however, you can also count on billions because, in addition to U.S. viewers, people around the world whose second language is English are part of your potential market. Not surprisingly, Americans make more movies, TV shows, and recordings than anyone else and American pop culture has become globally pervasive.

Similar dynamics apply in other areas. U.S. military power means that America is far and away the world's top arms supplier, but it also creates a huge flow of resources to support American technological leadership. The Internet, for example, originated as ARPA-Net, the network of the Defense Department's Advanced Research Projects Agency (ARPA). That single development, begun over twenty-five years ago, means that today 75 percent of global Internet traffic is switched through the United States and handled at some point by U.S. carriers.[24] Finally, U.S. military might reinforces the role of the dollar by making America the safest of havens. Even though it is swimming in dollars, the world continues to hold them because, in a time of uncertainty, where else would you put your money?

From this position of strength, American negotiators like me have marked out the playing field. Early in the game, the United States gained exemptions from the free-trade rules for its politically sensitive agricultural and textile markets, effectively allowing them to remain highly protected. In the first twenty years after the establishment of the GATT, U.S. negotiators assumed the superior competitiveness of other U.S. industries and freely opened U.S. markets without reciprocal opening from trading partners. As imports surged in the late 1970s, however, American diplomats toughened their stance. In industries such as autos and color television, they demanded "voluntary" restraint from exporters such as Japan and strongly suggested that the establishment of factories in the United States would be a wise course of action. This was a cynical and hypocritical way of continuing to profess the virtue of free trade while enjoying the forbidden fruit of protectionism. Of course, our trading partners were outraged, but they had few choices. The U.S. consumer, even if restricted, was the main buyer in town, and anyhow, all the exporters needed those U.S. carrier task forces over the horizon to protect them. The charade served even more to dampen pressures for protectionist measures from American political constituencies that were losing jobs to imports.

The preferred course for U.S. negotiators, however, was to push hard for opening of foreign markets and establishment of rules that would benefit particularly competitive (or influential) American industries and companies. This was a sensible policy, but its implementation could lead to bizarre results. Because the United States rejects as a matter of principle any notion of industrial policy or economic strategy, its negotiating agenda is largely determined by chance and intense corporate lobbying. Thus the U.S. tobacco industry, whose products are very competitive, enlisted the U.S. Trade Representative to open global markets for American tobacco even as the Attorney General was suing the industry for misleading the public about the carcinogenic effects of smoking. Some commentators wondered why the United States wanted to export cancer.

Intellectual property protection has been another area of great emphasis. The whole concept is distinctly western. In much of the rest of the world, the view is that we only stand on the shoulders of those who have gone before us. Thus the notion that I, all by myself, may invent and own a particular idea is seen as egoistical. Nevertheless it is the lifeblood of the U.S. high-technology industry, and U.S. negotiators have made it a high priority to incorporate strong patent and copyright protection in the international trade rules and to strictly enforce them. To take another example, firms making strategic products such as airplanes or semiconductors object to the investment requirements that some developing countries try to impose as a condition of selling into their markets. U.S. negotiators have succeeded in getting prohibition of such requirements incorporated into the global trade rules. Another instance of deft U.S. diplomacy occurred in the late 1980s when the Japanese banks looked as if they would run away with the international store. The U.S. Treasury led negotiation of the Basle Accord, requiring banks to increase the core capital in their balance sheets. This not only leveled the playing field for U.S. banks, which typically adhered to higher capital requirements than Japanese banks, it also induced substantial buying of U.S. Treasury notes at a time when the United States badly needed to finance its deficits.

There was a moment in the 1980s when it appeared that Japan might be on the brink of taking the game away from the United States as, along with its banks, its electronics, auto, steel, and machinery firms took the lead in key world markets. But in the Plaza Accord of 1985 (after New York's Plaza Hotel, where it was concluded) , the United States persuaded Japan to revalue the yen, setting in train a series of events that eventually resulted in the bursting of the Japanese bubble in 1992. That, along with the end of the Cold War and the spectacular rise of the American stock markets in the 1990s, erased any doubt about whose game it was. Fukuyama's end-of-history argument that liberal democracy linked to market capitalism has proven itself the ideal national model developed an important corollary: that it was specifically the American form of market capitalism that would serve as the example others could ignore only at their peril. In this model, the overriding purpose of the corporation is to maximize returns to shareholders. Management's interests are aligned with those of shareholders through generous grants of stock options that raise management's compensation to more than 400 times that of production workers (compared with more than 40 times in 1980) because top managers are seen as business-world equivalents of major sports stars.[25] The role of government is to deregulate, privatize, and get out of the way. Above all, the free, unbound market is seen as the best allocator of resources and the engine of development.

As this model produced an estimated 33 percent productivity growth

and seemed to have repealed the business cycle in the 1990s, it lent powerful support to the aforementioned Washington Consensus, which had
emerged as the dominant view of a developing country's best path to riches.
From this perspective, developing countries should open their markets to
free trade; liberalize their financial systems to encourage a free flow of capital; privatize, deregulate, and maintain high levels of savings and investment; and keep exchange rates stable in order to attract foreign investment.
When crises arose like those in Asia in 1997, the IMF's first instinct was to
try to maintain currency values by imposing austerity and high interest
rates as a condition for emergency loans. Far from providing system stability, the IMF had become the enforcer of the market fundamentalist views
of the Washington Consensus. Globalization clearly meant Americanization, and what was wrong with that? As Tom Friedman noted in 1996, no
two countries having McDonald's restaurants have ever gone to war.[26]
(This, of course, is no longer true.) Globalization as Americanization was
assumed to lead to rising standards that would lead to democracy that
would lead to global peace and stability.

BACKLASH

During the week of November 29, 1999, in Seattle, a lot of things were
happening but peace and stability were not among them. I stood on
Spring Street choking on tear gas and watching antiglobalization protest-
ers shatter shop windows and taunt police; meanwhile, most of the
world's trade ministers were gathered in the Seattle Convention and
Trade Center trying to launch a new round of international trade talks.
This was the first major meeting of the new World Trade Organization
(WTO), created as the successor to the GATT at the end of the last
round of trade talks in 1994.

In the past, only a few aficionados had even known when trade talks
were taking place. But globalization had become such an important issue
that some 50,000 protestors had converged on this meeting to voice their
concerns. A disparate gathering of unlikely bedfellows passed in front of
me. Burly workers from the docks and nearby Boeing plants shouted
"Teamsters love turtles" to environmentalists dressed in Save the Turtles
outfits. College students looking for a cause joined professional leftists in

condemning corporate exploitation, even as their Nike shoes betrayed their lack of commitment. Quite committed, on the other hand, were representatives of developing countries who complained that the global system had been unfairly tilted toward the interests of the developed countries. One Third World trade minister noted bitterly that he and many of his colleagues could not even get into most of the negotiating sessions. The meeting eventually foundered on the issue of developed country agricultural subsidies, but not before it had made the world aware that the road to globalization could be very rocky.

Although developed countries are widely thought to be the great beneficiaries of globalization, some of the strongest opposition to it comes from organized labor. Unions see globalization as threatening their hard-fought gains by enabling capitalism to evade the rules and institutions that national governments have established over the years to tame it. The fact that a country may benefit from globalization in an overall sense does not mean there are no losers. For example, inexpensive clothing imports into the United States are a boon to consumers and the overall economy, but they come at the expense of workers in the U.S. apparel industry. These are largely minority women like Maria Consuelo Garcia, who lost her $4.75 per hour job after fifteen years of stitching Polo jeans at the Sun Apparel plant in El Paso, Texas, when the company announced it would move much of the work to Mexico, where seamstresses are paid about $1 per hour. Although American consumers benefit from this move, the United States has no effective method for compensating women like Maria for the loss of their jobs. Not surprisingly, she and her colleagues and their unions are not cheerleaders for globalization. Particularly galling is the fact that these jobs often go to places like the Qin Shi plant in China, where the National Labor Committee found guards beating workers if they were late in turning out Kathie Lee Gifford handbags for Wal-Mart.[27] Labor in the advanced countries thus demands compensation for the costs of globalization, and the incorporation of basic labor rights in the international trade agreements.

Like labor, environmentalists see in globalization an environmentally catastrophic return to an era of raw capitalism. They fear that the inexorable pressure to reduce costs will inevitably result in production's moving to environmentally unregulated regions. This fear is not unjustified. I have been involved in many cases in which a factory location decision was to some extent influenced by the nature of the environmental regulations and their enforcement. Some analysts note that China's export-led growth has come at a cost of environmental degradation equivalent to 8 to 12 percent of China's GDP.[28] In Indonesia's tropical forests, an area the size of Connecticut is cut down every year to feed the flooring, furniture, and office stationary markets in Japan, China, the United States, and Europe. This trade, 80 percent of which is illegal, will entirely eliminate Sumatra's lowland forests along with the orangutan and Sumatran tiger in the next ten years.[29] In Brazil, the great mahogany forests are melting away for similar reasons. Then there are the turtle and the fish stocks, which according to marine scientists are already suffering catastrophic collapse worldwide as a result of subsidized over-fishing.[30] While voluntary efforts like the UN-backed Global Compact have made progress in getting multinational companies to endorse environmental principles, environmentalists remain pessimistic in the face of comments like those of the first President Bush, who noted before the Earth Summit in Rio de Janiero in 1992 that "the American way of life is not up for negotiation." His son's decision to keep the United States out of the Kyoto Treaty on Global Warming because "it would be bad for the U.S. economy" only confirmed environmentalists in the view that globalization needs to be drastically changed.[31]

For the professional left and for college students looking for a cause now that communism and socialism lost their cachet, antiglobalization is merely another way of attacking the same capitalist target. Another factor is an element of cultural homogenization that causes resentment, the more so because it is often the result of ambivalent surrender to temptation. Bambang Rachmadi knows a lot about this. The owner of eighty-five McDonalds restaurants spread throughout Indonesia, he quickly put up signs in the wake of September 11 saying: "In the name of Allah, the merciful and the gracious, McDonalds Indonesia is owned by an indigenous Muslim." Mr. Bambang believes his restaurants are good for Indonesia, but he also knows they symbolize a shift away from a stable, predictable lifestyle for which there is much nostalgia.[32] Added to this sense of loss is the feeling on the part of many that this shift is occurring in a most undemocratic way. As the Indian economics professor Kaushik Basu argues, globalization means that even if individual countries are becoming more democratic, the sum of global democracy is shrinking because under globalization peoples and nations exert asymmetric influence.[33] Korea, for example, had little choice during the financial crisis of 1997 but to accept a U.S.-crafted rescue package that required it to open up its banking sector to acquisitions by foreign banks. Poor countries and small countries have little say about the terms of globalization, which, as it spreads, increasingly eliminates their freedom of choice.

The biggest problem, however, is simply that many do not see American-led globalization as working for them. While many of the countries of East Asia and the Pacific, including most recently China, have dramatically raised their standards of living over the past fifteen years, much of the rest of the developing world has not. Per capita GDP in the Middle East, North Africa, and Latin America has grown at only about 1.5 percent per year. In sub-Saharan Africa, central and eastern Europe, and central Asia, per capita GDP has actually shrunk.[34] While a good deal of this failure is due to inappropriate domestic policies and lack of openness to the outside, the forces of globalization have also played a role.

Furthermore, some important countries are failing despite apparently following the prescribed globalization regime. Take Mexico, for example. The conclusion of the NAFTA treaty brought Mexico fully into the global economy, with reduced trade barriers, open financial markets, and full adherence to measures like protection of intellectual property that are thought to attract foreign investment. Mexico also became democratic after seventy-one years of one-party rule. Of course, NAFTA had no provisions for infrastructure construction, special development funding, or labor mobility such as the European Union has typically implemented when bringing less developed countries into the EU. But America's faith in free market solutions made those seem costly and unnecessary. On the one hand, NAFTA has spurred dramatic increases in Mexican exports and in foreign investment in Mexico. Between 1991 and 2001, Mexican exports increased by $120 billion, and FDI increased by $16 billion. And yet few in Mexico feel better off. After twenty years of free market reforms and ten years of NAFTA, 50 percent of Mexicans live on about $4 per day.[35] When I worked in Mexico in the 1970s about 60 percent of the population could be considered middle and working class. Today, the proportion is 35 percent and falling. Of many domestic problems, a major one is that jobs are leaving Mexico as factories close and move to countries with lower labor costs. In the summer of 2002, for example,

Callaway Golf Club cut its Mexican employment in half as it shifted production to China.[36] Later that fall, I met with Mayer Zaga, one of Mexico's leading textile manufacturers, who told me it was becoming extremely difficult to compete with imported Chinese textiles in the Mexican market.

Brazil is another example. Pressed to democratize its politics and globalize its markets, it suffered an economic crisis in the middle of its presidential elections in the fall of 2002 as foreign investors withdrew money, fearing that the leftist candidate, Luis Inacio "Lula" da Silva, would win and renege on debt obligations. As Brazil's ambassador to Washington Rubens Barbosa said to me at the time, "It doesn't seem fair that you should make us pay a price for having a democratic election. Worse, you make it difficult for us to earn the money to pay our obligations by erecting trade barriers against over half the products we want to sell you: soy beans, sugar, orange juice, and steel."

This issue of barriers and harmful restrictions is echoed in many places. Pakistan is bitter that after its staunch support in the wake of September 11, the United States made only a token increase in the strict quotas it has placed on imports of Pakistani textiles. New Zealand, Australia, and the Philippines complain of strict limits on U.S. agricultural imports.

A different complaint comes from Africa and India, where AIDS is having a devastating effect. Although drugs exist and are used in the rich western countries to enable AIDS patients to live productively with the disease, they are far too expensive for the developing world. Here the problem is that the WTO's rules protecting patents make it impossible for generic drug producers in developing countries to supply the medicines inexpensively. As a result, some in these countries actually see globalization as a major cause of death.

Beyond these complaints, however, lies a deeper issue of the validity of globalization theory. George Soros recently told me, "The conventional wisdom holds that markets are always right, but in my experience they are almost always wrong, although they can validate themselves." Mexico's problem with China provides a telling example. Globalization doctrine holds that if countries open their markets to the free flow of goods and money, privatize, deregulate, institute a strict rule of law, maintain transparency, and practice fiscal and monetary prudence, the world will come crowding to their doors. In fact, however, China is sucking up the lion's share of foreign direct investment as the world's producers flock to its shores. Yet China has no rule of law, little transparency, is heavily regulated and has a banking system second only to Japan's in fragility. The truth is, as the World Bank noted in *The East Asian Miracle: Economic Growth and Public Policy*, the East Asian countries followed a formula for success, pioneered by Japan, that bears little resemblance to the standard tenets of globalization. It calls for enforced high savings rates (Singapore, for example, sequesters nearly half of every worker's pay check for its provident fund) , suppressed domestic consumption, technology transfer conditions on foreign direct investment, government intervention in capital allocation, protection of most domestic markets, and emphasis on exports as the growth leader.

Yet it is doubtful that even this formula can succeed in the face of the China phenomenon. In the past, the pattern was for a developing country to begin making labor-intensive products like apparel and then move up the ladder of sophisticated manufacturing. But China can produce at both the low end and the high and be the low-cost producer at both. That leaves little room for other developing countries.

MAKING IT WORK

It has become a mantra that globalization, driven by technology's shrinkage of time and distance, is unstoppable. Yet this has been said before. In 1910, Norman Angell wrote *The Great Illusion*, a book that proclaimed war to be a thing of the past because the global economy was so integrated at the time. It took over sixty years after the end of World War I for the world to regain the level of globalization it had enjoyed in 1911. For globalization to work this time, it must address in a practical, non-ideological manner the complaints and inconsistencies I have noted above. Calling for free trade and openness is not enough. People don't hate American-led globalization per se. In fact, hundreds of millions if not billions love it. But if it is to last, it must spread benefits widely and equitably while being sensitive to the social and political needs of many different societies.

4

RUNNING ON EMPTY

Twelve yards long, two lanes wide
Sixty-five tons of American pride
Canyonero, Canyonero!

—The Simpsons
(parody of an SUV advertisement)

On Sunday, March 10, 2002, the lead story in the day's papers and on the talk shows was Afghanistan. The Taliban had been deposed, and the chase was on to catch Osama bin Laden in the jaws of a giant trap, known as Operation Anaconda, being sprung in the rugged Tora Bora mountains. About half the front page of the *Washington Post* was taken up by a photo showing massive bombing of mountain redoubts, along with a story detailing the progress of the operation and noting that American casualties so far totaled fifty-eight. It was an important, must read, breaking news story.

Less noticed was an article, buried on page A12, about that week's Senate debate on applying gasoline mileage requirements to sport utility vehicles (SUVs). These requirements had first been introduced for cars in 1975, after the oil shocks of 1973–1974, when the average U.S. auto got 13 miles per gallon of gas. Known as the CAFE standards, they required that the fleet of new passenger cars produced by U.S. makers achieve an average fuel economy of 27.5 mpg by 1985 and that light trucks average 17.2 mpg by 1979.[1]

The initial result had been dramatic. Within seven years, the average mileage of new American cars climbed from 13 mpg to 25.1 mpg and hit a peak of 26.2 mpg in 1987.[2] Since then, however, sport utility vehicles and pickup trucks had grown so popular as everyday family vehicles that by 2002 they made up more than half the total number of vehicles sold. While very profitable for auto producers, whose profits are much higher on SUVs and trucks than on cars, this change in the market played havoc with fuel economy. By the time the Senate took up the question, the average gas mileage of new vehicles had slid to 24 mpg and American gasoline consumption and oil imports were soaring. In an effort to correct this situation, the Senate was considering a bill to extend application of the standards from cars to SUVs with the goal of increasing total fleet mileage by 3 mpg, to about what it had been in 1987.[3]

The *Post* article quoted Senate Minority Leader Trent Lott as saying that raising the standard would be unacceptable because "this is still America," and if it happened he wouldn't "be able to drive my grandchildren around the ranch anymore."[4] This is a tragedy that would tear at the heart of every American were it not shamelessly exaggerated. Still, no one seems to have seen the connection between Lott's comments and the Operation Anaconda story on the front page. How many lives are we willing to pay for a barrel of oil and a spin around the ranch in an SUV? It's an unfair question, of course. But it's hard to escape the conclusion that Lott thinks gas should be cheap because this is America and Americans have a right to cheap gas. That the material and human costs of Operation Anaconda are, in part, a result of that sentiment is kept well hidden.

One sees few SUVs in London or in the rest of Europe and Japan. One major reason is that in all those places gasoline at the pump sells for between $3.97 per gallon (in Japan) and $4.66 (U.K.).[5] It costs much less on a pre-tax basis. In fact, the United States has the highest pre-tax price at $1.20 per gallon, compared with an average of about $1.10 in the other developed countries.[6] But whereas the United States adds only about 38 cents in taxes, the rest of the developed world imposes a tax over six times larger.[7] Not surprisingly, Europe and Japan produce cars that get about 34 mpg—or ten mpg better than the U.S. fleet.[8] If U.S. vehicles got the same fuel economy as European and Japanese vehicles, the United States would need to import no Persian Gulf oil at all.

Nor is the difference in energy efficiency limited to cars and trucks. You can go from Brussels to Paris on the TGV (Train à Gran Vitesse, or high-speed train), the European improvement on Japan's famed bullet trains, in about an hour and twenty minutes. The distance is about the same as between Washington and New York, yet the ride takes about half as long as the Amtrak Metroliner. As a result, many more people take the train from Paris to Brussels and back than fly. By building a modern, high-speed rail system, Europe has dramatically reduced the need for energy-inefficient flight in favor of extremely efficient rail.

Just as gasoline is more expensive outside the United States, so is electricity, and not surprisingly U.S. per capita electricity use is double that of Japan, the next highest user.[9] In fact, the Japanese have put such emphasis on energy efficiency that they can produce a dollar of GDP with less than half the energy of the United States.[10] Of course, Japan is a small country, with most of its people and industry located in a narrow strip between Tokyo and Osaka, so distances and climate variances are less than in the United States. But in the European Union, a large area with great climactic and topographical differences, a population larger than that of the United States, and a similar-sized GDP, the story is the same. To create the equivalent of $1 of GDP, Europeans use only about two thirds as much energy as the Americans.[11] If America had the same energy efficiency as the EU, it could not only do without oil imports from the Persian Gulf, it could do without oil imports period. This would cut $100 billion a year off the U.S. trade deficit, stop the flow of U.S. money that gets recycled through oil-producing countries in the Middle East to fund terrorism and the spread of radical Islam, and greatly reduce the need for U.S. military deployments in the Persian Gulf. These deployments, which cost $60 billion annually, raise the real cost of Gulf oil to about $200 per barrel.[12] Many observers around the world wonder why America isn't more serious about conserving energy purely in its own interest. As I will explain, the reason has to do with America's sense of entitlement. It also has to do with our love of personal freedom. But the price of that independence is a dependence that has made us vulnerable. In turn the vulnerability has led to war, destruction, and death, and finally to a hint of soul searching.

BUBBA'S BIRTHRIGHT

The standard definition of a "Bubba" is a man who feels it's his God-given right to drive his pickup truck down the highway at 80 miles an hour with the windows open, the CD player and air-conditioning both on at full blast, and an open can of beer in his lap. While he's generally thought of as a white man from the South, the truth is that Bubbas can be found from Connecticut to California among all races and both genders. There's some Bubba in all of us Americans (full disclosure: I myself drive an SUV). Leave aside the stereotype's nonessentials for a moment—the music, the beer can, the large dog in the passenger seat, the hunting rifle in a gun rack behind the rear window, the patriotic bumper stickers—and pay attention to the overpowered and over-accessorized vehicle (mostly provided by American industry), the road (provided by American government), and the sense of entitlement (provided by American history). Where do these things come from, and where are they taking us?

We often draw a picture of America as a country that started poor and through hard work and enterprise made itself into the most developed of nations. In truth, however, America was rich almost from the start. The technology of Europe in the seventeenth century was fully available to the settlers in the New World. In particular, the primary sources of energy at that time were wood, wind, and water, and nowhere was there more wood, wind, and water than in the new colonies. The Pilgrims and other early settlers had discovered the Saudi Arabia of their day, for just as Saudi Arabia has the biggest and least-costly energy reserves today, so at that time did North America. So from its birth the nation enjoyed cheap energy, and future generations came to assume that as a birthright.

When joined to the techniques and tools the settlers brought with them from Europe, this cheap, plentiful energy powered a surge of economic growth that quickly enabled living standards in the New World to match or exceed those of the old countries. By 1820, the United States was the fourth-richest country in the world with a per capita GDP (in 1990 dollars) of $1,257. It trailed only the Netherlands at $1,821, the United Kingdom at $1,707, and Belgium at $1,319. France was about the same as the United States, while Germany and Italy were well behind at about $1,100, and Japan was at about half the U.S. level. In average life expectancy, the United States was third at 39 years, trailing Germany's 41, and the U.K.'s 40.[13]

As the nineteenth century and the industrial revolution progressed together, the world's energy sources shifted from wood, wind, and water to a new era of steam, coal, and whale oil. Once again, the United States was the Saudi Arabia of the age. U.S. coal production rose from negligible levels in 1820 to almost 200 million metric tons by 1900.[14] The whaling fleet, which began in New Bedford, Massachusetts, in 1755, hit a peak of 329 ships in 1857.[15] This plentiful and inexpensive energy was a major factor in giving the U.S. economy the fastest growth rate among the world's major economies in the mid-nineteenth century. By 1870, the United States, was poised to more than double its standard of living over the next forty years to take over the top spot in per capita GDP.[16] Its rise would be greatly aided by what had been found a few years earlier at Oil Creek, near Titusville, Pennsylvania.

Seepages of a gooey black substance from the earth had been recorded as far back as 3000 B.C. in Mesopotamia, at Hit on the Euphrates, not far from Babylon and present-day Baghdad. Known as bitumen, it was used as a building mortar in the walls of Jericho and Babylon and very likely covered the seams of Noah's ark and Moses' basket to make them waterproof. It was also used for road building, lighting, medicine, and, of course, war. Homer notes in the *Iliad* that the Trojans shot unquenchable flames over the ships of the Greeks. The Persians used fire in their conquests, and the Byzantines used Greek fire, a mixture of bitumen and lime that caught fire on contact with water. Petroleum and its applications were largely forgotten in the West after the fall of Rome. By the 1850s, however, kerosene derived from crude oil found in Galicia and Rumania was used for lighting in Vienna and just being introduced in the United States.

It was this development that made the seepage of oil into the springs and salt wells around Oil Creek so interesting to the New York lawyer George Bissell and a small group of investors he had gathered. For some time the oil that coated the creek's surface had been gathered by skimming or by wringing out rags that had been soaked in the oily waters. The tiny supply of oil thus gathered was used mostly to make medicines, but Bissell's group saw their fortune in selling it as a competitor to kerosene and whale oil for lamps. Skimming and soaking could not produce nearly the volume of the product they envisioned selling, however, nor would digging do. To get at the source of the oil economically, they decided to adopt the techniques then in use for drilling salt wells. Work began in the spring of 1858, and after a year of exhausting work, there was absolutely nothing to show for it. With growing despair, the group pushed the work through the summer until late August. Then, with money running out, the investors sent a final money order to their drilling overseer, "Colonel" E. L. Drake, along with instructions to halt operations. By Saturday afternoon, August 27, 1859, when the drill fell into a crevice, Drake had not yet received the letter and work was halted only for the rest of the weekend. On Monday, still without the letter, Drake arrived at the site to find his drillers standing over tubs and barrels filled with black liquid. The age of oil had dawned.[17]

The extent of the American energy bonanza was not clear at first. For a quarter century the industry was fragile, uncertain, and wholly dependent on the oil fields of Pennsylvania. In 1885 the Pennsylvania state geologist warned that oil was "a temporary and vanishing phenomenon," and a top executive of Standard Oil became so concerned about declining production that he sold some of his shares in the company at a discount of 25 percent. No sooner had he done this than new oil was discovered at Lima, Ohio, in an oil field that straddled the Ohio-Indiana border. This field was so productive that by 1890 it accounted for a third of total U.S. production.

For the next sixty years, all concern about adequate supplies vanished as more giant oil fields were discovered. In 1893, the citizens of the small Texas town of Corsicana began drilling new wells to augment their dwindling water supply. Instead of water, however, they hit oil. This was just a prelude. In the fall of 1900, drilling began on top of a salt dome hill near Beaumont, Texas, called Spindletop. By Christmas, some oil had showed, and it was estimated that the well might produce fifty barrels a day. Not bad, but nothing like what was about to happen. After taking off for Christmas, the drillers resumed work on New Year's Day and on January 10, 1901, the earth exploded, sending the drill pipe, rock, and oil hundreds of feet into the air. It was the first gusher in the United States, flowing at a phenomenal seventy-five thousand barrels a day. Others followed: Signal Hill in California, Greater Seminole in Oklahoma, and then the granddaddy of them all, Dad Joiner's Black Giant in east

Texas. America was truly the Saudi Arabia of this era. How could anyone doubt that cheap energy was indeed an American birthright?

The trouble, in fact, was too much oil. Every time a new gusher came in, prices collapsed and threatened producers with bankruptcy. This problem had arisen soon after the first strikes at Oil Creek. Oil that was selling for $10 a barrel in early 1861 was down to 10 cents by the end of the year.[18] By gaining control of distribution and transport through his Standard Oil of New Jersey trust, John D. Rockefeller was able to take advantage of low prices to make huge profits and also to bring a measure of order to the market. But the vast Texas fields, particularly the Black Giant, overwhelmed even Standard Oil. Oil that had sold in Texas in l926 for $1.85 a barrel was going for as low as 6 cents a barrel by the end of May 1931. Even the largest producers could smell bankruptcy, and they cast about for a way of limiting production and stabilizing prices.

The Texas Railroad Commission had been created in 1891 as a populist attempt to gain some control over monopolistic railroads. In 1931 it was also granted some power to regulate "physical waste" in oil production. From that narrow base, through many difficult twists and turns, it came effectively to ration production and stabilize prices globally until the Saudi-led Organization of Petroleum Exporting Countries (OPEC) was established in 1960. In effect, the Texas Railroad Commission was the American OPEC of its day.

America's massive supply of inexpensive energy powered it to global leadership. By 1913, the U.S. per capita income of $5,301 was well above the $4,921 of the then superpower Great Britain, and the United States had become the world's largest producer of steel and many other key industrial products.[19] For a moment in the 1880s, the oil industry had been thrown a scare when Thomas Edison's electric light bulbs began to replace oil lamps. But the invention of the "horseless carriage" in 1885 saved the day, and the growth of the automobile industry changed the face of America and the world. By the time of America's entry into World War I, there were already 3.5 million autos on U.S. roads. This number grew to a bit more than 23 million by the end of 1929, when Americans owned 78 percent of all the autos in the world.[20]

Nor was the oil important only as an economic force. World War I began in 1914 with steam-powered trains carrying troops into battle and horses pulling artillery and supply wagons. It ended four years later with gasoline-powered British tanks crashing through German trenches, and German U boats choking for lack of diesel fuel. As the director of the French Comité Général du Pétrole put it, oil was "the blood of victory," and 80 percent of it came from the United States.[21] More than the late entry of American troops, it was the early and continuous participation of American oil that gave the allies the victory.

If oil was a key part of the game in World War I, it was the whole game in World War II. As Japan pushed further into China in 1940, the United States debated whether to impose an embargo on the oil exports that were essential for Japan's military machine, lest doing so only trigger a Japanese invasion of the Dutch East Indies to gain control of its oil fields. Finally, in July 1941, the Japanese takeover of Indochina resulted in a de facto embargo on July 25. From that point, the attack on Pearl Harbor and the war in the Pacific were only a matter of time. Even with the East Indian oil fields in their hands, however, the Japanese needed to move the stuff to their home islands. It was a long and vulnerable supply line, and Japan lost the war because it could not keep its oil tankers running. In the end, Japanese tankers were being sunk as fast as they were launched, and the Japanese fleet became inoperable for lack of fuel. The atomic bomb may have provided the coup de grace, but it was lack of oil that led to Japan's defeat.

It was the same story in Europe. Hitler failed to take Moscow largely because he had to divert a large part of his forces in an attempt to capture the Baku oil fields that were essential to keep his entire war effort going. At the same time, the poor quality of the Russian roads caused the German forces to use twice as much fuel as initially estimated. They failed to get to Baku, and Hitler's armies literally ran out of gas about twenty miles from Moscow.

In the Battle of the Bulge, his last-ditch effort to drive the allies back into the sea, Hitler again failed for lack of fuel. Indeed, once the U.S. and Great Britain managed in 1943 to defeat the Germans' North Atlantic submarine fleet, which had been attacking the tanker convoys to England, the fate of the Axis was sealed. Oil flowed unopposed from America to power the allied forces. In all, the allies consumed about 7 billion barrels of oil to fight the war, and 6 billion of them came from America.[22]

When wartime gasoline rationing was lifted in the United States, shortly after Japan's surrender, the cry of "fill 'er up" became the new national slogan. Between the end of the war in August 1945, and the end of 1950, U.S. auto sales, which had declined during the war, exploded as Americans began to create a whole new lifestyle.[23] For three centuries Americans had built the country. Then for a decade and a half, through depression and then war, the country had scrimped and denied itself. Now it was time to enjoy the nation's birthright of cheap energy.

BUBBA MORTGAGES HIS FREEDOM

Flatbush, Brooklyn, is a typical suburb, 1890s style. Built within a twenty-minute train ride from downtown Manhattan, it has short, straight blocks with sidewalks; close-set houses from whose verandahs neighbors can easily chat with one another; stores, schools, and train stations within easy walking distance. Cars are not really necessary and, in fact, only cause a nuisance by cluttering up the street. Flatbush was not built with automobiles in mind.

America's post-war boom was largely driven by construction of a very different kind of suburb. New housing developments mushroomed far from central cities in what most people had thought of as the countryside. But the countryside grew a new kind of suburb, with long, curving blocks, no sidewalks, plots of half an acre or more, within walking distance of nowhere, and with no nearby shops or train stations. The houses started big and got bigger over time as family rooms, country kitchens, and dens became necessities. And, of course, these houses were completely climate controlled and stuffed with the latest electric appliances. In the ten years after the war, over 9 million people moved to suburbs like these, and by 1976 more Americans were living in the suburbs than in either rural towns or cities.[24]

All these people, of course, had to get their shopping done somewhere, and the suburban strip mall arose to answer the demand. Again it differed significantly from the old downtown business district. In place of rows of stores in several-story buildings fronting a common sidewalk, suburban zoning ordinances mandated clumps of low-rise shops in the middle of vast parking lots—frequently making it impractical to walk from one store to its next-door neighbor. Meanwhile, the face of downtown was changing too. With so many people living in suburbs, the central cities became compounds of high-rise office buildings. But these buildings were not the brick-and-stone structures of an earlier day. They were gleaming glass towers that acted as heat sinks in summer and ice boxes in winter and were made habitable only by the climate control systems enabled by cheap energy.

At first, the suburbs typically did not have large enough concentrations of people to justify the investment of a private rail line, and they were located beyond the jurisdiction of cities that might have installed public transportation systems. So the only way to get to and around them was by car. There was another factor at work. While private companies had to invest in, maintain, and pay taxes on railroad lines, roads were a public good provided by government. Along with home building, road construction became a boom industry. The prototype for all this was Los Angeles. There, a fledgling public transportation system was destroyed when a consortium of automobile, fuel, and tire companies bought up the streetcar companies, shut them down, tore up their tracks, and turned the streetcar routes into bus routes. The idea was to increase the market for buses, cars, tires, and fuel. It worked.

In 1947 California undertook to build a massive road system that would be interlinked into a whole regional network. New Jersey soon followed with the Garden State Parkway and New Jersey Turnpike, and most other states came along shortly afterward. In 1956, President Eisenhower inaugurated the granddaddy of all road projects by signing the Interstate Highway Act, which aimed to create a 41,000-mile national network of superhighways. The project was promoted primarily as a national security measure that would enable quick evacuation of cities in the event of atomic attack; it was, however, not the military but rather a vast array of lobbyists from the auto, oil, rubber, real estate, trucking, and parking industries who pushed it through. Eisenhower said it "would change the face of America,"[25] and it did.

People not only moved their residences to the suburbs, they began to move their offices there as well. Increasing air travel made offices near airports attractive. Like roads, the airways and airports were built and maintained by the government, and travelers were turning in droves to the new jets that not only cut travel time dramatically but also cut prices as a result of their low fuel costs. Meanwhile, public transport and railroads dwindled as Americans took to the subsidized roads and skies.

By 1975 the country was designed and built to favor cars and airplanes over trains and buses, private transportation over public. Most of us lived in large, widely spaced houses far from our jobs, recreation, or any place else we might go. The lifestyle that cheap energy had given us was no longer a choice: The very architecture of the country demanded it.

The proximate cause of this transformation, the car, also metamorphosed. Because people spent so much time in their cars and saw them as an expression of their own personalities, the vehicles gradually became bigger, more powerful, and more luxurious. Tail fins and wraparound chrome bumpers adorned cars that grew to 25 feet in length. Automatic shift and air-conditioning became the standard, as did the V–8 engine with more than 250 horsepower. What difference did it make that by 1973 the average car got only 13 miles per gallon? Gas was no problem.

SHOCKS

Actually, it had been getting to be a problem for some time. As early as 1943, Interior Secretary Harold Ickes had written an article entitled "We're Running Out of Oil!" The discoveries of the 1920s and 1930s were not being repeated, and with consumption rising, it was inevitable that the United States would become a net importer. That situation materialized sooner than most expected—in 1948, when for the first time ever U.S. imports of oil exceeded exports.[26] Not since the arrival of the first settlers in Jamestown had America been energy dependent. Now it was becoming so.

But aside from representing a historic change, the switch was not immediately of much concern. The Texas Railroad Commission maintained price stability by keeping actual production well below capacity. As a byproduct, this practice provided a surge capability in time of crisis. It was this surge capacity that had provided the margin of victory in both world wars, and from 1948 until the late 1960s, it remained at several million barrels a day. But consumption rose beyond all expectation, not only in the United States but around the world, as Europe and Japan recovered and other countries began to industrialize. Between 1960 and 1972, free world oil consumption climbed from 19 million barrels a day to more than 44 million barrels a day.[27] In 1970, when U.S. production peaked at 11.3 million barrels per day, the surge capacity was down to 1 million barrels per day.[28] From there it was all downhill. In 1971 the Railroad Commission authorized production at full capacity. Imports nevertheless rose rapidly, from a little more than 2 million barrels a day in 1967 to 6 million, more than 35 percent of U.S. consumption, by 1973.[29] In 1968, the State Department had notified the Organization for Cooperation and Development (OECD) in Paris that in the event of a future crisis there would be no surge supply from the United States.[30] The world and the United States were now heavily reliant on production from the Middle East, one of the most insecure regions in the world, and this reliance would only increase.

Although it had been known since ancient times, oil did not become a focus of commercial interest in the Middle East until 1900, when the impecunious Shah of Persia, in an attempt to shore up his ever-precarious financial condition, approached a retired British diplomat about the possibility of selling a concession for oil exploration in Persia. After many adventures, William Knox D'Arcy, a British entrepreneur who had made a fortune in gold mining in Australia, bought the concession and with financial backing from the British government brought in a gusher on the morning of May 26, 1908. In 1909, D'Arcy's company made what a later generation of American entrepreneurs would call an "IPO" (Initial Public Offering), going public as the Anglo-Persian Oil Company. As the British rivalry with Germany intensified over the next five years, the British government, at the strong urging of the young Winston Churchill, bet heavily on oil-fired naval vessels to replace coal-fired ships. Then in June 1914, His Majesty's government bought 51 percent of the shares of Anglo-Persian. It turned out to be a wise purchase, for during the war that began in August of that year, the Anglo-Persian Oil Company came to produce 20 percent of the oil consumed by His Majesty's fleet.[31]

The story of the discovery and development of the great Middle East oil fields is a fascinating and complex tale, too long to tell here in detail. Suffice it to say that after D'Arcy's strike in Persia the race was on, and destitute Sheiks all over the Middle East suddenly became the objects of affection of western oil entrepreneurs in search of drilling concessions. Due to their imperial reach, the British got most of those in what became

Iran, Iraq, and Kuwait. But they somehow managed to convince themselves there was no oil in the Arabian peninsula. Thus, when Standard Oil of California (Socal) went calling on King Ibn Saud for a drilling concession in Saudi Arabia, a British diplomat told the King, who was reluctant about having foreigners poking holes in his kingdom, to take the money because there was no oil and he could therefore get the money and the foreigners would soon be gone. But in March 1938, Damman No. 7 well gushed, and the rest is history.

That it was an American company that found the oil in Saudi Arabia later turned out to be very significant, although at the time the U.S. government dismissed as unnecessary Socal's suggestion of U.S. diplomatic representation in the kingdom. By the beginning of World War II, everyone knew there was a lot of oil in the Middle East and especially in the Arabian peninsula. In the course of the war, the United States did, after initially dismissing the proposition as unimportant, use Lend Lease funding to support maintenance of the Saudi oil fields. Still, Middle Eastern production was of only marginal significance during the war.

That changed rapidly as the 1940s became the 1950s. In 1946, three-fourths of Europe's oil came from America. By 1951, more than half came from the Middle East.[32] The shift toward Middle East production, the end of colonialism, the rise of nationalism in the region, and the establishment of the state of Israel created a complex pudding with two major themes. One was a continuing struggle (destined to be successful) by the governments of the producing countries to wrest control of the oil and its pricing away from the oil companies. The other (still unsuccessful) was to erase or severely constrict Israel.

The first oil crisis arose in 1951 when Iran (formerly Persia) nationalized the Anglo-Persian Oil Company. This gave rise to much turmoil and an actual embargo by Britain against the newly nationalized company, which greatly curtailed the flow of Middle East oil to world markets. The still significant surge capacity of the Texas Railroad Commission filled the gap easily, however, and consumers were not hurt. The second crisis arose in 1956, when Egyptian leader Gamal Abdel Nasser moved to nationalize the British- and French-owned Suez Canal Company and take control of movement on the waterway. In response, Britain and France, in league with Israel, landed troops in an attempt to seize the canal zone.

This, of course, closed the canal and again halted the flow of oil from the Middle East to Europe. The British and French had counted on U.S. support for their action, but a surprised President Eisenhower was convinced it would only push the Arabs toward the Soviets. He not only told the Brits and the French to get out but refused to make U.S. surge capacity available unless they did. That was a decisive threat, and once the invaders left Egypt, the Texas Railroad Commission again saved Europe's bacon.

The third crisis arose as a result of the Six-Day War that began on June 5, 1967, when Israel launched a preemptive strike against threatening Egyptian and Syrian forces. Talk of the "oil weapon" had circulated in Arab circles for some time, and now it was unsheathed. On June 6, the oil ministers of the Arab countries announced an embargo, and by June 8, shipments had already been cut by 60 percent.[33] With Europe now getting three-fourths of its rapidly growing oil needs from the Middle East, the situation was critical. Again, however, the Railroad Commission rode to the rescue, unleashing a million barrels a day of surge capacity. By July it was clear that the "oil weapon" was a rubber sword.

By 1973, however, the world oil market had changed decisively. The United States was no longer the supplier of last resort. Saudi Arabia was, and even the United States depended on it for that last barrel of oil. OPEC, having been formed in 1960 as part of the exporting countries' struggle to wrest revenue and control away from the oil companies, was not yet a household name. While it had had some successes, the market condition of excess supply and the U.S. surge capacity continually undermined its efforts. The new circumstances, however, encouraged it to take a hard line at its annual negotiating meeting with the companies, scheduled for October 8, 1973, in Vienna. On October 6, Yom Kippur in Israel, Egyptian leader Anwar Sadat launched a surprise attack on Israeli forces occupying the Sinai and Gaza. At the negotiating table in Vienna, the companies offered a 15-percent price increase, to about $3.45 a barrel.[34] The OPEC oil ministers laughed. Double or nothing was their response. Meanwhile, in an effort to put pressure on the U.S and Europe to force Israel to retreat, Sadat was begging his Arab brethren to try the "oil weapon" one more time. Saudi Arabia, torn between reluctance to alienate the United States and the sense of injustice it shared with other Arabs over the creation of Israel, hesitated but then agreed. On October

17 the embargo was announced. This time the "oil weapon" proved to be a sword of Toledo steel.

In Belgium, where I was living at the time, people actually hitched horses and oxen to their cars for lack of gas. During a trip to my company's Philadelphia headquarters, I stocked my rental car with books and magazines for whiling away the time in gas lines. On October 16 the price of crude oil had been $5.40 per barrel. By mid-December it was $17 a barrel. At the pump in the United States, prices soared by 40 percent.[35] Eventually, Henry Kissinger negotiated an end to the hostilities, and Sadat, now looking to establish new ties to the United States, called on the Arabs to sheathe the sword, which they did on March 18.

But although the embargo was over, the new power structure stayed. It was the beginning of OPEC's golden age. For the next five years, stability returned to the markets, though at much higher prices than anyone had envisioned. Then came the overthrow of the Shah of Iran, the rise of Ayatollah Khomeini, and the closure of the Iranian oil fields at the end of 1978. Again, prices soared and panic ensued. The impact on the global economy was enormous. The industrial countries went into deep recession, with U.S. GDP falling by 6 percent and unemployment doubling to 9 percent.[36] Japan's economy stopped growing for the first time since the end of World War II. Even worse was the plight of the developing countries that didn't produce oil and had little ability to carry the burden of the higher prices. As the global economy stagnated, torrents of money flowed into OPEC coffers, to be recycled largely through U.S. and European banks in the form of loans to increasingly indebted developing countries. The global public demanded to know if there was a better way.

SHOCK THERAPY

The question had actually been asked almost thirty years before. As it was becoming clear in the mid-1940s that U.S. oil reserves might have limits, there was much discussion of alternatives to ensure security of supply. Some advocated increasing imports in peacetime so as to preserve domestic reserves for emergencies. Not only was this idea discarded, but quotas were actually imposed on imports in an effort to keep domestic producers profitable and theoretically drilling for more. With vast amounts of coal and oil shale in the Rocky Mountains, the United States seemed ideally positioned to develop a synthetic oil industry that could guarantee supplies indefinitely. In 1947 the Interior Department had proposed a $10-billion Manhattan-style project to develop a synthetic fuel industry over the next four or five years. Eventually, $85 million was authorized for research, but the program died as it became clear that synthetic oil would cost substantially more than the inexpensive foreign oil that was then readily available.[37]

Over the next two decades, the success in handling the early oil crises created a sense of security that prevented the "better way" question from being asked. Certainly none of the nation's national security advisors asked it when Eisenhower, in what must be one of history's great ironies, sold the Interstate Highway project that would greatly exacerbate America's vulnerability to foreign oil suppliers, in the name of national security.[38] Writing his memoir, *Present At The Creation*, after the Six Day War, former Secretary of State Dean Acheson did comment that if "a fraction of our investment in the space program had been put into the development of a practical electric automobile and of nuclear power plants here and in Europe, we could have done much to solve our air pollution problems and free Europe from dependence on the Middle East and the Soviet Union from its motive in penetrating it."[39] No one paid attention. But now the question was back, and more urgent than ever.

In Tokyo and Europe, the response to the 1978 crisis was immediate and drastic. Japan's powerful Ministry of International Trade and Industry (MITI) took elevators out of service at its headquarters building and reduced both the heat in the winter and air-conditioning in the summer. I remember literally sweating through negotiating sessions in those days or alternatively shivering in the presence of my comfortably sweatered Japanese colleagues. These measures were symbolic, of course, but they set the tone that enabled Japan to adopt tough new policies. On the supply side, Japan committed to a major program of construction of nuclear power plants, development of liquid natural gas supplies from Southeast Asia and Russia, and shifting from oil to coal wherever possible. Even more significant, however, were the country's efforts to cut demand by conserving energy. High efficiency standards were set for new appliances. Gasoline taxes and electricity prices were hiked. Government and industry worked to create more efficient processes and equipment. Perhaps most importantly, the Japanese government convinced its public that the future of Japan depended upon conserving energy and thereby enlisted the legendary ability of the Japanese to get just a little bit more out of nothing. It was at this time that MITI began to draw up plans for shifting the structure of Japanese industry from energy-intensive to the knowledge-intensive high technology sectors in which Japan would dramatically challenge the United States in the 1980s. Naohiro Amaya, MITI's vice minister at the time, once told me the whole experience had been a blessing in disguise. Certainly, the policies to reduce oil use and increase energy efficiency worked better than anyone had expected. By 1985, Japan was using 31 percent less energy to produce one dollar of GDP and fully 51 percent less oil.[40]

Nor did it stop there. By imposing heavy fuel and vehicle taxes that are partially rebated for energy efficient models, Japanese authorities have introduced enormous efficiency in their auto and truck fleet. Almost all Japanese taxis, for example, run on liquid natural gas. Toyota and Honda sold a combined 36,000 hybrid gas-electric vehicles, which get more than 50 miles per gallon, in the United States in 2002.[41] Their global competitors, meanwhile, have sold none. Since 1985, Japan has reduced its dependency on oil for overall energy needs from nearly 60 percent to about 50 percent, and its energy use per dollar of GDP is by far the lowest among major industrialized countries. Moreover, it has a long-term energy policy that puts it on track to improve energy efficiency by another 30 percent by 2010.[42]

Europe, led by France, imitated Japan, by raising its already high gasoline taxes and electricity prices. Even more than Japan it committed to nuclear power, with France adopting an extremely aggressive policy. The Europeans also imitated Japan's emphasis on conservation. Again, France led the way. Buildings were to be heated to no more than 20 degrees centigrade and inspectors would make unannounced visits to assure compliance. The French even banned any advertising that might be seen as encouraging more energy use.[43] High energy prices as well as government programs also spurred discovery and development of the North Sea oil fields and efforts (bitterly opposed by the United States) to bring natural gas from the Soviet Union into northern Europe. As in Japan, the policies proved more effective than expected. Whereas 63 percent of France's electricity in 1973 was supplied by oil, natural gas, and coal combined, today

75 percent of electricity is nuclear, while oil accounts for less than 1 percent.[44] Europe shifted most cars from gasoline to diesel power and thus raised its already high fleet fuel economy for new models from 28 mpg to about 35 mpg.[45] Europe's already comparatively low energy consumption of 8400 BTU per dollar of GDP was steadily cut to 7400 BTU by 2002, and Europe's per capita electricity consumption has been held at less than half that of the United States.[46] Like Japan, Europe also has a clear plan for further energy diversification and conservation, a plan that also puts great emphasis on development of alternative energy sources.

The American response, on the other hand, was fitful, confused, and often divided. In 1973, President Nixon announced Project Independence: In the spirit of the Manhattan and Apollo projects, the U.S. would achieve energy independence by 1980.[47] But Nixon soon disappeared in the Watergate scandal, and the project never even got to the planning stage. In any case, it had little popular support. The public saw the American way of life being threatened, and congressional hearings at the time convinced many that the shortages were created by the big oil companies. People wanted Washington to do something, but "something" seemed to mean getting rid of gas lines and bringing back the good old prices while making the companies pay. Following Nixon, President Ford proposed a ten-year plan to build 200 nuclear plants, 250 major coal mines, 150 coal-fired power plants, and 20 synthetic oil plants.[48] Vice President Nelson Rockefeller, grandson of the founder of the modern oil industry, upped the ante with a proposal for a $100 billion program to underwrite synthetic fuels and other economically uncompetitive energy sources.[49] Opponents of all kinds saw to it that none of this even got onto the drawing boards.

Amid all the controversy, however, two important steps were taken. The Trans-Alaskan Pipeline was authorized to enable development of the Alaskan oil fields, and fuel efficiency legislation was passed that required new cars to average 27.5 miles per gallon by 1985.[50] President Carter made energy his number-one issue upon taking office in 1977 and introduced his policies as "the moral equivalent of war."[51] Some wags pointed out that the acronym for this is MEOW, and certainly the debate occasionally sounded like the whining of cats. Aside from the auto fuel efficiency requirements there had been little emphasis on conservation. Oil, in fact, was still under price controls that kept it artificially cheap in order to please the public. Carter made it a priority to let domestic oil rise to world market prices, only to find that the public didn't think there was a crisis. He eventually won on this but paid a high political price. Other Carter proposals included a "gas guzzler" tax on very fuel inefficient cars, a tax rebate for high mileage cars, an increase in the gasoline tax, a series of tax incentives and regulations aimed at forcing conversion to coal-fired generating plants, a plan to double the number of nuclear power plants in operation, tax credits for investment in solar energy equipment and insulation, a change from voluntary to mandatory standards for appliance efficiency, mandatory performance standards for new buildings, a big increase in R&D funding and incentives for development of energy from renewable sources, removal of barriers to use of industrially generated electricity in the public grid, formation of a Strategic Petroleum Reserve to hold ninety days of oil supply, and, that old standby, a $20 billion synthetic fuel project to produce eventually 2.5 million barrels a day of oil from Rocky Mountain shale.[52]

Interestingly, there was no mention of mass transit or railroads. But if there had been, it probably would not have survived. As it turned out, Congress eliminated the gas tax and the high mileage car rebate, while the nuclear accident at Three Mile Island in 1978 essentially killed any expansion of nuclear power by making construction of a nuclear plant in the United States prohibitively expensive as a result of new and extremely rigorous environmental requirements, not to mention the liability of lawsuits. Still, the Carter program did add important incentives for greater efficiency and for a shift from oil to other energy sources. And there were results. Along with millions of other Americans, I took advantage of the tax credits to double the insulation in my house and to equip it with a solar water heater, and the paper company for which I was working took important steps to increase efficiency. Auto gas mileage had doubled by 1985, and energy consumption per dollar of GDP fell from 18,400 BTU to 13,400 BTU (compared with Japan's decline from 5,000 to 3,946).[53] At the same time, supplies rose as Alaskan oil came on line, and higher prices and other incentives sparked more discovery of oil and natural gas in the United States.

But the advent of the Reagan administration marked a shift in U.S. policies that was more in line with the underlying populist ethic of the country. I was Counselor to the Secretary of Commerce at the time, and

I remember the frenzy to dump things like the Synfuels project, which had been pilloried during the election campaign as a government white elephant. (Canada, an oil exporter, persevered with its project, and today 20 percent of the oil it produces is synthetic.)[54] Federal funding for energy conservation was cut by 70 percent, energy R&D was slashed by 64 percent, and proposals for higher efficiency standards for new vehicles were dropped.[55] The emphasis was all on the supply side: Tax incentives and regulations were used to spur drilling and enhanced production. Supplies did increase but mostly because of the Alaskan pipeline, of the Saudi policy of keeping prices low enough to make investment in alternative energy unattractive, and of major expansion of production in the North Sea, Malaysia, Nigeria, Mexico, and elsewhere.

As prices fell and leaders ridiculed the need for any kind of government industrial policy, consumption trends began to reverse. The energy required to produce a dollar of GDP continued to decline as old cars were gradually replaced with new and as the effects of the new building standards and new industrial processes continued to work their way through the economy. But the decline was slowing, even as the United States remained far less energy efficient than other industrial countries. Per capita energy use had fallen from 366 million BTU in 1973 to 314 million BTU in 1983, but it was back to 352 million by 1997—more than double the rates for Japan and Europe, which were 165 million and 170 million BTU, respectively.[56] The gas mileage of new cars, light trucks, and SUVs peaked at 25.9 in 1988 and then declined as real retail prices for a gallon of gasoline, $1.08 in 1972, rose to $2.05 in 1981 and then fell to $1.15 in 1997.[57] After falling from 1977 to 1987, oil imports resumed a steady climb and topped the 1977 level in 1997.[58] The average horsepower of new vehicles rose steadily after 1982.[59] Renewable energy use fell from nearly 10 percent of total U.S. energy consumption in 1984 to 7.6 percent in 1997, while the real retail price of electricity, which had risen 53 percent between 1973 and 1982, fell back to nearly the 1973 level in 1997.[60] Coincidentally or not, refrigerators achieved a 294 percent improvement in energy efficiency between 1972 and 1993, and then, once the mandatory standard had been reached, the curve turned completely flat.[61] No nuclear plants have been ordered since 1978, and the existing ones are aging. Meanwhile, the size of the Strategic Oil Reserve fell from a high of 115 days' supply in 1985 to 52 days' supply at the end of 1999.[62]

In short, as the United States entered the twenty-first century, its energy picture was looking increasingly like that of 1973.

TO THE GULF AND BACK: THE 1990s

On September 22, 1980, OPEC ministers were gathered in Vienna making plans for the organization's twentieth anniversary celebration later in the year, scheduled for Baghdad, the city in which OPEC had been founded. The party never happened. On that same day, long-simmering hatreds between Iraq and the new revolutionary Iran of the Ayatollahs erupted into war with a massive Iraqi attack on Iran's oil facilities. Led by President Saddam Hussein, of whom the world would learn more later, the Iraqis anticipated a quick victory. But the war lasted seven long years, during which it virtually removed both Iranian and Iraqi production from world markets. It was a measure of how markets and the mechanisms for handling crises had changed that the world avoided another panic, although prices did rise. More importantly, however, the United States was forced to put the U.S. flag on Kuwaiti ships and convoy them in order to prevent the Iranians, haters of the Great Satan, from dominating the Gulf. When the Iraqi military used poison gas (later termed a weapon of mass destruction) in the spring of 1988 to gain the upper hand and force an armistice, there was no outcry from Washington, the United Nations, or the media. Although another oil shock was avoided, this war marked the beginning of a massive buildup of U.S. naval forces in the Persian Gulf. By 1985, it was costing the United States about $50 billion a year just to keep the shipping lanes open.[63]

Five years later, however, happy days seemed to be here again. The Berlin Wall had come down and so had oil prices. Americans were paying less for gas than at any time since the late 1940s.[64] Nor did there seem to be any long-term concern. World oil supplies had increased by about 50 percent, from around 600 billion barrels in 1985 to more than 900 billion in 1990.[65] Few stopped to note that the additions to reserves had occurred mostly among the major producers of the Persian Gulf.[66] In fact, if you looked closely, the picture resembled the 1970s more than the 1980s. Global demand was growing rapidly, most of the lines on graphs of U.S. consumption had turned up, American production was in free fall, and there were no major non-Gulf oil sources waiting to come into the system. But no one was looking closely.

Except, that is, for one key person. At 2 o'clock on the morning of August 2, 1990, America's erstwhile ally Saddam announced he was back by sending 100,000 troops to occupy neighboring Kuwait, only recently his supporter in the battle against Iran. Two weeks later, in a coincidental but revealing juxtaposition, the front page of the *Wall Street Journal* of August 17 carried a story saying the Bush administration was stoutly resisting a major energy conservation effort for fear of reminding voters of the Carter years, when lights were switched off at the White House.[67]

Although the United States bought only 12 percent of its oil in the Gulf at that time, a takeover of Kuwait would have given Saddam direct control of 25 percent[68] of world oil reserves and put him in a position to threaten Saudi Arabia, which held another 26 percent. He might then move on to settle accounts with Iran, which had another 9 percent of world reserves. While Saddam posed no direct threat to the United States or its allies and would in any case have to sell the oil to gain any benefit from it, President Bush responded in the most forceful manner. "Our jobs, our way of life, our own freedom and the freedom of friendly countries around the world would all suffer if control of the world's great oil reserves fell in the hands of Saddam Hussein," he declared.[69] The president, of course, gathered a great coalition and launched Operation Desert Storm, in which 500,000 troops, under the command of General "Stormin'" Norman Schwarzkopf, decimated Saddam's forces within one hundred hours, restoring the independence of Kuwait and an uneasy peace in the Gulf. Amazingly, the victory was achieved with just over six hundred casualties, and although the war cost $61 billion, $54 billion of it was paid by Japan and other allies, in lieu of their sending their own troops.[70] Of course, the Gulf now had to be patrolled even more vigilantly.

None of this brought any change in U.S. policies or attitudes about energy. The curves on the consumption graphs kept moving smartly upward, and although Secretary of State James Baker told the House of Representatives in February 1991 that "we must do more to reduce our energy dependence,"[71] the president, when presenting his new energy strategy in March, made no mention of conservation or efficiency. The plan called for drilling for new oil in the Arctic National Wildlife Refuge, but it cut spending for mass transit and rejected any increase in auto fuel efficiency standards.[72] While President Clinton resisted the push to drill in the Arctic and other national parks and tightened many environmental controls, he did not significantly change the nation's energy policies and practices.

The Gulf War did, however, bring one very significant change. The scion of a wealthy Saudi family, one Osama bin Laden, became extremely upset by the establishment of a huge U.S. airbase and the deployment of a major U.S. force south of Riyadh on the sacred soil of Saudi Arabia. Taking this as an outrageous insult not only to Arabia but to Islam itself, he vowed jihad (holy war) on the United States. Unlikely as it may sound for even a very rich man to imagine that he could defeat the world's only remaining superpower, bin Laden's experience with another American war gave him reason for confidence. In 1979, the old Soviet Union invaded and occupied Afghanistan. Fearing the spread of communist influence, the United States helped organize and arm the mujahedin, the Islamic Fighters of God who would wage jihad against the Godless Soviet communist armies and, with the help of Allah and American money and Stinger missiles, defeat them. Bin Laden was one of those fighters, and he became convinced that the subsequent fall of the Soviet Union had been a direct consequence of its humiliation in Afghanistan. This further convinced him that if Allah was with him no one could successfully stand against him. Thus when he decided in the wake of the Gulf War to take on the remaining undefeated superpower, he had complete confidence in ultimate success.

Saddam, a real rogue with no saving ambiguity at all, is, of course, back again today. Or perhaps it is we who are back again, since Saddam never went away. In any case, we say the issue today is not oil but weapons of mass destruction. While that has its truth, you have to wonder whether Saddam would matter so much if his coffers were not filled by the world's need for his oil, or if he did not sit on top of and next to 70 percent of the world's petroleum reserves. Our attitude reminds me of the definition of insanity—someone repeating the same procedure over and over and, each time, expecting a different result. With many developing countries, including China and India and their huge populations, on the road to energy-intensive industrialization, demand for energy is expected to triple over the next fifty years.[73] At the same time, declining production in the North Sea, Alaska, and elsewhere, combined with big new finds in the Middle East, mean the world's dependence on Persian Gulf oil will almost certainly grow. That implies further conflict and entanglement in the dangerous politics of the region.

CHANGING BUBBA'S WAYS

As I write this chapter, in the fall of 2002, my neighbor has just fired up his leaf blower to get the late-falling leaves off his lawn by Thanksgiving. He is a little paunchy and raking would probably be good for him, but using the blower is easier, and it only costs pennies after all. Convinced that abundant, inexpensive energy is part of its birthright, the American public resists any restraint on its "freedom" to consume and disbelieves any suggestion of crisis or need for even minor changes in the "American way of life." Energy use per capita has resumed its climb, pushing the U.S. share of global energy consumption up again and driving U.S. oil imports toward 15 million barrels a day, the equivalent of the total output of the world's two largest producers, Russia and Saudi Arabia. The annual U.S. trade deficit, currently $500 billion and rising, grows increasingly unsustainable. But few seem concerned. The leaders of both political parties are focused on doing whatever is necessary to keep things going as they are for as long as possible.

Thus, in the wake of the attacks of September 11, the president announced a new national energy plan that was all supply side. It called for oil drilling in the Arctic National Wildlife Refuge, relaxation of restrictions on exploration in other national parks, construction of one thousand power plants over the next twenty years to be fired largely by coal, and incentives for natural gas development.[74] At the same time, funding of research on new energy technology was slashed, and the vice president rejected any notion that Americans could do more with less, and suggested that while conservation may be a private virtue, it cannot solve the nation's energy problems.[75] The plan contained no gas taxes, no mileage requirements, or any other conservation measures of any kind. While this program was being presented, the administration was also beefing up U.S. military forces worldwide, but particularly in the Persian Gulf in view of the need to assure the unhindered flow of oil.

In its debates, the Congress followed along. Objecting to any increase in fuel economy standards, Senator Barbara Mikulski, Democrat of Maryland, said soccer moms need big vans to be safe from road rage.[76] Senator Zell Miller, Democrat of Georgia, said that the "back of a pickup truck is the think tank of rural America"[77] where more problems are solved at the end of a day's work than in all the halls of Washington, D.C. As if trying to uphold its side of Miller's formula, Congress chose to do nothing about gas mileage but voted overwhelmingly to authorize the president to go to war with Iraq.

The pattern, then, is to use as much as we want, produce as much as we can, and fight for the right to do both with whatever military muscle it takes. When we invite our allies to fight with us, we mark any hesitation as wimpish and anti-American. But many of our foreign friends wonder whether it would be necessary to fight if we acted more like them and less like a spoiled rogue.

In any case, there is a real problem with the traditional U.S. approach to energy: It threatens to become prohibitively expensive. Consider the global situation over the next ten to fifty years. The current world population of about 6 billion people is expected to hit 9.3 billion around 2015.[78] This growth, coupled with increasing global industrialization, will drive a rapid rise in global oil demand, from the current 77 million barrels per day to 120 million in 2012.[79] The Middle East currently contains 63 percent of the world's oil reserves, and unless massive new fields are found, the decline of U.S. and North Sea production will drive that figure to 70 percent within ten years.[80] Saudi Arabia alone will contain 25–30 percent of global reserves.[81] The increase in world demand will thus be met almost entirely from the Middle East and primarily by Saudi Arabia. Because it is the only player with substantial spare capacity, Saudi Arabia, like the old Texas Railroad Commission, will have enormous market leverage. Former CIA Director James Woolsey has called this leverage the "equivalent of a nuclear weapon."[82] Japan is already completely dependent on this oil. Europe, the United States, China, India, and others will soon be nearly so.

For years, the United States has had that special relationship with Saudi Arabia. Not only do the Saudis sell oil to the United States for a dollar a barrel less than to anyone else,[83] they also price their oil in dollars, which helps the United States to maintain the dollar as the world's main unit of account. This is a great advantage. If oil were priced in euros, for example, and the United States had to pay in euros instead of dollars, the implications for us would be dire: Given our huge trade deficit, we would run out of euros very quickly. The Saudis have also been there when the United States needed money for forming the mujahedin in Afghanistan or the Contras in Nicaragua, or to pump extra barrels when the market needed stability. In return, the United States has protected Saudi Arabia and assured a safe haven for its investments.

But in the future, will the Chinese, Indians, and others be comfortable with the U.S. Navy as the main guarantor of Gulf stability? Keep in mind that for ideological and geopolitical reasons, the United States may from time to time find itself at odds with suppliers who have perfectly good relations with other customers. Will the United States be able to maintain the special quality of its relations with Saudi Arabia in the future? In the wake of September 11, relations have become strained as Americans lament the kingdom's promotion of Islamic extremism and its lack of democracy, women's rights, and religious freedom. Many Saudis have been shocked and hurt by the new American hostility and could easily decide to reciprocate it. In any case, the huge flow of funds to regimes that may be hostile to American interests and values is not desirable. Finally, the U.S. trade deficit and the current value of the dollar may not be sustainable under the pressure of the U.S. oil import levels being forecast for 2012. All this, of course, is not to mention the environmental consequences of burning all that oil.

So America faces a choice. To do nothing is to choose higher trade deficits and, ironically for a nation that prizes independence and freedom above all, greater economic and strategic dependence. To balance this, we will have to maintain and even increase our military power so that in the end, if we have to, we can just take what we need. Down this road lies further entanglement in various jihads, confrontation with Islam, and sticky involvement in the court politics of the Saudi royal family.

If this seems like a can of worms to you, there are two alternatives: to get serious about energy conservation, and to get serious about nonpetroleum-based energy development. The two are not mutually exclusive. At the moment, however, the United States is doing neither.

Any serious effort at conservation has to reckon with the United States' energy-intensive infrastructure and with not only the American but also the global economy's perverse dependence on that infrastructure. The U.S. economy is the only engine driving the global economy. When you hear critics complain that America has 5 percent of the world's population but uses 25 percent of its energy, the proper response is that it also produces more than 25 percent of the world's GDP. Without that production, much of the world would hardly have any GDP to speak of. America's big houses may be energy inefficient, but they contain not one but two or even three imported TV sets, stereos, computers, and cars. Any quick, dramatic change in this lifestyle is going to hit not just Americans but the whole world.

Still, probably the biggest energy reserves in the world are in American cars, homes, factories, and office buildings. What is required is not so much downsizing as reengineering. During the infamous Senate debate on SUVs and the proposed fuel economy legislation, Senator John Kerry, Democrat from Massachusetts, noted a Ford Motor Company advertisement saying that you can have in your future an SUV that provides all the room and power you want while using half the current amount of gasoline.[84] Also cited was a study by the National Academy of Sciences concluding that with technologies currently available, improvements in gas mileage of more than 40 percent are achievable for SUVs and minivans on competitive economic terms with no sacrifice in size or horsepower.[85] Such improvements alone would reduce projected U.S. oil imports by 6 million barrels a day, nearly as much as Saudi Arabia produces. Even more importantly, that technology, if adopted broadly around the world, would dramatically change all the energy projections.

Even more spectacular conservation gains may be possible with electricity. In the first place, the largest present usage of electric power is for waste. Enormous losses occur as electricity is transmitted over the power grid. As Amory Lovins of the Rocky Mountain Institute explains, decentralized micro power plants could greatly reduce these losses while also making the power supply much less vulnerable to terrorist sabotage. Even more simple and powerful is the example Lovins cites of the contrast between Seattle and Chicago in the 1990–1996 period. Annual electricity use fell nearly four thousand times faster in Seattle than in Chicago even though a kilowatt-hour cost twice as much in Chicago.[86] The reason was that the utilities in Seattle helped people save, while those in Chicago discouraged them from doing so. As Lovins further notes, a decade ago nine U.S. states rewarded the utilities for helping customers reduce usage instead of selling them more power. Today, many states have dropped the practice, but in New England, a regional approach that has utilities doing on-site inspections, and offering rebates for installing more efficient equipment, has prevented blackouts that would otherwise almost certainly have occurred. In the United Kingdom, businesses are allowed to take a tax writeoff for energy-saving investments just as they write off the energy they waste. Applied in the United States, this practice could have dramatic results. Lovins also estimates that adoption in the United States of European-style combined heat-and-power plants could cut U.S. fuel usage by a third. I could go on, but the point is that even without draconian measures we can dramatically reduce the usage of energy and the importance of oil, not only for the U.S. economy but for the global economy as well.

By the same token, there are promising technologies that could greatly increase the supply of energy without using fossil fuels at all. Europe and Japan have already demonstrated that nuclear power can be safe and economical, and new technologies for handling nuclear waste promise to greatly reduce its dangers. Denmark already gets nearly 20 percent of its energy from wind power, and the European Union plans to get fully 22 percent of its electricity mostly from wind power by 2010.[87] Wind power could also meet a large part of U.S. needs at competitive costs. In recent years, it has been demonstrated that genetically modified biocatalysts can produce ethanol from virtually any kind of woody plant material. The potential exists to obtain large amounts of an environmentally friendly fuel from simply fermenting agricultural and logging wastes. Thermal depolymerization also turns wastes such as animal carcasses and used tires into high-grade diesel fuel.[88] Perhaps the most dramatic potential lies in deriving energy from hydrogen through the use of fuel cells. This technology can provide power for plants, buildings, and homes as well as replacing gasoline in autos and trucks. Buses in some cities already run on hydrogen, as do some buildings, like the Condé Nast building in Manhattan.[89] All of the auto companies are experimenting with hydrogen-powered vehicles. General Motors recently demonstrated a prototype called the Hywire at the Paris Motor Show. Again, the point is that much can be done with technology to solve many problems at once. While the U.S. government is working in conjunction with the auto companies on fuel cell technology, and President Bush just boosted support for that by $1.2 billion,[90] the contrast with our recent military build-up is telling. In the wake of September 11, Congress instantly passed a $40 billion supplemental budget increase, much of which went to the Pentagon, with the Bush Administration proposing an additional $46 billion increase in 2003, the single largest annual increase since 1982.[91] The $60 billion we spend as a matter of course on patrolling the Persian Gulf will also be increased to deal with the problems of Iraq. However necessary this may be, we are not spending $50 or $60 billion on developing alternative energy resources. Yet this would seem like a good time to reconsider the proposals that have been made over the years to launch an Apollo- or Manhattan-style energy project. Of course, development of some technologies like hydrogen fuel cells will take time regardless of the amount of investment. But that is precisely why we should start now. In the meanwhile, interim technologies like hybrid cars could be much more vigorously promoted.

For if Bubba cannot change his ways and become a good global citizen, he risks looking more and more like the rogues he is trying to discipline.

5

WHO LOST KYOTO?

"Come see us while we're still here."
—Ministry of Tourism,
Maldive Islands

If you are looking for the ideal spot to get away from it all, you could do a lot worse than the Maldive Islands. Mere flecks in the Indian Ocean about one thousand miles due south of India, these coral and sand atolls have a beautiful subtropical climate, great beaches, and a population of 275,000 people whose goal in life is to make sure you are completely relaxed and satisfied. If you're tempted, book your flight now. The islands' highest point is 5 feet above sea level, and they seem to be visibly vanishing as the coral dies, the sea rises, and the beaches wash away. In 1987, President Maumoon Abdul Gayoom's car was nearly swept away by a freak wave, and ever since, the islanders have had a more than passing interest in topics like global warming and the melting of polar ice caps.

At the Rio Earth Summit in 1992, President Gayoom told then U.S. President George H. W. Bush that "a few feet of rise is the end of our country." Not to worry, Bush replied, in unconscious imitation of King Canute. "The United States will not allow that to happen to the Maldives."[1] The president then joined with nearly all the leaders of the world in committing his country to take steps that would reduce emissions of so-called greenhouse gases and abate global warming.

Imagine then the shock in the middle of the Indian Ocean on March 28, 2001, when the administration of President Bush the younger announced that the United States would not support ratification of the Kyoto Protocol to reduce global warming. Concluded after laborious negotiations in December 1997 in Kyoto, Japan, the protocol called on its signatories to reduce by 2010 their emissions of climate-altering greenhouse gases to a level 7 percent below the levels of 1990. Although this reduction was substantially less than the 60–80 percent necessary to save the Maldives from drowning, the Maldivans and citizens of other low-lying countries considered it better than nothing. Now Bush's Environmental Protection Agency chief, Christine Todd Whitman, was saying the Kyoto treaty was "dead" so far as the administration was concerned and that if the Europeans and Japanese wanted an agreement they would have to take a different approach.[2] If the Maldivans were dismayed at this news, much of the rest of the world, particularly Europe, was incensed.

The timing did not help. Whitman's statement came two days before German Prime Minister Gerhard Schröder, who governed by dint of a coalition with Germany's Green Party, made his first visit to the new Bush White House. (Could this have had something to do with Shröder's later reluctance to support Bush on Iraq?) It also came only a week after the European Union had sent a letter urging renewed efforts at agreement on global warming issues, and about two and a half months before Bush was scheduled for his first consultations with Europe's leaders in Stockholm, Sweden. The announcement came across as a slap in the face. Nor was anyone mollified by the president's speech on June 11, made just a few hours before he left for Stockholm. Calling the Kyoto Protocol a "fatally flawed" treaty with "unrealistic targets not based on science," the president said he would not comply with mandates that "would have a negative economic impact, with layoffs of workers and price increases for consumers."[3]

The response from the diplomatic world, where an "expression of concern" counts as a sharp rebuke, was unusually harsh. In Stockholm, the Swedish government called the U.S. decision "appalling and provocative." Britain's Environment Minister, Michael Meacher, described the American announcement as "extremely serious" and "an issue of trans-Atlantic, global, and foreign policy," while the European Union said it was "very worried." The European Parliament went further, saying: "We are appalled that the long-term interests of the majority of the world population are being sacrificed for short-term corporate greed in the United States." Japan urged Washington to reconsider; Australia emphasized that, in view of America's enormous consumption of resources, it had a responsibility to cut emissions of greenhouse gases.[4] The *Guardian*, somewhat less restrained, shrieked that renouncing the treaty was a "Taliban-style act of wanton destruction."[5]

During the 2000 presidential campaign, candidate Bush had actually said he would clamp down on the emissions of power plants, thus giving the impression that as president he would be concerned with the environment. Barely six weeks after his inauguration, however, the new administration had withdrawn certain measures that had been announced previously for protection of endangered salmon and trout. Then, on March 13, 2001, in a reversal of his campaign pledge to reduce carbon pollution, Bush relaxed rather than tightened regulations on power plant emissions. He did this despite a note from EPA Administrator Whitman saying, "I would strongly recommend that you continue to recognize global warming is a real and serious issue." She added, "Mr. President, this is a credibility issue for the U.S. in the international community" and "also an issue that is resonating here at home. We need to appear engaged."[6] The president argued, however, that we had an economic emergency due to lack of electricity, and getting additional power was thus more important, at the moment, than dealing with emissions. He followed this with orders on March 20 to relax regulations limiting arsenic in drinking water and, on the following day, delayed mining regulations designed to protect watersheds.

In the wake of these moves, the Kyoto decision appeared to epitomize a profoundly anti-environment spirit within the administration and became a metaphor for American profligacy, unconcern, and arrogance. Yet this was a great irony. Heretofore, America had always been a leader on environmental matters. Indeed, it had invented environmentalism. Now suddenly we were being seen as the bad guys with our environmental policies somehow symbolic of everything wrong with America. How, I wondered, did we get here?

ENVIRONMENTALISM: MADE IN AMERICA

Early Americans fought the French, the Indians, and then the British, but what they fought most was trees. The axe ranked with the rifle as an essential tool of the frontier, and the odor of burning wood hung over the new settlements. It was Charles Dickens who first brought attention to the devastation all this cutting was wreaking in *American Notes*, his account of traveling over the National Road in 1842. By 1864, concern with overcutting was becoming serious, and George Perkins Marsh became America's first conservationist with the publication of *Man and Nature*, a book arguing that felling the woods was having disastrous consequences for the soil and local climate. In the same year, Henry David Thoreau's *The Maine Woods*, published posthumously, called for the establishment of national forests. And Congress obliged with legislation granting the Yosemite Valley to the state of California as a public park. Then in 1872, Congress created Yellowstone as the first national park— the first in the world—an act that has been much imitated around the globe since. But the greatest imitator was none other than President Theodore Roosevelt who made himself the conservationist president by establishing seventeen national parks and monuments and laying the foundation for the establishment of the National Park Service. His cousin, President Franklin Roosevelt, followed in Teddy's footsteps by creating the Civilian Conservation Corps during the Great Depression to provide jobs by building much of the environmental infrastructure on which we still rely.

Then in 1962, Rachel Carson burst on the scene with her blockbuster best-seller *Silent Spring*. Termed the environmental movement's "shot heard round the world," it made an airtight case that the chemical agents we had come to view as the basis of our modern, progressive lifestyle were, in fact, poisoning large parts of the food chain, including humans. In particular, Carson traced the deadly trail of DDT from the spraying of elms to control disease to the death of birds, to malignancies of fish, to liver and central nervous damage in humans. When Carson died of cancer in 1964, she had started a ball rolling that led to President Richard Nixon's establishment of the world's first Environmental Protection Agency in 1970.

I could go on with more examples, but the point is that for more than a century it was the United States that led the way on environmental questions. Its initial focus was domestic, but it also came to take the lead on the critical global issue of the ozone hole as well.

A HOLE IN THE SKY

The June 1974 issue of *Nature* contained an article by F. Sherwood Rowland, a professor of chemistry at the University of California, Irvine, and Mario J. Molina, a postdoctoral fellow in Rowland's laboratory on a group of chemicals called chlorofluorocarbons. Considering both its subject, the gases invented in the 1930s for use in refrigeration and air-conditioning, and the catchy title, "Stratospheric Sink for Chlorofluoromethanes-Chlorine Atomic Catalyzed Destruction of Ozone," it's no surprise that most people missed it. The paper began innocuously by noting what everyone already knew, that these compounds, whose main advantage was that they were chemically almost inert and therefore non-toxic, were being released into the atmosphere in steadily increasing amounts; that their extreme stability meant they would remain there for sixty to one hundred years. The only way these chemicals were destroyed, the authors noted, was if they drifted into the upper atmosphere and were broken apart by ultraviolet rays, a process known as photodissociation. Then the authors unleashed their Sunday punch: "Photodissociation of the CFCs in the stratosphere produces significant amounts of chlorine atoms, and leads to destruction of the atmospheric ozone."[7]

Well, so what? Few people at the time cared about ozone, a highly unstable form of oxygen that has a bluish tint and an acrid odor and happens to be poisonous. At sea level, it's used in a number of products such as bleaches, disinfectants, and decontaminants. It also forms naturally about thirty miles above the earth in the stratosphere through a reaction of solar ultraviolet light with oxygen.[8] Though extremely thin and tenuous, this stratospheric ozone is nevertheless critical to most life forms, because it blocks most of the solar ultraviolet rays that are harmful to plants, insects, and birds, and that cause cancer in humans. What Rowland and Molina were saying, then, was that an invisible layer of molecules that is more or less essential to life on earth was being eaten away by the action of ultraviolet radiation on CFCs in the stratosphere.

But this was all highly theoretical. Nobody had actually seen any of this bad stuff happening. The overwhelming reaction of industry, the public, and political leaders was if it ain't broke, don't fix it. And it didn't seem to be broken.

Until 1985. On May 16 of that year, *Nature* published another paper on ozone, this one by Joseph Farman, a member of the British Antarctic Survey and a faculty member at Cambridge University. Farman had visited Antarctica for twenty-seven straight years between 1957 and 1984, and each year one of his tasks was to measure the level of ozone in the sky overhead. Though aware of the article by Rowland and Molina, Farman was nevertheless dubious when his 1981 readings showed a substantial decline in the ozone layer over Antarctica during the Southern Hemisphere spring. Maybe the instruments were out of calibration, he thought, and he had them readjusted. But they showed the same thing in 1982 and again in 1983. By 1984 the readings were 40 percent below average and the "ozone hole" had enlarged to reach Tierra del Fuego at the tip of South America. Further review of his readings showed Farman that the decline had actually begun about 1977.[9]

At about the same time as Farman's paper, the National Academy of Sciences published a paper estimating that the ozone layer would decline only moderately if at all in the coming century.[10] But then NASA weighed in. Its Nimbus 7 satellite had been orbiting the earth over the poles every hour and a half since 1978 and was supposed to be monitoring the ozone layer. It had found nothing amiss, but after Farman's article, NASA checked its instruments and found that the satellite had been told to ignore, as obviously erroneous, any numbers below a certain level. When NASA reprogrammed, its satellite confirmed that the "erroneous" readings were correct, and even worse than what Farman had measured. Of course, there was some initial effort to discount the significance of the findings. President Reagan's Secretary of the Interior recommended that people just put on hats, dark glasses, and sunscreen. But when doctors projected 130 million additional cases of skin cancer on top of everything else and other damage predicted by other scientists,[11] it was hard to be happy.

The sky was, in fact, broken, and it needed to get fixed—fast. International discussions of ozone depletion had actually begun in 1976 under the aegis of the United Nations Environment Program (UNEP), and negotiations for an agreement to phase out ozone-depleting substances had started in 1981. They concluded in 1985 with adoption of the Vienna Convention, which encouraged intergovernmental cooperation on research, observation of the ozone layer, and exchange of information. In other words, it was a typical diplomatic toothless tiger with no targets, no controls, and no binding obligations. As a member of the Reagan administration at the time, I remember the concern among staffers over the gravity of the situation. Many thought that because of its general opposition to government regulation and its close relationship with industry, the administration would avoid or water down any remedial action. But EPA administrator Lee M. Thomas insisted that this was something on which the United States had to take the lead. He worked closely with major American CFC producers, and DuPont led the way in committing to develop alternatives and phase out CFC production. At the same time, Ambassador Richard E. Benedick was dispatched to Montreal in the summer of 1987 to lead the U.S. delegation in negotiating a binding international agreement on cutting and eventually eliminating CFC usage and manufacture. On September 16, agreement was reached on the Montreal Protocol, which called for a 50-percent reduction in the 1986 level of CFC consumption by 1999.[12] The agreement was intended to be universal, but developing countries were granted an exemption from its provisions for ten years because of both their relatively low level of consumption and the difficulties of converting to the replacement technology. In fact, compliance was much more rapid than anticipated. By 2003, most experts anticipated that the ozone layer would be back to normal by the middle of the twenty-first century.[13]

When warnings of a second problem with the atmosphere grew loud and frequent, many people expected it to be solved as the ozone problem had been, with a clear, effective treaty enjoying widespread international support, led again by the United States. At least, they didn't see why this wasn't possible. But as global issues go, the ozone hole was in many ways unique: It had a single cause whose sources were few and easily identifiable, the consequences of inaction were easy to estimate, and a perfectly adequate replacement for CFCs already existed. With global climate change and the putative role of carbon dioxide in raising temperatures worldwide, none of the above was true. The sources are infinite: you emit carbon dioxide, and so do your dog and its fleas and the bacteria in your shower drain, not to mention your car and your furnace. And all the major questions—the consequences of global warming, how much of it is caused by human activity, even whether it's happening at all—are still in the process of being answered.

FROM OZONE TO GREENHOUSE GASES

Before 1820, no one asked how the earth is warmed. It was in that year that Jean-Baptiste-Joseph Fourier attacked the question of how the earth retains the sun's heat instead of simply reflecting it back into space. Fourier had contracted myxedema—a disease that makes one feel perpetually cold—while serving in the *corps des savants* that accompanied Napoleon on his Egypt campaign. After his return to France, he wore an overcoat throughout the year and devoted much time to the study of how heat spreads. His conclusion was that while much heat does bounce back, the earth's atmosphere traps some of it and re-reflects it back to the earth's surface. He compared this to a giant bell jar whose dome is formed of clouds and gases that trap sufficient heat to make life possible. His article, "General Remarks on the Temperature of the Terrestrial Globe and Planetary Spaces," was published in 1824. At the time, it was not considered his best work and was forgotten until the end of the century.[14]

In 1895, the Swedish physicist Svente Arrhenius, who had read Fourier's work developed the first theoretical model for calculating the influence of carbon dioxide on the earth's temperature.[15] His conclusion was that a decrease of about 40 percent of the carbon dioxide in the atmosphere would cause temperatures to drop by 4 to 5 degrees Celsius (7–9 degrees F) and trigger a new ice age. By the same token, a doubling of those levels would raise temperatures by 5 to 6 degrees (9–11 degrees F). He further estimated that it would take about three thousand years of burning fossil fuels to accomplish this doubling. To a man accustomed to the harsh Nordic winters of the Little Ice Age, ending about then, a long, gentle warming must have seemed a pleasant prospect.

A few years after Arrhenius published his calculations, Spindletop blew in, followed by the other giant oil field finds in Texas and Oklahoma. Henry Ford's Model T displaced horses much faster than anyone had expected, while Edison's electric light drove demand for electric power production. Fossil fuel-burning accelerated far faster than Arrhenius had anticipated, but no one was concerned with whether this might affect the weather. Except, that is, for George Callendar, who in 1938 published an article entitled, "The Artificial Production of Carbon Dioxide and Its Influence on Temperature."[16] Based on data he had collected from two hundred weather stations around the world between 1880 and 1934, Callendar calculated that the earth had warmed by about 1 degree Fahrenheit (0.55 C) in that time. He predicted that it would warm another 2 degrees (1.1 C) over the next century as a result of the continuing discharge of carbon dioxide into the atmosphere. In 1956, after eighteen years of further data collecting, he published calculations showing the atmospheric concentration of carbon dioxide rising from 290 parts per million (ppm) in 1900 to 325 ppm in 1956. This level was very close to the 315 ppm that Charles Keeling, a young postdoctoral student at the California Institute of Technology announced the same year. These numbers and curves sparked a landmark article the following year by Roger Revelle and Hans Suess, both of the Scripps Institution of Oceanography, who noted that "human beings are carrying out a large scale geophysical experiment by returning to the atmosphere within a few centuries the concentrated organic carbon stored in the earth over hundreds of millions of years."[17] Keeling's measurements over the next twenty years only underlined this point. From 315 ppm in 1956, the Keeling Curve climbed steadily to 365 ppm by 1997.[18]

As the Keeling Curve rose, so did concern with its implications. Already sensitized to environmental hazards such as water pollution and pesticides, people began to take notice of the weather. Beginning in the 1960s, John McGowan of the Scripps Institution began to notice that the waters off the California coast were gradually warming and by 1995 were nearly 3 degrees F. warmer than in 1960. The ice cover on Mount Kenya began to disappear visibly around 1963 and had shrunk by 40 percent by 1987. Arctic summers grew cozier by 6 degrees F. over twenty years, and the glaciers in the Peruvian Andes tripled their rate of melting between 1960 and the early 1980s.[19] These portents stimulated a broad discussion of potential implications and policy measures. As early as 1965,[20] a White House report on environmental issues mentioned the possible consequences of global warming. In 1971, William Kellogg of the National Council on Atmospheric Research organized a conference in Stockholm on what he called "inadvertent climate modification."[21]

Over the next two decades, both analyses and signs multiplied. Writing in *Science* magazine in 1975, Columbia University's Wallace S. Broecker predicted a substantial acceleration of the warming trend over the next ten years.[22] Two years later the National Academy of Sciences released a report entitled "Energy and Climate," which concluded that possible global warming should produce neither panic nor complacency, but intensified research. In the same year, William Kellogg and Margaret Mead published "The Atmosphere: Endangered and Endangering"[23] in which they called for a "law of the air" whereby all nations would agree to reduce their carbon dioxide emissions to some negotiated level. As the 1970s faded into the 1980s, the weather seemed bent on fulfilling the predictions. The rate of retreat of mid-latitude glaciers accelerated from 30 to 45 meters per year.[24] Toolik Lake at the base of the Brooks Range on Alaska's frigid North Slope showed a 3-degree F (5.4 C) rise in summer temperatures between 1979 and 1994.[25] The arctic ice sheet shrank by 6 percent,[26] the snowline continued to retreat, and computer models of the atmosphere predicted yet more warming. In 1987, a conference sponsored by the United Nations, Canada, and the World Meteorological Society gathered 330 scientists and policy makers from forty-six nations who released a statement saying: "Humanity is conducting an enormous, unintended, globally pervasive experiment whose ultimate consequences could be second only to a global nuclear war."[27] They went on to urge the nations of the developed world to act immediately to reduce greenhouse gas emissions.

But 1988 was the bell ringing year for global warming. For starters, it was the hottest year on record, topping three other years in the 1980s that had all briefly held the record. Sixty-nine U.S. cities recorded their highest one-day temperatures ever, as did Moscow. In Los Angeles, four hundred electric transformers blew up on a single day as the mercury hit 110 degrees F (43 C).[28] The Midwest suffered its worst drought since the Dust Bowl days, while Yellowstone National Park literally burned. In the midst of this holocaust, James Hansen, director of NASA's Goddard Institute of Space Studies, stood up before the U.S. Senate Committee on Energy and Natural Resources and said: "The greenhouse effect has been detected and it is changing our climate now." Hansen was 99-percent certain that current temperatures represented a real warming trend as opposed to natural variability, and added, "We're loading the climate dice."[29] Coming from an expert like Hansen in the august chambers of the U.S. Senate that statement can be said to have marked the real beginning of the battle over global warming. Meeting in Toronto later that interminable summer, the United Nations Environmental Program established the Intergovernmental Panel on Climate Change (IPCC) and launched preparations for a global Conference on Environment and Development (that would become known as the Earth Summit) to be held in Rio de Janeiro in June 1992. It would be one of the seminal meetings of the last decade of the twentieth century.

To comprehend what did and didn't happen at Rio, you need to understand some of the key forces and attitudes that were developing in the late 1980s and early 1990s. One key factor was the debate over the science. While no one disputed Keeling's data on rising carbon content in the atmosphere, there was much debate about the effect. On the one hand were those like Hansen, who drew an analogy with the experience of the ozone hole. In that case, actual measurement data had confirmed earlier scientific predictions, and steps had been taken immediately to fix the problem through internationally agreed reductions of CFC emissions. Here again, these people argued, the unusual weather is demonstrating the validity of scientific theory, and something dramatic and similar to the Montreal Protocol needs to be done now. On the other hand were people like Richard Lindzen, a climatologist from M.I.T., who argued that cause and effect were not so clear nor was the future so easily forecast.[30] In the first place, many of the recent climatic events were the "highest temperature since . . ." or "the worst storm since . . . ." But "since" meant there had been an earlier dramatic event before the accumulation of atmospheric carbon and the supposed onset of warming. Moreover, a period of warming greater than today's had occurred in the Middle Ages, when the Vikings settled in Iceland and Greenland. This had been followed by the Little Ice Age of about 1350–1850 and then by renewed warming, all without greenhouse gas emissions. Even worse, meteorologists had recorded a distinct *cooling* between 1940 and 1970, even though, according to the theory, this should have been a time of accelerated warming. It had also long been known that physical events, such as the wobble of the earth's orbit and the dimming and brightening of the sun, affect temperature and climate. Might these be partly or totally responsible for the changes? Then there was the fact that while surface records showed warming, weather balloons showed no change in atmospheric temperatures at high altitudes. To address these issues, the scientists of the IPCC built computer models to simulate the climate.

The first report of the IPCC, issued in 1990, concluded with certainty that atmospheric concentrations of greenhouse gases were increasing. It forecast that under a "business as usual" scenario the twenty-first century would see a 0.3 degree C (0.54 F) increase in temperature per decade along with a sea-level rise of 6 centimeters per decade. Thus at the end of the twenty-first century average temperatures would be 3–4 degrees C (5.4–7.2 degrees F) higher than at present, and sea levels would have risen 60–70 centimeters, about 2 feet. The IPCC went on to conclude that to stabilize current concentrations of carbon dioxide, present greenhouse gas emissions would have to be cut by 60–80 percent, meaning essentially a shutdown of most significant industry and transportation.[31] Although this conclusion had the authority of two thousand of the world's leading scientists behind it, there was a problem. The computer said there should already have been a warming over the last one hundred years of about 1 degree C (1.8 F). But the actual warming had been measured at about 0.5 degrees C (0.9 F). Moreover, the computer could not explain the cooling from 1940 to 1970. The IPCC acknowledged it had trouble simulating cloud behavior in its computer and that there were levels of detail the computer simply couldn't reach. The battle of the scientists raged on.

Meanwhile, environmentalism was on the rise in Europe. Although Europe had no history of environmentalism similar to that of the United States, London's killer fog of 1952 had resulted in clean air legislation in 1956, and people on the Continent were noticing that the rivers and streams as well as the air were more and more foul. I was living in the Netherlands in the late 1960s and remember discussions in the Dutch press about the poor quality of the Rhine River water when it finally reached Rotterdam after traversing the length of Europe. Perhaps more importantly, acid rain began to become a problem in Europe as it was in the United States. In April 1974, the acidity of the rain in Scotland was measured at 1500 times normal.[32] By 1982, 7 percent of the trees in Germany's Black Forest were dead or dying, and within three years the figure had climbed to 50 percent.[33] In Sweden, four thousand lakes were dead by 1980, and another five thousand were dying.[34] Environmental concerns led France to create a Ministry of the Environment in 1971.[35] Other European countries soon followed suit.

The growing public preoccupation with environmental issues dovetailed with another political trend. Although historically Judeo-Christian, much of Europe had embraced the godless religions of communism, fascism, and socialism in the twentieth century. Fascism, of course, failed in World War II, and by the 1970s communism was failing and socialism had been so co-opted by the mainstream bourgeoisie that it differed little from conservatism. The anticapitalist left had lost its home and its cause. It found the Green cause. Environmentalism was perfect in many ways. Protecting the environment automatically aligned one with the good. It legitimized being anticorporate and antiglobalization, and, of course, it required big government and regulation to impose a whole new lifestyle on western society. Much of the European left embraced the fledgling Green movement, and it quickly became a significant political force. Greens entered the Swiss parliament in 1979 and four years later became a significant force in the German parliament with nearly 6 percent of the national vote. Eventually the German Greens would form part of Germany's ruling coalition and hold the post of foreign minister in the person of Joshka Fisher, a former radical left street demonstrator. This strain of environmentalism was much more ideological than the mainstream American environmental groups, and less interested in practical solutions than in grand revolutionary agendas and policies. The environmental ministries in most European countries came to be dominated by the views of the Greens if not by the Greens themselves. It was they who were the chief representatives of Europe in the various UN working bodies and at Rio.

In the United States, by contrast, politics had jogged to the right with the two Reagan administrations and then the first Bush administration in 1988. One of the main expressions of this new conservatism was suspicion of big government and opposition to regulations, particularly those that were thought to shackle productive business at the hands of unproductive bureaucrats. Reagan's first Secretary of the Interior, James Watt, cut funding for programs to protect endangered species, pushed to open wilderness areas for oil and gas leases, and removed a number of environmental regulatory responsibilities from the jurisdiction of the federal government. More important were the views of John Sununu, who as White House chief of staff in the first Bush administration played a key role in the preparations for Rio. A former governor of New Hampshire, he had been a leader in establishing regulations to control acid rain and counted himself an environmentalist. But he also felt that environmentalist positions are often ideological and block economic development on the basis of insufficient scientific evidence of the danger of damage or of proof that a proposed remedy will work. In the case of global warming, Sununu argued that significantly reducing fossil fuel emissions would be very costly, and that the scientific evidence didn't yet prove the problem to be serious enough to warrant the expense. "If you're going to make a trillion-dollar decision, if you're going to make a decision that's going to affect a million jobs, you ought to make it on the basis of what you know and not on the basis of what your emotions may lead you to feel," he said.[36] In this, Sununu probably reflected the views of the U.S. Senate, which would have to ratify any international treaty. The Bush administration entered the preparations for Rio warily, looking hard at the cost/benefit equation.

Industry was also looking at the evidence and the potential costs. In the case of the ozone hole, manufacturers fought against CFC replacement as long as the danger was only theoretical. But as soon as the evidence of the ozone hole became clear and the nature of the danger certain, industry moved with alacrity to make the necessary changes. Global warming was more complex. Any regulations would hit major industries and thousands of companies across the economy. The evidence was uncertain, the potential damage unclear (some even said the effect might be beneficial), and the costs of a fix would be very high. Thus, American industry prepared to lobby against all but the most flexible of conclusions.

European industry took a somewhat different attitude. It was not unworried, but it had neither the American companies' history nor their capacity for active lobbying of its governments. Moreover, it faced a less costly problem. The ongoing nuclearization of France meant it would be greatly reducing fossil fuel emissions in any case. So French industry was really not going to be required to do very much. The situation was similar in Britain and Germany. For decades Britain had subsidized its coal mines and thereby artificially kept coal alive as its primary power-generation fuel. But the Thatcher government had earlier made the decision to halt the subsidies. At the same time, the discovery of vast natural gas reserves in the British sector of the North Sea made it both convenient and economical to switch from coal to much cleaner-burning natural gas. Thus Britain too was going to be greatly reducing emissions as a natural course. German industry had the best deal of all. With reunification, Germany had inherited the old, inefficient coal and peat-fired factories of the East, which it was systematically closing down and replacing with modern plants. The old East German plants were so bad that companies from West Germany could actually increase their emissions while dramatically reducing the country's overall emissions. As for the rest of Europe, since it all fit under the EU umbrella, it benefited from the emissions reductions in Britain, France, and Germany. Many European countries would be able to increase their individual emissions because the EU as a whole would nevertheless experience a reduction.

Finally, there were the developing countries. Many saw the West's "concern" over the environment as a plot to curb their growth. In any case they wanted to be paid with large amounts of development aid for any commitments they might make. OPEC countries represented a special subset of the developing countries and—surprise, surprise—they didn't want to hear about limitations on emissions.

As these forces prepared to tango in Rio, the UN designated an Intergovernmental Negotiating Committee (INC) to develop the agenda and hold preliminary talks on the agreements to be signed by the heads of government at the full "Earth Summit" planned for June 1992. The final agenda included a treaty on protecting biodiversity, a program for preservation of forests, an ambitious Agenda 21 framework to guide comprehensive environment and economic development policy, and the UN Framework Convention on Climate Change. It was this last item that was the major focus of debate and that eventually led to Kyoto. The approach was heavily influenced by the experience of the Montreal Protocol. All the discussions essentially boiled down to two questions: Would there be targets and timetables for reduction of greenhouse gas emissions *à la* the Montreal Protocol on Ozone? And would the developing countries be required to participate?

The play began in the winter of 1991 when the INC held the first of its preparatory meetings on the proposed climate change treaty. Setting the tone was the UN Environmental Project's Director Mostafa Tolba, who said that "people everywhere look to 1992 as our best chance, perhaps our last chance, to save our Earth."[37] But although the IPCC's scientists had concluded that a cut of 60–80 percent in carbon dioxide emissions would be needed to stabilize atmospheric carbon concentrations, few were prepared to consider such cuts in the face of economic reality. The strongest proposal considered was to freeze carbon dioxide emissions at 1990 levels by 2000. This was proposed by the European Community and supported by the Alliance of Small Island States as well as by Canada, Australia, and the Nordic states. It was not a scientifically or economically derived target, but simply the best they thought they could do. The United States, in a rare alliance with the OPEC countries, opposed any emissions targets or timetables. The developing countries, led by China and India, made it clear they could accept no commitments that might restrict their growth, and emphasized the need for financial assistance and technology transfer if they were to achieve anything.

By summer 1991, the battle had hardened into trench warfare. At the London G–7 meeting in July, the European Community, Canada, and Japan all called on the United States to join them in making the commitment to freeze emissions. The U.S. refusal, citing lack of sufficient scientific evidence, elicited a rare on-the-record criticism from European leaders. Said one top official: "The United States wants to avoid anything other than generalization. Everybody else wants to make a commitment."[38] Particularly striking was the position of Great Britain, which not only committed to emissions reductions but made clear its view that as the world's biggest polluter the United States should do its part. It was also noted that U.S. skepticism was making it easy for future polluters like India and China to ignore the whole thing. As if on cue, a month later a group of developing countries issued a statement disclaiming responsibility for environmental problems and demanding large financial assistance in return for any environmental cooperation. Malaysia went so far as to threaten to boycott the conference if it focused too much on developing-country responsibilities.

In the ensuing months, Bush, who had said he would be "the environment president," came under increasing pressure from domestic environmental groups to prove it. Rio became a cause for celebrities. The actor James Earl Jones told audiences that "the entire human race is at stake,"[39] and the Sierra Club organized a grass-roots campaign to urge the president to take the leadership of the summit by agreeing to sign strong agreements. The World Resources Institute suggested that if the president didn't act forcefully he would be vulnerable to charges of antienvironmentalism in the upcoming election campaign, and Democratic Party leaders in the Congress introduced legislation calling for stabilization of U.S. emissions at 1990 levels by 2000—the commitment for which the

EC was lobbying. Despite this pressure and Sununu's departure from the chief of staff job, Bush held firm to making no target and timetable commitments. At the UN, U.S. negotiators insisted there had to be quantification and a suitable scientific basis for making what could be very expensive commitments. Their position was strengthened when the American Association for the Advancement of Science issued a report with mixed conclusions about the potential effects of greenhouse gas emissions. It advised taking action to reduce emissions but said the information available did not warrant drastic action.

If it was good enough for the scientists, it was good enough for Bush, and his administration stuck with its position. The United States favored a treaty that would commit signatories to reducing emissions—but in a manner and at a time based on well-established scientific findings and consistent with the basic needs and institutions of each country. As the date for the Rio meeting approached, the other industrial countries threatened to conclude a treaty based on the commitment to freeze emissions without the United States. Bush threatened in turn not to attend the meeting if it appeared the United States would be isolated and a target for attack. In the end, the European Community concluded it would be better to have a weak treaty with the United States in than a strong treaty with the United States out, and relented on the demand for targets and timetables. The final agreement of the UN Framework Convention on Climate Change acknowledged the harmful effect of human greenhouse gas emissions and committed the signatories to reduce such emissions to 1990 levels by 2000, but the agreement was nonbinding. Developed countries were expected to provide financial and technical assistance to developing countries, from whom nothing but goodwill was required.

Bush eventually joined the party, literally—the 1992 Rio Earth Summit—on June 13. Ted Turner and Jane Fonda were there, along with Shirley MacLaine and Jerry Brown. Jimmy Cliff sang while Native Americans sat around a campfire softly beating drums. The Europeans announced a $4 billion package of environmental aid that put to shame a small U.S. offering, and issued a statement affirming their commitment to reduced emissions. When asked if the EC was assuming a new leadership role, European Community Director General for the Environment Laurens Jan Brinkhorst said: "It's logical that we are moving into that position." Bush insisted, however, "We are the leaders, not the followers."[40] But this wasn't his crowd to begin with, and he lost any remaining sympathy when he said, "The American way of life is not up for negotiation."[41] As a matter of fact that is exactly what was up for negotiation.

FROM RIO TO KYOTO

The road from Rio to Kyoto turned out to be tortuous. One of the first curves came up fast as Democratic Party candidate Bill Clinton defeated Bush in the 1992 election only five months after Rio. The Democrats had always had more support among environmentalists than the Republicans, and this time Clinton's vice president, former Senator Al Gore, counted himself among the environmentalist true believers. As a student, Gore had been deeply impressed by Keeling's research and its implications, and was a champion of environmental legislation in the Senate. In his best-selling *Earth in the Balance*, Gore set out detailed proposals for a new environmental policy that would include a kind of carbon tax, higher gas mileage requirements for vehicles, and a fee on manufacturers' use of nonrenewable materials.[42] As vice president, Gore had a chance to put these ideas into action; he became the captain of the new administration's environmental team and lost no time in putting together a Climate Change Action Plan, announced in October 1993. Among other things, it committed the United States to achieving 1990 carbon emission levels by 2000, exactly what the rest of the world had been demanding of the United States in Rio. A few months later the Rio treaty came into force as it was ratified by the requisite number of countries, including the now very supportive United States.

But the road was about to get bumpy. In November 1994, the Republicans gained control of the House of Representatives for the first time in forty-two years and elected the fiery Newt Gingrich as Speaker, arguably the second most powerful position in the U.S. government. His attitude toward environmentalism was best captured in a newspaper interview in which he said, "I love the environment, but I'm cheap at loving the environment."[43] The class of '94 was the most conservative group of Republicans that Washington or the world had seen since the 1920s. They hated big government, and to them, environmentalism was big government. Speaking shortly after the election, Utah Representative Jim Hansen said, "The question is not whether to close the [national] parks, but how to accomplish this goal."[44] The Chairman of the House Resources Committee Don Young, a Republican from Alaska, noted that "when I see a tree, I see a paper to blow your nose."[45] He added: "Environmentalists are a socialist group of individuals that are a tool of the Democratic Party. They are not Americans, never have been Americans, never will be Americans."[46] Congresswoman Helen Chenoweth of Idaho chimed in that "environmental policies are driven by a kind of emotional spiritualism that threatens the very foundation of our society, by eroding basic principles of our Constitution."[47] Whether these Republicans were right or wrong could be debated, but they were certainly not in doubt.

The other side of the Atlantic, meanwhile, saw an opposite political dynamic. Socialist governments had come to power in Britain, Germany, and France, as well as in some of the smaller European countries. Long sympathetic to the environmental cause, they now found themselves relying more and more on the Greens for political support. In Germany the government was now a Socialist-Green coalition. Part of the Greens' appeal was that they identified problems, like acid rain and pollution, that were of everyday concern. It also owed something to the sense of virtue people derived from fighting for clean air and water and healthy food. Beyond this, however, it also stemmed from and fed, in a kind of positive feedback loop, an emerging sense of European identity. As the European Community morphed into the European Union and focused on "deepening" its economic and political integration, certain policies became vehicles for expressing Europeanness. One of these was, of course, the proposal for a single European currency. Another was environmental policy. Here was a good thing for which all Europeans could pride themselves on taking a leadership position. It was also a way of expressing their resentment of the United States. In a sense, environmentalism, and particularly climate change policy, became an expression of European nationalism and a declaration of European independence.

The weather continued to cooperate nicely with the prophets of doom. January 1995 found Dr. Rodolfo del Valle, director of the Earth Sciences Department at Argentina's National Antarctic Institute, heading for an observation station on James Ross Island off the Antarctic peninsula to do research during the frigid continent's brief summer. In the middle of the month, colleagues at an Argentine base on the Larsen Ice Shelf radioed to say they were being shaken by constant ice quakes. On January 23, they called again to say, "Rudi, something's happening, the ice shelf is breaking."[48] Flying in a light plane over the thousand-foot-thick Rhode Island-sized shelf del Valle witnessed the unbelievable. The ice shelf collapsed before his eyes. "It was spectacular," he said. "What was once a platform of ice more than forty miles wide . . . looked like bits of polystyrene foam smashed by a child. The first thing I did was cry."[49] Looking then at the northern part of the shelf jutting into the Weddell Sea, del Valle and his colleagues predicted that it, too, would crack within ten years.

That was the most shocking climate event of the year, but hardly the only one. After a fifth consecutive winter without frost, New Orleans was overrun by mosquitoes, cockroaches, and termites. Across the Atlantic, Spaniards were suffering through the fourth year of the worst drought on record, and in Russia the asphalt melted at Moscow's Sheremetyevo airport.[50]

That was the backdrop to the opening of the first Conference of the Parties (COP 1) in Berlin pursuant to the undertakings of the Rio treaty. The objective of this meeting was to both determine if the signatories' announced plans for emissions reduction were likely to be adequate and to recommend further steps if they were not. In view of the hardening attitudes in the European Union and the changed attitudes in the United States with the arrival of the Clinton administration, it would have been surprising if the COP had found that everything was dandy. In fact, the Berlin Mandate ruled that the plans and processes were inadequate, and called for further strengthening of commitments, perhaps through a binding protocol or other legal instrument. This declaration effectively opened the Rio negotiation all over again.

That more needed to be done seemed to be confirmed by the release of the second report by the now 2,500 scientists of the IPCC. Their computer models were getting better. They could now predict the past, meaning that what the computers said should have happened in past years matched pretty closely what had actually happened. The new results tended to strengthen those of 1990. The key sentence read: "The balance of evidence suggests a discernable human influence on global climate." The scientists predicted a warming of 1–3.5 degrees Celsius by the year

2100 and said that this would result in continually rising sea levels, increased precipitation and more violent storms in some places, and severe drought in others. The cautiously worded report admitted that skeptics had some good points when they pointed to the weaknesses of the models in dealing with clouds, ocean currents, and small particles.[51] Nevertheless, the picture of earth's future painted for the delegates to COP 2, in Geneva in July 1996, was not a pretty one. The United States delegation, led by Undersecretary of State Tim Wirth, moved quickly to take the lead in doing something about it. The Geneva Declaration was based primarily upon a U.S. policy statement, and it recognized and endorsed the IPCC assessment and called for parties to set legally binding, medium-term targets for limitations and significant overall reductions of their greenhouse gas emissions. Here was the United States not only climbing on board but leading the charge for targets and timetables. It remained only to agree on the details and cut the actual deal at COP 3, scheduled for Kyoto the following year.

Wirth and the administration had made themselves popular with the European Union, but not with many others. The Australians, New Zealanders, and Russians rejected the call for binding targets, while the Canadians and Japanese waffled. Unlike the Europeans they would have a hard time hitting the targets being discussed. The G–77 developing countries, led by China again, emphasized that they would neither pay for the emissions sins of the developed countries nor allow them to use climate change as a latter-day colonial mechanism to keep the developing countries down. They would come to Kyoto only as interested bystanders and possible recipients of assistance. But the loudest objections came from U.S. businessmen, who saw the deck stacked against them. To begin with, they had nothing like the British natural gas, French nuclearization, or German shutdown of old East German power plants to help them meet a target. In fact, the environmental community would stoutly oppose any French-style nuclearization in the United States. One CEO jokingly suggested annexing Mexico and closing some of its ancient power plants. Beyond that, the base year of 1990 had been a recession year, when emissions were abnormally low. Now the country was in the midst of a great economic expansion and also experiencing strong immigration and population growth. So there had been a large increase in U.S. emissions since 1990, something the stagnant European and Japanese economies and declining populations had not experienced. Hitting some target of emissions below 1990 levels was going to hurt U.S. businesses harder more than others. Finally, they thought the yardstick was wrong and that they were not getting credit for what had actually been a good performance. Over the preceding fifteen years, U.S. industry had reduced emissions per unit of output far more than most of the rest of the world, and over 50 percent more than Britain or France.[52] Focusing on tons of emissions rather than on emissions per ton of output seemed to penalize the fastest growing and most efficient producers and economies. So American business formed the Global Climate Coalition to fight what it feared would be an unfavorable agreement in Kyoto.

The coalition made essentially two arguments. The first was that the deal would cut economic growth and cost jobs. The administration had done an economic analysis indicating that measures equivalent to a $100 per ton carbon tax would reduce U.S. emissions in 2010 to 1990 levels while reducing GDP less than 1 percent in the first ten years after enactment, and actually result in increased growth thereafter. But a number of independent analysts took the administration to task for making heroically optimistic assumptions. One study, based on a well-known Wharton Economic Forecasting Associates model, showed that instead of a $100 carbon tax equivalent, it would take a $200 equivalent to hit the target level of emissions. This would result in a cut in GDP of over 2 percent and the loss of 1 million jobs. The second business argument was that even if the deal were done as proposed, it wouldn't work because the greatest future growth in emissions would be from the developing countries, which had already been excused from any obligations. Worse, in the event of a deal, they would become magnets for U.S. companies relocating factories abroad, exacerbating the loss of U.S. jobs while cutting global emissions not at all.

Environmentalists pointed out that all these calculations did not include the potential costs of doing nothing, costs that would be catastrophic if even half of the IPCC predictions came true. This may have made sense to European leaders and certainly to leaders in the Association of Island States—but the U.S. Congress wasn't listening. The congressional attitude was well reflected in a House Subcommittee on Energy and Environment hearing on rising sea levels chaired by the avid surfer Dana Rohrabacher, Republican from California. When told that scientists project a 3-foot rise in sea levels that will drown up to 60 percent of U.S. wetlands and inundate an area the size of Connecticut over the next century, Rohrabacher responded: "I am tempted to ask what this will do to the shape of the waves and rideability of the surf. But I will not do that. I will wait until later, when we get off the record."[53] More serious were former Senate Majority leader Robert Byrd, Democrat from West Virginia, and Republican Nebraska Senator Chuck Hagel. In July 1997 on the eve of the Kyoto meeting, they introduced a resolution affirming that the Senate would not consider passing any treaty that would harm the U.S. economy or that excluded the developing countries. This resolution passed by a vote of 95 to 0 as a kind of bon voyage note from the Senate to the U.S. negotiators about to board their planes for Kyoto.

Three groups gathered in Kyoto that December. Over one hundred delegates came from the developing world—mainly, I suspect, to visit the old temples and see the sights of Japan's ancient capital, as they had already made it clear they wouldn't agree to any emission reductions. The second group was the Europeans and their close allies from the small island nations, who were seeking substantial reductions below the 1990 levels. The core of the final group was the Americans, with the Australians, Canadians, New Zealanders, and Japanese on the perimeter. The Americans were under the most pressure not to make painful cuts, but the others in the American group were also wondering how they would meet the targets and hoping the Americans would shield them from too much pain—both economically and politically. The debate was essentially between the United States and the EU. The negotiations were eye-glazingly complex and ended around 4 A.M. the morning after the deadline. But there were really only four issues— gases to be covered, sinks, emissions trading, and targets and deadlines.

Gases

The popular discussion of greenhouse gases focuses on carbon dioxide emitted from the burning of fossil fuels. But carbon dioxide makes up about 65 percent of the greenhouse gas concentration in the atmosphere. The other 35 percent is composed of methane (significantly derived from rice paddies in developing countries), CFCs, HFCs, and nitrous oxide. Because CFC emissions were already being cut by the Montreal Protocol, the American group wanted them included as a way of making the ultimate target easier to reach.

Sinks

Forests and oceans soak up about 55 percent of the carbon dioxide currently emitted into the atmosphere. They thus constitute "carbon sinks" that help reduce growth in atmospheric concentration. Reforestation such as that taking place in the northeastern United States thus contributes significantly to reducing net emissions. Indeed, there is some evidence from the Carbon Modeling Consortium that if sinks are counted into the calculation, the United States may not be a net emitter. In any case, the American group wanted sinks to be counted for the purpose of reaching the ultimate targets.

Emissions Trading

Emissions trading is a mechanism for harnessing market forces to achieve maximum reductions at minimal cost. It can be very complex but the concept is simple. Once a target for emissions is established, emitters would be issued permits or coupons for the amount of their allowed emissions. If one emitter found it unnecessary to use all the coupons, he or she could sell them to an emitter in danger of exceeding the limit. This device works particularly well if developing countries are included. To close an existing power plant ahead of schedule in order to meet an emissions reduction target in a developed country is very costly, amounting to throwing away a part of the capital invested. But developing countries are adding new plants for the first time. By selling their emissions permits, developing countries can get the money necessary to invest in more expensive but cleaner plants, while the developed country's plant is able to operate until the end of its financially viable life. This can be a win-win situation, but the more players who play the better, particularly if many of them are developing countries. Since the Americans, of course, wanted trading, they began urging the developing countries to participate, if only on a voluntary basis.

Targets and Timetables

The Americans were still willing to aim for 1990 levels, but they didn't want to go below them. It was already obvious that no one, including the

Europeans, could hit even this target by 2000 as originally planned in Rio, so the issue became whether the deadline should be 2010 for a 15-percent reduction below 1990 emissions levels for three greenhouse gases (the EU position) or 2008–2012 for a reduction to 1990 emissions levels for six greenhouse gases (the U.S. position). Obviously, a later date gave more time for new technologies to come into play. That, of course, was what the Americans wanted.

The Europeans and the island states began with a view of the American lifestyle as bloated and wasteful and of U.S. economic policy as selfish and exploitative of America's privileged international financial position. They saw all these sinks and gases and trading schemes as artful dodges by which America sought to evade its responsibilities to the global community. Here was the very essence of U.S. hypocrisy, claiming to be the virtuous world leader while looking for loopholes. With 4 percent of the world's population, America accounted for more than 25 percent of global pollution. It was time for America to stand up or shut up. So Europe opposed the flexibility sought by the Americans and again cast them as the only thing standing between the humble masses of the world and their environmental salvation.

The tone of the sessions was set by German Foreign Minister Klaus Kinkel's opening remarks. He started by praising the Americans for their tradition of innovation, and then slipped in the knife by saying, "Pioneers would be expected to set high standards. Future generations must not be burdened with the costs of our carelessness."[54] Acting as the spokesman for the European Union, he then proposed a 15-percent cut in the 1990 level of emissions by 2010. This was less than the 20 percent the island states had proposed but far more than the American camp was contemplating. Given the boom in the U.S. economy, such a target would have meant a nearly 35-percent cut in the present level of U.S. emissions.

Then, not to be outdone, Britain's Environment Minister Michael Meacher called on his American colleagues to make a "bigger effort," and to help them propose a cut of 20 percent in transport and industry emissions below the 1990 level by 2010. Moreover, the Europeans didn't want to hear about sinks or trading or gases other than the three main greenhouse gases. They wanted real reductions of actual emissions and no fakery. Undersecretary of State Stuart Eizenstadt, who was leading the U.S. team, knew he'd be lynched if he came back to Washington with a deal like that. He had said before arriving in Kyoto that "we want an agreement, but not at any cost."[55] Now Vice President Gore chimed in, saying, "We are perfectly prepared to walk away from an agreement we don't think will work."[56] But it was the vice president's bluff that didn't work. The Europeans refused to compromise, and after a week it looked as if the conference might fail. In a desperate effort to salvage the conference and his environmentalist credentials, Gore flew to Kyoto to address the gathered delegates. More important, he directed the hard-nosed Eizenstadt to "show flexibility." The result was a kind of Japanese compromise. The American camp got its gases, including methane, nitrous oxide (laughing gas), and three halocarbons used as substitutes for CFCs. The American camp also got sinks, but with the definitions and absorption accounting standards to be worked out later. (God is always in the details.) But there was to be no emissions trading, and on the all-important targets and timing, the agreement was for emissions reductions below 1990 levels of 8 percent for the EU, 7 percent for the United States, and 6 percent for Japan, to be achieved between 2008 and 2012. The developing countries were excused from any obligations but were invited to "opt in" on a voluntary basis. The protocol was to take effect once ratified by at least fifty-five countries that collectively would account for 55 percent of carbon dioxide emissions.[57] Champagne corks were duly popped, and the deal celebrated by weary negotiators and most of the environmental establishment. But it wasn't so much a deal as a ticket to The Hague.

AT THE HAGUE

The whole discussion in Kyoto had had a surreal quality. Here were the United States and Europe, probably the world's closest allies, villainizing each other over a difference of 15 percent in targeted emissions reductions. But the scientists of the IPCC had been saying for a long time that to stabilize atmospheric carbon concentrations at 1990 levels and avoid further human-induced warming by 2100, emissions would have to be immediately reduced by 60–80 percent. No one at Kyoto proposed anything near that. Moreover, it was already clear that the developing world would soon overtake the developed world as the leading greenhouse gas emitter. To the extent warming was humanly induced, it was therefore going to continue, and Kyoto would make a difference of only a few tenths of a degree in the world temperature by 2100. So what was going on?

Except in the island states, mostly posturing. Certainly there was much sincerity on the European side, but this was a situation where Europe could both do good and look good at America's expense. Eizenstadt and others were convinced that the Europeans and developing countries saw as well an opportunity to put the United States at a certain disadvantage in economic competition. As for the developing countries, since they stood to be the big losers in most of the warming scenarios, their tactic of blaming and defying the old colonial exploiters may have been emotionally satisfying, but it was ultimately self-destructive. The perimeter countries of the American camp were trying to be liked by everyone—their domestic constituencies, the Americans, and the Europeans. It was the Japanese who eventually brokered the deal. The Americans, finally, were trapped by their own institutions and politics. Unlike the leaders of the European and other parliamentary democracies, they could not just sign a deal and be assured either that it would pass the legislature, or that, once passed, it could not be challenged in the courts. They had to show Congress they were protecting U.S. interests while also showing their own environmental supporters they were also doing the right thing.

But economics was a common denominator. No one really wanted the U.S. system to change, despite their complaints about the bloated American lifestyle and the criticism noted earlier that with only 4 percent of the world's population America accounted for 25 percent of global emissions. As noted earlier, the proper response to the latter charge was that the United States also accounted for more than 25 percent of global GDP and was the lone engine driving world economic growth. Did anyone want that engine to slow down? No. Moreover, even the truest of true believers were making a cost-benefit calculation. If you really expected catastrophe for your children, you had to accept the 60– to 80–percent cuts recommended by the scientists—unless, of course, that meant catastrophe now. But it did. That's why even the Europeans' suggested cuts were so low. And then, without the developing countries, it wasn't going to work anyhow, which further lowered the price anyone was willing to pay for an uncertain benefit. So if Kyoto had any point at all, it was really about buying time to enable the only practical fix—the effect of new technology. But that argued for a big umbrella system under which everyone could be comfortable and even enthusiastic. Everyone had agreed in principle at Kyoto, but the actual system remained to be worked out.

As structured, the deal was dead on arrival in the United States. A number of studies put its cost at anywhere from 1 to 4 percent of GDP in order to avoid a warming catastrophe that few believed was likely to happen.[58] As one poll reported, more than 50 percent of Americans thought global warming was a big problem, but only 17 percent said they'd be willing to pay an extra 50 cents per gallon of gasoline to avert it. On top of the cost, this deal wasn't going anywhere in the U.S. Senate without a commitment from the developing countries.

But between Kyoto and ratification there were a number of interim negotiating sessions to work out the details, and for any negotiator worth his or her salt, such "detail sessions" are always a good chance to reopen the deal. The key meeting took place in the Dutch capital of The Hague on November 13–24, 2000. With the outcome of the U.S. election now up to the courts, this might be the world's last chance to negotiate with a U.S. administration that was essentially committed to the environmental cause. The U.S. negotiating team was now under the leadership of Undersecretary of State Frank Loy, a veteran of environmental causes and international negotiations. Loy desperately needed help from the Europeans. He needed the forest sinks to be accounted for generously, and as much emissions trading as he could get. He also hoped to put a little pressure on the developing countries, which were suffering from their own emissions in the form of huge smog clouds that blanketed whole regions for days at a time.

Loy later admitted to me that the United States had not helped its cause by doing so little to reduce emissions throughout a decade of negotiations. On the other hand, he believes many EU negotiators wanted to force a change in the U.S. lifestyle and even to punish the United States. The European negotiators were all from the environmental ministries. Loy noted that when he met with officials from the foreign ministries or trade ministries of Europe, they would roll their eyes over the positions of their own environmental ministries.

On the other hand, the European negotiators genuinely feared concluding a cynical deal that would be vitiated by loopholes. Any fakery by the developed countries, they thought, would kill their hopes of getting a commitment from the developing countries. In any case, after days of the toughest bargaining, Loy and Britain's Deputy Prime Minister John Prescott came to an agreement that gave Loy not what he wanted but at least what he needed on sinks and trading. At 4 A.M. on Thanksgiving Day a three-page working paper was initialed, and again, the champagne corks popped. But Prescott had to clear it unanimously with the other EU delegates, and the whole thing fell apart when he tried to do so the next day. A month later, the United States had a new president whose name was not Al Gore.

TO MARRAKESH

George W. Bush could have allowed the sleeping dog of Kyoto simply to continue its nice nap. Given the resistance of Canada, Japan, Russia, and Australia, it would have been next to impossible to achieve the necessary fifty-five signatures covering 55 percent of emissions for ratification. Thus the treaty would have never come into force. Or Bush could have launched a renegotiation. Instead, he achieved satisfaction by publicly announcing that the United States would never ratify the agreement.

There were three reasons for this. First, Bush had little sympathy with the environmental crowd in either the United States or Europe. As an oil man and a businessman he believed in drilling and growth, and was suspicious of government regulation. His energy plan called for drilling for oil in the Arctic National Wildlife Area, boosting federal funding and support of research and development in coal technology, and relaxing regulations on coal-fired plants. As one State Department official told me, "The Bushies think environmentalism is where all the commies went after the collapse of the Soviet Union. They hate 'em." Second, Bush didn't believe the science on global warming and really thought the Kyoto measures would hurt the U.S. economy. His economic advisers were from the supply side and the aluminum industry. Third, Bush had made campaign promises to the coal, power, oil, and steel companies in

order to win critical states like West Virginia. Now it was payback time.
That his announcement came just before his first official trip to Europe
had the added benefit of letting the European wimps know that a new
wind was blowing from Washington.

Beyond arousing a diplomatic and media firestorm, however, the
Bush rejection of Kyoto galvanized the Europeans to take the lead as
they had never done before. They resolved to show the United States
that it was not indispensable, and to press ahead with ratification. Bush
only hardened their determination when he tweaked them during his
visit about not meeting their own goals. Without a U.S. signature, the
EU had to get all the others from the perimeter of the U.S. camp on
board. They proposed that forest sinks credits be negotiated country by
country rather than allocated on the basis of fixed criteria, which led to
very generous credits, especially for Canada and Russia. The Japanese
and Australians wanted more emissions trading and that too was expanded. In the end, to bring everyone else under the umbrella, the EU
agreed to everything Frank Loy and Stu Eizenstadt had been asking for,
and more. The revised Kyoto Protocol was ratified and put into effect
on November 10, 2001, in Marrakesh. Undersecretary of State Paula
Dobriansky sat watching as the other delegates signed. Much of the
world now saw the United States, the inventor of environmentalism, as
its enemy.

WHAT IS TO BE DONE

In March 2001, the IPCC issued its third assessment, in which the
findings of the first two were largely confirmed and strengthened. The
report states authoritatively that over the twentieth century temperatures have risen by 0.6 degrees Celsius; that the rise has occurred in the
lowest 8 kilometers of the atmosphere (resolving the earlier discrepancy
between surface temperature data and atmospheric temperature data);
that sea level has risen by 0.1–0.2 meters; and that ocean temperatures
have also increased. There has been more precipitation, more heavy
precipitation events, and an increase in cloud cover. Emissions due to
human activities continue to alter the atmosphere in ways that are expected to affect the climate, and there is new and stronger evidence that

most of the warming over the last fifty years is attributable to human activities. The confident tone of this report is based on improvements in the computer climate models and in their abilities both to predict the past and to capture elements, such as solar activity, previously not included in the calculations. The scientists admit they cannot simulate all aspects of climate, and note that there remain uncertainties with regard to clouds and their interaction with other elements. Nevertheless, they can confidently predict a surface temperature increase of 1.4–5.8 degrees Celsius over the next century. This is larger than what the world experienced in the twentieth century and probably unprecedented in the last ten thousand years. All these projections assume business as usual by humans, meaning continually rising atmospheric carbon concentrations. On that basis, the implications are continually rising sea levels, more extreme weather events, more extensive droughts, and continued retreat of glaciers and snow lines. There is also the possibility of a tipping point or points to make these changes sudden and drastic rather than gradual.

No one really knows how much of this will occur because both human and natural activity are sure to change. Perhaps they will ameliorate the problem, but they could also exacerbate it. Given the state of knowledge today, ignoring the issue would seem to be a complete roll of the dice. On the other hand, to be sure of preventing the problem means immediate emissions reductions on a scale whose economic consequences no one can reasonably contemplate. Somewhere in the back of their minds, most observers think new technology or other changes in human behavior will occur to relieve the problem. And that, indeed, seems to be the only real answer. Since we can't really save our way to salvation, we will—in the American way, in the best sense—have to invent our way there.

But that will take time. In the meantime the problem is getting worse. Some action aimed at abatement and buying time seems wise as a kind of insurance policy. The only question then is the cost and effectiveness of the policy. A very expensive policy that will result in little abatement and buy little time is not attractive unless it is a step toward a less expensive policy or more abatement or both. The original Kyoto deal was certainly an expensive policy for the United States and one that aimed at little abatement. Whether it was a step along the way is another question. But the more important point is that Kyoto *à la* Marrakesh is very different and much less expensive. The United States can easily afford it and should have signed up at Marrakesh. It would have made economic sense and would have avoided enormous international ill will. Since we missed the opportunity at Marrakesh, it would have been a brilliant move if we had, in the wake of September 11, signed the treaty as a sign of U.S. solidarity with the friends who were dramatically expressing their support for us at the time. We missed that opportunity also, but it is still not too late.

6

In Arms We Trust

*"America always preaches rule of law, but in the end it
always places itself above the law."*

—A British ambassador

The United States is quintessentially the country of law. Lawyers
thrive here as nowhere else, and we have several times as many
lawyers per thousand people as any other country. It has truly been said,
for example, that there are more lawyers in any medium-sized American
city than in all of Japan. Anyone who has engaged in business internationally knows that considerations of the legal aspects of any commercial
deal are far more extensive in the United States than anywhere else and
the documentation several orders of magnitude more voluminous. Only
in America are most legislators and top government officials lawyers and
only in America is law routinely the way to the top of major corporations. In the diplomatic arena too, the United States is a champion of the
rule of law, particularly preaching it as the *sine qua non* for free trade and
economic development. (I know, having often been the preacher.) And,
of course, the expansion and protection of human rights internationally
is part of the foundation of American foreign policy. From the time of
Woodrow Wilson, America has been the leader in initiating negotiation
of international treaties.

Yet, in an April 2002 report entitled "Rule of Power or Rule of Law"
that reviewed the U.S. reponses to eight major international agreements,

the editor Nicole Deller noted that the United States had "compromised or acted to undermine in some crucial way every treaty that we have studied in detail." Of course, America is party to thousands of international agreements, and it would be wrong to say it never keeps its end of a deal. But in recent years, America has rejected or weakened several landmark treaties, including the ban on use of landmines, the ban on trade in small arms, the comprehensive test ban treaty, the ABM treaty, the chemical warfare treaty, the biological warfare treaty, the nonproliferation treaty, the International Criminal Court, and others. As one of the major factors causing alienation from America in the world today, we need to examine both our resistance to international limitation of a variety of weaponry as well as what our dependence on the military means for the U.S. economy.

SOWING THE FIELDS WITH MINES

It burrows into the ground and sits, sometimes for years, waiting for an innocent child at play, a mother seeking the child, young men playing football, or farmers plowing new fields. Always it waits for someone who is unaware. Then, when the unsuspecting are at last in just the right spot, it explodes without warning, eviscerating the victims' bodies or tearing off arms and legs.

Though first developed during the American Civil War, the landmine was little used until the end of World War I, when it blossomed as the antidote to the newly invented tank, which was upsetting the long stalemate of trench warfare. The antagonists in World War II deployed more than 300 million antitank landmines. Early in the war, however, they revealed a dangerous weakness: They could be dug up and redeployed by the enemy. To counter that, a new kind of landmine was quickly developed—the antipersonnel mine. It was typically placed around the antitank mines to prevent their removal. Perhaps the most effective of these was the German "Bouncing Betty," which could jump to hip-height when activated and spew thousands of deadly steel fragments into any soldiers within a wide arc around it. So effective were landmines that they soon began to be used for offensive as well as defensive purposes.

After World War II, weapons technology advanced rapidly. In the

1960s, so-called scatterable landmines were developed that could be dropped from airplanes and automatically activated as they hit the ground. Rather than laboriously planting each mine by hand, an air force could quickly deploy large numbers of mines. Scatterables were first introduced by the United States during the Vietnam War, and they became a major weapon driving wedges between the opposing forces and their bases and channeling them into adverse terrain. They were also used by both sides to displace villages, make fertile land unusable, and destroy roads, bridges, and water sources. They sometimes had perverse consequences. U.S. troops often found themselves retreating through their own mine fields, and it is estimated that nearly one-third of all U.S. casualties during the war were caused by friendly landmines.[1]

As low-intensity wars spread throughout the 1960s and 1970s, landmines were widely used not only by government troops but by paramilitaries, police, and guerillas.

In 1979, the Soviet Union invaded Afghanistan with a new, improved scatterable, called a butterfly mine, that it dropped pretty much all over the country. Although in World War II mine fields had been rigorously marked and mapped so that they could be avoided and eventually removed, the advent of scatterables and their increasingly indiscriminate use made adequate mapping and marking impossible. Nowhere was this more true than in Afghanistan. For, although the Soviets were eventually driven out in 1989 by the Mujahedin, the mines stayed.

This fact became painfully clear to a former British army officer, Lieutenant Colonel Colin "Mad Mitch" Mitchell, in the 1980s when he was sent to Afghanistan to help the Afghanis recover their agricultural production. He found so many mines that it was impossible to do any serious farming until they were cleared, an extremely dangerous undertaking in view of the fact that no maps or markings of the mine fields existed. Mitchell persevered, nevertheless, and launched the Halo Trust with the mission of carrying out a humanitarian mine clearance program.

Afghanistan was far from being the only country with a landmine problem. Cambodia, Vietnam, and about seventy other mostly developing countries were still hosts to about 110 million mines left over from long-ceased activities. These mines were killing or injuring about 26,000 people annually.[2] In January 1991, after months of caring for landmine victims in refugee camps along the Thai-Cambodian border, the leaders of the Women's Commission for Refugee Women and Children called for a ban on antipersonnel mines in testimony before the U.S. Congress. That summer, the Vietnam Veterans of America Foundation opened its first prosthetics clinic in Cambodia. Then in September, Human Rights Watch and Physicians for Human Rights published *The Coward's War: Landmines in Cambodia* and added their voices to those calling for a ban. These and other groups eventually came together in the fall of 1992 to form the International Campaign to Ban Landmines (ICBL); to head the effort they chose a determined and energetic woman from the Vietnam Veterans of America Foundation, Jody Williams.

Williams threw herself into an unprecedented campaign that eventually brought together 1,300 NGOs in more than eighty-five countries under the ICBL banner. The campaign put great emphasis on building as large a coalition as possible and met early and often with religious, labor, business, academic, military, and political leaders. Among the most important early converts to the cause was Senator Patrick Leahy, Democrat of Vermont. Leahy, along with Congressman Lane Evans of Illinois, introduced legislation, passed by Congress in 1992, to put a one-year moratorium on American exports of antipersonnel mines.[3] This proved to be a powerful catalyst. Politicians everywhere began to think that if the United States could take such a step, significant progress was really possible. During a trip to Cambodia in February 1993, French President François Mitterand announced that France would ban exports of mines; this was quickly followed by similar announcements from more than a dozen countries. Then in June of 1994 the Swedish Parliament called for a total ban on landmines. In August it was the turn of the Italian Senate, which ordered its government to work to ban all exports of mines. Then came the biggest gun of all. At the UN General Assembly's annual opening meeting in September, President Clinton called for the "eventual elimination" of landmines.[4] He followed all this with a new policy statement in May 1996 saying that the United States would end the use of "dumb" mines by 1999 except in Korea, would continue to use "smart mines" (mines that self-destruct after a pre-set time) indefinitely until an international agreement was reached, and would negotiate to reach an international agreement to ban antipersonnel mines.[5]

That set the stage for the dramatic Ottawa Conference of October

1996. Canada invited all those governments in favor of a total ban on mines to meet to discuss strategy. Fifty governments participated along with twenty-four observer states and other participants from the NGO community and the UN. At the end of the conference, Canadian Foreign Minister Lloyd Axworthy announced the intent of the Canadian government to convene the same countries, along with any others who might want to join, one year later in December 1997 to sign a treaty completely and immediately banning antipersonnel landmines of all kinds. This effectively established an alternative, fast-track process to the ponderous UN talks on the same subject.

But as the Ottawa process gathered steam, U.S. statements began to sound just a tad tentative. Said U.S. Deputy UN Ambassador Karl F. Inderfurth, "We're not prepared to set a date, but we are prepared to start work immediately. If this Ottawa process can take place within that time frame and if our concerns can be met, we'll be very supportive."[6] Positive, but a lot of "ifs." Actually, the United States was leading in mine destruction, having destroyed 3 million of the mines in its own stockpile and provided more financial support for de-mining around the world than any other country.[7] The United States had also continually extended its moratorium on exports and sponsored a UN resolution calling on all nations to "vigorously pursue" a ban on mines. As the Ottawa process moved forward, however, U.S. officials began to express preference for the slower UN process.

This was because the U.S. Defense Department, in an effort to square a treaty with key defense needs, requested three exceptions. Mines must be permitted in the Demilitarized Zone (DMZ) between North and South Korea; the United States must be allowed to continue mine use in mixed antitank systems; and the United States must reserve the right to use "smart" mines. Korea, it was argued, should be exempted from any treaty because it was the last battleground of the Cold War and the mines were all that stood between the 37,000 U.S. troops guarding Seoul and 1 million North Korean soldiers on the other side of the DMZ.[8] In any case smart mines were not the problem: since they self-destructed, they shouldn't be banned.

This position called forth a hail of criticism from Leahy and other congressional leaders, as well as from much of the world's press. Princess Diana of Great Britain implicitly criticized the U.S. position with her visits to landmine victims during a tour of Angola. In response, Clinton changed course in August and agreed to join the Ottawa process talks that were to take place in Oslo in about two weeks. These were to prepare the treaty for final completion and signing in Ottawa in December. But although the United States had agreed to work within the Ottawa process, it continued to request the exceptions, at least temporarily. The pressure to maintain that position was only increased by a letter Clinton received from ten retired U.S. four-star generals calling the treaty "clearly defective, unverifiable, unenforceable, and ineffectual."[9] After agonizing for another week, Clinton announced on September 17, 1997, that the United States would not sign the mine ban treaty as then constituted. Thus when 122 nations, including all of America's closest allies, gathered in Ottawa in early December to sign the Mine Ban Treaty, the United States watched from afar. Said President Clinton: "Our nation has the unique responsibility. . . . As Commander–in–Chief, I will not send our soldiers to defend the freedom of our people and the freedom of others without doing everything we can to make them as secure as possible."[10] But that was not the last word. Shortly after the signing of the treaty, Jody Williams was awarded the Nobel Peace Prize.

The Clinton administration later announced its intention to develop alternatives to present systems, to end the use of all landmines outside Korea by 2003, and to sign the Mine Ban Treaty by 2006. In May 2001, eight retired U.S. military leaders, including several former commanders in Korea and the former Superintendent of West Point, wrote the new President Bush urging that he sign on to the Mine Ban Treaty. Among other points, they emphasized two: far from being critical to defending Korea, mines were more likely to slow and obstruct the movements of U.S. and South Korean troops; and in any case the landmines in the DMZ are under the jurisdiction of the South Korean government and thus unaffected by U.S. accession to the treaty. More generally, their letter argued that antipersonnel mines are outmoded weapons that do more harm than good to U.S. forces. This sentiment followed statements by people like former Army Captain Ed Miles, who, having lost both legs to a landmine in Vietnam, said that "the weapon has outlived its usefulness, whatever usefulness it ever had."[11] In August, President Bush announced a White House review of landmine policy; several officials emphasized America's special security burdens and the priority of protecting our troops and allies (all of whom have already signed the treaty and destroyed their mines).[12] At the end of February 2002, the Vietnam Veterans of America Foundation launched a series of full-page ads and TV spots to urge the president to sign on to the treaty.[13] As I write, the matter remains under review.

IN OUR GUNS, MISSILES, BOMBS, GASES, AND GERMS WE TRUST

Small arms are another category of weapon whose use the United States hesitates to curb. While the developed countries pay much attention to chemical, biological, and nuclear weapons, small arms are the poor man's weapons of mass destruction. The United Nations estimates there are presently about 500 million such weapons in circulation around the world. Out of forty-nine significant armed conflicts in the past twelve years, small arms have been the weapons of choice in forty-six.[14] They are easy to obtain, legally or illegally, easy to conceal, simple to use, and difficult to control to the point where the black-market price of an AK–47 has become a leading indicator of conflict. Normally the price is $230–$400. Anything under $100 indicates an outbreak of peace after a period of intense violence. Conversely, prices above $1000 are a strong warning of coming trouble.[15]

Because we are numbed by repetition, we watch the consequences every night on TV without seeing them. But in the killing fields of Sierra Leone, the jungles of East Timor, the deserts of Somalia and elsewhere, 4 million people have been killed by small arms in the past decade, 90 percent of them civilians and 80 percent women and children.[16]

In an attempt to curb this mayhem, the UN General Assembly created a special panel in 1995 to consider the problem of small arms. Over several years the panel's work eventually led to the convocation of the United Nations Conference on the Illicit Trade in Small Arms and Light Weapons in All Its Aspects, held in New York in late July 2001. Merely holding the conference was itself a major accomplishment in the face of resistance from several major arms-exporting countries, including the United States. At the same time, the focus on "illicit trade" revealed the compromises that were necessary to get the meeting off the ground. Most participants believed the problem goes far beyond mere illicit trade, but all knew that any effort to address anything else would founder on the unyielding rock of U.S. opposition. Even dealing with illicit trade would turn out to be extremely difficult. The conference's objective was stated broadly as being to deal with "all relevant factors leading to the excessive and destabilizing accumulation of small arms and light weapons in the context of the illegal arms trade."[17] The main immediate goal was to formulate political—not legally binding—accords that would limit production and trade of these weapons solely to registered manufacturers and brokers, and that would provide for marking the weapons, tracing and verifying supply lines, collecting and destroying weapons in "hot spots," and disarming, demobilizing, and reintegrating former combatants. Particularly important to many countries like South Africa and Norway were possible measures to limit civilian possession of such weapons and to prevent their sale to nongovernmental entities.

U.S. Undersecretary of State for Arms Control and International Security John Bolton lost no time in giving the conference delegates a dose of reality. Speaking early in the conference, he noted that "the abstract goals and objectives of this Conference are laudable." But he went on to emphasize that he was talking only about military arms, not hunting rifles or pistols, and only about illicit trade: "We . . . do not begin with the presumption that all small arms and light weapons are the same or that they are all problematic." In response to the South Africans, Norwegians and others uneasy about a gun in every closet, Bolton emphasized that "just as the First and Fourth Amendments [to the U.S. Constitution] secure individual rights of speech and security respectively, the Second Amendment protects an individual right to keep and bear arms." So much for limiting arms sales to government-recognized entities. Just in case anyone mistook his meaning, Bolton added: "We do not support measures that would constrain legal trade and legal manufacturing of small arms and light weapons. We do not support the promotion of international advocacy activity by NGOs. We do not support measures that prohibit civilian possession of small arms. We do not support measures limiting trade in small arms solely to governments, and the United States also will not support a mandatory Review Conference."[18] Other than that, he thought there might be some good in the proposals.

The conference ended by declaring victory with the publication of a watered-down "set of norms to guide the actions of states in addressing this problem."[19] These contained no mention of restricting civilian gun ownership. But only the Americans were happy. "The United States should be ashamed of themselves," said South African delegate Jean Du Preez. Mexico's delegate, Luis Alfonso de Alba, called the U.S. position "regrettable," while the conference chairman, Camillo Reyes of Colombia, vented his frustration by saying, "I must express my disappointment over the conference's inability to agree due to the concerns of one state."[20] Many left believing that the sacred right of every American to own an AK–47 would probably lead to several million more deaths in the next decade. But the Americans figured they'd be okay.

Landmines and small arms were arms limitation agreements the United States chose to avoid. But on December 13, 2001, President Bush gave notice to Russia that the United States would actually abrogate a treaty—the Anti-Ballistic Missile Treaty then in force between the two countries—six months hence in June of 2002.[21] First proposed by the United States in June of 1967, this treaty mutually to restrict deployment of antimissile defenses was concluded in May of 1972. It was thought to provide security by assuring that neither country could feel so invulnerable to missile attack that it would be tempted to try a first strike in the belief that it could escape devastating retaliation. Because the treaty had seemed to provide precisely the nuclear stalemate it was designed to produce, the possibility—first mooted in the early days of the Bush administration—of its nullification caused an international firestorm, in conjunction with the administration's plans to push ahead with a National Missile Defense (NMD) that would be incompatible with the provisions of the treaty. Russian Defense Minister Igor Sergeyev spoke for virtually all the leaders of Europe, China, Japan, and South Korea when he said that "this will destroy the entire system of international treaties aimed at ensuring strategic stability."[22]

But three developments muted this reaction. The Russians knew, first, that for financial reasons they would have great difficulty maintaining their full inventory of nuclear warheads. So, they were open to mutual warhead reduction proposals. They also knew that any NMD system the United States was likely to build would not be a threat to them, because they would always retain more than enough warheads to overwhelm it. And they wanted closer relations with the West to help their economic development. So they came to an agreement with the United States under which both sides would cut their nuclear arsenals by two-thirds to 1700–2200 warheads,[23] while the United States undertook to bring Russia into closer cooperation with NATO and to facilitate that nation's economic development. In return, the Russians agreed that they would swallow the U.S. abrogation of the ABM treaty.

The second event was the terror attacks of September 11, 2001, which provided justification for the U.S. argument for deployment of the NMD—namely that it was necessary as a defense against attack by "rogue nations." Finally, the Chinese, who—because of their relatively small nuclear arsenal and their designation as a "strategic competitor" by the administration—could justifiably see themselves as the real target of the NMD, decided to go along with deployment, at least for the time being, because in the wake of September 11 relations with the United States had become much more cooperative and much less adversarial, and the Chinese preferred to keep it that way. Thus, when the nullification eventually became official on June 13, 2002, criticism was restrained. The Russians and Europeans repeated that nullification was unwise, but said they could live with it. The Chinese just said quietly that it was unwise.

The reaction was quite different, however, when Undersecretary Bolton told a Geneva press conference on January 24, 2002, that the United States is opposed to the Comprehensive Nuclear Test Ban Treaty (CTBT). The effort to ban nuclear testing is, of course, nearly as old as nuclear testing. The recent history of the effort and of the CTBT began with an announcement by Soviet President Gorbachev on October 5, 1991, that the Soviet Union would observe a one-year moratorium on its nuclear testing and that it was inviting the United States to refrain from testing as well. Shortly afterward, the United Nations began preparations for eventual negotiation of a CTBT. The following year France announced a unilateral testing moratorium and the U.S. Congress passed the Hatfield-Exxon Amendment calling for a nine-month testing moratorium, test ban negotiations, and a prohibition on all U.S. testing after September 1996 unless another nation conducted a test. President George H. W. Bush reluctantly signed the legislation. In 1993 the new Clinton administration pledged to observe the moratorium and to pursue completion of a CTBT by the end of 1996. Congress followed this with a resolution in support passed by an overwhelming majority. The French announcement, in mid-1995, of new tests and Indian reservations about the CTBT, threatened to halt momentum, but then China dropped its insistence on so-called "peaceful explosions"; and by the end of September 1996, the CTBT was completed and opened for signature at the UN in New York. The United States was among the first signers, along with seventy other countries, including Russia and China, and the treaty was quickly passed to the U.S. Senate for what promised to be easy ratification.

But supporters reckoned without the Senate Foreign Relations Committee Chairman, the extreme American exceptionalist Jesse Helms, Republican of North Carolina. Helms bottled the treaty up in committee for two years and it did not come up for consideration until the fall of 1999. By this time, more than 150 countries had signed it.[24] The Chairman of the Joint Chiefs of Staff, General Henry Shelton, and four former chairmen, including General Colin Powell, all endorsed it, as did a large number of other active and retired military, diplomatic, and scientific leaders. Paul Nitze, the Reagan administration arms control negotiator, even called for U.S. unilateral nuclear disarmament on the grounds that our superiority in conventional weapons actually made nuclear weapons a danger to our own forces.[25] The public supported the treaty by an overwhelming 82 percent.[26]

Still, there were arguments against the deal. Senate Majority Leader Trent Lott argued that it would be unverifiable and thus open to cheating. He also noted that simulation alternatives to testing are unproven and therefore risky for maintaining the efficiency and reliability of U.S. weapons. A final argument was that the treaty was just a first step on the "slippery slope" toward nuclear disarmament. Former National Security Advisers Henry Kissinger and Brent Scowcroft called for delaying the vote on the grounds that the treaty was not sufficiently enforceable and failed to include countries like Iraq and Iran.[27] But partisan politics was also at work. The Republican leaders in the Senate had been reluctant to bring the treaty up for consideration. Despite a letter from sixty-two senators requesting more time for debate, only one day was allotted for discussion.[28] When the treaty finally came to a vote on October 13, 1999, it was defeated on a party line tally of 51–48. Most countries expressed great disappointment. Some hoped that a new Bush administration would try again and have more luck with the Republican Senate. But as Bolton made clear in Geneva, there was never a chance.

The administration's focus on deployment of the NMD (whose viability many scientists doubt) stems from both its strategy of preemption and hegemonic dominance and its desire to escape the vulnerability inherent in the concept of mutual assured destruction, or MAD. NMD is an attempt to free the United States to intervene militarily almost anywhere in the world. This is coupled with the desire to develop more flexible forces and particularly to recast nuclear weapons for use against hardened underground bunkers and in retaliation for biological and chemical attacks. Achieving this may require new weapons, and testing to develop them.

The mention of chemical and biological weapons brings us to a final treaty the United States has rejected. Attempts to control these weapons date to the Geneva Protocol of 1925, adopted as a reaction to large-scale use of poison gas in World War I. In 1962 the United States and the Soviet Union both made proposals to the UN for elimination of all chemical and biological weapons. As international talks dragged into the fall of 1969, President Nixon declared a U.S. policy of unilateral renunciation of biological warfare and a no-first-strike policy for chemical weapons.[29] By the mid-1980s the United States had decided that possession of chemical weapons was not in its national interest, and in November 1985, Congress mandated the destruction of the U.S. stockpile of unitary chemical weapons.[30] In the aftermath of the Persian Gulf War in May 1991, President Bush declared that the United States would forswear using chemical weapons for any reason, including retaliation, once the on-going UN talks had concluded in a Chemical Weapons Convention (CWC).[31] These negotiations did conclude in January 1993 with a very straightforward and tough treaty that called for destruction of chemical weapon stockpiles, a ban on further manufacture, and creation of an inspection and verification body.[32] The United States signed immediately, but doubts about cheating by other nations and concerns in Congress about giving up a weapons option delayed U.S. ratification until April 1997. The U.S. chemical industry played a key role in lobbying for U.S. ratification because it feared losing business if the treaty came into force without U.S. membership.

Having ratified the treaty, however, the United States then moved to gut it by passing legislation that permitted U.S. officials to refuse on-site inspections, prohibit removal of chemical samples from U.S. territory for independent analysis, and sharply limit the number of U.S. facilities subject to declaration and routine inspection. The United States also refused to pay its share of the costs of the convention and neglected to provide adequate financing to help destroy Russia's vast stockpiles.

In his 1969 statement, Nixon had treated biological weapons separately from chemical ones. In 1972, UN discussions led to conclusion of a Biological and Toxins Weapons Convention (BWC) committing each party "never in any circumstances to develop, produce, stockpile or otherwise acquire or retain" biological agents or toxins for military purposes. This treaty came into force upon U.S. ratification in 1975 and has remained the controlling convention ever since. Unfortunately, it has no enforcement or verification provisions; and in the 1990s, Russian President Boris Yeltsin's revelations of illegal Soviet anthrax programs as well as concern about Iraq's germ warfare capabilities led to creation of a UN committee for developing a new protocol to put teeth into the agreement in the form of a legally binding verification regime. The committee hoped to have a document ready for signature by 2001. The United States provided significant support and called the plan "a major step forward." In December 2000, however, a new tone sounded from Washington when private analysts and some U.S. defense officials suggested to *New Scientist* magazine that the treaties banning chemical and biological weapons should be rewritten to allow "non lethal" versions that could put entire armies to sleep or disable vehicles and weapons by eating their plastics or making their tires brittle.[33] Still, when the final document was presented for signature in March 2001 the major problem for the United States remained inadequate detection and verification. Its allies pushed hard for U.S. acceptance of the proposed system of regular reporting and inspection, including challenge inspections. But having simulated the proposed system on its own chemical and biological installations, the U.S. had concluded that it not only didn't work but could actually lead to increased suspicions. On July 25, 2001, U.S. Ambassador Donald Mahley told the UN committee that the United States was ceasing negotiations because "in our assessment, the draft Protocol would put national security and confidential business information at risk."[34] Japanese Ambassador Seiichiro Noboru spoke for the international community when he said, "I was rather surprised by the U.S. argument at this stage."[35]

At a subsequent BWC review meeting in November, Undersecretary Bolton made several suggestions for strengthening the BWC that he claimed had never been considered. In fact, however, all but one of them were contained in the Protocol the United States had just rejected. None of that deterred Bolton, who proposed on the last day of the conference that the committee simply be disbanded. A few months later, the United States insisted on having the head of the Chemical Weapons Convention inspection unit fired on grounds, we said, of financial mismanagement.[36] But no one believed that. As Lord Rea of Britain pointed out, much of the financial difficulty was the result of U.S. refusal to pay its dues.[37] The real reason, many believed, was that the inspections director was planning unannounced inspections in the United States.

SOVEREIGNTY TRUMPS HUMAN RIGHTS

In similar fashion, the United States has rejected a protocol to strengthen the 1987 Convention Against Torture (many believe out of reluctance to allow inspections of the condition of Taliban prisoners at Guantanamo Bay); the Convention on Elimination of All Forms of Discrimination Against Women; and the International Convention on the Rights of the Child (out of conservative fears that it would interfere with "family values").

But the pièce de résistance of all these international treaty and convention battles is the struggle over the International Criminal Court (ICC). Here the various conceptual and institutional difficulties the United States has in its intercourse with the international community all combine in one dramatic and revealing picture.

The ICC had its origins in the 1948 Convention on Genocide, which was prompted by the post–World War II revelations of the Holocaust. The UN resolution calling for adoption of the Convention also invited the UN's International Law Commission to look into the desirability of establishing an international court for putting on trial persons charged with genocide. To make a long story short, the atrocities in Yugoslavia and Rwanda in the early 1990s gave rise to two developments. At the urging of the United States, the ad hoc International Criminal Tribunals on Yugoslavia and Rwanda were established to prosecute the perpetrators of genocide in those two countries. At the same time, the International Law Commission developed a draft statute to create the long-discussed International Criminal Court, and this statute was presented for adoption by the UN at a special conference in Rome in June and July of 1998.

It is important to understand the main issues at stake at this seminal conference. First was the question of the independence of the court. Would its jurisdiction require case-by-case approval of the UN Security Council and thus be subject to the veto power of its permanent members (U.S., Russia, China, U.K., and France), or would it have a degree of independent authority? A second question concerned the independence of the prosecutor and whether he or she could launch prosecutions at will. Then there was the so-called consent regime issue. Would there be universal jurisdiction such that the court would have authority to prosecute any pertinent crime committed anywhere in the world? Or would jurisdiction require the case-by-case approval of the country where the crime had taken place or of the country of the nationality of the accused? Would the court have jurisdiction over crimes committed during civil wars? Fourth was the question of national versus ICC jurisdiction. Could the ICC prosecute if national courts have initiated their own criminal proceedings? Finally, there was the question of the past. Would the court be able to prosecute Henry Kissinger, for example, over alleged responsibility for the 1971 coup in Chile?

Each of these questions was, of course, fraught with implications for sovereignty and with, in American eyes, the potential for politically motivated action against U.S. citizens by anti-American regimes. The effort to establish the court was driven by the so-called Like Minded Group of sixty countries under the chairmanship of Canada and including most U.S. allies around the world. While the United States insisted it supported the ICC in principle, it categorically opposed a court that could indict U.S. citizens without prior U.S. approval. In particular it abhorred the notion of universal jurisdiction, which had been introduced by Germany, and threatened active opposition if any variant of it was codified in the statute. U.S. concern was so strong that Secretary of Defense Cohen was reported to have linked U.S. troop deployments in Germany to the issue.[38] In the debate that ensued over the five major questions, it was pretty much the United States against the Like Minded Group with the rest of the world watching. Nonetheless, the Americans scored many

points and got much of the draft statute watered down. With regard to
independence, the United States wanted case-by-case approval by the Security Council. Initially, the other permanent members of the Security
Council backed the U.S. position, but when Britain abandoned this position as legally and morally untenable, the dam was broken and eventually the United States was left isolated. The decision was that, to ensure
its credibility as an independent court, the ICC would have to be able to
prosecute without prior Security Council approval. To prevent frivolous,
politically motivated suits, however, it was agreed that in order to launch
an investigation the prosecutor would have to have the approval of a
panel of ICC judges. It was also agreed that the Security Council could
adopt a resolution to stop any ICC investigation. On the question of jurisdiction the United States scored a partial gain. Universal jurisdiction
was deleted. Under the final wording of the statute, the ICC can act only
if the state in which the crime took place or the state of nationality of the
accused consents or is a party to the ICC Convention. On the question
of civil wars, the agreement was for the ICC to have jurisdiction, a small
defeat for the U.S. position. But on national versus ICC jurisdiction the
United States scored a major win with the agreement that the ICC can
prosecute only if national courts fail to act. It was also agreed that there
would be a nonrenewable seven-year period during which states could
opt out of ICC jurisdiction over war crimes.[39] At the last minute the
United States sought a special exemption for nationals of nonmember
states who were carrying out official duties. This would have allowed a
government to block prosecution of its citizens at will and would have
undermined the court's credibility. It was defeated. But the United States
did succeed in having national security adopted as a ground for refusal to
cooperate with the court, and in having superior's orders established as a
ground of defense. Two opportunities for states to challenge and appeal
the court's jurisdiction were also provided.

None of this, however, was enough for the United States, and it voted
against creation of the court, along with China, Iraq, Libya, Yemen,
Qatar, and Israel. The final vote was 120 in favor, 7 against, and 21 ab-
staining. The court would become effective when the accord was ratified
by the sixtieth country.

The international community's defiance of U.S. wishes led to a veritable U.S. jihad against the court's establishment. President Clinton signed the convention on the very last day of his administration, but only as a means of giving incoming President Bush the option of working with the UN to shape implementation of the court. The Bush administration, however, gave early indication that it might go so far as to unsign the treaty.[40] In the fall of 2001, the Senate adopted the American Service-members Protection Act, submitted by Senator Helms, which would have prohibited the United States from cooperating in any way with the ICC, and barred U.S. military assistance to any country supporting the ICC. The bill also directed the United States to use any means, including force, to release any American citizens held by the court. It was this clause that gave the bill its nickname "The Hague invasion act." It did not become law, but the other measures restricting cooperation with the ICC did.

As it became apparent in the winter and spring of 2002 that the needed sixty ratifications would soon be achieved, the U.S. government ran an increasingly high-pressure campaign to discourage ratification, but to no avail. On April 11 the sixtieth signature was affixed and the court went into force. At that point the U.S. government went into overdrive. In an unprecedented letter to UN Secretary General Kofi Annan, Under-secretary Bolton informed him that the United States was effectively removing its signature from the court treaty. The United States, he explained, "has a unique role in the world in helping to defend freedom and advance the cause of humanity," and Americans might therefore become targets of politicized prosecutions. Thus, the United States refused to be a party to the treaty.[41]

But there was still a problem. While the court would have no jurisdiction in the United States, American citizens might be operating in countries that are parties to the ICC, and the court could still wind up with jurisdiction over Americans without the consent of their government. U.S. officials argued it was unfair to subject Americans anywhere to jurisdiction of a treaty to which their government was not a party. Opponents pointed out that if an American commits an ordinary crime abroad, the foreign government has the right to prosecute without U.S. approval. In the event of an atrocity, the same government would be well within its rights to delegate prosecution to the ICC. Moreover, the United States could gain great influence over the course of any such prosecution if it simply ratified the ICC treaty. It was also noted that while the United States does play a key role in global hot spots, it is not entirely alone. France, Britain, and others have troops and personnel in various trouble spots, and they seemed to have no problem with the court. Finally, even in the event of an American being accused in another country, under the rules of the court, the United States would have the right to prosecute first. Only if it refused to investigate would the ICC have any ability to step in. The counter to this was that the United States might have good reasons not to investigate if it thought the charge fraudulent.

But this dispute was not about debating points, it was about power. U.S. officials launched a campaign to pressure many countries that ratified the treaty to sign special bilateral agreements exempting U.S. citizens from the court's jurisdiction in their domains. In Europe this put the U.S. government on a collision course with the EU, which told countries like Romania and Poland that acceding to U.S. pressure could endanger their candidacy for EU membership.

The United States threatened to veto routine renewal of all current UN peacekeeping missions, beginning with Bosnia, if the Security Council did not grant all UN peacekeepers permanent immunity from the court. In the end, the Security Council reluctantly granted a one-year immunity to American nationals. This was a face-saving, halfway solution, but the Council also expressed the intention to renew the exemption annually. So the United States seemed to have won. But Mexican Ambassador Adolfo Aguilar Zinser spoke for many when he said: "The general opinion of the international community is that this is wrong."[42] Another ambassador from one of America's oldest and closest allies, told me privately in the words of this chapter's epigraph: "America always preaches rule of law, but in the end it always places itself above the law."

John Bolton and Jesse Helms, who have appeared several times in this narrative, represent a critical institutional peculiarity. Both are what are known as "conservative Republicans," generally meaning that they are devoted to "freedom" and suspicious of government. They see the United States as having the most democratic form of government, are firm apostles of the American creed, and see American power and the American way of life as the ultimate model toward which the world will converge over time. Although Helms was on the Foreign Relations Committee and served as its chairman for many years until his retirement in 2002, and

Bolton has had high-level positions in the State Department, they are suspicious of foreign governments, believing them to be less democratic and more welfare-oriented than the U.S. government, and also tend to see other countries as envious of American freedom. They have no use for the UN or other multilateral institutions, seeing them as corrupt, undemocratic, and dedicated to restraining or obstructing the benevolent power of the United States. They place complete faith in American power and put the highest priority on maintaining absolute sovereignty and freedom of action.

The influence of such views is greatly enhanced by the separation of powers in the U.S. government. Treaties must be ratified by the U.S. Senate before becoming law, and before they can be voted on in the Senate, the chairman of the Foreign Relations Committee must put them on the schedule and conduct hearings and debate. The chairman can bottle up a treaty for years without taking action. Or he can insist on some other action as the price of bringing the treaty up for a vote. It is often the case that the president and a majority of the American people support a particular treaty or piece of legislation, but cannot obtain its passage because of the opposition of a powerful committee chairman. This combination of ideological views and institutional power is one reason America has frequently been at odds with the world.

THE ARMED ECONOMY

The third important aspect of American militarism is economic. Just as it has sought to keep key countries as quasi-client states, so the United States has sought to dominate key weapons and military technology. In 1948, U.S. defense spending was $9.1 billion, about 3.6 percent of GDP, having fallen from well over half of GDP in 1945.[43] The outbreak of the Korean War led to a quick doubling of the military budget, and during the Cold War, defense spending of about 6–7 percent of GDP became a kind of rule of thumb. Given the size of the U.S. economy this resulted in a prodigious amount of arms spending—over the entire Cold War, the equivalent of $15.8 trillion in today's dollars.[44] This was not the unbearable burden for the U.S. economy that it would eventually prove to be for the Soviet Union. Nevertheless, there were regular outbreaks of angst over falling behind and of euphoria for the silver bullet weapons system that would make the United States invulnerable, and each of these cycles unleashed a new flood of spending.

The first panic came in 1954, when pictures of the Soviet May Day parade seemed to show a whole fleet of new Soviet bombers not derived from U.S. or British design and capable of reaching the continental United States. It was later shown that in fact the Soviets had only a few of these planes but had flown them in continuous circles over the May Day parade, making it appear that the supply was endless. At the time, however, there was great concern over the "bomber gap" and powerful pressure to build more B–52s to "catch up with" the Soviets. This pressure continued until the first U–2 spy plane flights over the Soviet Union in 1956 showed that the gap was in favor of the United States. This fact did not stop presidential candidate John F. Kennedy from emphasizing, during the 1960 campaign, the need to close the dangerously widening "missile gap" by creating an invulnerable retaliatory force of ICBMs to the tune of about $300 billion.[45] After Kennedy was elected it was discovered that there really wasn't a missile gap, but that fact, too, did not stop the appropriation of billions of dollars for further expansion of U.S. missile forces. In the missile and nuclear warhead race of the 1960s and 1970s, it is impossible to say whether we or the Soviets were the generator.

A modicum of stability seemed to be established in the 1970s with the ABM Treaty and various undertakings to limit testing. But the election of Ronald Reagan as president in 1980 again unleashed the American search for invulnerability. Reagan said the doctrine of MAD (Mutual Assured Destruction) that then guided U.S. nuclear deterrence strategy was itself mad. The notion of voluntarily accepting vulnerability was just un-American, and Reagan launched the $50 billion Strategic Defense Initiative, better known as Star Wars, to develop a system capable of knocking down any missiles launched at the United States before they could arrive. Few scientists thought the system could ever be made to work effectively, but neither doubts nor cost were any object when the goal was invulnerability. The end of the Cold War slowed this program but did not kill it. Rather it metamorphosed into the current National Missile Defense system, for which the United States abrogated the ABM treaty in 2001. As noted earlier, it was promoted as a defense against missile strikes from "rogue nations," but looks suspiciously as if it were aimed at China. Again, there are grave doubts about its effectiveness. As former Undersecretary of Defense for Acquisition and Technology Jacques Gansler told me in August 2002, the system has not worked under the simplest of controlled situations and is very susceptible to decoys and other evasive measures.

Of course, if it can truly provide protection against the destruction of major U.S. population centers, it would be worth a substantial investment. But there are several ironies in the situation. First, despite years of research and billions of dollars of expense, the proposed system would have been useless against the kind of missiles that struck the World Trade Towers on September 11. It would be useless, too, against the hand-held Stinger missiles that helped bring the Mujahedin victory in Afghanistan and that nearly brought down an Israeli airliner over Nairobi on November 28, 2002. There are an estimated 700,000 of these missiles available around the world, many of them supplied by the United States to countries and groups with terrorist connections.[46] These are truly the weapons of rogues: cheap, easy to carry and conceal, and capable of bringing air travel to a complete halt. Yet there has been virtually no effort, certainly nothing comparable to SDI and NMD, to control or defend against these weapons.

From another perspective, the attempts of designated "Axis of Evil" states like North Korea and Iran to obtain nuclear weapons and missiles may be more to defend against, than to threaten, us. Our tendency to replace regimes and our emphasis on overwhelming military power send a clear message of danger to many governments. And our recent experience in North Korea cannot have gone unnoticed. It has a few nuclear weapons and missiles and holds Seoul hostage. We have been forced to back away from our threats here while continuing to threaten Iraq with attack at any moment. The message couldn't be clearer. Obtain nukes and the Americans will become more reasonable. NMD won't change this tactic, because the nukes don't have to be aimed at American soil.

The persistence of this and other systems demonstrates a depressing aspect of the American political system. You can't kill a weapons system or a base. Once a project gets launched, it picks up bureaucratic and congressional champions who direct money to key congressional districts. The arms industry purposely spreads work widely around the country to assure the support of as many congresspersons as possible, particularly those who chair key committees. For example, in 1998, the Speaker of the House, Newt Gingrich, Republican of Georgia, managed to have $2.5 billion added to the defense budget for procurement of airplanes even the air force said it didn't want, because the planes were produced in his state.[47] Various regions' economic and political need to keep weapons systems going perpetuates their proliferation, which in turn creates pressure for their deployment and use. Thus, although the F–15 is often described as the world's most advanced aircraft and the United States has more than one thousand of them, but the U.S. defense establishment is planning their replacement with the more advanced F–22. Another example of this process is a proposal to deploy space weapons that could ward off attack on U.S. space-based hardware and destroy the satellites and space hardware of other countries. There is no known threat to America in space, but the temptation is there to militarize it because we can, and for somebody the project means research grants and jobs and votes.

The arms industry is also a major exporter and provider of jobs. An iron law of business economics is that one seeks to amortize capital and R&D investments over as large a production run as possible, thereby reducing the per unit cost of these investments. With the United States spending approximately 70 percent of military R&D worldwide, it is not surprising that arms exports are a big American business. The Commerce, State, and Defense departments all maintain large staffs to sell and facilitate the export of American weapons to the world. In 1999, the last year for which statistics are available, the world's arms trade rose to nearly $52 billion, after declining from $70 billion in 1989 to a low of about $40 billion in 1994. A little more than half of this was imports by developed countries, the rest by developing countries. U.S. exports, which accounted for 64 percent of these sales, are likely to approach 70 percent in the future based on sales agreements already signed.[48] The top buyers of U.S. weapons are Saudi Arabia, Taiwan, Japan, Britain, Turkey, Israel, South Korea, Egypt, and Greece. If it looks to you as if the United States is sometimes arming both sides of a conflict, you're right.

Much more than selling is involved. The United States uses arms arrangements to cement relationships with key countries, to standardize equipment and procedures globally, and also to gain a degree of control over foreign government policies. For example, Poland announced in

January 2003 that it would procure forty-eight new F–16 fighters from the United States as part of its program to beef up its forces to meet its obligations as a new member of NATO.[49] This is obviously good for General Dynamics, which makes F–16s, and for the U.S. economy, but it has several other implications. For one thing, it further weakens competitive European aircraft makers by depriving them of a sale, thus raising their costs and making other customers more likely to buy the F–16. (This is counter to U.S. pressure for more European defense reform.) It makes the Polish Air Force interoperable with the U.S. Air Force but not necessarily compatible with other NATO forces. Because parts are to be supplied from the United States, it also gives U.S. officials leverage in the event that Poland wants to do something with those airplanes that is at odds with U.S. wishes. But that, of course, is the biggest question of all. What, exactly, is Poland going to do with those planes? Neither NATO nor Poland faces any significant threat that F–16s can address, and one might think that as a developing country Poland could make better use of the money. That was certainly the position of Brazil, whose new President "Lula" announced at nearly the same time that he would cancel delivery of U.S. fighter planes ordered by the previous administration because Brazil has better ways to spend the money. This kind of behavior gets a head of state branded a "dangerous leftist."

Poland may have been anticipating future arrangements such as those the United States has concluded with Japan, Korea, and a number of other countries under which they co-produce and even co-develop the weapons. U.S. deals to sell weapons systems, and especially aircraft, are often predicated upon the conclusion of what are known as "offset" arrangements. This means that the buying country—say, Korea—will receive a license to produce part or all of the airplane in its domestic factories, and that the technology necessary to do so will be transferred from the original U.S. producer. A number of countries have used procurement of U.S. aircraft in this way to develop an indigenous aircraft industry where none previously existed. Japan has proven particularly adept at gradually making more and more of an airplane until finally it has become a full partner in the development of the next generations. This process actually raises the cost of the final product because it makes production runs shorter than if they were all made in the United States and exported off the shelf. Japan's new FSX fighter will go for about $150 million per copy, while simply buying an equivalent off the shelf would cost less than half that.[50] Beyond the immediate cost, the transfer of technology not only diminishes American industrial leadership but also makes critical weapons systems more easily available. This is all done in the name of improving U.S. security.

Whether it actually does that is not clear, but it certainly reduces the productivity of the U.S. economy. By spending 3–5 percent of our GDP on defense, we are in effect taking that much and investing it in products and services we will mostly never use. Thus at the first level, we lose the returns we would get by investing in productive assets. At the second level, we would gain more by simply exporting off the shelf, but we lose much of that gain through offset arrangements and joint development deals. Finally, at the third level, our inexpensively transferred proprietary technology is used by foreign competitors to improve a wide range of products and services that compete commercially with U.S. offerings. We lament that we have to do this because of our special responsibilities and burdens and complain that our allies don't spend to maintain equivalent force capabilities. But the truth is that we want these responsibilities. We demand them, and the proof is the offset deals. The official story is we do these deals to defend our allies. But the allies demand bribes to accept the deals. Obviously they don't see the threats the same way we do. They are taking advantage of our need to shoulder special burdens, and we beg them to do it.

We also make it extremely difficult for them to collaborate with us even if they wanted to. The Pentagon is far and away the biggest arms buyer in the world, accounting for more than half of global procurement. As a supplier, if you can't sell to the Pentagon, you can't stay competitive. You can't get the volumes of production or the big R&D dollars to allow you to remain at the leading edge. But the Pentagon makes it extremely difficult for foreign producers to sell to it.

The mid–1990s saw one of the defining moments in the American arms industry structure. With the end of the Cold War there was a drop in weapons spending and a necessary shrinkage of the defense industry. Secretary of Defense William Perry convened what came to be known as the "last supper," a dinner with defense industry CEOs to advise them to start thinking merger and shakeout. This would have been a time to consider globalizing the defense industry through international mergers, but it didn't happen, partly because of resistance abroad, partly because it might have impaired U.S. weapons dominance and reduced imperial leverage.

TEACH THEM TO FIGHT—NOT TO WRITE

The United States is not only the world's premier weapons exporter, it is also the leading instructor on war. The School of the America's, for example, was first established in the U.S.-controlled Panama Canal Zone in 1946 and since then has graduated more than sixty thousand officers, cadets, and noncommissioned officers from all the Latin American countries as well as the United States. There are several objectives. One is to establish close relations between the military personnel of Latin America and those of the United States. It is thought that this not only can inculcate U.S. concepts of civilian control of the military but also enable training in human rights and democracy along with instruction in such things as special operations, civil military operations, and so forth. That's the theory, but in practice, the school has been labeled the "school for dictators" because of the high number of former Latin American dictators among its graduates and the high number of human rights complaints they have generated. To be fair, it is also true that some of the school's graduates like Paz García of Honduras have been instrumental in transferring power back to civilian democratic rule, and that all the countries of Latin and South America have become democracies over the past decade as the dictators have failed. But this owed little to the School of the Americas.

The same mixed bag can be seen in a more recent and diversified program. In the post-Cold War environment, the mission of the U.S. military has been in part and importantly to "shape the international environment." That has meant a proliferation of military-to-military relationships involving military training, counternarcotics programs, antiterrorist activities, education programs, and equipment transfers. These activities are primarily carried out by U.S. Special Operations Forces (SOF) who are now deployed in more than 140 countries with a budget of well over $3 billion. These forces operate under the 1991 Joint Combined Exchange Training (JCET) law that both allows them to train abroad with foreign forces, and also allows the U.S. SOF to pick up the expenses of the foreign forces if they are unable to pay their own way.

This law was ostensibly aimed at providing critical training for U.S. SOF personnel. It may indeed do that, but it has also morphed into a broad program under which the United States is training virtually all the world's armies. With about 4,500 U.S. troops deployed around the globe at any given time, JCET personnel outnumber the 4,000 Foreign Service officers of the State Department.

Looking at the other side of the ledger only makes clearer how strong our trust in arms is. In 1948, the first year of the Cold War, U.S. spending on aid and other diplomatic and nonmilitary international programs totaled $6 billion 1948 dollars or more than 3 percent of GDP, about the same as the U.S. military budget at the time[51] or $104 billion in 2002 dollars. Today, America's total overseas nonmilitary spending, including the cost of embassies, aid, education, and everything else, comes to less than $17 billion or about 0.17 percent of GDP. Moreover, of that, nearly $4 billion is for military assistance, mostly through the Foreign Military Financing program, which operates as a grant program to enable foreign governments to buy U.S. military equipment.[52] So, in fact, only about $13 billion or 0.13 percent of GDP is aid in the normal sense. Of this about $3 billion goes to Israel and $2 billion to Egypt (still part of the payoff for the 1979 Egypt-Israel peace deal), with the rest divided among everybody else.[53] These pitiful numbers—despite the end of the Cold War, the Peace Dividend, the global explosion of AIDS infections, and the spread of famine in Africa—are actually down from where they were in 1990, making the United States the smallest donor of aid as a percentage of GDP of the industrialized countries.[54]

We are also the most remiss contributor to international organizations. As of December 31, 2001, for example, we still owed back dues to the UN of nearly $900 million even after having paid off some of what we previously owed.[55] Is it any wonder that our allies tire of all our talk about special burdens?

But then, if we actually decided to spend some money, there would be hardly anyone left to spend it, and many of those who remain couldn't talk to the recipients anyhow. Over the past decade the State Department has slashed the number of its consulates and overseas offices. We now have fewer consulates in China, for example, than we had in 1939. Still, according to the General Accounting Office the State Department faces serious personnel shortages at many critical posts, and the people who are there are frequently unqualified. For example, the GAO found in its survey that 62 percent of the Foreign Service officers assigned to China did not meet the language proficiency requirements of their posts, nor did 41 percent of those in Russia. In Saudi Arabia, the head of the Public Diplomacy Section could not speak Arabic at all. Of course, the United States Information Agency, created during the Eisenhower administration for the purpose of telling America's story abroad, was dismantled in 1999. In the wake of September 11, the Bush administration created something called the "Office of Global Communications" and hired a Madison Avenue advertising executive to run it. Whether it will be slick and savvy or just slick, however, remains to be seen. None of this should be surprising when we consider that only 14 percent of Americans carry passports, and that many universities no longer include a foreign language as a graduation requirement. In recent polls, 87 percent of Americans couldn't locate Iraq on a map.[56]

At the end of the Cold War, America had an opportunity like the one briefly imagined immediately after World War II, when it could consider a new world order based on a community of nations genuinely sharing responsibility for maintaining peace. With the demise of the Soviet Union and the transformation of China into a market economy increasingly integrated into the global trading and investment system, the UN became potentially a more workable body. There was also time to review the rationale for key alliances like NATO and the Japan-U.S. Security Treaty, as well as the basis for American military deployments abroad. None of this was done. To be sure, defense spending fell back finally to the 3.5 percent of GDP levels of the late 1940s, and the military services shrank somewhat in size. But with the rapid decline of Soviet forces and the size and growth of the U.S. economy, U.S. forces actually grew in a relative sense, and the basic deployments and missions remained. Samuel Huntington has noted the tendency of America to define itself in opposition to outside threats and to look for enemies. In the absence of specific enemies after 1992, the United States still perceived threats sufficient to justify keeping more than 200,000 troops abroad.

Oddly for an ever-changing capitalist country like the United States, "instability" became an enemy. Any change in existing alliances or deployments might lead to dangerous "instability" and was to be avoided at all costs. The events of September 11 and the advent of the War on Terror, along with the focus on regime change in Iraq have provided new and, in a sense, less-dangerous enemies. But they also highlight another point, noted by Immanuel Wallerstein: The United States relies very heavily on one card in the international poker game, the military card. We don't like to think of ourselves as a warlike people, but can we expect others to accept us as "peace-loving" when it is really only in arms that we trust?[57]

7

PEACEFUL PEOPLE,
ENDLESS WAR

In February 2002, in the face of mounting tensions with North Korea, President Bush stopped for talks with South Korean President Kim Dae Jung while traveling in the Far East. During the obligatory visit to U.S. troops stationed at the Demilitarized Zone just north of Seoul, Bush gave a speech in which he strongly emphasized that "we're peaceful people."[1]

The statement was unremarkable in the sense that it is true. Americans don't think of themselves as warlike or as having territorial or imperial ambitions. Few of America's wars have enjoyed great public enthusiasm, and public opinion polls consistently show that Americans as individuals care little about what happens overseas. If there were a referendum on U.S. deployments and commitments abroad, the American people would probably vote against most of them. Yet Bush's speech was made in a context in which tensions had risen at least in part because the U.S. government had opposed South Korea's "Sunshine Policy" toward the North, in favor of greater pressure to force the fall of the hated communist regime. This situation illustrated another aspect of America, namely that despite the peace-loving nature of the American people, the country was not only founded in war but has been almost continuously engaged in war or preparations for war since its birth. According to my count, from the signing of the Constitution in 1789 until the present, there has been scarcely a year when the United States was not engaged in some overseas military operation. Admittedly, these include a number of small skirmishes and guarding operations, but the sum comes to 235 separately named events of which perhaps 25 to 30 could be characterized as full-scale wars.

Even before the Revolutionary War, Americans were engaged in fighting the native American Indians. From the founding of the country until the closing of the frontier a hundred years later, there was hardly a year without conflict between the United States and the various tribes. One of George Washington's first duties as president was to put down Indian uprisings in the Northwest (then Ohio and Michigan), although he was troubled by the need for doing so. He hoped that "all need of coercion in the future might cease," and urged Congress to adopt philanthropic regulations regarding the tribes. Thomas Jefferson also struggled with the problem and, while mourning the Indians' fate, also promoted the westward expansion that sealed it. Andrew Jackson, who made his mark by driving the Seminoles out of Florida, had no patrician qualms, believing that Indians "can not live with a civilized community and prosper." Sadly, he proved to be right but perhaps for the wrong reasons. In any case, by 1890 the Indians were all dead or on reservations.[2]

Aside from the Civil War and the War of 1812 that consolidated U.S. independence from Britain, America fought two kinds of engagements with foreign adversaries during the nineteenth century. There were two full-fledged wars with foreign countries and numerous incursions, skirmishes, and interventions around the globe arising from the perceived need to protect Americans and their commerce. Many were initiated by the United States and nearly all resulted in gain for the country. The determinedly unilateralist America fought none in alliance with other countries. The first skirmishes were with the pirates of the Barbary states of North Africa to whom the United States refused to pay the bribes that had become part of the cost of doing business in the Mediterranean. By the 1820s, America had Mediterranean, Pacific, African, and South Atlantic naval squadrons doing everything from ensuring the rights of American seal hunters in the Falkland Islands to punishing Sumatrans for stealing opium from American traders. Three incidents had particular later significance. In the 1840s, America obtained a concession for trade with China at Shanghai and began a century of Yangtze River patrols aimed at enforcing the opening of China's markets and the protection of missionaries. In 1853 Commodore Matthew Perry showed up in Tokyo Bay with his famous fleet of "Black Ships" and demanded that the Japanese open their market upon pain of bombardment and possible invasion. And in 1871, Admiral John Rodgers tried the same thing, but with less success, in Korea.

The real wars were the one with Mexico in 1846 and that with Spain in 1898. In the case of Mexico, war arose in connection with the U.S. annexation of Texas when President James Polk sent the U.S. army far south into Mexican territory. With minimal casualties, the United States won and gained not only Texas, but New Mexico, most of Arizona, and California. As for the Spanish-American War, in response to alleged Spanish brutality in putting down Cuban independence fighters and in the wake of the mysterious explosion of the U.S. battleship *Maine* in Havana Harbor, U.S. troops were dispatched to Cuba. In what Secretary of State John Hay called "that splendid little war," the United States again suffered few casualties and gained an empire that included Puerto Rico, the Virgin Islands, the Philippines, and Guam. Ironically, American control of the Philippines entailed both refusing to recognize a Filipino Declaration of Independence modeled on America's and putting down Filipino independence fighters with at least as much brutality as the Spanish had used in Cuba. But it did give us a chance, as President William McKinley said, "to Christianize" the Filipinos who had been Roman Catholics for 350 years.

The history of the twentieth century for America centered on three crusades to save the world from militarism, genocidal fascism, and totalitarian communism. The first, of course, was America's entry into World War I. Whether the Germans were really more at fault than the Russians, French, and British is a subject of debate. But there is no doubt that the American intervention saved France, Britain, and much of the rest of Europe from a militaristic German hegemony.

It also marked a major transition in the rationale of American foreign policy. While America's nineteenth-century wars (except for the Civil War) had been largely about territorial expansion, protection of trade routes, or the defense of some vague notion of "honor," its motives in the Great War were more idealistic. Woodrow Wilson's high-minded Presbyterianism would not allow the United States to fight a war for mere material gain. Rather it had to "vindicate the principles of peace and justice in the life of the world" and "to make the world itself at last free."[3] If you think that sounds like President Bush, you're right. Idealism had permanently entered U.S. foreign policy.

Wilson's idealism foundered in the losing battle to get the U.S. Senate to ratify his beloved League of Nations. In a scenario that would be repeated frequently, the United States conceived of and sold the world a plan and an institution that the United States itself in the end rejected. Senators William Borah and Henry Cabot Lodge, who led the vote against the League in the U.S. Senate, have been cast in later history as isolationists, a term that has since become pejorative. But they were not isolationist, and Lodge had in fact been an enthusiastic supporter of U.S. imperialism. Rather, as noted in Chapter 2, they were unilateralists, jealous of America's sovereignty, sure of its superior virtue, and suspicious of the motives and reliability of other nations. America, they believed, was better off walking alone as it always had.

If there was ever a just war, it was World War II. There is no doubt that America saved the world from what truly was an evil empire. This too was a war fought for freedom and justice and to end all wars. Thus, the objective was unconditional surrender, and we rationalized the use of some terrible weapons to obtain it. Having emerged as the world's dominant power militarily, technologically, and economically, the United States determined that the idealism of Wilson would not be denied, and did something it had never done before. It led the creation of and actually joined the United Nations, the IMF, the World Bank, and other international bodies that would entangle it in long-term agreements with other countries and cause it to forego a measure of freedom of action. Of course, the United States remained the senior partner and had effective veto power over all of these bodies, but their creation represented an important evolution of American foreign-policy thinking.

It is axiomatic that all countries pursue their national interest. The critical question is how they define that interest. Hitler defined Germany's interest as the conquest of much of the world and the extermination of Jews. The United States, which had long focused on the unilateral pursuit of its own freedom and happiness, now began to define its interest in terms of improving global economic conditions, rebuilding devastated countries, and establishing a community of nations on the basis of global rule of law and due process. In effect, the United States defined its interest in terms congenial to a world order based on a consensus of the community of nations. So multilateralist was the United States at this time that it even proposed to put control of atomic energy under the new

UN. For perhaps the first time in history, a dominant power was actively promoting the dilution of its own power. Before the experiment could go very far, however, the century's third crusade intruded.

THE COLD WAR

Less than a year after the end of the war in 1945, American military forces, which had comprised some 15 million personnel, melted away to about 1.5 million, and the intent was to shrink further. The war had been won and now it was time to "get the boys back home." No one was planning on empire. The Cold War changed that completely.

The war started in earnest in early 1946. On February 9, Joseph Stalin made a speech declaring cooperation impossible between the imperialists of the west and the peace-loving peoples of the socialist countries. On February 22, the American diplomat George Kennan cabled his famous Long Telegram from the U.S. embassy in Moscow explaining to Washington that, in the view of the leaders in Moscow, there could be no permanent peace with the United States. They therefore saw it as necessary that the international authority of the United States be broken if Soviet power was to be secure. At the same time, Kennan emphasized, the Soviets were not schematic or prone to adventurism. On March 5, Winston Churchill spoke in Fulton, Missouri, saying, "From Stettin in the Baltic to Trieste in the Adriatic an iron curtain has descended across the Continent." The key event occurred on February 21 when the British Ambassador to the United States announced that Great Britain was broke and could neither maintain its support for the Greek and Turkish governments battling communist insurrections nor continue to hold many of its other posts in the Middle East.

Thus, the Truman administration faced a momentous decision. Would it assume the mantle of Great Britain and take on broad responsibilities for shaping the world? Truman answered on March 12 before a joint session of Congress:

At the present moment in world history nearly every nation must choose between alternative ways of life. . . . Our way of life is based upon the will of the majority, and is distinguished by free institutions, representative government, free elections, guarantees of individual liberty, freedom of speech and religion, and freedom from political oppression. The second way of life is based upon the will of the minority forcibly imposed upon the majority. It relies upon terror and oppression. . . . I believe it must be the policy of the United States to support free peoples who are resisting attempted subjugation by armed minorities or by outside pressures. . . . If we falter we may endanger the peace of the world—and we shall surely endanger the welfare of this nation.[4]

George Bush couldn't have said it better. In quick succession the United States proposed the Marshall Plan, launched the North Atlantic Treaty Organization, and, in the wake of the Soviet Union's first atomic explosion, moved to develop the hydrogen bomb. By 1949 the United States was beginning a major build-up of forces that would last into the present.

The policy Truman articulated was not preemption or preventive war, but containment, on the Madisonian premise that "A bad cause never fails to betray itself."[5] But it lasted so long on such a titanic scale that it became much more than containment. All national priorities were subordinated to the overriding objective of hermetically sealing off Soviet, Chinese, and any other communists wherever they might be. A new "gospel of national security"[6] guided the nation to a new doctrine that wonderfully synthesized all of its old and new foreign policy traditions. Containment fueled the superpatriotic, us-against-them sentiment never far from the surface of the American personality and convinced the country that its most sacred value, "freedom," was under attack. It also gave a new lease on life to the American proclivity for unilateralism that had been briefly suspended after World War II. The United States still made commitments to others and entered into "entangling alliances," but always made sure to maintain its freedom of action. Containment also provided a justification and rationale for the progressive brand of imperialism America had employed in the Spanish American War and lesser conflicts by validating the need for far-flung bases, which turned large parts of the world into client states of the United States. It incorporated Wilsonianism by invoking liberal internationalist values and using them as weapons, and finally it served the ends of expansionist commerce by opposing both colonial and communist empires and pushing for open markets. As Tony Smith has said, "American hegemony constituted a form of anti-imperialist imperialism."[7] James Warburg called it isolationism turned inside out and said, "We are willing to become citizens of the world, but only if the world becomes an extension of the United States."[8]

There should be no doubt that the Cold War was a noble crusade carried on with the best of intentions, without hope of material gain or conquest, against foes that perpetrated great evils. If we had to face the same decision again, we should, in my judgment, unhesitatingly make the same choice. But we might consider different methods of implementation. We are paying today for serious mistakes made out of ignorance, paranoia, and an excessive trust in arms and power. This is not the place for a history of the Cold War, but the Korean War and a series of American interventions show why, despite its sacrifices in the cause of freedom and justice, America is often viewed from abroad with fear and distrust.

THE KOREAN WAR

The first shooting war of the Cold War was the Korean War. It began when Soviet-trained and -supplied North Korean forces invaded the South in June 1950. While this act of unprovoked aggression may have been partly induced by U.S. statements and actions indicating that Korea was outside the U.S. defense perimeter, Truman rightly announced that it could not go unchallenged, particularly in the context of Soviet threats elsewhere at the time. U.S. troops were committed and fought desperately to stem the North Korean tide. This they did quickly and then brilliantly counterattacked with the famous Inchon landing behind North Korean lines. By September, U.S. forces had secured all of South Korea and occupied much of the North, including the capital city of Pyongyang. What remained of North Korean forces were broken and scattered. At this point U.S. casualties were 3,614 dead, 4,260 missing, and 16,289 wounded.[9]

As the defeat of the North Koreans became clear, China warned against an American advance to its border with North Korea on the Yalu River. Such an advance was unnecessary: The communists had been contained, and the allies were in effective control of Korea. But General Douglas MacArthur, commander of the allied forces, believed in total victory and also in the need to replace the communist regime in China with Chiang Kai-shek's Nationalist Chinese government, which had recently fled to Taiwan. As he had ordered U.S. troops to Korea, Truman had also directed the U.S. Seventh Fleet to position itself in the Taiwan Straits between mainland China and Taiwan, thus intervening in the Chinese civil war on the side of the corrupt Chiang Kai-shek regime. Without any decision having been made regarding war with China, MacArthur visited Taiwan to coordinate his war effort with Chiang's continuing attempts to regain a foothold on the mainland. MacArthur also directed the U.S.-led forces to drive to the Yalu. As they said they would, the Chinese attacked. Three years later, with the death toll at 54,246, the wounded at 103,284,[10] and the U.S.-led forces no longer in control of North Korea, a fragile armistice was concluded and a Demilitarized Zone established that is still policed by U.S. troops and their South Korean allies. Thus, our ignorance about our foe and our paranoia about Chinese communism combined with our readiness to resort to arms to lengthen the war, adding to the casualty lists while actually weakening the U.S. position. And there was other fallout, whose effects we are still feeling.

The Chinese communists were not predestined to become a major enemy of the United States. During the war against Japan, they had made friendly overtures to U.S. officials and had actually fought harder against the Japanese than Chiang's forces. They naturally resented U.S. support of Chiang in the civil war that ensued after Japan's defeat and were angry that the United States continued to recognize the remnants of Chiang's forces in Taiwan as the government of China (I discuss Taiwan further in Chapter 8), even while Britain and most of the rest of the world recognized the communist regime in Beijing. But China was not looking for a fight with the United States. There were major differences between the Chinese communists and the Soviet communists. Some U.S. Foreign Service officers, such as John Service and John Patton Davies, tried to make this clear to Washington and the U.S. press at the time, but in the hysteria about communism that gripped the country then, they were ignored. Their careers were soon ruined by the advent of McCarthyism. The march to the Yalu had locked the United States into more or less permanent intervention in China's civil war and into an attitude of unrelenting suspicion and hostility. Not until the 1970s was it possible for then President Richard Nixon and National Security Adviser Henry Kissinger to take advantage of the differences between China and the Soviets to make their opening to China. Despite the modus vivendi that has governed U.S.-China relations since then, there remain deep wells of suspicion on both sides that periodically threaten a return to the old hostile relations. It didn't have to be that way.

The armistice that stopped the fighting cemented in power the dictatorship of Synghman Rhee, whom the United States had intervened in South Korea to back. Ironically, the regime was heavily staffed by former collaborators with the Japanese. Although it had saved the South Koreans from an oppressive communist future, the United States quickly demonstrated a preference, which it would display time and again during the Cold War, for reliable dictators to messy democracies. In 1960, Rhee was overthrown by Koreans attempting to establish a democracy, but the attempt failed when the United States supported a takeover by General Park Chung-hee. Then in 1979, the United States not only encouraged a coup d'état by General Chun Doo-hwan but actually gave Chun permission to use the 20th division of the Korean Army (formally under U.S. command) to put down a 1980 student uprising in Kwangju. Before it was over, hundreds of South Korean democracy advocates had been killed in what became known as the "Kwangju Massacre," an event that Koreans will always associate with the United States. Among other things, Chun arrested long-time democracy advocate Kim Dae-jung and sentenced him to death on charges of collaborating with North Korea. The Reagan administration persuaded Chun to commute the sentence. The United States did promote the economic development of South Korea both by welcoming thousands of Korean students and by opening its markets and technology to Korea. Eventually in the late 1980s Korean democracy advocates managed to achieve a change to democratic government and Kim Dae-jung ultimately returned from U.S. exile to become president. It was he who initiated the "Sunshine Policy" aimed at gradual warming of relations with North Korea and consummation of economic ties as a way of loosening the iron grip of Pyongyang's rulers.

Americans who feel the South Koreans are ungrateful for all we did for them should keep in mind the above events. They should also consider what began in 1994 when the Clinton administration headed off a North Korean threat to build nuclear weapons by concluding an "Agreed Framework." Under the deal, the United States was to replace North Korea's plutonium-producing reactors with two light-water reactors (which could not produce weapons-grade plutonium) that would give North Korea the same amount of electricity. The United States was also to provide a certain amount of fuel oil, pledge not to use nuclear weapons in Korea, and open trade and some form of diplomatic relations. In addition to closing its old reactors, North Korea pledged to remain party to the Non-Proliferation Treaty and to allow IAEA inspections. The United States had difficulties on all points. It delivered the oil, but not on schedule, and did not open diplomatic or economic relations, although it did provide enough food to keep North Koreans from starving. The promised light-water reactors fell far behind schedule. Aware of these problems and frightened that North Korea might collapse and inundate South Korea with starving refugees—or worse launch a desperation attack—Kim began providing economic assistance to the North. With the advent of the Bush administration in 2001, the U.S. policy changed from vacillating rapprochement to seeking the collapse of the Northern regime. It quickly became clear that the North Koreans had also reneged on the deal and were continuing their nuclear weapons development, that news justified the administration's position in some eyes. But military retaliation was out of the question because Seoul would likely be destroyed in any conflagration. The United States was forced to revert to a version of the Clinton-Kim policies, but with the added handicap that by now such a strong anti-American sentiment had developed in South Korea that its new president was elected on a platform to revise the SOFA.

In response, some Americans, believing that our troops in Korea are primarily there to defend the South against the North, called for a U.S. withdrawal. They should be aware of Secretary of Defense William Cohen's statement in April 1997 that the United States intends to keep its forces in Korea even if the two Koreas unite.[11] U.S. troops are in Korea as much for America's purposes as for protection of Korea. The Koreans know this even if most Americans don't.

U.S. INTERVENTION: FROM INDONESIA TO IRAQ

After the Korean War, there followed a long series of American interventions to change democratically elected regimes in favor of authoritarian governments more compliant with U.S. wishes. In 1953, the CIA played a key role in the ouster of Iranian Prime Minister Mohammed Mossadegh and the restoration of the Shah. In 1954, the government of Jacobo Arbenz, elected to replace thirty years of bloody right-wing dictators in Guatemala was overthrown with U.S. assistance after complaints by the Chiquita Banana Company that the new government was dangerously left wing. The result has been another fifty years of bloody right-wing dictators. In 1955, the United States encouraged the South Vietnamese ruler Ngo Dinh Diem to ignore the agreement that settled the French Indo-China war and that called for elections to unite North and South Vietnam. Since everyone knew that Diem would have lost to the North Vietnamese leader Ho Chi Minh, America favored no elections. The domino theory—that if South Vietnam went communist, all Southeast Asia would automatically follow—was then holy writ in Washington. Exactly why the theory would hold was never well explained, but it guided U.S. policy toward war with North Vietnam. In fact, we were so determined to "bear any burden and pay any price" that we manufactured a justification for going to war. We now know that the North Vietnamese "attack" on the destroyer *Maddox* that served as the pretext for a congressional resolution authorizing the use of force caused little damage and occurred only after the *Maddox* fired first. The rest is, of course, a sad history.

On September 11, 1973 (this is the 9-11 remembered in Chile), the U.S. helped spark the overthrow of the democratically elected socialist government of Salvador Allende and put in place a military dictatorship under General Augusto Pinochet. Thousands of persons simply disappeared under the regime, in circumstances that the world later learned were shockingly barbaric. Zaire, Indonesia, the Dominican Republic, Lebanon, Greece, the Philippines, Taiwan, Thailand, and Afghanistan round out the list of countries where the United States either installed dictators or lent them vital support. This is not the place to review all of these in detail, but four countries in particular have come back to haunt us: Indonesia, Iran, Afghanistan, and Iraq.

Indonesia

Indonesia, the world's fourth-largest country and largest Muslim country, is much in the news today as a result of the War on Terror and the terror

attacks in Bali. It was also in the news in the late 1950s and early 1960s as
a result of U.S. fear that it might go communist and that it needed protection against China. Given that Chinese Indonesians are a small, dis-
criminated-against minority and that China at that time could barely feed
itself, it seems amazing that anyone feared the Chinese in Indonesia. But
the American government did because Sukarno, the leader who had gained
independence in a bitter war with the Dutch, saw capitalism as a system in
which the Dutch owned everything and the Indonesians nothing in their
own country and adopted socialism, along with nonalignment in the
Manichaen U.S.-Soviet contest. This development created quivers of fear
along the Potomac, and in 1958 the CIA trained Indonesian dissidents
and mercenaries at bases in the Philippines and infiltrated them into Indonesia where they briefly established a rebel government in conjunction
with some dissident local army commanders.[12] This gambit eventually
failed; Sukarno strengthened his position and made himself President for
Life. He also nationalized some U.S. property, took Indonesia out of the
UN, and didn't seem upset when mobs attacked the U.S. AID mission.

Then, in September 1965, a still murky incident changed the whole
game. A squad drawn from the Indonesian Air Force and suspected of
communist ties raided the homes of the army's high command, killed six
generals, seized the radio station and announced they were saving the
country from a CIA takeover. Somehow, General Suharto, commander of
the Army's strategic reserve, survived and led a counterattack that crushed
the takeover attempt. The U.S. ambassador at the time, Marshall Green,
noted that "the Indonesian Army had many people in it who were our
friends."[13] These included Suharto, whom embassy personnel supplied
with lists of names that helped the army's retribution to be thorough.[14]
The ensuing blood bath resulted in 200,000–500,000 deaths. In quick
succession U.S. property was returned, the Bank of America was invited
in, and the United States urged the IMF to make a $200 million line of
credit available to Indonesia.[15] For the next thirty-two years Suharto destroyed every potential opponent as he maintained strict military rule leav-
ened with nepotism. As generations of Indonesian army officers learned
how to keep dissidents under control at American military schools,
Suharto's wife, sons, and daughters became fabulously rich acquiring huge
industries and swathes of prime real estate. The Dutch had left Indonesia
with no institutions, and Suharto introduced none except the army. The

United States trained Indonesia's soldiers but did little to promote concepts like rule of law and democracy. In 1975, during a visit to Indonesia, President Gerald Ford and Kissinger let Suharto know that an invasion of East Timor, recently granted independence by Portugal, would not be opposed by the United States. Unsurprisingly, Suharto's troops moved the following week. The only institution in which it was possible to voice dissent at this time was the mosque. Islam, increasingly funded by Arab oil dollars and increasingly fundamentalist, began to spread.

In 1997, Indonesia was hit by the same financial crisis that devastated Thailand. The crisis was bad, but the prescription of the U.S.-led IMF was worse. As a condition for essential emergency loans, the IMF demanded that Indonesia halt food subsidies and raise interest rates in an attempt to keep the currency from devaluing. It also directed the closing of many banks. The remedies were completely at odds with the needs of the Indonesian economy and everyone immediately dumped their rupiahs, sending the currency plummeting despite the sky-high interest rates. More than 20 percent of the population fell into poverty almost overnight. Meanwhile, Washington was becoming uneasy with Suharto, especially because his army continued to terrorize East Timor. Eventullly, Australian and New Zealand troops were called in by the UN to quell the situation created by the Indonesian army. With the acquiescence of Washington demonstrators and leaders of his own party, Suharto was pushed out of office in May 1998, and engineered a shift to a civilian administration that eventually held elections and began creating a democracy.

Bad experiences with the Indonesian army had led the United States to end its training and liaison programs in 1998. But as the new democracy developed, it became apparent that Islamic parties would be powerful and that the Indonesian government was having trouble establishing order. In the wake of September 11, some U.S. officials began to push for resumption of the old training and support relationships with the military. About this time, I was traveling in Indonesia and had dinner one night with the U.S. ambassador and a group of about thirty Indonesian political, academic, and media leaders. I was particularly impressed by their pleas to the U.S. ambassador that military ties not be reestablished. "What we need," they emphasized, "is training for mayors, police officers, judges, and teachers, not soldiers." They also asked that the United States take the trouble to understand their needs. Several months later, however, some military ties had been renewed, and when I met with a high-ranking Indonesian official in Washington, he noted in despair that the United States was looking at Indonesia only through the prism of terrorism. "They want us to stop money-laundering," he said. "But how can we do that when we can't even collect taxes?"

A few months later, a terrorist bombing of a nightclub in Bali killed several hundred tourists, making clear that Indonesia needed to address terrorism along with its other needs. Yet Indonesians hesitated to act because many of them believed the bombing had been organized by the CIA as a way of persuading President Megawati Sukarnoputri to crack down on Islamic activisits. Said a member of Parliament from Megawati's own party, "The police will only be able to determine the actors in the field and will not be able to reveal the mastermind behind the attack. But I think the CIA was involved in this case."[16] This view was echoed by other important leaders who said the attack was probably organized by a foreign intelligence agency for the purpose of creating a "certain image of Indonesia." It sounded crazy to Americans, but in view of the Indonesians' previous experience with the CIA and American manipulation, who could blame them?

Iran

Mohammed Mossadegh headed an Iranian political movement known as the National Front in 1951. An ardent nationalist, he had played a major role in driving the Soviets out of Northern Iran after World War II. Now, as head of a parliamentary committee on the oil industry, he proposed that Anglo-Iranian Oil Company pay Iran a royalty of 50 percent of its profits. This was identical to the arrangements between the major oil companies and Saudi Arabia and Venezuela, but more than the company had been paying. Anglo-Iranian, half owned by the British government and with exclusive marketing arrangements with Exxon and Mobil, refused. They had a monopoly on Middle Eastern supplies and were not about to let the Iranians change the deal. Mossadegh then persuaded Parliament to nationalize the company, a move that was wildly popular with the Iranian people. But the big oil companies boycotted Iran, refusing to buy or market Iranian oil pending some kind of settlement. For two years

Mossadegh tried without success to sell his oil. The Iranian economy sank, and the U.S. government, even while pursuing a case against the oil monopoly domestically, put more pressure on Iran by cutting off aid. Unable to sell its oil and with its finances floundering, Iran had begun to turn to the Soviets for help. Given its history, the United States might have been expected to line up with the Iranian nationalists against the British imperialists, but the fear of communist influence in Iran trumped everything else. The CIA arranged a coup and a mob uprising in Tehran and reinstalled Shah Reza Pahlevi on the Peacock Throne. He immediately received an emergency grant of $45 million from Washington to help him get reestablished,[17] as well as another $850 million over the next six years along with CIA and Mossad assistance in organization and training of the dreaded SAVAK Iranian secret police service.[18]

The Shah repaid this kindness by playing a key role in organizing the first OPEC oil price hike at a meeting in Tehran in 1971, which laid the groundwork for the embargo and quadrupling of prices in 1973–1974. With oil now suddenly seen as a strategic commodity and with the British steadily reducing their presence in the Persian Gulf, Washington began to fret about maintaining the region's stability. Not wanting to deploy a large American contingent, it turned to its old and now oil-wealthy friend the Shah as a possible regional enforcer. The Shah loved the idea and ordered nearly $80 billion (in today's dollars) of U.S. military hardware.[19] It seemed like a great deal. The Shah became America's agent in the Gulf, and the U.S. got the weapons sales. In addition, said the CIA, "A continuing and growing supply of oil from Iran appears as certain as anything can be in an uncertain world."[20]

Even as it wrote those comforting words, the CIA should have been aware (but characteristically was not) that an explosion was building in Iran as its devout Muslim people came increasingly to resent the brutality of the Shah and the Americans who backed him. It came in 1979, when the Ayatollah Khomeini led a powerful uprising that toppled the Shah, threw out the Great Satan Americans, captured their embassy and its staff, and established an Islamic Republic in the name of Allah.

Now the United States had to worry about Iranian Islamic radicalism and its anti-American influence in the newly unstable Persian Gulf as well as, increasingly, the Israeli-Palestinian imbroglio. When Iraqi dictator Saddam Hussein launched an invasion across the Shatt Al-Arab waterway into Iran's oil fields in September 1980, the United States welcomed the attack as something like a godsend, as I shall shortly discuss.

Afghanistan

The story of America and Afghanistan began on the night of December 27, 1979, when Soviet tanks, artillery, and trucks carrying some 100,000 troops rumbled into Afghanistan to prop up a faltering communist puppet regime. In the wake of the fall of the Shah and the rise of the Ayatollahs, this invasion was interpreted in Washington not as a disastrous march into quicksand but as a threat to vital U.S. interests. The Soviets had taken a step toward the Persian Gulf and the 30-mile-wide Straits of Hormuz, whose shipping lane is so narrow that a single sunken supertanker would plug the channel through which passes 60 percent of the oil used by the United States, Europe, and Japan. In a nationally televised speech, President Jimmy Carter called the Soviet invasion the gravest crisis since World War II. It is not clear why he said that, since if the Soviets really wanted to stop shipping through the straits they could easily have sent a submarine to sink a tanker. But never mind that, it was time for tense situation room conferences and high-level international consultations.

There was no way the United States was going to engage Soviet troops directly—the potential for escalation made it far too dangerous. Luckily, the problem had an easier solution. Afghanistan, with its wild mountains and wild people, had been the cemetery of armies from the time of Alexander the Great to that of Queen Victoria. The Afghans, who had never been conquered by foreigners, no more welcomed the Soviet troops than they had the others. They began fighting back guerilla style using everything from hoes to nineteenth-century British Enfield rifles. The spirit was more than willing but the arms were weak.

That was a problem Washington could easily fix. It could also help on the spirit side. Motivating the Afghans, in addition to their fierce rejection of foreigners, was their Islamic faith, which the godless communists of the Soviet Union not only denied but denigrated. Washington mounted an effort in conjunction with Pakistan to build up the Islamic Mujahedin resistance to the Soviets. Beginning with small arms shipments in January 1980, the United States eventually spent $5 billion on getting weapons, including shoulder-fired anti-aircraft missiles and anti-tank guns, to the Afghans.[21] It printed thousands of textbooks and training manuals with pictures of militant Islamic students attacking Soviet targets, and set up training bases in Pakistan for Islamic fighters from Saudi Arabia and elsewhere who flocked to defend the faith by fighting with the Afghans. Among these was Osama bin Laden. The Saudi government also answered Washington's call for financial help and saw to it that the Mujahedin fighters were not lacking for funds.

Afghanistan became a huge, bleeding wound for the Soviets. After ten years they had had enough and withdrew in February 1989 as a prelude to the collapse of the Soviet Union itself. Champagne corks were popped at the White House and at CIA headquarters in Langley, Virginia. Even if the war had been unnecessary, it was a great tactical success.

But the celebration was premature. Victory led to the establishment, with Pakistani and at least tacit U.S. backing, of the medievally repressive Taliban regime in Afghanistan. It also gave confidence to the Arab Islamic fighters who attributed to divine intervention their victory over one of the world's two superpowers. With God on their side, there was nothing they couldn't do, including taking down the other superpower.

Two years later, in the wake of the Gulf war of 1991 (about which more later), there were thirty thousand U.S. soldiers in Saudi Arabia, many of them stationed at the huge Prince Sultan base south of Riyadh, the Saudi capital. Their seemingly permanent presence on what many Muslims consider sacred soil aroused acute anger among the Islamic fighters. Although he was the scion of a wealthy Saudi family, Osama bin Laden saw Saudi royalty and its government as corrupt obstacles to the cleansing of Islam and the restoration of the culture's ancient glories. The United States was the Saudi government's prop and its shield as symbolized by the heretical presence of American troops in the country of Mohammad's birth. He determined that this second Great Satan of a superpower had to go also, and that with God on his side, it would. Al Qaeda was born and would etch itself into the pages of history on September 11.

Iraq

Even in 1980, Saddam was known as a not very savory character. The State Department had included Iraq on a 1979 list of states that sponsor

terrorism, and in late summer 1980, 5,000 Iraqi Kurds were detained
and never seen again—killed, the *Independent* of London reported, in gas
and chemical weapons experiments.[22] This event was consistent with
U.S. Defense Intelligence Agency documents that had been reporting
Iraqi acquisition of chemical weapons since the mid–1970s.[23] But not to
worry: it was only Kurds and fanatical Islamic Iranians who were being
killed, and besides, the war would surely end quickly because most of the
Iranian weapons, acquired from the United States during the time of the
Shah, were crippled for lack of spare parts. But the Iranians fought back
with human wave attacks and by 1982 had not only pushed the Iraqis
out of Iran but were pushing into Iraq. Frightened that the Army of God
was now threatening to topple Saddam and take the Iraqi oil fields, President Reagan ordered his Department of Defense and CIA to supply Iraq
with military intelligence, including U.S. spy satellite photos, and with
sufficient weapons to ensure that it would not lose the war. To clear the
way for U.S. military aid, Iraq was removed from the list of states spon-
soring terrorism, even as the State Department was reporting unabated
Iraqi support of terrorist groups.[24] By November 1983, Secretary of State
George Shultz knew that Iraqi troops were using chemical weapons almost daily.[25]

Nevertheless, on December 19, special U.S. envoy Donald Rumsfeld
was dispatched to Baghdad to inform Saddam of the administration's intention to resume diplomatic relations with Iraq. Rumsfeld also relayed a
message from Israeli Prime Minister Yitzhak Shamir offering assistance in
the war against Iran.[26] Over the next several years, the United States re-
opened its embassy in Baghdad, sent CIA and U.S. military officers to as-
sist Iraq in various aspects of its war effort, and in May 1986 even
shipped two batches of anthrax bacillus along with two batches of botu-
lism bacteria to the Iraqi Ministry of Higher Education.[27] At about the
same time, U.S. intelligence learned of Iraqi efforts to develop ballistic
missiles. This did not deter further U.S. computer exports to the Iraqi research center engaged in the missile development.

Skipping ahead to 1988, we find that in January and February of that
year the U.S. Commerce Department licensed the export of equipment
to Iraq for its SCUD missile program, while in March, U.S.-supplied Bell
helicopters were used to spray deadly chemicals on the Iraqi Kurds of the
village of Halabja, causing about five thousand deaths.[28] In response to

increasing reports of Iraqi use of chemical weapons during the summer, Secretary Shultz said there was no conclusive evidence, and Assistant Secretary of State Richard Murphy wrote that "the U.S.-Iraqi relationship is . . . important to our long-term political and economic objectives. We believe that economic sanctions will be useless or counterproductive to influence the Iraqis."[29] In September, the U.S. Senate unanimously passed the Prevention of Genocide Act of 1988 making Iraq ineligible to receive U.S. loans, military or nonmilitary assistance. It also made importation of Iraqi oil illegal, but the Reagan administration launched a major effort to kill the bill in the House of Representatives and succeeded.[30] In March 1989, CIA Director William Webster told Congress that Iraq was the largest producer of chemical weapons in the world,[31] but this did not prevent the continued issuance of licenses for export of dual-use equipment to Iraq. As late as July 1990, the first Bush administration okayed nearly $5 million in sales of advanced technology equipment to Iraqi research centers known to be involved in development of chemical and nuclear weapons.[32] It was apparently also in July that Saddam decided on war with Kuwait. Before moving, however, he first tried to determine how the U.S. would react. On July 25, he met with U.S. Ambassador April Glaspie who assured him that President Bush "wanted better and deeper relations, and that we have no opinion on the Arab-Arab conflict like your border disagreement with Kuwait."[33] This was followed on August 1 by approval of the sale of nearly $700,000 worth of U.S. advanced data transmission devices to Iraq.[34] On August 2, Iraqi troops stormed across the border into Kuwait.

Imagine Saddam's surprise when the United States reacted to his aggression by likening him to Hitler and organizing, under UN auspices, a global coalition and military operation known as Desert Storm to stop it. But then imagine what he must have thought when the coalition forces halted their destruction of his armies on February 27, 1991, at the order of President Bush. Even more, imagine Saddam's thinking when the United States and coalition forces did nothing to stop him from using his U.S.-supplied helicopters as gunships to snuff out the uprisings the coalition had incited among northern Kurds and southern Shiites. The reason for this cowardly betrayal was apparently the coalition's fear that collapse of Saddam's regime might strengthen Iran's influence in the region. So Saddam survived because the coalition still wanted him as a shield against the Ayatollahs. Also surviving was the huge Prince Sultan airbase and surveillance establishment, with the thousands of U.S. troops that the Bush administration had put in Saudi Arabia as the first major foreign base ever in that country. It was this presence that outraged Osama bin Laden and came back to haunt us on September 11 and afterward. After conclusion of the Gulf war, UN resolution 687 directed Saddam to destroy his chemical and biological weapons as well as his equipment for developing nuclear weapons, and to permit outside verification that he had done so. A system of UN inspections was established along with no-fly zones in the north and south of the country, in a belated effort to protect the Kurds and Shiites. The inspections were never completely successful in finding and destroying all the weapons; and in response to Iraqi noncooperation, the UN imposed economic sanctions that resulted in the impoverishment of much of the Iraqi population but not in the destruction of further weapons. The inspections were also compromised by insertion of U.S. intelligence agents as well as by gradually increasing Iraqi obstructions, which the U.S. spying only served to rationalize. From time to time, the United States made unilateral cruise missile strikes at suspected Iraqi weaposn sites, but by 1998 the inspectors had been completely removed. They stayed away from Iraq for four years.

The events of September 11 caused concern that containment might no longer work if there were an alliance between Saddam and terrorist groups under which Iraq would transfer weapons of mass destruction to Al Qaeda. The new Bush administration, which contained many holdovers from the old Bush administration, thus quickly turned the spotlight on Saddam and the necessity for regime change as the destruction of the Taliban regime was coming to conclusion in Afghanistan. Saddam, they argued, had to go because he had, among other things, used chemical weapons on the Iranians and even gassed his own people. It seemed so obvious that such a bad actor should be gotten rid of that President Bush's top security officials even told him there was no need to get congressional support for an action to do so. The same Donald Rumsfeld who had solicitously asked Saddam in 1983 if there was anything more the United States could do for him, now as Secretary of Defense urged an immediate, unilateral U.S. attack to remove this thorn from our side as quickly as possible. He claimed as the basis for attack alleged Iraqi violation of the UN's inspection resolutions and of the agreement ending the 1991 hostilities. So great was the threat, the administration argued, that it required a preemptive war. In response to a global outcry against such a move as well as to substantial domestic opposition, the administration asked for and got resolution 1441 with the unanimous vote of the Security Counci as noted in Chapter 1. This resolution called on Saddam to provide complete data on the extent and whereabouts of his weapons of mass destruction and to make this information available for verification to a new contingent of UN inspectors.

The outcry reflected a number of concerns. In the United States, there was great popular reluctance to go to war alone and without the backing of the UN Abroad there was growing fear of unbridled American power. Many observers in both places felt that Iraq was less of a threat than the administration argued. It didn't have nuclear weapons or ballistic missiles, and evidence of ties to Al Qaeda was very thin. There was also concern that an invasion of Iraq would cause more problems than it solved, destablizing much of the region and perhaps the larger Islamic world, and requiring a long and costly occupation.

The Arab and Islamic countries in particular believed that the U.S. stance was another example of Western double standards and of putting the Iraqi cart before the horse of Israel and Palestine. Why was it unacceptable for Iraq to ignore UN resolutions but perfectly okay for Israel to do so? Before attacking Iraq, they said, you should make a real effort to resolve the Israeli-Palestinian issue so that an eventual, if necessary, attack on Iraq will not be seen in the Muslim world as an attack on Islam in favor of the Israeli occupiers of the West Bank and Gaza.[35] In the face of these kinds of concerns, the implementation of 1441 became terribly contentious. It was when the initial results indicated less than full Iraqi compliance that Powell made his plea to the Security Council for an ultimatum to Saddam. Instead, led by France and Germany, a number of countries developed plans for intensified inspections. But these were rejected by the U.S., and when attempt at compromise in the Security Council failed, U.S. determination for war, alone, and at odds with others around the world, became a certainty.

As a final note to this part of the tale, in Iran, where the United States has feared to tread for twenty years, the rule of the Ayatollahs is faltering in the face of demands for freedom from the Internet-loving, rock-singing youth of the Islamic Republic. Just as in Vietnam, the further away our troops and guns are the better they like us.

8

WAGGING THE DOG: TWO TALES

B ecause the subjects of this chapter are politically radioactive, I hesitated long before starting to write. But there is no getting around the
huge significance of Israel and Taiwan, both for American foreign policy
and for foreign perceptions of the United States. Despite their tiny populations—6.2 million and 22 million, respectively—I have often felt that
America's differences with the world could be largely explained in four
words: Israel, Taiwan, religion, and lobby.

ISRAEL

On no subject do the views of the United States and those of virtually all
other countries diverge more than on Israel and its interminable conflict
with the Palestinians, and there is no greater source of alienation between
ourselves and the others. This divergence became very clear in the spring
and summer of 2002, when in response to escalating Palestinian suicide
bombings, Israeli Prime Minister Ariel Sharon ordered his army to carry
out reprisals in Gaza and the West Bank. Its destructiveness evoked an international uproar. Despite the prime minister's defiance of repeated
presidential demands for an Israeli withdrawal, Bush said he continued to
support Sharon and called him a "man of peace." On June 24, the president gave a much-anticipated speech calling for eventual creation of a
Palestinian state next to Israel, but making such an event contingent on

a halt to terror attacks and on the Palestinians' holding elections to choose new leaders—the current leaders (i.e. Yasir Arafat) being "compromised by terror." Although the speech referred in passing to eventual Israeli withdrawal, it was clear the onus was on the Palestinians to change if they wanted U.S. help in promoting a peace process. Congressional leaders fell in behind the president, with Democratic Leader Richard Gephardt saying, "We will stand with Israel," and Republican Senator Mitch McConnell proposing legislation to formally designate the Palestinian Liberation Organization a terrorist group. Significantly, the president closed his speech with the Biblical passage, "I have set before you life and death, therefore choose life."

In using a scriptural reference, Bush reflected the thinking of most Americans whose perspectives on Israel and Palestine are strongly shaped by the Old Testament or Torah story of the land promised by God to the Jews. Americans, both Christian and Jewish, tend to see the Israelis as the heirs of that covenant, with an ancient historic right to at least the land of present-day Israel and perhaps to whatever else was included in the biblical map.

Americans also view Israel as a lot like America—an immigrant nation, a haven for the oppressed, a society of pioneering settlers, a strong and brave country willing to fight for the right, a democracy with a rule of law (the only one in the Middle East), and an oasis of Western consumer culture in an otherwise alien desert. And there are, of course, a lot of Americans in Israel. The ties are close enough that for many Americans, Israel is something like a fifty-first state. Palestinian terrorist attacks are widely reported in the U.S. media and are quickly equated, as in Bush's speech, with the Al Qaeda attacks on the World Trade Center and the Pentagon and interpreted as an existential threat. The U.S. media are so sensitive to Israeli criticism of their coverage that CNN, in a historic first, actually apologized in response to complaints that its reporting of Israeli-Palestinian battles in the town of Jenin was too favorable to the Palestinians.[1] Israeli attacks on Palestinians get less attention and are easily accepted as legitimate self-defense. Israel's war is seen as America's war.

The view from the other countries is quite different. While condemning them, few outside the United States see the Palestinian terror attacks on Israel as connected to Al Qaeda. The fear of some analysts in Europe is that continued Israeli pressure on Palestinian areas may generate precisely that highly undesirable fusion of terrors. Commenting on Israeli reprisals, the Lutheran Bishop of Jerusalem said, "It seems this is not a war against terrorism. This seems to be a war against the hope and future of the Palestinian people."[2] He went on to add that Israeli use of U.S. weapons and the closeness of U.S.-Israeli ties sometimes gives the impression of U.S. support for this war.

This is the prevalent view in much of the world. I was traveling in Asia at the time of the Israeli reprisals, and the scenes shown on Japanese, Singaporean, Malaysian, and Indonesian television made CNN look one-sidedly pro-Israel. Pictures of U.S.-supplied helicopters and other weapons being used against Palestinian civilians, and of Sharon defying Bush's demand for withdrawal of Israeli forces, made a deep anti-American impression everywhere, as did the characterization of Sharon as a "man of peace." It is widely known that Sharon is one of Israel's toughest hawks with a history of violence against Palestinians and of opposition to peace talks. Said the leading Malaysian writer Dato' Mohamed Jawhar bin Hassan, "How can Bush call a man like that a man of peace? Even pro-American Muslims like me are beginning to think badly of America because it ignores Israeli oppression."

The Economist noted that "U.S. newspapers don't print Israeli bulldozings of Palestinian homes, and the United States doesn't realize the extent to which it is held responsible as the armorer of Israel."[3] Everywhere I went, my interlocutors were quick to note double standards. "If America is so upset about weapons of mass destruction, why doesn't it object to Israel's nuclear arsenal?" "Why does America insist that some countries strictly observe UN resolutions while making no mention of Israel's defiance of UN resolutions?" "The United States insists on some countries being democracies, but Israel is not really a democracy."

Clearly there is a major disconnect. There are two possible explanations. One was voiced recently by Sharon, who called European criticism of Israel biased (implying that it was anti-Semitic)[4]—but maybe it's just a global bias against Israel. The other possibility is that Israel and the United States are isolated on this issue for good reasons. While no person is capable of perfect objectivity, let me, as someone with experience of living with many different peoples, at least try to provide a more balanced view than one often sees either on Fox News or in *Le Monde*.

Tel Aviv and Jerusalem

I arrived in Tel Aviv's Ben Gurion Airport on September 27, 2002. Even for Americans—and Israel is the one place where one finds not an ounce of anti-Americanism—there was tight security, including a double passport check. There had been another suicide bombing a few days before on a municipal bus in the heart of town that had killed five people and injured another fifty. On the way to the hotel my cab passed Allenby Street, close to where the bus had been blown to pieces. There was no sign of the blast, and the sidewalks were full of people shopping and sipping cappuccinos as if nothing had happened. But everyone knew something had occurred, and that it had done so just a day after another suicide attack had killed a policeman in northern Israel. These had been the first attacks after a six-week lull following the Israeli reoccupation of the West Bank and Gaza and Bush's speech in June. Just to be sure everyone understood that neither the president's speech nor Sharon's military tactics had changed anything, Islamic Jihad and Hamas, two extremist Palestinian organizations, had claimed responsibility for the new attacks and promised more. Looking at the fashionable street and its harmless activity, I had to wonder what kind of people would actually advertise that they had carried out a mass murder of victims happily engaged in looking for a bargain. Arafat and his Palestinian Authority (PA) had hastened to say they had had nothing to do with it, but few in Israel or the United States believed him.

To the casual observer conditioned by scenes of horror broadcast on CNN, the first impression of Israeli life is one of surprising tranquility. Certainly, every office building and hotel has a security force who give you a hard look as you enter, metal detectors and special passes are ubiquitous, and the government offices look like fortresses. But to anyone who does a fair amount of international travel, the security measures are, if anything, surprisingly unobtrusive. Tel Aviv looks like a Mediterranean version of Santa Monica and goes about its business in the same informal, sun-dappled way. The streets are clogged, and the restaurants and omnipresent Starbucks are sufficiently full to make one puzzle over the newspaper reports of 10-percent unemployment and government deportations of illegal foreign workers. Neither Tel Aviv nor Jerusalem seem like war zones in a country living on handouts.

But you don't have to dig very deep to find signs of an anxious, troubled life. My morning *Jerusalem Post* has poll results showing that 60 percent of Israelis believe they are in a war for their very existence.[5] The background noise is a constant flow of reports of violence. A typical news day here contains stories about a 95-year-old Arab woman shot while riding in a taxi on the West Bank, another suicide bombing in Jerusalem, demolition of Palestinian homes in retaliation for earlier attacks on Israelis, and an Israeli Arab's successful prevention of a West Bank Arab's attempt to bomb a bus. This creates constant anxiety. My lunch companion is visibly uneasy. We eat quickly and leave the restaurant, whereupon he tells me there was a diner at a nearby table who made him nervous.

Despite the hustle and bustle, the economy is a disaster. In Jerusalem, I checked in at the Marriott, a large hotel with more than seven hundred rooms overlooking part of the Old City. The Israeli Travel Minister had been gunned down here a few months earlier. I discover I am one of perhaps ten guests. The restaurant is closed except for a continental breakfast. Later, a stroll on the Mount of Olives provides a spectacular panorama of the city and its landmarks, Al Aqsa, the Western Wall, the Old City, and much more. It is one of the great views of the world. Tourism accounts for slightly more than 3 percent of Israel's GDP, and this is what the tourists come to see. But I am alone except for some forlorn Israeli Arab boys who swarm around trying to sell me a souvenir. I resist until I hear one stage-whisper to another, "He's an American. He won't buy because they hate us." I relent and buy a map and a book. It's clear that I'm all they'll be eating on tonight, and they don't care if I leave the stuff behind in my hotel.

But my little stimulus package won't do it for the Israeli economy. Forecast to shrink by nearly 3 percent this year, it is also experiencing 8-percent inflation.[6] Despite a government debt second only to that of Japan and declining credit ratings, the Israeli government is asking for U.S. guarantees for further loans as well as for $4 billion in new military aid—about $645 for every Israeli. Maintaining a military establishment and occupation of the West Bank and Gaza keeps a large proportion of the population tied up manning checkpoints, rooting out terrorists, and protecting settlers. The burden is enormous and unsustainable without aid from the United States. As James Bennet of the *New York Times* told me, "the Israeli economy doesn't add up, but all the contradictions are masked by fighting." And supported by private and official donations from the United States. This is the embattled, besieged Israel that largely shapes the American perception.

Jewish Settlers and Israeli Arabs

Yet while a majority of Israelis say they are fighting for their very existence, many have different existences in mind. One powerful force is the Israeli settlers. In the Six-Day War in 1967, Israel's preemptive attack on threatening Arab armies in Egypt, Syria, and Jordan resulted in its occupation of the West Bank of the Jordan River, East Jerusalem, the Gaza Strip, and the Sinai desert. The Israelis swapped the Sinai for peace with Egypt in 1979 but held onto the rest, pending peace agreements with the other parties, which have yet to materialize. In truth, they did much more than hold onto the territories. They annexed East Jerusalem, with its historic holy sites, in 1967 and moved their capital to Jerusalem from Tel Aviv. They also began to plant new Israeli settlements in the West Bank, Gaza, and around Jerusalem with two objectives in mind: to establish a security belt against future attack; and to fulfill the Biblical designation of Palestine as the land God had promised to the Jews. From their beginning, these settlements have been the source of great conflict and controversy. Most experts consider them illegal under articles of the Fourth Geneva Convention stipulating that an occupying power cannot annex occupied territory or move part of its population into the occupied area. They are also arguably at odds with UN Resolutions 242 and 338, which call for Israeli "withdrawal from occupied territories" in the context of an eventual peace agreement. They are certainly in defiance of the demands of every U.S. president from Jimmy Carter to the current President Bush, and their doubling during the past few years has certainly been in violation of the spirit if not the letter of the Oslo peace process commitments of 1993.

More importantly, the settlements mean taking land from Palestinians, building checkpoints and special access roads, and doing a hundred other things that cause friction between Israelis and Palestinians. The first settlements were few, small, and mostly strategic. But under Prime Minister Menachem Begin and Agriculture Minister Ariel Sharon in 1977, the Likud Party sponsored a major effort to expand the settlements. Begin was a firm believer in what he called "Eretz Israel" or "Greater Israel," meaning all the territory of Mandatory Palestine. The Israeli government began to provide financial incentives to settlers, offering them housing and other amenities they could never afford in Israel proper. As a result, the settler population has grown from a few thousand in the late 1970s to nearly 400,000 today,[7] and the full territorial reach of the settlements, including military zones and special access roads, is estimated at about 42 percent of the West Bank.

The settlers and their supporters include two groups of people. One is religiously inspired. Many of this group come from the United States and are backed by fundamentalist Christians as well as Jewish organizations. Their view was well expressed by one who told Molly Moore of the *Washington Post* that "until all the land of Israel belongs to the people of Israel as promised in the Bible there can be no peace."[8] The other, more materially oriented group, is represented by the settler who told Ms. Moore "the question is not if the settlements are legal or illegal. The issue is whether one leaves these hills to Arabs or whether Jews will live on them. That is the issue. The question of legality is secondary." In either case, the settlers are a powerful force, and the existence for which they are fighting is the incorporation of the West Bank and perhaps Gaza into Israel proper.

The majority of Israelis are not fighting for the settlers' existence. Poll after poll has shown that a majority are willing to pull out of most of the settlements and turn them over to the Palestinians in exchange for a true, lasting peace. Most Israelis would be satisfied to live within slightly modified borders of 1967 Israel, and a wall to fence Israel off from the West Bank along that line is already under construction. But many don't believe the Palestinians are interested only in getting the Israelis out of the West Bank and Gaza. They think the Palestinians won't be satisfied until Israel has been destroyed.

This belief has waxed and waned. After the beginning of the Oslo peace process, launched in September 1993 with a historic handshake between Israeli Prime Minister Yitzhak Rabin and Palestinian leader Yasir Arafat on the White House lawn, there was a wave of euphoria and hope that gradually diminished as roadblocks, literal and figurative, kept cropping up. In the summer and fall of 2000, meetings at Camp David and then at Taba in Egypt seemed agonizingly close to achieving a settlement, and hope swelled again. It was the collapse of this effort that plunged Israelis into their present mood of grim determination. The strongly held view in Israel is that Prime Minister Ehud Barak offered Arafat a deal he couldn't refuse at Camp David, bettered it at Bolling Air Force Base in December 2000, and then added cherries on top at Taba in January 2001. According to both Barak and President Clinton, if Arafat could have just taken "yes" for an answer he would have had withdrawal of nearly all the settlements, an independent Palestinian state with East Jerusalem as its capital, 97 percent of the land area of the West Bank, sovereignty over Haram al-Sharif (the Temple Mount), and a right of return to a Palestinian state of the refugees from the 1948 war that established Israel. Instead, goes the argument, Arafat did refuse and unleashed the suicide bombings of the second Intifada. This refusal lies behind the reluctant conclusion that the Palestinians' true goal is the ultimate destruction of Israel. The editor and writer Yossi Klein Halevi told me: "This was the last straw for me. You know I have been all over the map in the last twenty years. At first I thought there was no hope of peace, then I began to accept some of the Palestinian points and to believe in their sincerity, but this does it. We have no choice but to fight back." A sign in Haifa made the same point: "Now we are all Settlers." Much of the middle of the Israeli political spectrum feels the Palestinians have left Israel no choice but to cast its lot with the settlers.

Some, however, have begun to ask a question to which we shall return. Could it be that the continuing expansion of the settlements creates on the Palestinian side a similar distrust and despair that feed the attacks the Israelis believe have left them with only an existential choice? Could it be, as some Israeli analysts suggest, that the Eretz Israel hawks actually foment strife in order to radicalize the Palestinians in order to unite Israel behind the existential fight? Is it, as an Israeli peacenik asked that "they want all the land, but without the Palestinians?"

This debate engages two other critical aspects of the existential question. One concerns the preservation of "the Jewish state." This point is not well understood in the United States. In Israel one hears the term "the Jewish state" so often that it almost sounds like an echo of the Islamic identification of many Arab states. The whole point of the Zionist movement that led to the founding of Israel, was, after all, to create a country where Jews would not be persecuted because it would be theirs and under their control. Today, that control is increasingly at odds with local demographics, both inside Israel proper and in the occupied territories. The citizens of Israel include about 5 million Jews and 1.2 million Arabs, but the Arabs are reproducing much faster than the Jews. In the past this Jewish shortfall was more than made up by immigration, but that has fallen off in the face of the continuing conflict as well as rising living standards in places like Russia. Thus, more and more Israelis are likely to be Arabs.

This prospect poses excruciating questions. If the Israeli Arabs are to be fully integrated into Israeli society, they will inevitably dilute and challenge the concept of the Jewish state. If they are not to be fully integrated, the inevitable implication is for a kind of apartheid rule that is inimical to the fundamental values of Judaism and the state of Israel. Yet, ominously, one increasingly hears talk in Israel of "transfer," meaning transfer of Israeli Arabs out of Israel. It sounds uncomfortably like ethnic cleansing. The settlements only make this issue more complex. In the occupied territories there are another 3.5 million Palestinians, who are also reproducing much faster than the Jewish Israelis. By 2010, it is estimated, more Israeli Arabs and Palestinians will be living in the old mandatory Palestine than Jews.[9] If the settlements are to remain and expand, what will be the status of the Palestinians, now a majority, in Greater Israel? As one Israeli professor said to me, "If Arafat were smart he would reject the Palestinian state idea and say the Palestinians want to be Israelis on a one person one vote basis."

It was precisely that prospect that led Prime Minister Rabin to resurrect Yasir Arafat from exile in Tunis in 1993 and initiate the Oslo Peace Process, with Arafat as his main interlocutor. He saw that a Jewish, democratic state could be viable only as a small Israel within some modification of the 1967 borders. He needed a Palestinian entity and someone with whom to make peace, and Arafat, with all his warts, was the only possible choice.

That leads to the final question. Even in a small Israel, the status of the Israeli Arabs and whether Israel is a Jewish state or a secular one are searing questions. Lev Grinberg says that "by any standard Israel is not a democracy." That is a huge overstatement. For its Jewish citizens, Israel is one of the most raucous and vibrant democracies around. In fact, as we will see later, some Israelis believe one problem in reaching a settlement with the Palestinians is "too much democracy." But it is also true that Israeli Arabs are distinctly second-class citizens. Raheek is an impressive young Israeli Arab woman from Jaffa who speaks Arabic, Hebrew, French, and English fluently and who works for a group protecting the rights of Israeli Arabs. She points out that schools, public services, and road repairs are substantially underfunded in Arab neighborhoods compared with Jewish areas, that there are severe restrictions on the buying of land and starting of businesses by Arabs, that school text books reflect only the Israeli view of history, and that Arabs are not subject to the military draft and not encouraged to join the Israeli army. Although the reasons for this later situation are obvious and understandable, in Israeli society service in the army is a sine qua non for advancement. This second-class citizenship has gone so far that in the Israeli parliamentary elections of early 2003, two Israeli Arab Knesset members were initially barred from running for reelection by the Central Election Committee. The Supreme Court later overturned this ruling, but it demonstrates dramatically what Nissim Calderon calls the contradiction between the notion of a Jewish state and a democracy.

The West Bank

But the complications don't really begin until you get to the West Bank. I began to appreciate this when I got a call one day at about 3 P.M. telling me, "Chairman Arafat can see you, but you must be at the Ramallah checkpoint at 5 P.M." Since Ramallah is essentially a suburb of Jerusalem, under normal circumstances it shouldn't take more than a half hour to get there.

But nothing about the West Bank is normal. This area has essentially been under Israeli occupation for thirty-five years. The need to protect increasing numbers of settlers has resulted in a crazy system of 400 kilometers of special roads bypassing Palestinian population centers so that settlers and Israeli military traffic can pass quickly and safely. At the same time, many of these roads are cut off or have long detours, and the ubiquitous military checkpoints require frequent stops. As a result of all this, I just made it in time to meet my guides, the Mayor of Bethlehem, his brother, and the Palestinian Ambassador Designate to the United States. We moved slowly to the checkpoint in a long line of trucks, bicycles, donkeys, and people on foot. The Israeli soldiers were kids, maybe 18 to 25 years old. They were polite and thorough, but it wasn't hard to feel the humiliation of my companions, mature, experienced officials, at being questioned by children about what they were doing in their own back yard.

Once through the checkpoint, I discovered what tank trucks do to city streets—grind them up and spit them out. Our car jumped and lurched over ruts and holes to Arafat's partially bulldozed headquarters, the Muqata. A few days earlier, Sharon, in a fit of rage, had dispatched his tanks and bulldozers for another go at squeezing Arafat even tighter. As we approached, we passed the tanks ringing the now dilapidated building, and then parked and entered through barbed wire and past sandbags.

Arafat is a small man, and at seventy-seven and afflicted with Parkinson's disease, he shows his age. It is difficult to imagine him as the frightening scourge of the Israelis. But his mind is still sharp, and on that day it was focused on the latest American outrage, the bill just passed by Congress directing the president to move the American embassy in Israel from Tel Aviv to Jerusalem. This had been reported, with glee bordering on euphoria, in the Israeli press that morning. For the Palestinians, the relocation of the U.S. embassy would legitimate Israel's annexation of East Jerusalem and further reduce Palestinian hopes of retrieving lost ground. I explained that the whole thing was a political exercise. The bill had a loophole allowing the president to ignore the directive if he deemed that moving the embassy would harm U.S. national security, and he would surely deem precisely that. The vote was a way for Congress to satisfy its pro-Israel constituency without running the risk that the move would actually occur. Clever American politics, but try to explain that to a suspicious foreign audience.

Arafat was at pains to explain that he was not directing or instigating terror attacks on Israel. Noting that the Israeli army had more or less destroyed all the Palestinian Authority's police stations and public offices, including closing Palestinian universities and taking computer hard drives, he argued that he had little capability to direct anything. "Bush," he said, "calls for reform and elections, but how can we hold elections when we can't even make a telephone call?" He attributed the suicide bombing to the extremist Hamas and Islamic Jihad organizations that are competing with his Palestine Liberation Organization (PLO) for the support of Palestinians, and noted that the more Israel attacks him and undermines the Palestinian Authority, the stronger Hamas becomes. He also denied that he had rejected the Clinton and Taba peace plan ideas. Rather, he said, it was Barak who had backed away from the Taba talks after admitting he couldn't sell the ideas to the Israeli public. (In fact, he lost to Sharon in the next election.) One is instinctively skeptical of an old survivor like Arafat, but his comment that he would welcome a settlement imposed by the United States or the international community policed by U.S. and international forces, was arresting because it matched the comments of some Israelis who told me that the only hope is a U.S.-imposed settlement.

Saab Erekat is the Palestinian chief negotiator. A University of California graduate with a Ph.D. in economics, he lived for eight years in San Francisco and participated in all the negotiations at Camp David and Taba and in between. He is also the Mayor of Jericho, and I arranged to meet him there the following afternoon. My Israeli Arab cab driver got me to the Jericho checkpoint the next day but was not allowed to take me through. I had to leave the cab, walk through, and pick up another cab on the other side to get to Erekat's office.

I asked Erekat immediately why the suicide bombings and terrorist attacks couldn't be stopped, and noted that as one who knew America he surely recognized how devastating each of those attacks is to any American support for the Palestinian cause. His response was deeply troubling. Of course he knew, he said. "But, Clyde, listen to me. I am supposed to have some authority in Jericho, but I am being made more irrelevant every day. The real head of Jericho is Lieutenant Allon down at the checkpoint. It is he who decides who gets into the city and who gets out, whether an old woman gets to the hospital or not, whether fuel oil comes in or not. And just as he is undermining me, the guys over here"—pointing to the mosque—"are also making me irrelevant by telling the people that Erekat can do nothing for you and only God can help. Let me tell you something about terror attacks. Life on the West Bank is hell. Unemployment is near 80 percent in most areas. Half the people are living on $2 per day in hovels and have to wait at checkpoints so the Israeli settlers can have priority. The Israelis complain about suicide bombings, and I agree that they are immoral, but more Palestinians are being killed by Israelis than the reverse. Every time Sharon orders reprisals and assassinations, he creates more support for Hamas and Islamic jihad. Let me tell you, I have a teenage son. He is harassed at school and taunted because I, his father, am seen as a pro-American softie. I just pray every night that he doesn't become a suicide bomber, hoping in some crazy teenage way to save the family honor. How can we stop anything when Sharon has dismantled our entire infrastructure? Is Bush joking?"

As for Camp David, Erekat emphasized that he and Arafat had begged Clinton for more time to prepare before starting the talks, but to no avail. Clinton was in the last six months of his presidency, and Barak was hoping to use the talks to strengthen his weakening position in the upcoming Israeli elections. Erekat noted that it had been the Palestinians who made some of the imaginative proposals such as swapping land in Israel with the Palestinians in exchange for incorporating some of the major West Bank settlements into Israel proper. He also stressed that the Palestinians knew the Israelis could not accept a massive return of all refugees, and had therefore suggested optional return mechanisms that would allow the PLO to claim to its people that it had addressed this very emotional issue, yet avoid flooding Israel with new Palestinian arrivals. Finally, although he admitted that failure to reach closure on the Clinton proposals had caused difficulties, he also insisted that the two sides had been very close to agreement at Taba, only to fail because of Barak's imminent election defeat. He adamantly denied that Arafat had ordered the second intifada. After the breakdown of Camp David, he said, when it became known that Sharon planned a walk on the Temple Mount that was bound to antagonize Palestinians, Arafat had gone to Barak's home and begged him to stop the walk, saying he couldn't control the consequences. Moreover, Erekat noted that the first shootings, after the inevitable demonstrations generated by the Sharon walk, were of Palestinians by Israeli soldiers, and that in the first few months of the intifada nearly all of the dead were Palestinian youths.

To see the Palestinian picture fully, it is important to look at several points more closely. First, outside observers confirm and even strengthen Erekat's comments about the economic and social situation. The leading Israeli newspaper, *Ha'aretz*, has noted that more than a fourth of Palestinian students are no longer able to go to school,[10] while the UN and other international agencies report $4 billion in Palestinian losses of various kinds in an economy that had a GDP in 1999 of only $3.5 billion. Much of this loss appears to be due to the Israeli army's destruction of orchards or buildings that might provide cover for possible Palestinian attackers near settler roads.[11] The UN also reported declines in admissions at Palestinian hospitals and in performance of various medical procedures on the order of 30 to 70 percent, along with increasing signs of malnutrition in children.[12] This is almost entirely due to curfews and restrictions on movement within the West Bank and Gaza. In short, the Palestinian economic and social situation is even more of a disaster than that of Israel.

A second point is that while Israeli-Palestinian interactions in the occupied areas are bound to be irritating under the best of circumstances, they are worsened by the fact that settlers are subject only to Israeli courts, and the Israeli military has broad latitude to seize land for security purposes. The UN Human Rights Commission found that Palestinians have little hope of restitution from Israeli courts for damages from violence committed by the increasingly militant settlers. They have no hope at all when the damage is done by the military. The situation is often so bad that a movement has grown up within the Israeli military of soldiers who refuse to serve in the occupied areas. Says David Zonsheine, the leader of this group, "You stand at a checkpoint, and you know that Israeli settlers go right through and Arabs don't, and you remember South Africa."[13] Even more striking are the comments of former Israeli negotiator Uri Savir, who wrote of his surprise at discovering in the Oslo pre-negotiations that a Palestinian "couldn't build, work, study, purchase land, grow produce, start a business, take a walk at night, or visit his family in Gaza or Jordan without a permit from us."[14] The myth of an "enlightened occupation" had hidden all this from him.

The final point is the complex politics of the Palestinians. Because he has come to symbolize the Palestinian movement, and also because Sharon paints him that way, Arafat is seen by much of the world as a kind of dictator in full control of every Palestinian movement. The truth is otherwise. Arafat is the head of the PLO and the chairman of the Palestinian Authority, the executive body established under the Oslo process to administer the areas that were to be relinquished gradually by the Israelis. He also presides over the Palestinian Parliament, described by Nissim Calderon of Tel Aviv University as the most democratic in the Arab world. But he has at least three powerful challengers. The first is Hamas, a group that ironically was initially created with support from Israeli officials hoping to weaken Arafat. It has certainly done that but not as the Israelis perhaps hoped. Linked to international Muslim groups that run large charities and are amply funded, Hamas in Israel has two arms, a charitable one providing food, medicine, and other help to the poor, and a military one that specializes in suicide bombings. Islamic jihad is a less well-organized group, but with the same militant Islamic philosophy and the same terrorist modus operandi. Hezbollah is another militant Islamic group. Founded in Lebanon, it has ties to Iran and operates much like Hamas, with both military and charitable arms. All these groups are philosophically dedicated to the destruction of Israel and have no interest in peace or a Palestinian state on the West Bank and Gaza. In demanding all or nothing, they are the mirror image of the Israeli hawks who favor Eretz Israel.

Israelis and many Americans often say that Arafat wants it all too, and at one time he probably did, but most experts agree that in the Oslo process Arafat decided, however reluctantly, to accept the fact of Israel and to seek a separate Palestinian state. Thus for him and the Palestinian Authority, the fight with Israel is essentially over land, not existence. But Arafat's failure to get any land has given rise, as Palestinian pollster Khalid Shikaki notes, to an increasingly powerful young guard that is challenging the old PLO leadership. This generation is not necessarily dedicated to the erasure of Israel, but it increasingly believes the Israelis will not halt the occupation until the price becomes too great for them to bear.

In this dynamic, actions by Sharon and Bush that weaken Arafat and frustrate achievement of legitimate Palestinian objectives feed resentment that greatly strengthens Hamas and all the other challengers. That Sharon knows this, and continues to squeeze Arafat, has led all Palestinians and a lot of Israelis to believe that he prefers to make the fight truly existential, in order to unite Israel in a war that will push the Palestinians into Jordan and eventually realize the borders of Biblical Israel. Many in the region fear that a U.S.-led war on Iraq will give Sharon the cover to annex the West Bank while cleansing it of Palestinians.

Not Getting to Peace

The current conflict is rooted in the late nineteenth century, when Jewish leaders like Theodore Herzl, Leo Pinsker, and Moses Hess became convinced that the only way for Jews to escape pogroms and discrimination was to have their own nation in the ancient homeland of the Jews around Jerusalem. Beginning in 1878 they began arranging for European

Jews to emigrate into Palestine, then part of the Ottoman empire. These early Zionists seemed not to recognize an indigenous Arab presence and spoke naively of "a land without people for a people without a land."[15] Friction with Arabs arose quickly as it became clear that the newcomers did not intend to become part of the local life but aimed rather to create their own separate and very different society. Chaim Margalit Kalvarisky, who managed the Jewish Colonization Association, said he felt compassion for the Arabs and twenty-five years of dispossessing them was hard, but the Jewish public demanded it. The Jewish philosopher and writer Ahad Ha'am stated prophetically, "We have to treat the local population with love and respect. . . . And what do our brethren in the Land of Israel do? Exactly the opposite. . . . They behave toward the Arabs with hostility and cruelty. . . . Should the time come when the life of our people in Palestine imposes on the natives, they will not easily step aside."[16]

World War I resulted in a crucial new development for Palestine, as British Foreign Minister Lord Balfour, in an effort to marshal Jewish support for the allied cause in Europe and the United States, issued the "Balfour Declaration" saying Britain would support the "establishment in Palestine of a national home for the Jewish People." He added that "Zionism, good or bad, is of far profounder import than the desires and prejudices of the 700,000 Arabs who now inhabit that ancient land."[17] Unfortunately, that was not the opinion of Henry McMahon, Britain's High Commissioner in Egypt, who was trying to incite an Arab revolt against Germany's allies, the Ottoman Turks. In a letter to Arab leader Sharif Hussein, McMahon promised independence to the Arabs in the Ottoman-ruled provinces if they would rise up against the Turks. He also sent T. E. Lawrence (Lawrence of Arabia) to help organize the uprising.

These conflicting promises collided at the Versailles Peace Conference. Despite his devotion to national self-determination, President Wilson noted that "undeveloped peoples" would need "guidance" from administering powers under mandates from the League of Nations.[18] The British, having long ago forgotten Lawrence and the Arab revolt, pushed to get the mandate for Palestine. Wilson's King-Crane Commission was sent to investigate local sentiment and found strong opposition to the Zionist program among the area's Christian-Muslim majority as well as a desire for an American mandate. This idea was opposed by the Zionists, who surmised that America would insist on majority rule that would put Arabs in control. They thus preferred Britain and the Balfour Declaration. (This prompted Tom Segev to note that "the Zionist dream ran counter to the principles of democracy.") Wilson went along, and Britain wound up in charge of Palestine.

It was an unhappy tenure. As immigrants poured in from Europe, tensions with the Arab population led to frequent riots. Eventually, the British tried to restrict immigration, but this caused conflict with the Zionist groups. These problems got lost in the tumult of World War II, but with the end of the war millions of Holocaust survivors turned their steps toward Palestine. Now fearful of massive displacement, the Arabs resisted further Jewish immigration and the British again imposed restrictions. At that point the Irgun, the Jewish underground army that had been fighting Arabs, turned its guns and bombs on the British, who turned their mandate back to the UN and left in 1948. The UN (at that time a body of fifty-six mostly western and Latin American countries) came up with the original two-state solution by proposing to divide Palestine into Jewish and Arab entities with Jerusalem internationalized. The Arabs rejected this plan, declared war on the newly formed Israel, and lost, leaving Palestine and Jerusalem divided along an armistice line that now constitutes the internationally recognized Israeli border. About 750,000 Palestinian refugees from the area that was now Israel were left stranded in camps on the West Bank, in Gaza, and other countries like Jordan and Lebanon.[19] From then until now the conflict has waxed and waned more or less continuously, and from this history has grown the Arab sense of injustice, the longing for "return," the Israeli sense of besiegement, and the continued muddling of the international community.

Nothing fundamental changed until 1967, when the Six-Day War left Israel in charge of the West Bank and Gaza and gave rise to the Israeli Settler movement, setting the stage for decades of struggle, terrorist attacks, war in Lebanon, UN resolutions calling for peace negotiations and Israeli withdrawal from occupied territories, and various peace talks. The first intifada of 1987–1989 and the Gulf War of 1990–1991 actually began to create movement. An uprising of Palestinian young people throwing stones against the now twenty-year-old Israeli occupation, the intifada gained sympathy in the international community and also among Israelis, many of whom were questioning the morality of the occupation and the settlements. The Gulf War highlighted the urgency of settling the long conflict. The first President Bush called for a peace conference in Madrid and also for a halt to settlement construction, which U.S. aid inevitably was underwriting. Israeli Prime Minister Yitzhak Shamir was a "big Israel" man and steadfastly refused to freeze settlements, whereupon Bush suspended certain aid flows to Israel. The Madrid conference produced little, but it did get Israelis and Palestinians talking directly to each other for the first time, and the cutoff of aid played a role in Shamir's election defeat by Yitzhak Rabin, who continued the talks secretly until they resulted in an agreement between the two sides at Oslo in August 1993.

The Oslo arrangement committed the Israelis to gradual withdrawal of their army from some occupied areas and to transfer some authority for things like education, health, and police to the Palestinians. It committed the Palestinians to recognition of Israel's right to exist and to renunciation by the PLO of all acts of violence. The gradual transfer of limited authority was to lead to a permanent settlement based on Security Council Resolutions 242 and 338. The initial Israeli withdrawals were to be from Gaza and the Jericho area. As long as Rabin was in charge, things moved as agreed, if slowly. But after his assassination by an Israeli fanatic in late 1995, the process began to unwind. The heart of the difficulties was two hidden assumptions in the deal. Although the Israelis had made no written commitment, it was expected that expansion of settlements would be halted since their continued growth was clearly against the spirit if not the letter of the deal. By the same token, while the PLO had undertaken to renounce its own violence, the Israelis expected it would also stop that of Hamas and other groups. In the event, the settlements more than doubled over the years of the Oslo process and although violence diminished dramatically—to the extent that the Israelis became the high rollers at the Jericho Casino—it did not disappear.

The reason was that this deal was the last thing Hamas and the other radicals wanted, and terror was the best tool of sabotage. Terror also served the Big Israel hawks, who could use it to refuse withdrawals and to justify their own violence. While many in Israel and the United States saw Israel as giving up land for uncertain Palestinian promises, many international observers saw the Palestinians as making the major concessions. According to this view, they gave up any claim to the bulk of the old Mandatory Palestine, got no commitments on removal of the hated settlements, and received no guarantees for the future except the right to negotiate an uncertain "final settlement." As one Israeli commentator noted, "Arafat must have been desperate to take such a chance." In any case, by late 1999 all the timetables had been pushed back, violence was rising on both sides, and it was clear the process was in deep trouble.

The Lobby

A central fact of the Israeli-Palestinian story is the continuous increase in the amount of land under Israeli control. Since 1967 this has largely come from unceasing expansion of settlements. While Palestinian terror attacks would probably not completely stop even if the Israelis dismantled all the settlements, surely the Palestinian perception that the Israelis mean to take all the land contributes to the violence. Over dinner recently, a former U.S. National Security Adviser not only agreed with that perception but told me how frustrating it had been to be unable to bring about a freeze on settlement expansion. Why, I asked, can't the president of the most powerful country in the world get a freeze commitment from a much smaller country that is totally dependent on U.S. money and protection? "Clyde," he said, "that's the first time you've asked me a question to which there's an obvious answer: New York and Florida." What he meant was the importance of the American Jewish vote in those two states and more broadly the powerful Israeli lobby. I told him I would add the powerful influence of the Christian Coalition and other fundamentalist Christian groups as well, and he quickly agreed.

A major factor in the collapse of the peace efforts has been these lobbies' ability to prevent U.S. pressure on Israel. The American Israel Public Affairs Committee (AIPAC) is one of the strongest of the pro-Israel groups, and it has claimed that any legislation important to Israel starts with a dependable base of two hundred supporters in the House of Representatives and up to forty-five senators.[20] In a speech to the Christian Coalition in October 2002, evangelist Pat Robertson added the weight of the evangelical community, saying, "We will stand with Israel," and adding that a "Palestinian state would be anathema."[21] Former congressman Paul Findley has written that the lobby assures that "open discussion of the Arab-Israeli conflict is non-existent,"[22] and former National Security Council official William Quandt says 70 to 80 percent of all members of Congress will go along with AIPAC.[23] As if to bear this out, FoxNews reported in

early May 2002 that pro-Israeli resolutions, including $200 million for Is-
raeli military activities, passed the House by 352–21 and the Senate by
94–2.[24] Prior to that, when Bush called for withdrawal of Israeli tanks
from the West Bank in April, the White House received more than
100,000 angry e-mails from Christian conservatives.[25] As an Israeli political analyst told me, "the space for debate on Israel is less in the United
States than in Israel." He could have added that the level of the debate that
does take place is sometimes laughable. House Majority Leader Richard
Armey said on *Hardball* in May 2002 that he was for a Palestinian state,
as long as it didn't mean giving up Israeli-controlled territory.[26]

The Blame Game

In March 2000, with the Oslo process on its deathbed and his own reelection prospects sinking, Israeli Prime Minister Ehud Barak called President Clinton with a bold new proposal—leapfrog the tedious Oslo
arrangements and call a summit at Camp David for all-or-nothing talks
on a final settlement. Despite the lack of time for preparation, the limited time left in both his own and possibly Barak's tenure in office, and
the risk that failure would intensify the conflict, Clinton saw a historic
opportunity for an agreement and perhaps a legacy for himself, and bit.
The ultimate failure of this gamble produced the suicide bombings, the
election of the hawkish Big Israel proponent Sharon as Israeli Prime Minister, and brutal Israeli reprisals. More importantly, the inevitable attribu-
tion of blame has led to broad acceptance among Israeli and American
leaders of an orthodox view that the Palestinians rejected generous Israeli
offers because they truly hate Israel and prefer to seek its violent destruction rather than peace.

This argument is actually best stated by Barak himself. Over a breakfast with me, Barak insisted he had offered Arafat the deal of a lifetime: a
demilitarized Palestinian state on 92 percent of the West Bank and 100
percent of the Gaza Strip with some territorial compensation for the
Palestinians from pre–1967 Israel; the dismantling of most of the settlements and relocation of settlers to an 8-percent portion of the West Bank
to be annexed by Israel; creation of a Palestinian capital in East
Jerusalem; custody (not sovereignty) of the Temple Mount; a return of
refugees to the Palestinian state (but not to Israel proper), and a massive

international aid program. But that the obdurate old Palestinian leader had said no. Barak insists Arafat was just "performing" and seeking maximum Israeli concessions without "negotiating in good faith." He profoundly distrusts not only Arafat but Arabs in general, saying that in their culture there is no such thing as "truth" and they therefore have no qualms about lying. As for why Arafat would turn down such an apparently good deal, Barak says it's because the Palestinians don't believe Israel has a right to exist and that they seek a Palestinian state in all of Palestine. He believes Arafat sees demographics as his main weapon, and says the Palestinians will take advantage of Israeli democracy to turn Israel into "a state for all its citizens" and then push for a bi-national state until demographics gives them a majority and thereby an end to the "Jewish state." He also says Arafat planned all along to milk the talks for as much as he could get and then to unleash violence as a way of putting more pressure for concessions on the Israelis.

While he doesn't say it exactly the same way, Clinton's top Camp David negotiator, Dennis Ross, agrees that Arafat earned most of the blame for the failure by turning down the offer and then unleashing violence. He describes Arafat as a "surfer" who missed the Big Wave because he was more interested in continuing to surf than in riding into shore, perhaps because the shore of a limited Palestinian state is not the one he is seeking. Clinton, too, has pointed the finger at Arafat, saying that for the first time in history a U.S. president proposed a deal close to long-standing Palestinian demands and Arafat refused even to consider it as the basis for negotiations.[27]

More important even than what these key people say is that the current President Bush believes them. Hence Bush's patience with Sharon's defiance, hence his oxymoronic call for free Palestinian elections of a new leader who cannot be Arafat, hence his equation of Palestinian violence with global terror and his demand that all violence cease before peace negotiations proceed, and hence his refusal to meet with Arafat or even to shake his hand at the UN. If the orthodoxy is true, even if Bush's actions and attitude tend toward the inflammatory, there is little alternative. But what if it's not true?

Having spoken with most of the key negotiators on all sides, my impression is similar to that of the Japanese movie *Rashomon*, in which several participants in a single event each relate what seem to be several completely different events. Arafat and his chief negotiator deny rejecting a deal and point the finger at Barak, who insists they did reject it. More interesting is the analysis of Robert Malley, who was part of the U.S. negotiating team and who subsequently has written "revisionist" accounts of the negotiations that tend to square with my own research and interview findings.

To begin, Malley confirms Arafat's concerns about lack of preparation time and the risks of failure. On June 15, 2000, he told Clinton of his fear that everything could "explode in the president's face," and said that "the summit is our last card. Do you really want to burn it?"[28] The answer was yes, and Arafat went along in order not to incur U.S. anger but without great expectations. The background of Barak's urgency and Arafat's caution is critical to understanding what actually seems to have happened. The Israeli Prime Minister was deeply suspicious of the gradualist Oslo process. To him it meant military withdrawals, for which Israel paid a heavy price, without anything tangible in return and without any idea of eventual Palestinian demands. On top of this, increasing Palestinian unrest was creating pressure for faster movement and a dramatic peace deal offered a chance to rescue his declining position in pre-election polls. For all these reasons, he considered it better to avoid the salami machine and go for the whole sandwich. Because of his focus on the end game, he neglected a number of interim steps—most important, a third partial withdrawal of troops from the West Bank and transfer to Palestinian control of three villages near Jerusalem, to which Israel was formally committed by Oslo and subsequent agreements. At the same time, expansion of West Bank settlements accelerated. In Barak's mind, none of this need matter, because by definition a final settlement would resolve the problems.

Arafat, of course, saw things differently. He also found Oslo a painful process, but for different reasons than Barak. To the Palestinians, the promise of Oslo had turned into an endless series of unfulfilled and deferred commitments. "Six years after the agreement, there were more Israeli settlements, less freedom of movement, and worse economic conditions." Against this background, Barak's neglect of the required interim withdrawals and the continued rapid pace of settlement only confirmed Arafat's suspicions of the Israelis and of Barak himself. To reassure himself about the summit, Arafat asked Clinton for more preparation time and also for Israeli execution of the previously committed partial army withdrawals. Clinton, who shared some of Arafat's concerns, responded by getting a promise from Barak that the Israeli withdrawal would proceed with or without a final deal. The president also promised Arafat that he would not be blamed in the event of failure, saying "there will be no finger pointing." As it turned out, there was no additional preparatory time and no Israeli withdrawal, but Arafat went along because he had no choice.

The procedure at Camp David was very different from the public image of the Israelis and Palestinians facing each other across the bargaining table and hammering out proposals under American supervision. Barak and Arafat never had a substantive conversation and spent most of the time in separate rooms with the Americans shuttling back and forth conveying ideas and responses. I use the term "ideas" advisedly because there never were any formal written proposals from one side to the other. Notes were taken by the American messengers and read back to the two sides to assure understanding, but everything was conditional. The ideas were presented as U.S. rather than Israeli proposals and couched in terms of an Israeli willingness to use them as a basis of negotiation if Arafat would do the same.

In this procedure, the U.S. team was not pushing a plan of its own but acting as a very high-class facilitator without knowing either side's bottom line. To move the ball toward a goal, the U.S. moderators needed counterproposals to take back to the other side. Here the Palestinians' great weakness was revealed. Although, as Erekat told me in Jericho, they had been creative in devising the idea of land swaps in order to enable Israeli annexation of some major settlements, in suggesting ways to limit actual return of refugees to Israel as part of a recognition of the right of return, and in granting Israeli sovereignty over Jewish areas of East Jerusalem, the Palestinians ultimately proved unable to give the U.S. negotiators a coherent peace plan. It is not entirely clear why, although several factors played a role. One was the feeling they had been burned in the past by ambiguous, contingent agreements and that if this was the final ball game it had to be crystal clear and written down with nothing left to the imagination. Yet it wasn't clear that this was indeed the final ball game, because Barak never finally committed to a position. It was a catch-22. Barak didn't want to show his bottom line until Arafat demonstrated he was serious, and Arafat didn't feel he could afford to do anything until he could see the bottom line.

Another factor was the fractious domestic political situation of the Palestinians, which caused divisions in a negotiating team that was beginning to anticipate a successor to the aging Arafat. Finally, the Palestinians saw acceptance of the U.S. ideas, even as "bases for further negotiation," as fraught with subtle but important dangers. The ideas, while interesting in some respects, were silent regarding refugees and unbalanced regarding land exchange, and they left the Temple Mount and much of Arab Jerusalem under Israeli sovereignty. Accepting the proposed ideas, the Palestinians feared, might undermine the fundamental Palestinian position by shifting the debate from the Israelis' obligations under the various UN resolutions to the fuzzy U.S. ideas. Nevertheless, the agonizing question is why Arafat didn't come back with better suggestions. Several important Palestinian leaders have told me they think he missed a great opportunity.

At the same time, however, Barak faced no pressure from the United States to stop, let alone dismantle, the settlements the United States had been calling illegal for thirty-five years. Clinton and his team acted more like messengers than as powerful leaders with a vital stake in a just resolution and the means to achieve one. Thus, for a variety of reasons, the Camp David summit ended without conclusion.

But that was not the end of the discussion. Talks continued between the three sides throughout the fall of 2000, and on December 23, with less than a month left in his presidency, Clinton offered a new set of proposals that would give the Palestinians more land, a right of refugee return to a possible new Palestinian state (though not to Israel), and a stronger position in Jerusalem. Arafat remained cautious but told Clinton, when they met on January 2, 2001, that the president could tell Barak that "I accept your parameters and have some views I must express. At the same time, we know Israelis have views we must respect."

At this point, Barak appears to have developed reservations of his own, which he communicated privately to Clinton. Three weeks later Clinton was off the stage, but the Israelis and Palestinians continued direct talks at Taba. These ended not because either side rejected a deal but because the Israeli elections came before the talks could be concluded. Barak, who had campaigned for a mandate to continue the talks, authorized a joint statement with the Palestinians saying: "The two sides declare that they have never been closer to reaching an agreement and it is thus our shared belief that the remaining gaps could be bridged with the resumption of negotiations following Israeli elections."[29]

Ariel Sharon, the new Prime Minister, immediately declared Taba dead and announced his opposition to any further peace discussions. Barak had lost, in part, because since the end of September violence had escalated rapidly, undermining the credibility of his peace initiative. The second part of the orthodoxy of blaming Arafat is the charge that he had planned this violence and unleashed it in the wake of the failure to reach agreement at Camp David, in order to put more pressure for concessions on the Israelis. But a careful look at the circumstances again suggests a more complex picture.

In late September, it became known that Sharon was planning a walk on the Temple Mount/Haram al-Sharif. Arafat made his visit to Barak's home to plead with him to stop the walk, but Barak, according to Arafat, said he could do nothing. In subsequent statements, Barak has said that it was an internal Israeli political matter, that it was coordinated with Palestinian security officials, and that it had nothing to do with the outbreak of violence that ensued. This was not the view of knowledgeable observers at the time. Dennis Ross said of Sharon's walk, "I can think of a lot of bad ideas, but I can't think of a worse one." Given his anti-peace, anti-Palestinian reputation and the prevailing unrest, it was clear the event would be provocative, and it seemed calculatedly so at a moment when provocation might pay Sharon electoral dividends. On September 28, Sharon took his little stroll accompanied by one thousand Israeli police officers. The next day, demonstrations resulted in violence that was to explode over the next few months. According to the report submitted by former Senate Majority Leader George Mitchell, as head of a commission established to determine the cause of the violence, the conflict began when a large number of unarmed Palestinian demonstrators were confronted by a large Israeli police contingent. "The Palestinians threw stones in the vicinity of the Western Wall. Police used live ammunition to disperse the demonstrators, killing 4 persons and injuring 200." Fourteen Israeli police were also injured. Over the next three months the number of Palestinian deaths rose rapidly. According to the Mitchell report, "most incidents did not involve Palestinian use of firearms and explosives."[30]

By the end of the first week, more than sixty Palestinians had been killed along with five Israelis, and several international groups complained of excessive use of force by the Israeli army. Many Palestinians, as well as some Israelis with whom I spoke, believe that the army, increasingly dominated by right wingers and devoted to Sharon, purposely used excessive force in order to provoke an intifada that would justify ending peace talks and moving back massively into the occupied territories.

Regardless of the truth of that speculation, my point is not to whitewash the Palestinians or absolve them from blame for either the failure of Camp David or the violence that has devastated the region for the past two years. I believe, and a number of Palestinians agree, that Arafat made a huge mistake not to respond more positively and creatively at Camp David. But the failure and the violence were not solely due to Arafat and were certainly not a manifestation of an unremitting dedication to the destruction of Israel.

This brings us to the real problem: Although the orthodoxy is wrong, U.S. policy is based on it. As a result, our actions are accelerating the global alienation from America at just the moment when we need a few friends. Here is how a top official in the U.S. embassy in Tel Aviv explained the situation to me: "Israeli governments are always coalitions, a fact that gives extremist parties disproportional power and that effectively makes Israel a hostage of the settlers and the Big Israel crowd. They also want a Jewish state, and the desire for the land coupled with the desire for a Jewish state inevitably implies either some kind of ethnic cleansing or a South African-style apartheid. The only practical solution is an imposed settlement of some kind by the United States, perhaps in conjunction with NATO. But because the U.S. Israeli-Christian lobby is 2000 percent behind Israel and controls the U.S. Congress, that won't happen." I can only add that unless the lobbies and the Congress and the White House wake up, the prospect is for the United States to pour more billions of dollars into expansion of Israeli settlements. This policy will catalyze violence and lead to brutal reprisal that will bring more global disdain for the United States. And the peace all sides desperately want will only recede.

* * *

TAIWAN

Given that it involves the world's most populous and rapidly developing country and its richest and most powerful one, America's relationship with China is probably the most important bilateral relationship in the world. Ever since the "Opening to China" in 1972, U.S. China policy has been aimed at normalizing relations and weaning China away from central planning economics and communist politics. By any measure, this policy has had substantial success. China has become the location of choice for global manufacturers, and U.S. companies alone have invested almost $40 billion.[31] It has also become a member of the World Trade Organization with full U.S. backing and a significant investor in the United States. In addition to adopting capitalism, China has also dramatically opened its social and political system. While it is by no means a democracy, the rights and freedoms of everyday people have greatly increased.

On the face of it there should be few problems between the United States and China. Only one thing could negate this progress, and that is U.S. intervention in Taiwan-China relations.

For the Chinese, the status of Taiwan is a fundamental matter of national sovereignty and of throwing off the last vestiges of quasi-colonial rule. It is also a matter of finishing the Chinese civil war, which ended on the mainland in 1949. The Chinese see any foreign intervention regarding Taiwan as unacceptable interference in their internal affairs. While it's a bit of a stretch, an analogy may be helpful here. My daughter has a home on the island of Maui overlooking the Maui channel and the uninhabited island of Kahoolawe. In recent years a Hawaiian independence movement has arisen among some of the descendants of the original Polynesian inhabitants of the Islands. Imagine that the Hawaiian independentistas should occupy Kahoolawe and declare a new independent Monarchy of Hawaii. No doubt the U.S. Coast Guard or Navy would be sent to quell the uprising. Now suppose the Chinese were to dispatch their navy to patrol the Maui channel in order to protect the new Hawaiian state from harm. I know it's unlikely, but if it happened you can imagine the outrage that would grip every American.

It was precisely that outrage I met when I made a swing through China in the spring of 2002. No meeting could begin or end except on the issue of U.S. interference in Taiwan and why the United States wanted to risk war over a matter that was wholly the concern of the Chinese. Why indeed? Before we get to that, let's turn to what caused this uproar.

On April 24, 2001, the United States announced a massive sale of weaponry to Taiwan. The $4 billion package was to include four destroyers, a dozen antisubmarine airplanes, and up to eight submarines capable of launching not only torpedoes but cruise missiles. This was the first time a U.S. administration had sold unambiguously offensive weapons to Taiwan, and the sale was coupled with an unprecedented agreement to expand U.S. training of Taiwan forces in using advanced weapons systems. The announcement came only hours after China's ambassador to the United States had told a luncheon audience that "China-U.S. relations are at a crossroads; continued U.S. sales of advanced weapons to Taiwan threatens China's national security, violates its sovereignty, and emboldens the separatist forces on that Chinese island."[32] The sale was seen as a big victory for Taiwan (especially for the Taiwanese pushing independence) and its U.S. lobbyists (including Senator Trent Lott, Republican of Mississippi, where the ships would be built, and a couple of major U.S. think tanks that get large grants from Taiwan), who had been frustrated by Clinton's deferral of their proposals while he pursued engagement with China.

Even more surprising were the president's comments the following day: Bush said the United States would do "whatever it took to help Taiwan defend herself" even if that required the full force of American military power.[33] Although China called this an "open provocation," it was followed in succeeding months by unprecedented visits of top Taiwanese military officials to meet "unofficially" with top U.S. defense authorities and by expansion of U.S training of and coordination with Taiwan's military forces.

The problem with all this, and the reason it infuriated Beijing, was that it was a complete violation of the spirit and probably the letter of the Joint Communiqué of August 17, 1982, one of the three key documents that govern U.S.-China relations. In that document, the United States reiterated "that it has no intention of infringing on Chinese sovereignty and territorial integrity, or interfering in China's internal affairs, or pursuing a policy of 'two Chinas' or 'one China, one Taiwan.'" The United States also said that "it does not seek to carry out a long-term policy of arms sales to Taiwan, that its arms sales to Taiwan will not exceed, either in qualitative or in quantitative terms, the level of those supplied in recent years since the establishment of diplomatic relations between the United States and China, and that it intends gradually to reduce its sale of arms to Taiwan, leading, over a period of time, to a final resolution."

This was not the first time the United States had appeared to breach this agreement. In the heat of the 1992 presidential election campaign, the first President Bush had announced the sale of 150 F–16 fighters to Taiwan (planes far superior to anything in the mainland Chinese inventory) in an apparent effort to solidify his political base in Texas, where the planes are made, and also to curry favor with anti-China right-wing Republicans often known as the China or, more recently, the Taiwan lobby. To understand what's going on here you need to know a bit of history.

In the late nineteenth and early twentieth centuries, China was the destination of choice for American Protestant missionaries. "Saving" China was the missionary equivalent of the commercial goal of providing the oil to light the lamps of China. I can remember from my boyhood the occasional visits of the missionaries in China being supported by my own church. Among the missionaries were the parents of Henry B. Luce, the founder and editor of *Time* magazine, whom Theodore White described as the most powerful opinion-maker in America. White also noted that "in Luce's mind, the purpose of Christ, and the purpose of America joined in a most simple, uncomplicated fashion, and the purpose of both embraced the Chinese people."[34] Among the Chinese it embraced were Generalissimo and Madame Chiang Kai-shek, who were named "Man and Wife of the Year" by *Time* in 1937. Chiang, the leader of the Kuomintang or Nationalist Party of China, had managed to gain loose dominance over China's warlords and was moving to unite the country, with some success except for the stubborn resistance of his erstwhile allies, the Chinese Communists under Mao Zedong. Madame, or Mei Ling, was the daughter of T. V. Soong, one of China's richest men, who had made his fortune from publishing Bibles. Madame, a graduate of Wellesley College and a Methodist, had persuaded Chiang to convert to Christianity. It was these two who led China as the World War II threatened, and to whom Luce and the missionaries rallied. Said the *Missionary Review of the World*, "China has now the most enlightened, patriotic, and able rulers in her history."[35]

That was not the view that evolved in the mind of General Joseph Stilwell after he dealt with Chiang and Madame as Commanding General of U.S. Forces in the China-Burma-India theater and as chief of staff to Chiang. A fluent Chinese speaker, Stilwell was known as "Vinegar Joe" for his blunt opinions. After years of frustration with Chiang, who seemed more interested in husbanding his resources for an eventual showdown with Mao's communists than in fighting the Japanese, Stilwell pithily described the problem: "The trouble in China is simple: We are allied to an ignorant, illiterate, superstitious, peasant son of a bitch."[36] While Stilwell found the communists disciplined, tough, and eager to fight the Japanese, he found Chiang's soldiers unfed and unpaid because the generals stole the money, and deployed more against the communists than against the Japanese. While Stilwell fought valiantly to reform Chiang's graft-ridden dictatorship and for a degree of control that would allow him to field a real Chinese army in harness with the communists against the Japanese, Madame used her charm, contacts, and Luce's doting press to have Stilwell removed. White's conclusion says it best: "I was beginning to believe the Chinese government was totally incapable of governing. He [Chiang] was not only useless to us but useless to his own people, which was more important. If Stilwell had had his way, the Communists might not have won China or if they had, would have won as our allies or at least not regarded us as enemies."

But Stilwell didn't have his way. After the Japanese surrender, the civil war between Chiang's Nationalists and Mao's Communists broke out with renewed fury. Despite billions of dollars of U.S. aid and tons of U.S.-supplied equipment and weapons, it was no contest. The communists marched through Chiang's forces like a hot knife through butter, capturing and turning on the Nationalists all the U.S.-supplied weapons. It was as if the Americans were supplying the Communists with the Nationalists acting as deliverymen. White described the decaying system and regime to which America was bound as combining "the worst features of Tammany Hall and the Spanish Inquisition."[37] But Luce wouldn't print the bad news because "it destroyed his philosophy of the world."

Luce wasn't the only one who couldn't face the truth. While White was sending copy that *Time* wouldn't print, a group of China specialists in the U.S. Foreign Service, including John Service, were sending to Washington similar messages that officials wouldn't read. In the end, White quit *Time*, the communists took mainland China, Chiang fled with China's gold bullion to the island of Taiwan where he and Madame remained Luce's darlings, and John Service was fired as Senator Joe McCarthy and the conservative right wing blamed him and other China experts for "losing China."

Once on Taiwan, Chiang ordered the execution of several thousand opponents and established a Nationalist dictatorship that imposed martial law for nearly forty years. He maintained that his government remained the legitimate government of all of China and that he would return to recapture the mainland. Most countries quickly recognized that, like it or not, Mao's communist regime controlled all of China except Taiwan, and established formal diplomatic relations with Beijing. Not, however, the United States. It maintained the fiction of the Chiang regime on Taiwan as the legitimate government of China for twenty-three years, until Nixon finally began to bring the country back to reality with his opening to China in 1972.

What lay behind this exercise in fantasy was the China lobby in conjunction with the Korean War. Immediately after Chiang's flight to Taiwan in 1949, Secretary of State Dean Acheson declared that Formosa (i.e. Taiwan) was outside the U.S. defense perimeter. Had it remained so, the communists would undoubtedly have ended the civil war by taking the island fairly quickly. But with the outbreak of the Korean War, the U.S. Seventh Fleet was sent to patrol the Straits of Taiwan; and for the next generation, *Time*, religious organizations, and political leaders like Senator Walter George, John Foster Dulles, and Dean Rusk convinced the American public that Chiang's corrupt dictatorship on Taiwan was a champion of freedom and democracy.

The trick for Nixon in achieving a rapprochement with Beijing was how to dump Chiang without making the United States look as if it were backing out on a generation of support. This was accomplished through "creative ambivalence" and rhetorical sleight of hand. In the Shanghai Communiqué issued at the end of the 1972 Nixon visit, the United States took advantage of the fact that Chiang still nursed the fiction that his was the legitimate government of China and would soon return to take control of the mainland. In the statement, China identified the Taiwan question as the crucial issue obstructing normalization of relations and emphasized its opposition to any status for Taiwan other than as an integral part of China. Since Chiang's view was the same, albeit for different reasons, the United States declared that it "acknowledges that all Chinese on either side of the Taiwan Strait maintain there is but one China and that Taiwan is a part of China." That was clever though disingenuous, but what followed actually put an obligation on the United States. The Communiqué affirmed "the ultimate objective of the withdrawal of all U.S. forces and military installations from Taiwan." Still, "ultimate" could mean a long time hence, especially since U.S. weapons sales and military relations with Taiwan continued unabated, as did the maintenance of America's ambassador to China in Taipei.

Not until 1979 and the issuance of the Second Joint Communiqué did the United States and China agree to establish normal relations. In doing so, the United States reaffirmed the one-China principle and agreed to sever formal relations with Taiwan, establish its embassy in Beijing, end its mutual defense treaty with Taiwan, and withdraw all U.S. forces from the Island. The issue of arms sales was left unresolved. This looked as if it might make Chiang's son Ching-kuo, now the head of the Nationalist regime, no more than the governor of a Chinese province. But Madame and her stepson still had fans in the U.S. press who portrayed them as champions in the struggle for freedom despite thirty years of press censorship and martial law in Taiwan.

They also had friends in Congress. The Carter Administration had drafted a bill to handle the myriad legal details of the shift of U.S. diplomatic recognition from Taipei to Beijing. This initially bland legal document was transformed into the Taiwan Relations Act of 1979 by a bipartisan group of pro-Taiwan congressmen led by our old friend Senator Jesse Helms along with Senator Ted Kennedy, Democrat of Massachusetts. At the heart of the act was a provision for sale to Taiwan of arms sufficient for self-defense (whatever that meant) and a commitment from the United States to resist any resort to force or coercion against Taiwan. The act also created a quasi-official embassy in Taipei, the American Institute in Taiwan, a private organization incorporated in Washington, D.C., and funded by the U.S. government with a board of trustees appointed by the secretary of state.

If you were Chinese, you would probably see this act as undermining the promises the United States had just made in the Second Communiqué. That, in fact, is just how the Chinese saw it. They demanded clarification, and that resulted in the Third Communique of August 1982. Of course, the Chinese were not without blemish in all this. They built up a missile force opposite Taiwan, demonstrated some missile shoots in 1996, and warned of war if Taiwan were to declare independence. They were frustrated because U.S. guarantees enabled the regime on Taiwan to resist serious discussions regarding any kind of Hong Kong-style reunification. Their actions were thus sometimes unpleasant and even frightening, but then they thought it was their country. An analogy like my Maui fantasy is one often cited by Chinese debaters: How would the United States have felt if China had sent forces to support the Confederacy during the American Civil War?

With luck, however, we won't have to answer that question. With the end of the Cold War, China's usefulness as a semi-ally of the United States against the Soviet Union disappeared. That, together with development at long last of a democratic regime on Taiwan, led to a movement among American conservatives to back a Declaration of Independence for Taiwan, something that despite much discussion has not gained majority support there. But as China's economy has developed rapidly over the past ten years, businessmen from Taiwan have flocked to move their factories to the mainland. At first, the Taiwan regime tried desperately to limit the investment and the flow of sophisticated technology, but it was like telling the tide not to go out. Businesses from Taiwan are now the biggest investors in China, and about half a million former residents of Taiwan are now living in Shanghai with more joining them every day. Bush may thus find himself "doing whatever it takes" to defend Taiwan just as the last resident of Taiwan turns out the lights and ships out to the mainland. In fact, as I write, the first commercial flight between Taiwan and mainland China since 1949 took place this week (January 26, 2003). So that last resident won't have to ship out, but can fly first class.

MORAL OF THE STORIES

In its policies toward Israel and Taiwan, America continues to do itself enormous damage and create intense, needless enmity toward itself by allowing its view of reality to be distorted by intensely self-interested groups and by willfully averting its eyes from contrary evidence. Our system of government, with its separation of powers, facilitates capture of key positions by dedicated minorities that are sometimes heavily influenced by foreign elements whose interests are directly at odds with those of the United States. A senator from a state with fewer than a million citizens can capture U.S. foreign policy if he or she holds the right chairmanship at the right time. Our great power enables us, as I have indicated, to avoid facing reality for long stretches of time and can result in our doing great damage not only to others but also to ourselves.

In this regard, our press has much to answer for. It took a long time before the press reported the actuality of Vietnam. It still does not fully report the actuality of Israel, Palestine, Taiwan, and many other critical regions because it is too often blinded by its own preconceived ideology or afraid to challenge the prejudices of its audience. Ultimately, however, the problem lies with that audience, which too often cares about countries selectively, temporarily, or as an expression of its own ethnic, religious, or political biases. Americans tend to think of other countries not as real places with real people but as vehicles for their ideas either of how the world should work or for the redress of their historical grievances. Don't even get me started on Cuba.

9

FRIENDS AND FOES

On November 9, 1989, like millions of others around the world, I watched CNN with joy and disbelief as Germans from East and West Berlin popped champagne corks from atop the Berlin Wall. Long a symbol of tyranny and division, it was now suddenly an emblem of the triumph of freedom and hope. The forty-year Cold War, the sinister backdrop of my generation's whole life, had ended not in Armageddon but in the laughter and singing of free people. It was a great moment, for me, for my generation, for the United States that had led the struggle, and for Western ideas and values.

Things got better. On March 2, 1991, Iraq accepted the terms of the U.S.-led coalition for an end to the Gulf War that seemingly ended for all time the Iraqi dictator Saddam Hussein's threat to his neighbors. In July 1991, the Warsaw Pact disbanded. And on Christmas Day, 1991, the immense and indestructible Soviet Union, Ronald Reagan's "Evil Empire," collapsed. The ideological struggles between fascism, communism, and democratic capitalism, which had defined the twentieth century, were ended, with democratic capitalism the sole survivor. Francis Fukuyama famously called it "The End of History" and it quickly seemed that he was right. Democracy sprouted in the once barren soil of Latin America, while China adopted something called a socialist market economy, its peculiar term for capitalism. Even the Israelis and Palestinians seemed to get in the mood as they launched what came to be called the Oslo peace process. To top it all, world economic growth took off, powered by the greatest boom in American history. The peculiarly American model of capitalism, unleashed at last, emerged as the norm toward which the world would inevitably converge.

The United States seemed to have no enemies. The president was welcome anywhere, be it London, Paris, Riyadh, Moscow, Beijing, Seoul, Jakarta, Cairo, Mexico City, or Buenos Aires. It was a moment of opportunity and hope much like 1946–1948, when America had also towered over the world and begun to lay the foundations for a new order of multilateral cooperation, only to have its work rudely interrupted by the outbreak of the Cold War. Indeed, this moment was even better. The institutions and concepts established in the earlier period had won, and now there was no possible contender to even threaten a new conflict.

There was another important difference as well. Whereas Acheson and the leaders of that earlier postwar era thought consciously about being "present at the creation" of a new world order and of playing a direct role in shaping it, the leaders of the 1990s thought they would achieve nirvana automatically. They just had to follow Ronald Reagan's advice and "stay the course." Fukuyama argued that liberal democracy represents a political end state because it "accords the individual the self-worth he has been seeking throughout history."[1] A world of like-minded liberal democracies would have little incentive for war because as everyone knew, democracies don't go to war with each other. They'd rather trade and get rich. A world of such democracies would constitute a stable, peaceful order. The top U.S. priority should thus be to promote the expansion of the realm of democracy, and the question of how to do this was answered with the single intoxicating word "globalization." This seductive tune was considered so catchy that countries would be willing to adopt quite demanding common rules (Tom Friedman's "golden straight-jacket"[2]) in order to get rich. Globalization would automatically make countries become more democratic; and in becoming both richer and more democratic, they would become more modern and thereby more dedicated to peace, stability, and the innocent pursuit of happiness. It was a beautiful dream, the best part being that it required no one to be "present" at any kind of "creation."

No sooner had U.S. leaders won the war than they began mismanaging the peace. They continued acting as if the Cold War and the twentieth century had not ended. While U.S. defense expenditures did fall, at least briefly, they actually rose in relative terms because those of the old Soviet Union and other countries melted away. The old alliance structures were maintained under the old conditions, with Korea, Japan, and to some extent Europe remaining American protectorates and client states. Overseas commitments and bases were even expanded, particularly in the Persian Gulf with the establishment of the large aforementioned air base in Saudi Arabia. At the same time, nonmilitary foreign operations continued to be neglected. The amount of unpaid American UN dues continued to mount, while U.S. aid and overseas diplomatic post budgets fell. The United States continued aggressively to negotiate international trade agreements like the North American Free Trade Agreement (NAFTA) and the Uruguay Round that created the World Trade Organization out of the old General Agreement on Tariffs and Trade. But no thought was given to the underlying infrastructures and conditions of the newly participating and newly opened markets. The Washington Consensus taught that free trade would automatically take care of all that.

Other important developments were also neglected. Having defeated the Soviet Union, the United States did little to help the successor states make the shift from communism and central planning to democracy and free markets, and little to secure loosely guarded stocks of dangerous materials. Lulled by the belief that the nuclear club could be kept limited, America and its allies were caught completely by surprise when India and Pakistan announced their new membership with loud bangs. While globalization spurred economic growth in some areas, its tendency to do so unequally and to generate greater gaps between rich and poor was conveniently overlooked. Also overlooked was the fact that globalization made those gaps more visible and forced peoples with very different beliefs and values into intimate contact in ways that threatened their identity. The end of the Cold War and the development of the EU and its new currency, the euro, had dramatically changed the dynamics of the U.S.-European relationship, but this development was not recognized either, any more than was the corrosive impact on Latin America of U.S. drug use and policies; or the implications of Islam's sense of lost respect; or the significance of Japan's broken politics, Korea's new democracy, and China's resurgence. The rapid spread of the AIDS epidemic, along with even more widespread epidemics of malaria and tuberculosis, was seen as a far away problem, as were the forecasts that by 2025 one-third of the world's population would lack clean drinking water, and that rising sea levels and flooding would cut wheat production in places like Egypt and Pakistan by

20 to 50 percent.[3] To mention such things was uncouth, and a distraction from the far more important news coming out of Wall Street.

The result was that while the twentieth century may have ended on Christmas Day, 1991, the twenty-first century didn't begin until September 11, 2001, when the attacks on the World Trade Towers and the Pentagon made it clear that history was still on track and that globalization was not necessarily a magic elixir. These attacks triggered far-reaching shifts of global relationships, with some old American friends looking more like antagonists and old opponents looking more like allies.

EUROPE

Nowhere are these shifts sharper than in Europe, where America has long had its most important international ties. Although the United States was born in revolt against Britain and much that was European, the ideas expressed in the Declaration of Independence and the Constitution of the United States were all derived from European thought. It was the NATO alliance, founded on common values of democracy, human rights, and resistance to oppression, that won the Cold War. The U.S.-European alliance shaped such key global economic institutions as the IMF, the World Bank, and the WTO; it was the interaction of the U.S. and European economies that initially drove globalization. U.S. investment in Europe amounts to $80 billion,[4] far more than its investment in Asia and Latin America combined, and the output of U.S. firms operating in Europe accounts for about a quarter of European GDP. Europe's investments in the United States are of similar magnitude. With GDPs of $10 trillion and $9 trillion, respectively, the United States and Europe together account for nearly 60 percent of the global economy. As the former WTO chief, now chairman of British Petroleum Peter Sutherland told me, "The success of our alliance is fundamental to the working of the global system."

Sutherland is precisely right, and it is just that fact that makes the increasingly troubled state of the alliance so worrisome. While the Pew Opinion Polls still show majorities in Europe expressing positive attitudes toward the United States, the percentages are smaller than in much of the rest of the world, and falling.[5] At the World Economic Forum in Davos in January 2003, at the spring 2002 Bilderberg meeting, and at the spring

2002 meeting of the Trans-Atlantic Policy Network, top business, government, media, and academic leaders from both sides of the Atlantic noted that the gap between the United States and Europe has never been wider. After asking for and getting NATO's equivalent of a declaration of war, U.S. rejection of allied help in Afghanistan after September 11, on grounds that the Europeans would only slow things down, not only wounded European pride but raised questions of the alliance's purpose. While the United States pressed for a quick military solution to the problem of Iraq's weapons of mass destruction, Europe insisted on UN resolutions and verifications of promised Iraqi weapons destruction. Indeed, German Chancellor Gerhard Schröder vowed that Germany would not support military action in Iraq under any circumstances. The new U.S. doctrine of preventive and preemptive war rang alarm bells in a Europe with far more intimate experience of war than we have had. When the United States rejected the Kyoto accord, the International Criminal Court, and other treaties, Europe moved ahead to assure their coming into force even without U.S. ratification. On top of this, trade disputes over emotional issues like genetically modified foods mushroomed.

Moreover, the tone in which these issues were debated became harsher than at any time in the past. Old European friends of America expressed betrayal along with disappointment. The former EU Commissioner Etienne Davignon told me that "America is blowing up NATO in favor of coalitions of the willing." And the *Financial Times* columnist Martin Wolf said that "The United States had such a fantastic asset in the world's identity of its interest with U.S. interests, but that is now all being thrown away. The United States today is frightening because it won't be constrained. The left has always thought of the United States as a rogue state, but now the center is thinking the same way."

For many Europeans, it seems the United States has turned its back on the values underpinning the global system and opted, in Wolf's words, for "might makes right." On the American side, Undersecretary of Defense Doug Feith has referred to U.S. NATO policy as "keeping the myth alive," while a White House official called the Europeans "fair weather friends."[6] In his much-discussed 2002 book *Of Paradise and Power,* Robert Kagan claims that "Europe is from Venus while the United States is from Mars," and argues that Europe's military weakness creates a tendency both to appease and to tie down America.[7] Europe is increasingly portrayed in America not only as appeasing but also as antidemocratic, antimarket, inward looking, free riding, and unwilling to spend money on defense while being envious and resentful of U.S. power and success.

Beneath these specific issues and frustrations lie deeper matters of values, motivations, and models. The French columnist Dominque Moisi commented in *Foreign Affairs* that "1970s anti-Americanism was a reaction to what America did, but today's anti-Americanism is in response to what America is."[8] U.S. commentators like *The National Review*'s John O'Sullivan have warned that the EU is drifting toward becoming a power hostile to the United States.[9] And Martin Wolf responds by saying that the EU, China, and India may have to align in order to balance the United States.

This is not just the spat of an old married couple. Large tectonic plates are in motion that could dramatically change, if not destroy, the global system Sutherland described. The "end of history" argument assumes that triumphant democratic capitalism is unitary, but in fact there are different strains. If history were to go forward as a contest between those strains, it would have to consist of a fight between the United States and Europe, because of all the world's powers only Europe has the size, resources, institutions, and technology to challenge the United States. Indeed, some observers, including Fukuyama, are already asking if the term "the West" still has meaning.[10] Given America's declared policy of preventing the rise of challengers, this line of thinking suddenly makes the joke about a U.S. invasion of The Hague, coined as a result of U.S. opposition to the International Criminal Court, much less funny. Of course, actual invasion is not going to happen, but some kind of U.S.-European Cold War is a distinct possibility.

Few Americans recognize the magnitude of Europe's economic achievement. Instead, we tend to be impatient with Europe because of its difficulty in reaching a unified position, its endless committees, and its preoccupation with the eighty thousand mind-numbing pages of the *acquis communitaire,* the complete rules and regulations of the EU. But as President Kennedy noted in a 1962 speech in support of the effort, the task of building a United Europe is far more daunting than that of building the United States. I got a personal taste of this truth while working in Brussels in the 1970s, as head of Scott Paper Company's European marketing operations. We had affiliate companies in most of the major European countries and were trying to standardize our operations so that they could be run on a Europe-wide, rather than a national, basis.

This effort frequently involved calling together the marketing managers from the various countries to discuss changes. The first difficulty was language. English was supposed to be the working language, but it didn't always work. Beyond that there were a thousand reasons why Europe-wide strategies couldn't be adopted. For example, we had a paper mill in the north of Italy and another in the north of Belgium. We wanted to supply the French market from these two mills, but it happened that paper towel rolls were a little wider in Belgium than in Italy, making for chaos when shipments arrived in French supermarkets. Or the label in Britain had to have different information than that in Holland. I could go on, but you get the picture. It was a long, tedious, often maddening process, and I was dealing with only one company and one fairly simple product line. I marveled at the energy, patience, and dedication of the European officials who were building the EU one standard at a time.

And look at what's been accomplished. The EU conquered rampant inflation, reduced runaway national budget deficits and set limits on new deficits, established a single European Central Bank, and now uses only one currency. Today, you can travel all over Europe and never change money or show your passport. It is often said that the United States has the world's biggest economy, followed by Japan. But that is an out-of-date way of looking at things. On December 13, 2002, the EU decided to add ten new member countries, effective June 2004, bringing its total population to 450 million people and its GDP to $9 trillion—double the size of Japan and just behind the U.S. $10 trillion GDP. Moreover, if the euro strengthens much more against the dollar, the EU could become number one.

The significance of this development cannot be overestimated. In global economics, where Europe is a full-fledged superpower, the United States cannot act unilaterally. Where the EU speaks with one voice through one top official—as it does on matters of trade, agriculture, technology standards, competition policy, and currency—it is fully the equal of the United States and can in no way be pushed around. If anything, it sets the standard. Jack Welch, the former CEO of General Electric and former business icon, learned that the hard way when, as his swan song before retiring, he tried to bring off a merger of GE with Honeywell. When it sailed through the U.S. Justice Department's antitrust review process, he and Wall Street figured it was a done deal and ordered champagne. Too soon, as it turned out. They had reckoned without Mario Monti, the EU's Competition Policy Commissioner, who killed the deal and wrecked Welch's retirement party. Thus, he proved that no merger of two U.S.-based companies, assuming they have operations in Europe, can be consummated without European approval. In doing so, he also asserted the validity of a competition doctrine that focused on the impact on competitors rather than on consumers, as is typical in the United States.

Even more than competition policy, however, currency is king. Before it occurred, the line on Wall Street, and particularly on the pages of the *Wall Street Journal*, was that the unification of European currencies would never happen. When it did happen, the new line was that it wouldn't work and even if it did, the euro would pose no challenge to the dollar. Whether it will work over the long term, only time will tell, but we are already seeing an impact on the dollar. In late February 2003, Russia moved some of its reserves from dollars into euros as the dollar continued its weakening trend. The euro is emerging as something the world hasn't seen for sixty years: a viable alternative reserve currency to the dollar. As it does so, the United States will find its freedom of action on interest rates, savings rates, and trade deficits increasingly constrained. It may find itself wrestling generally with Europe for control of the IMF, the World Bank, and the international monetary system. This competition could become particularly intense if the gap between America and Europe widens on broader global issues. Ultimately it could affect America's ability to project power.

The two economies are likely to see increasing conflict in other ways as well. Just as Rome and Byzantium eventually developed very different societies after the split of the Roman Empire, so the United States and Europe have evolved quite different socioeconomic models that, owing to globalization, increasingly rub against each other. At the heart of the difference are the roles and responsibilities of the individual and government. America, of course, emphasizes the individual and distrusts government. It believes in equality of opportunity but embraces a vast inequality of results. In its lead editorial of August 26, 2002, *Business Week* magazine urged adoption of policies that would widen the gap between rich and poor in the United States, and did so on the grounds that despite the wider gap, the absolute level of income of the poor would rise also.[11] This would not be a popular argument in Europe, where emphasis is on modulating inequality of result and government is thought to have a positive role to play in promoting the welfare of the community. In the growth-versus-welfare-state debate, the United States has always argued that its laissez-faire approach fosters start-ups, innovation, growth, and productivity while keeping unemployment low. U.S. commentators point to the low growth and high unemployment rates of Europe, while Europeans argue that their unemployed live better than many Americans with jobs. Europeans lament the high numbers of Americans who lack medical insurance and live below the poverty level.

During the 1990s, it looked as if this argument might be settled in the Americans' favor. Europeans began to try to deregulate and privatize while speaking the word "shareholder" and creating Nasdaq clones. But with the collapse of the technology bubble, the American model looks less attractive, and the argument is going the other way. As Renault's chief executive Louis Schweizer noted in a recent conversation, "It is hard to believe the American idea that the price of a share in some short time period is the best way to measure the value of a company or of a manager's performance." Moreover, despite America's generally dismissive view of "eurosclerosis," many European economies with high taxes and welfare payments, like Sweden and the Netherlands, are doing quite well; and overall, the EU's performance does not lag far behind that of the United States. For example, when proper adjustments are made for accounting practices, it turns out that the recent, much ballyhooed increases in U.S. productivity growth are actually behind those of Europe.[12] More importantly, in many respects the EU's economic fundamentals look better than those of America. EU savings rates are 6.35 percent compared to America's roughly 3 percent,[13] while EU trade is roughly in balance compared with the large structural U.S. trade deficit.[14] Thus to get whatever superior economic growth it may have, the United States has to borrow about $500 billion a year from Europe and elsewhere. As Martin Wolf points out, U.S. borrowing is now so high that it is becoming unsustainable. Moreover, many see Europe as more advanced in the processes and techniques of globalization as a result of its own experience in thoroughly integrating its national economies into the EU. As globalization proceeds, the EU will vigorously promote its model and that model will be attractive. Thus instead of U.S. accounting standards, for example, the world may adopt those of the EU, and instead of U.S. rules on Internet privacy, the world may adopt those of the EU. Globalization may quickly cease to be America's game.

Europeans are justly proud of these accomplishments and of the values that produced them. It has long been a mantra of U.S.-European dialogue that we share the same values. But while we are heirs of the same broad cultural background and advocates of democracy, there are actually big differences in values. One of the biggest is religion. While half of all Americans attend a place of worship on any given weekend, in Europe the number is closer to 15 percent. Europeans generally find the American debates over abortion and evolution versus creationism hard to comprehend. Even harder to comprehend, and more irritating, are the frequent calls by U.S. political leaders for God to bless America, as if this nation were more deserving of God's favor than other nations. It is highly unlikely that Tony Blair or Jacques Chirac would ever in a public speech ask God to bless Britain or France.

Europeans are concerned that this religiosity imbues American foreign policy with a crusading, manichean element that can lead to unnecessary and unnecessarily violent conflict. Not believing so much in good versus evil, Europeans tend to look for the social and economic causes of problems. Just as Europeans do not share America's religious commitment, neither do they share its super-patriotism. A Swiss exchange student who stayed for several months with my family was shocked at the flag displays and frequent pledges of allegiance he encountered in the United States. Again, there is a feeling in Europe that this passionate Americanism can too easily turn into hostility. As a result of their history, Europeans downplay nationalism and seem to indulge in endless negotiations to resolve dangerous issues.

While Americans emphasize equality of opportunity, Europeans focus more on equality of results. Noting that Nokia is the world's leading producer of cell phones even though it pays its executives relatively modest salaries, Europeans wonder why American executives need to be paid so much more than their workers. They also question the shareholder-driven values of U.S. business and instead recognize a wide range of stakeholders in addition to a business's owners—including its employees, suppliers, customers, and local community. This community orientation includes a faith in government as an instrument for good. Europeans see the American emphasis on individualism and distrust of government as having created a violent, crime-ridden society whose incarceration rates (417 per 100,000 inhabitants for white men and 3408 per 100,000 for black men, compared with fewer than 100 per 100,000 men in Europe) are simply insane.[15] They particularly don't understand the easy availability of guns in America and the argument that guns are necessary to assure democracy. They deem their own democracy assured without every citizen's being armed to the teeth. They find the death penalty especially odious and have refused to extradite terrorist suspects to the United States if they face a possible death sentence. Indeed, it is puzzling to them how such a religious society can also embrace such an unforgiving penalty. Finally, they see American democracy, with its susceptibility to wealthy special interests, as very imperfect. Still, for all the flaws they find in American society, 61 percent of even the French have a positive overall attitude toward the United States.[16]

On the other side, Americans see the godlessness of the Europeans as the source of their susceptibility to the destructive secular religions of fascism and communism from which the United States had to save them repeatedly in the last century. They also see the Europeans as ungrateful free riders who have never met a dictator they wouldn't appease and take advantage of America's defense umbrella to posture smugly as morally superior. For Americans, the Europeans' resistance to immigration despite their declining populations, their hesitance over approving Turkey's application for full EU membership, and their criticism of Israeli policies smack of racism and anti-Semitism. From the American perspective, Europe is not a democracy at all, but a collection of bureaucracies run by quasi-aristocratic elites far removed from real people and bent on constraining the more dynamic United States out of envy and nostalgia for a lost global dominance that they will never regain. Again, I must emphasize that polls show Americans having overall favorable attitudes toward Europe. But again, their criticisms are also views expressed by leading commentators.

Which brings us to the crux of the matter—the future of Europe and of the alliance. From its inception the European project envisioned an eventual political union to be achieved through gradual economic integration. With that integration now virtually complete, European leaders are turning to the question famously posed by Henry Kissinger: What telephone number do you dial to reach Europe? As I write, former French

President Giscard D'Estaing is leading an effort to write a European constitution that will be presented for consideration to Europe's leaders in June 2003. If adopted, it will create a more unified EU structure with a more sincere voice. Its objective, however, has already been foreshadowed in documents and speeches. In accepting the Charlemagne Prize in May 1999, British Prime Minister Tony Blair said, "For Europe the central challenge . . . is the challenge posed by the outside world about how we make Europe strong and influential, how we make full use of the potential Europe has to be a global power for good."[17] Blair later emphasized that "this is about the projection of collected power and influence . . . that makes a superpower."[18] In September 2000, the European Commission issued instructions to the European Parliament saying that "our objective must be to make Europe a global actor, with a political weight commensurate with our economic strength, a player capable of speaking with a strong voice and of making a difference in the conduct of world affairs."[19] Achieving anything like this, of course, means submerging ancient sovereignties in the larger European whole. Thus EU External Affairs Commissioner Chris Patten noted in the 2000 Chatham lecture at Oxford that "sovereignty in the sense of unfettered freedom of action is a nonsense. A man naked, hungry, and alone in the Sahara is sovereign— and doomed."[20] He was echoed by Swedish Prime Minister Carl Bildt, who said that "the nation state is dead as an independent actor."[21]

That sentiment would not appeal to any American politician or statesman, but as *Die Zeit* editor Josef Joffe noted to me, "the European leaders are raging against their own impotence." That impotence was masked throughout the Cold War. Although World War II ended the era of European great powers, Europe's status as the main battlefield of the Cold War and the consequent need for the United States to consult and work closely with the Europeans, maintained the illusion of great-power status long after the actuality had passed. With the collapse of the Soviet Union, American interests turned elsewhere and European phones were not ringing nearly so often.

The impotence was reflected by the experience in Yugoslavia. Luxembourg was in the chair of the EU in 1991, when ethnic clashes broke out in Bosnia, and Luxembourg's Foreign Minister Jacques Poos flew to what he thought was the rescue, proclaiming that "this is the hour of Europe, not the hour of the Americans."[22] Poos is still choking on those words.

The EU proved hopelessly unable to cope with the situation, and it was the Americans who eventually crafted the Dayton agreement that ended the fighting. Even more significant was the embarrassment of Kosovo. Not only was the EU unable to mount a credible military operation in its own backyard, it could hardly even support the U.S. operations. Moreover, although it profoundly disagreed with the U.S. strategy of air strikes mainly on Belgrade and would have preferred using ground troops in Kosovo itself, the EU had no power to alter the American game plan. Europe's reaction was complex: relief that the American efforts brought down the Milosevic regime, embarrassment at its own inadequacy, and surprise and chagrin at the technological gap between the American and the European military forces. This experience sparked the decision, in 1999, to accelerate development of a Common Foreign and Security Policy (CFSP) by appointing Javier Solana as Europe's High Representative for the CFSP, responsible for, among other things, creating an independent EU rapid reaction force of some sixty thousand troops with the equipment and firepower to enable them to handle situations like Kosovo without calling in NATO and the Americans. Here was Kissinger's phone number, or at least the answering machine.

But given that NATO could easily create its own rapid reaction force, and in fact subsequently did so, one could reasonably ask what was the point of the EU force? Although cloaked in the garb of undying friendship and mutual cooperation, the answer seemed mainly to be that the Americans would not be in it. As Tony Blair asserted, "Whatever its origin, Europe today is no longer just about peace. It is about projecting collective power,"[23] which it promptly displayed with initiatives toward North Korea and the Middle East, traditional regions of American dominance.

Like the union itself, the EU foreign policy is a work in progress. Nevertheless, there are some important indicators of its likely tone and substance. The first major consideration is the ongoing enlargement of the EU. The addition of ten new members in 2004 will not only dramatically enlarge the EU but, as Elaine Sciolino noted, constituted the biggest voluntary surrender of sovereignty in twelve hundred years.[24] While this is important economically, it is a foreign policy initiative as well, for it extends the stabilizing and democratizing influence of the EU to the borders of Russia and Ukraine as well as toward the Middle East. Judging from its internal practice of building consensus through endless discussion, the EU will be relentlessly multilateral in foreign policy and will insist on dealing with global issues through the UN and other international bodies. Robert Kagan and other conservative U.S commentators argue that this may be partly a manifestation of a strategy of the weak using the UN Lilliputians to tie down the American Gulliver, but it is also an affirmation of the validity of the European post-World War II experience. After centuries of war, Europe became distrustful of claims of absolute sovereignty and found the conference room a better path to glory.

Thus the Europeans insisted on proceeding against Iraq through the UN Security Council in order to legitimize any action, and have reacted with concern to the U.S. call for coalitions of the willing to carry out preventive war. Javier Solana says, "Maybe terror needs a new form of containment, but preventive use of force needs wider legitimation either through the UN or some form of multilateral backing. If the United States claims that power for itself, it will only foster resentment and undermine its national interest."[25] Added to multilateralism will be a focus on attacking root causes of unrest through economic and social programs. Here Solana notes that while the United States tends to emphasize military solutions, the EU believes military operations alone cannot solve the problem of terror. "The EU," he says, "has a specific culture based on conflict prevention through dialogue and sensitivity to the economic and social roots of violence." His colleague, External Affairs Commissioner Chris Patten, adds, "I am not so naïve to think if you drop 20 million aid packages on Afghanistan that terrorism is going to disappear tomorrow, but I do believe there is a relationship between global inequity and state breakdown and violence and instability and terror."[26] In that context it is worth noting that Europe's $30 billion expenditure on development assistance is nearly three times what the U.S. spends.

Finally, the EU is skeptical of the moral passion that imbues U.S. foreign policy as well as of its "twists and turns" in places like the Middle East. The London School of Economics professor William Wallace says that "The United States thinks only it can promote democracy and that it is the only valid model, but its strident tone of moral and economic superiority creates a backlash while its policies like those of supporting Israel and at the same time building huge bases in the Saudi Arabian heartland of Islam make no sense."[27] Thus, in the words of Martin Wolf, "a balancer [read the EU] is a self-fulfilling prophecy."

The United States has long been ambivalent about Europe. Speaking at Independence Hall on July 4, 1962, President Kennedy said: "The United States looks on this valiant enterprise with hope and admiration. We don't regard a strong, united Europe as a rival but as a partner. To aid its progress has been the basic objective of our foreign policy for the past 17 years." He went on to call for a "Declaration of Interdependence" between the United States and Europe. But as Europe has become stronger, this view has changed. The EU Intergovernmental Conference of 1991 contained proposals to give the EU a security dimension and eventually a military capability. In view of frequent U.S. complaints that the Europeans were not sharing enough of the burden, many thought this would be welcome to the Americans. But Washington reacted with dismay and warnings about the dangers of undermining NATO, and the proposals were dropped. Six years later, in the wake of the Bosnia experience, the United States fully endorsed the proposal for development of an EU security and defense identity. At the same time, however, the United States pushed through, without consultation, the enlargement of NATO to include Poland, Hungary, and the Czech Republic. Then, as the EU's Common Foreign and Security Policy apparatus began to take shape and plans for its rapid reaction force moved ahead in 1999–2000, Washington again erupted with concern and warnings. Senator Jesse Helms attacked the "Euro army," calling it "a dangerous and divisive dynamic within NATO"; his comments were echoed by former Secretary of State Madeleine Albright and Secretary of Defense William Cohen.[28] The transition team of incoming President George W. Bush called the rapid reaction force "a dagger aimed at NATO's heart."[29] Thus U.S. policy has vacillated between urging Europe to share more of the defense burden and trying to block development of an independent European military force. The dynamics here are not complicated. As former National Security Adviser Zbigniew Brzezinski has noted, "Europe is a protectorate of the United States."[30] Washington needs Europe as a staging base for operations in the Middle East and as part of its global communications network. NATO is the American seat at the European table, so the United States wants more European support of NATO and of U.S.-led initiatives but is not at all keen on anything that might make Europe a real player.

As Europe has asserted its independence, commentary in the United States has turned distinctly negative. Even before September 11, analysts like the *National Review* editor John O'Sullivan were warning of the EU's "drift to a rival and hostile set of policies."[31] O'Sullivan wrote that "there is no need for a European security force or policy. It is a pure expression of burgeoning statehood and nationalism masquerading as anti-nationalism."[32] Moreover, he saw a separate European policy as arising from anti-Americanism and a desire to challenge the United States. In the wake of September 11, Europe's inability (with notable exceptions, like Britain's special forces) to field forces as quickly and as well equipped as U.S. troops, and its hesitance to back the United States on getting rid of Iraq's Saddam Hussein while insisting on elaborate UN procedures, confirmed to many Americans that Europe is not only a hopeless appeaser but also more interested in checking American power than in policing anyone else. Europeans, of course, noted it was they who provided the bulk of the peace-keeping troops and aid after the initial assaults in Afghanistan, and insisted that following the UN procedures is a fundamental matter of avoiding international anarchy. This argument cut little ice in the United States, which preferred Robert Kagan's view of Europeans as being from Venus and Americans from Mars.

Kagan's argument, in brief, was that, owing to America's protective power, Europe is able to indulge both in the luxury of low defense spending and in the delusion that military power is to be eschewed in favor of laws and rules and transnational cooperation. In this view, since Europe does not understand the Hobbesian world in which America must operate, it sees America as a threat that must be constrained, and does not realize that its own fantasyland existence is enabled only by U.S. power.[33] There is truth in this argument, but, unfortunately, not the whole truth. The Europeans, like the Japanese and others behind the U.S. defense shield, do not bear full responsibility for themselves and thus are able to see the world through rosier glasses. But this is how the United States prefers it. When Europe has moved in the direction of taking more responsibility, the United States has frequently objected and tried to undermine the effort.

For example, Europe is far more dependent on Persian Gulf oil than the United States, and any rational division of defense labor would have the EU countries deploying more aircraft carriers and troops there than the United States. But America has never asked for that help because it doesn't particularly want them there, lest their presence dilute U.S. influence and power. We believe it is easier, faster, and less complicated just to do the job ourselves: and, truth be told, we don't really trust them. Their interests would be a little different from ours. In particular, they do not see the Israeli-Palestinian conflict as we do. Letting the Europeans have a significant role in the region would not always comport with our perception of our own interests. But if we are not willing to let them take on the responsibilities of full-fledged sovereign powers, we can't simultaneously gripe that they are wimps. We complain that Europe does not spend enough on defense and that its level of weapons technology lags woefully behind ours. Both complaints have merit. Certainly, the Europeans much prefer to spend money on medical care and long vacations than on defense. On the other hand, in the case of a real player like China, we constantly emphasize that it spends too much on defense, and use that "threat" to justify our own buildups.

We also have systematically moved to hobble European weapons development. I worked in the Reagan administration at a time when licensing of technology exports was a hot issue. The United States restricts technology exports in a variety of ways that make it difficult or unattractive for foreign companies to do business with us. Moreover, the Pentagon, by far the biggest buyer of weapons in the world, works hand in glove with U.S. arms suppliers to help them maintain their global dominance. The restrictions on foreigners doing business with the Pentagon are such that the biggest foreign supplier, BAE Systems, accounts for less than 1 percent of Pentagon weapons and systems procurement. Pentagon funds for development of new weapons thus go overwhelmingly to American firms.[34]

Furthermore, the United States uses NATO as a way of trumping the EU in Europe. There was certainly no increased threat from Russia to justify the enlargement of NATO, and the new members added nothing to NATO's power; indeed, they only increased its load without adding to its resources. The enlargement was done partly for reasons of internal U.S. ethnic politics and partly to tie the eastern European countries directly to the United States. For a place like Poland, for instance, with strong ethnic ties to the United States, NATO membership is very attractive. But as a NATO member it then has to upgrade its air force, and the Pentagon is right there to help sell it F–16s, whose procurement by Poland undercuts the competitiveness of European aircraft producers. In addition, as noted earlier, it makes the Polish air force subject to numerous U.S. licenses, supply regulations, and usage requirements so that the United States effectively has some say in how Poland uses the planes. So if the Europeans are living in fantasyland, it is a fantasyland created and maintained by the United States.

A second cold war with Europe is unlikely, but continued friction is very much in the cards, particularly in view of U.S. efforts to create a split between "old" and "new" Europe. U.S.–Iraq policy has also resulted in a chasm between Britain and the Continent. The irony is that the Russians now seem to be our quite good friends. If we want to pull out of the ABM treaty they accommodate us. If we want to deploy a national missile defense system, they go along, if reluctantly. But the Russians are in no position to challenge us. This brings us back to Peter Sutherland's point. The global system rests not on a U.S.-Russian alliance but on the U.S.-EU Alliance, and if it really breaks down, the global system goes with it. All the differences we have recently discovered between us were there during the Cold War, yet we managed to submerge them in larger shared values and objectives. Because it is not in our interest, or the world's, that the system break down, it is a matter of the utmost importance that the United States review its European policies and work out a new structure of cooperation with the EU.

ASIA

As in Europe, so in Asia the United States is finding a new coolness in its relations with old friends while seeming to achieve better relations with old antagonists. Particularly striking, however, is the surprising similarity of perceptions of the United States throughout Asia. Whether in Tokyo, Beijing, or Jakarta, the analysis of U.S. objectives and motives is sharply at odds with the standard American rationale.

To begin, all believe the United States thinks of itself as the bearer of universal standards of morality, political philosophy, and organization, or, as one commentator put it, "the apotheosis and arbiter of civilized international conduct."[35] They see a United States bent on imposing and enforcing its brand of western values through hegemonic dominance as well as multilateral institutions. Moreover, allies and antagonists alike see a sharp difference between the individualism and materialism they believe lie at the core of U.S. values and their own more communal and hierarchical Asian values. They believe the American military is in Asia largely to assure U.S. dominance in the region and to prevent the rise of any competing power. In their view, the United States wants a strong and prosperous Asia-Pacific community but strictly on its own terms—economically sound, politically stable and democratic, and accepting of American leadership. They also believe the United States has a perhaps unconscious need for enemies to provide a justification for its large, high-tech forces and to serve as the focus of its geopolitical strategy. This, they believe, is why, with the end of the Cold War, the United States began to emphasize the concept of "rogue nations" and the need for "stability." They also believe the Bush administration was preparing to put China in the "enemy" category when Osama bin Laden conveniently made himself a better target.

The United States is also seen as exempting itself from the restraints that govern others because of its self-image as a benign hegemon. Thus, it explains its forward deployment of military forces as unthreatening, while it frequently cites as threats, justifying ever-greater U.S. defense expenditures, the far more limited deployments of other countries. Again, wherever I go in Asia I find extreme sensitivity to perceived double standards, particularly with regard to weaponry like nuclear arms that are seen as acceptable to the United States when owned by Britain or France or Israel, but as unacceptable in the hands of Asians.

None of these views should be taken to mean that Asians dislike America. Indeed, the Pew polls show generally positive attitudes and great admiration on a number of scales. Moreover, like others, Asians make a firm distinction between Americans, whom they overwhelmingly like, and America, whose policies and actions they find frequently baffling and odious. But there is a vast gap between the Asian view of what America is doing in the region and America's view of it. To understand the nuances and implications of this gap, let's take a tour, beginning with Korea, where the strains are most evident.

Korea

I have already noted in Chapter 7 the growing estrangement between the United States and South Korea, which culminated—to great annoyance in Washington—in the election in December 2002 of Roh Moo-hyun as

President of Korea to succeed Kim Dae-jung. Washington had been devoutly hoping for Roh's opponent, longtime U.S. friend Lee Hoi-chang to win on his platform of reversing Kim's Sunshine Policy toward the North.

And Roh not only won, he won with an overwhelming percentage of the vote of young people. His election coincided with the further escalation of tension between North Korea and the United States, as North Korea not only revealed a previously clandestine uranium enrichment program but expelled International Atomic Energy Agency (IAEA) inspectors and began preparations to restart its Yongbyon reactor. From this facility it would extract plutonium that could be used to make nuclear bombs, in violation of the nonproliferation treaty as well as of agreements with the United States. While Washington insisted it would not negotiate with North Korea until it halted these threatening activities, Roh announced that he both would continue the Sunshine Policy and undertake his own negotiations with the North. Behind this breach lies a view of the Korean situation that is never heard in Washington. It could, of course, be wrong, but it is important for Americans to understand it as one of South Korea's top negotiators explained it to me recently.

Americans know that the United States has no intention to invade North Korea, but North Korea doesn't know that. There has never been a peace treaty to end the Korean War. The United States has kept nearly forty thousand troops in South Korea as well as wartime command of the South Korean army for fifty years, and the obvious U.S. intention of attacking Iraq combined with North Korea's inclusion in the "Axis of Evil" leads the North to see the United States as a threat to its security. Fundamental to the American view is the conviction that North Korea cannot be trusted to honor any bilateral or multilateral commitments. That it initiated the uranium enrichment program in violation of the agreements it made with the United States in the Agreed Framework of 1994 is typically cited in support of this view. Yet the specific provisions of the 1994 agreement were for the suspension of the North's plutonium production facilities, and those provisions have been honored.[36] Moreover, the United States itself has failed to honor key provisions of the deal. The promised installation of 2,000 megawatts of nuclear powered electric generating capacity by 2003 has not been delivered, nor has the "full normalization of political and economic relations,"[37] nor have the "formal assurances against the threat or the use of nuclear weapons by the United

States"[38] been made. Thus in the eyes of the North Koreans, while the United States got what it wanted up front—namely, the suspension of the North Korean plutonium program—North Korea got mostly unfulfilled promises.

Moreover, when confronted with U.S. knowledge of the enriched uranium program by Assistant Secretary of State James Kelly during his visit to Pyongyang in October 2002, the North Koreans offered to shut down the program in return for a U.S. commitment not to attack and to go ahead with the promised normalization of relations. But Kelly told them they had to halt the program, period, and that there would be no negotiations. What North Korea wants most, according to South Korea's negotiators, is U.S. recognition and a nonaggression treaty to end the war. The South doesn't see why that is so difficult in view of the fact that virtually every country in the world, except for the United States, Japan, and France, recognizes North Korea. The South Koreans believe Washington's policy is driven by hard-line ideological hawks who want to bring about the collapse of the North and maintain hostility in order to justify broader U.S. deployment in the Pacific. Thus, in the view of many South Koreans, the United States is as much an obstacle to resolution as the North.

Beyond this, South Koreans resent what they see as Washington's highhanded approach. Recently it has come out that the Clinton administration seriously considered launching air strikes to destroy the North's nuclear plants in 1994. Ultimately it did not do so and instead negotiated the Agreed Framework that resulted in the shutdown of the plant. But South Koreans were shocked to find that their government was only informed of the attack plan at the last moment, when the government vigorously objected. Given that South Korea's capital, Seoul, is only about 17 miles south of the border and that North Korea has it targeted by the heaviest concentration of artillery in the world, any such attack would almost certainly have resulted in the leveling of Seoul. It was a real blow to Koreans not to be asked, by a supposedly staunch ally, what they thought about the destruction of their own capital.

Nor did anyone in Washington consult the South Koreans about including North Korea in the "Axis of Evil" or about undermining the South's sunshine policy with an American hard line. In short, the South Koreans think we take them for granted, and they resent it like hell. Iron-

ically, this sentiment is driven by the newly ascendant democratic ideals of
thousands of young people and business people who studied and worked
in the United States and came back wanting Koreans to have the same
rights as their American friends. The Koreans, like many Europeans, feel a
sense of betrayal when America does not live up to its own ideals.

An interesting twist is that South Korea has begun to send missionaries to the United States. Having become a Christian country over the
past fifty years, with a predominance of Protestant and especially Presbyterian churches, many Koreans have begun to see the United States as increasingly in need of spiritual rejuvenation.

Another important dynamic is the rise of the Chinese economy. China
has become a major importer of Korean products, so much so that Korea
can foresee the day when its exports to China will outstrip those to the
United States. This has resulted in much discussion in Korea of a regional
trade strategy and of regionalization generally. Along with this has come
public debate over the status of U.S. troops in South Korea. For fifty
years, Americans have been saying the troops are there to protect South
Korea. Of course, Defense Secretary Cohen's 1997 comment that U.S.
troops would stay even if Korea reunited let the cat out of the bag. The
fact is, the United States has those troops there as part of its overall projection of power into Asia. Now, insensitivity and ideologically driven
policy may undermine exactly the status of forces the United States has
been trying to preserve.

Japan

Across the straits from Korea, in Japan, is a much more complex and
slowly developing situation, but with similar characteristics. Japan is truly
in crisis, even if it is a quiet and largely invisible crisis. If you walk
through Tokyo or travel through Japan, all appears quite normal. The
traffic is impossible. Restaurants are crowded. The trains run exactly on
time and the subway stops right in front of the door-opening marker.
Construction cranes are everywhere, and even the tiniest villages are ser-
viced by expressways and fast trains. And that is the clue. Despite the
outward sheen, Japan's economy is on the edge of disaster and its politics
are rotten at the core, and the evidence of both is all those construction
cranes and expressways and trains to nowhere.

Japan has been governed by the Liberal Democratic Party (LDP) for all but about two of the past fifty-odd years. The party built its power on an iron triangle of support that includes farmers and rural residents, construction companies and their employees and related activities, and small business people and shopkeepers. The political system is rigged with rotten boroughs just like those of nineteenth and early twentieth century Britain. Because of the way votes are counted, a farmer's vote in Japan is worth about 2.2 votes from urban area residents. The LDP maintains this iron triangle by heavily subsidizing and protecting it. Farmers are protected from imports by some of the highest tariffs in the world. They are also heavily subsidized so that the domestic price of rice, for example, is ten times what it is on the world market. Small business is also subsidized in various ways and, best of all, pays virtually nothing in taxes. Construction lives on huge handouts from government contracts for roads that go to those farm villages and bridges that connect them. The result is that construction spending accounts for about 10 percent of the entire Japanese economy, about double the figure for the United States.

Beyond this, most of the Japanese economy has been highly protected for years both from imports and from foreign investors. After World War II, Japan adopted an export-led development strategy under which the government enforced high savings that were channeled through the banking system into mass production manufacturing industries like autos, electronics, and steel. Enormous production capacity was created, and much production was exported while the home market was reserved mainly for Japanese production. The system worked so well that by the mid–1980s, Japan was exporting so much and importing so little that the value of the yen was forced to rise in the 1985 Plaza Accord. The export strategy should have been changed, but it was hard to turn away from such a successful formula. Instead the government pumped money into the economy to offset the impact of a stronger yen and keep Japanese exporters competitive despite the stronger yen. The result was a classic bubble that burst in 1991–1992, leaving many companies virtually bankrupt and many banks with large nonperforming loans. But many of these companies were construction companies and banks closely tied to the LDP. Rather than aggressively clean things up, the LDP for the past ten years has been shoveling out more and more in subsidies. Meanwhile, the economy has stagnated because banks, already carrying too much bad

debt, lend mostly to keep zombie companies alive, thereby further increasing their bad debts. Japan's national debt is now the highest in the
world and rising. It is caught in a threatening deflationary spiral for which
the only solutions are substantial inflation, something likely to erode
household wealth, or a 1930s-style depression that will do the same.

Where does the United States come into this? The LDP is a creature of
the United States. Alfred C. Ulmer, Jr., CIA operations chief for East
Asia 1955–1958; Roger Hilsman, head of intelligence and research in the
Kennedy and Johnson administrations; and U. Alexis Johnson, Ambassador to Japan 1966–1969, have all acknowledged making payoffs to the
LDP from 1955 to 1972.[39] Moreover, there were close connections between the CIA, the LDP, and the Yakuza or Japanese Mafia.[40] From the
end of the Japanese Occupation to the present, Washington has favored
the LDP in Japan because it has been anti-Communist, has provided
bases, and has followed the American lead in foreign policy. There has
long been a deal. The United States takes care of security and has use of
bases in Japan, and in return the United States supports, or at least accepts, Japan's economic policies. In recent years, it has been a matter not
so much of accepting as of having become so structurally and financially
intertwined with Japan as to have little ability to do much about it. But
the point is that the United States has been an important factor (but far
from the only one or even the greatest one) in Japan's ills and particularly
in the suppression of a true democracy.

The United States has distorted Japan's development in other important
ways as well. Because the Tokyo War Crimes trials excluded any discussion
of the role of the emperor (by decision of the United States, which thought
it needed to govern Japan through the emperor), these trials have never
been accepted as anything other than victor's justice by the Japanese, and
Japan has never come to grips with the history of the war. For the most part
it doesn't even teach this history in its schools. This has made it impossible
for Japan to bring closure on the war in its relations with other countries.
The visits in recent years by Japanese prime ministers to Yasukuni Shrine
(where the spirits of Japan's war dead, including convicted war criminals,
are enshrined) cause outrage in many countries, but the outrage baffles
many Japanese, who see it as similar to visiting tombs in Arlington National Cemetery. Beyond this, the United States has created the same kind
of fantasyland in Japan as in Europe. Because it has no real responsibility

for the defense of the oil routes or overall strategic issues in Asia, Japan can indulge in low defense expenditures—only 1 percent of GDP—and avoid difficult issues. (Interestingly, the United States no longer complains about the level of Japan's defense expenditure even though it is far less than that of Europe.) The status of U.S. forces in Japan actually gives Japan's authorities more de facto jurisdiction than they have in Korea, but the issue is similar. Japan is a protectorate and a client state of the United States. It also was not fully consulted about U.S. policy toward North Korea even though it would surely be a target for North Korean missiles.

None of this has given rise to displays of anti-American feelings like those expressed in Korea, partly because Japan is a bigger beneficiary of the U.S. economic relationship, partly because Japan's democracy is not as well developed as Korea's, and partly because the Japanese tend to be less outspoken. But there are significant signals that should be noted. For example, one of the biggest hit movies in Japan in recent years was *Pride*, a film glorifying General Hideki Tojo, who led Japan during most of World War II and was convicted and executed as a war criminal. The producer, Hideaki Kase, who is now writing a book about kamikaze pilots, said, "Tojo was a superstar and still is."[41] Then there is Yoshinori Kobayashi, Japan's most popular cartoonist, who told me over coffee in Tokyo recently that for Japan World War II was about liberating Asia from western colonization. Most important of all is Shintaro Ishihara, the novelist and governor of Tokyo. Author with former Sony Chairman Akio Morita of the best-seller *The Japan That Can Say No*, Ishihara is an outspoken nationalist whose views, though sophisticated, are somewhat jingoistic. In the book, he suggested that Japan should cut off high-tech exports to the United States as an answer to U.S. complaints about Japanese trade barriers. In a country sick of the corruption and inarticulate leadership of the U.S.-backed LDP, he is now by far the most popular single political leader in the country, and his name keeps being mentioned as a possible prime minister. If he were elected, he would very likely join the South Koreans in moving to get the U.S. troops out. (I once debated him on Japanese TV, and he made sure to emphasize his opposition to U.S. military bases in his country.) Even without that there are increasing calls in Japan to reduce U.S. troop levels, and Japan's Foreign Minister, Yoriko Kawaguchi, announced on February 2, 2003, that the Japanese government would strive to reduce the number of American troops on Okinawa.[42]

It is important to understand that Japan's view of the role of the U.S. troops and bases is at great odds with that of most Americans'. While Americans think they are defending Japan and that Japanese should be grateful, the Japanese call the funds they provide for base maintenance "the sympathy budget." This budget is presented by political leaders in Japan not as the contribution of an ally to a critical joint mission but as a favor or a gift to the Americans, enabling them to indulge their hegemonic ambitions. Once again, perspective is of critical importance. Japanese like Americans. All the polls and all my forty years of contact with Japan confirm it. But we shouldn't ignore views like those of a Japanese friend of mine, a former ambassador to Thailand, who told me, "America needs conflict to keep its economy going." Japan is not going to renounce America tomorrow or perhaps ever, but those in the U.S. government who insist on betting on Japan as America's "strategic partner" may find themselves sorely disappointed.

China

As with Russia, so with China, U.S. relations are distinctly better today than before September 11. This continues the oscillating pattern of U.S.-China relations since Nixon's "opening to China" in 1972. During the Reagan administration, China's economic development and common interests in containing the Soviet Union drew the two countries together. As a Reagan administration official, I participated in some of the early economic negotiations with China and can attest to the immense interest of American business in the Chinese market. The end of the Cold War and the Tienanmen Square incident of 1989 then introduced a chill that the first Bush administration eventually corrected in response to business pressure as well as to broader strategic interests. During the 1992 presidential campaign, Bill Clinton accused the Bush administration of "mollycoddling" the Chinese and promised to take a sterner line. As president he initially did take a tough line on human rights and other issues, but he soon succumbed to the logic of economic development and initiated the policy of "engagement," calling China a "strategic partner." This angered some in Japan, who thought Japan was the "strategic partner," and many on the right wing of the Republican Party who still harbor the old hatred of the Chinese communists.

With the advent of the second Bush administration in 2001, the U.S. line hardened again. China was relabeled a "strategic competitor," and U.S. military surveillance of China was increased. It looked to many Chinese as if America needed an enemy to replace the Soviet Union and had chosen China. Osama bin Laden appeared to Beijing as something of a godsend. They quickly voiced sympathy and offered cooperation to Washington, after which relations warmed considerably. But the Chinese remain concerned that once the threat of terror is under control, they could once again become a target of American hostility.

By far the most important piece of the U.S.-China puzzle is Taiwan. As noted earlier, for mainland Chinese, putting Taiwan under the Chinese flag represents the last step in reestablishing the sovereignty and integrity that were lost to western colonialism in the Opium Wars of the nineteenth century. America's support of Taiwan is seen as intervention in a strictly internal matter and is inexplicable except in terms of a U.S. interest in weakening and containing China. In their view, every time a Taiwanese leader meets with a U.S. leader, and every time President Bush says something like "we will do whatever it takes" to defend Taiwan, it simply encourages Taiwanese leaders to resist China's efforts at reunification and so puts more pressure on the leadership in Beijing to take a tougher line. The Chinese have told anyone who will listen (and most experts believe them) that the one thing that would almost certainly cause a war would be a declaration of independence by Taiwan. In a mirror image of the American view that China's buildup of forces across from Taiwan poses a threat demanding a U.S. response, the Chinese see our gestures of support to Taiwan as posing a threat to which they have no choice but to respond. In their view, it was the United States that created the Taiwan problem in the first place, and they see our support for a separate Taiwan as part of a larger effort to contain and undermine China's rising power and influence.

That brings us to the second piece of the puzzle—hegemonic competition. Whether apocryphal or not, the story of the Chinese professor who commented that "China has had 150 bad years, but now we're back" is very telling. Once one gets past the inevitable Taiwan discussion, the second major topic on the minds of Chinese elites is the country's bright prospects and return to the front rank of nations. Without being Chinese you probably cannot fully understand the deep sense of historical humiliation brought by the troubles of the past century, but the sense of euphoria and anticipation in the wake of China's current success is palpable. Yet there is also an anxiety in China that the United States fears this success and wants to limit it.

Again mirror images are at work. Recall, for example, the incident in early 2001 when a U.S. EP–3 electronic surveillance aircraft was forced to land on Hainan Island. Americans saw this as an unprovoked act of hostility that proved once more why we have to beware of China. But the Chinese asked why U.S. planes are constantly patrolling their coast, deliberately triggering Chinese defense communications in order to monitor China's defense capabilities. They point out that they neither have such aircraft nor do they patrol the coasts of the United States or even neighboring countries in Asia. In their view, the United States gains benefits from being the hegemonic power and seeks to maintain that power, perhaps even by forcibly preventing the rise of a rival. This sense is powerfully reinforced by U.S. actions and, of course, by the president's West Point speech and statements of other officials calling for preventive war and the abrogation of the rise of any competing power. Looking at the world from Beijing, the Chinese see U.S. troops and fleets all over the Pacific, advanced U.S. weapons being sent to Taiwan, U.S. détente with Russia, and U.S. forces based for the first time ever in several non-Democratic central Asian countries bordering China as a result of the conflict in Afghanistan. They see a U.S. National Missile Defense effort ostensibly aimed at "rogue nations" like North Korea but also tending to negate the deterrent power of China's nuclear missiles; a unilateral move without UN backing in Iraq; and an arsenal of unparalleled sophistication and power. Altogether that makes a scary picture for the Chinese, indicating to them that America thinks they are a threat. They insist they are not an expansionist power and never have been and pose no threat to the United States other than economic competition, which the United States says it welcomes. Indeed, they say the U.S. posture forces them to waste resources on defense that they would much rather put into economic development. Many suspect the American threats are part of a strategy to reduce China's economic growth.

The third part of the puzzle is the issue of pride, respect, clash of cultures, and ultimate intent. The Chinese are perhaps more ambivalent about the United States than are any other people. Give a lecture at a Chinese university and, as an American, you will be sharply questioned and subjected to harsh criticism about American hegemonism, militarism, and intervention in Taiwan. But after the lecture, half of the students will crowd around to ask how they can go to M.I.T. or Stanford or get a job in America. They are endlessly fascinated by American technology, its industry and productivity, and its democratic government and spirit. Chinese also find Americans informal and expressive like themselves, easy to talk to. Yet they also have tremendous pride in their own culture and believe deeply that China must be ruled differently than America, and that Chinese ways must be incorporated into the framework of globalization. Time and again, Chinese officials, scholars, and students will express resentment that Americans take for granted that the American way or western way is the universally best way. They repeatedly insist that the world cannot run on an American standard only but must incorporate Chinese standards as well. In this discussion, they insist that China is no threat to anyone, that they have no desire to impose their standards.

This claim gets a mixed reaction in the rest of Asia. On the one hand, few in Asia outside of Taiwan fear a Chinese-armed attack. On the other hand, many have told me they feel threatened by the way China's hierarchical, authoritarian system will tend to reorder global structures as its power increases. Such people feel more comfortable with the United States in the neighborhood as well. One reason they do is demonstrated by a long conversation I had with students and faculty at Tsinghua University and the Unirule Institute of Economics in the spring of 2002. After having been berated for quite some time about the arrogance of America and the deficiencies of western standards, I asked if they could tell me exactly what the Chinese standard or system of future political and geo-political organization would be. They honestly admitted they could not.

Here then is the major issue. China wants to be a great power, and it aches for American acceptance and respect, a desire that offers us great potential influence. Yet China does not yet have institutions that can handle change in a systematic, predictable fashion, a fact that inevitably contains an element of risk. China is certainly not an enemy of the United States today, yet it might become so in response to its interpretations of our actions. In other words, we could make the hostility of China a self-fulfilling prophecy. It is thus a matter of the highest importance that we step carefully and do all we can to assure that China continues on a path of development and liberalization.

That brings us finally to the last piece of the puzzle: the economy. China's transformation since I went on that early trade mission in 1982 is staggering. It is not completely a market economy but it is getting there at high speed, and this development has dramatically changed Chinese society and politics. While it is still far from a democracy, for the average person, China today is a much, much freer place than it has perhaps ever been. This development has been powerfully promoted both by the United States government and U.S. industry through enormous investment and technology transfer. This trend is the best guarantee of peaceful, friendly U.S.-China relations in the future. Indeed, there is a great irony here. Even as we have swung back and forth on whether China is a "strategic partner" or a "strategic competitor," the U.S. economy has grown increasingly dependent on China in two critical ways. First, the U.S. trade deficit with China has reached $85 billion as America has come to rely more and more on China as the low-cost quality supplier of everything from paint brushes to cell phones.[53] Even more importantly, China is building up enormous dollar reserves and increasingly is an investor in U.S. securities. As we saw earlier, the U.S. economy is heavily dependent on a constant inflow of foreign capital, and as China becomes a bigger source of that capital, the United States will become more dependent on China. In Beijing, officials hope that by the time Osama bin Laden is out of the way, the United States will not be able to afford to see China as an enemy.

LATIN AMERICA

"There is a huge weapon of mass destruction located just South of the U.S. border, and it's about to explode. It's called Latin America." Those words, from former Mexican Finance Minister Angél Gurría, woke me up over breakfast in Mexico City in the fall of 2002. At the time, Argentina was in the process of defaulting on its loans from the IMF, unemployment was rising in Mexico, the endless strife in Colombia was intensifying, a coup attempt that looked as if it had at least tacit U.S.

backing had failed in Venezuela, and the Brazilian economy was teetering on the edge of disaster as international investors pulled out money in the midst of a turbulent presidential election campaign that might bring a leftist to power. Gurría, lamented that "market fundamentalists" in Washington with little knowledge of the circumstances in Latin America were delaying IMF assistance and making statements about the dangers of moral hazard (essentially enabling policies that are unwise in the long term in order to achieve short-term satisfaction) while paying no attention to the much greater risk of collapse of the whole system. "Brazil," he said, "is being penalized by investors from the democracies for carrying out a democratic election. How do you expect Latin Americans to hold fast to democracy when that happens?" He also blasted the Washington Consensus for prescribing policies according to the textbook rather than according to the realities of developing country situations. "The United States needs a Latin America strategy," he said, "but it never has had one."

That was the assessment of one of America's better friends in Latin America. Given the U.S. record in the region of alternating intervention and neglect, widespread cynicism and suspicion of U.S. motives should be no surprise. The United States is widely seen to have interests but not friends and to be primarily interested in material gain and power. It is in no way seen as peace-loving. Indeed, another Latin American ambassador to the United States asked, "Peace loving? Are you kidding? No one believes that nonsense in Latin America." Here as elsewhere, there is widespread criticism of U.S. double standards. Yet here, too, the United States is admired for its economic success and its great universities and institutions, and is widely recognized as Latin America's only hope. But as the Brazilian Ambassador Rubens Barbosa notes, making that hope materialize is difficult because "there is no security or nuclear threat in this hemisphere, and as a result Latin America is given a low priority in Washington."

That low priority has been especially frustrating to Mexican President Vicente Fox, who staked the success of his presidency on the bet that his good friend and fellow rancher George W. Bush would dramatically change the form and substance of the whole relationship. That this doesn't seem to be happening is beginning to hurt Fox. But leaders I spoke with in the region are still hopeful that Bush will address three major issues in the course of his administration—trade and economic development, drug traffic control, and support for democracy.

Economic development is the most pressing issue, and one on which the region sees Washington failing badly. The U.S. approach is to propose free trade agreements, along with domestic privatization and deregulation. The difficulty is that while NAFTA has brought a dramatic increase in trade between Mexico and the United States, it has not fulfilled many other expectations and forecasts. For example, Mexican salaries and wages have fallen considerably since 1994, and the numbers of those living below the poverty level have risen, along with unemployment and underemployment. Thus the attraction of illegal immigration in search of U.S. jobs remains strong. The problem is not solely due to NAFTA; it is also the result of the financial crisis of 1995 and the ups and downs of oil prices. But NAFTA has not been enough to offset any of this, and has brought its own problems. Mexican access to the U.S. market for products like sugar or services like trucking remains limited. At the same time, as Mexican agricultural markets open to heavily subsidized commodities like American corn, Mexican producers are increasingly faced with extinction. Unlike the EU, which provided substantial adjustment assistance, full market access, and new infrastructure funding when it took in Spain and Portugal, the U.S. under NAFTA has assumed that trade alone will provide the means for taking care of other necessities.

In the rest of Latin and South America outside of NAFTA, the problem is even more difficult. While various free trade agreements have been proposed, only one, with Chile, has been concluded. Brazil, with South America's largest economy, finds over half its export items under some restriction in the U.S. market. On top of all this comes the challenge of China. Factories that first moved from a U.S. location to Mexico are now beginning to leave Mexico for China, where wages are far below Mexico's low levels. And what is true for Mexico holds even more for the rest of the hemisphere. China's entry into the WTO is seen south of the Rio Grande as the beginning of the end of NAFTA, and no one in Washington seems to be addressing this issue.

By far the most troubling issue is drug trafficking, where the U.S. stance resembles its behavior on oil imports. In that case, U.S. addiction to cheap gas has embroiled it in the dangerous politics of the Middle East and led it inadvertently to fund the spread of fundamentalist Islam and terrorists to its own detriment. In the same way, U.S. addiction to co-caine and other narcotics is funding the drug cartels of Latin America and the corruption and corrosion of the societies of Peru, Colombia, Panama, Mexico, and elsewhere. Americans—an estimated 20 million to 25 million marijuana smokers, 6 million regular cocaine users, and half a million heroin users—spend about $64 billion annually on drugs.[44] Since 1909, the United States has taken a prohibitionist approach that ef-fectively requires "unconditional surrender from traffickers, dealers, and addicts." That the surrender has not occurred is evident from the size of the market and the fact that world production of opium and coca more than doubled just between the years 1985 and 1996.[45]

The U.S. government's interaction with drugs is complex and often corrupt. When the CIA helped organize the Mujahedin in Afghanistan after the Soviet invasion, it knew the guerillas were raising money by sell-ing opium. By 1980, 60 percent of the heroin in the U.S. market origi-nated in Afghanistan.[46] For many years, former Panama President Manuel Noriega was a CIA operative who also had a long collaboration with the Medellín Cartel of Colombia. In 1989, the first Bush adminis-tration invaded Panama and arrested Noriega, who is now in a U.S. prison serving a forty-year sentence for drug trafficking in a U.S. prison. Panama, however, remains a major money laundering and cocaine trans-shipment center.

The U.S. approach to drug trafficking has been not only prohibition-ist but also para-military and highly interventionist. Although U.S. courts and jails are clogged with people arrested on drug charges, major efforts to reduce drug demand through treatment have never really been implemented in the United States. The control effort has been focused on stopping production and interdicting shipments. This effort employs a vast armada of ships and planes to spot, track, and stop the flow of drugs. The United States trains Latin military units and funds them to stop drug production and trafficking in their countries. Spray planes are used to destroy the coca crops planted by campesinos in the jungles and farm lands of Peru and Colombia. Often this spraying destroys legitimate crops as well as coca and also engenders soil erosion. Efforts to help campesinos establish alternative crops have been wholly inadequate and unsuccessful. Moreover, the training given to Latin narcotics control per-sonnel is very similar to counterinsurgency training and has undoubtedly been applied for non-narcotics purposes in the region's endemic guerilla wars.

A major problem is the annual certification reviews for foreign governments. Every year, the White House has to certify to Congress that foreign governments are cooperating adequately with U.S. efforts on narcotics control. Decertified countries lose foreign aid and face trade sanctions. This peculiar policy effectively means that the war against drugs is waged not in partnership with allies but against them. The United States acts as prosecutor, judge, and jury in determining whether Mexico or Peru is acting properly to attempt to stop the flow of drugs across the U.S. border. The process is humiliating, maddening, and in the eyes of our Latin neighbors, full of U.S. hypocrisy. One bitter Mexican official told me, "The United States manages to excuse its banks for handling drug money, and although it can track trucks to the U.S. border, somehow they vanish once in U.S. jurisdiction." All over Latin America, people ask about the demand side of the equation. As long as the demand is so great and the trade so profitable, traffickers will find a way to supply. As a consequence, the police forces, judges, armies, and ordinary people of Latin America are being drowned in illicit money that eats away at the fiber of their societies. Yet they have no opportunity to certify us on our efforts to control our insatiable demand for drugs.

Which brings us to the issue of democracy. One of the bright aspects of the past fifteen years has been Latin America's turn to democracy. Yet there is increasing doubt whether it will work. "Policy takes time to show results," said one leader, "but democracy doesn't give you any time." Said another, "Look, the countries that have successfully developed like Singapore, Taiwan, and Chile were not democracies during the development stages." These leaders wonder how democracy can be sustained in an ocean of drug money. But most discouraging of all is their view that the United States doesn't really care that much about democracy in Latin America. Of course, they all note past U.S. comfort with and installation of dictators. But the prime example these days is Venezeuela, where in April 2002 U.S. officials seemed to lend support to the attempt at a coup to oust elected President Hugo Chavez. Of course, Washington backtracked and denied involvement, but no one in Latin America believes the denials for a minute. Here again, U.S. policies have not given much reason for faith.

MIDDLE EAST

If Latin America has little faith in the United States, the Islamic countries of the Middle East, South Asia, and Southeast Asia have virtually none left. This, too, reflects a great reverse. As deeply religious countries, they naturally rejected communist doctrine and were mostly allies of America during the Cold War despite their discomfort with U.S. backing of Israel. As noted in Chapter 4, Saudi Arabia has had particularly warm relations with the United States going back to the Americans' first discovery of oil in the Saudi desert when the British and others stoutly maintained the impossibility of any being there. The other key Middle East country, Egypt, has had a more up-and-down U.S. relationship, but after the end of the Yom Kippur War in 1973 it, too, became a firm friend. Jordan and Lebanon, while small, also played key roles as helpers of and friends of the United States. In particular, Jordan under King Hussein often acted as a moderating influence in the volatile politics of the region.

Today, as the Pew survey data noted in Chapters 1 and 2 indicate, good will has all been washed away. The immediate cause is the Iraq situation, but the longer-term and deeper factor is the perception of U.S. bias for Israel against the Palestinians. Also, undoubtedly an element of frustration and self-anger in many of these countries over their inability so far to cope with modernization gets redirected at the United States. But the loss of good will and respect I particularly refer to here is that of people who bet their careers and built their lives on the basis of being friends of the United States. Saudi Arabia is particularly important in this regard, because so many of its elite have studied and lived in the United States and because the country has, in its own eyes, done so much to be supportive in terms of providing backing for covert U.S. operations around the globe as well as disciplining oil prices. In the wake of September 11, the heretofore friendly, or mostly uninterested, American press suddenly turned a hard eye on Saudi Arabia because fifteen of the nineteen hijackers were Saudi citizens. After years of ignoring the kingdom or of favorably covering its strong support of most U.S. initiatives, newspapers like the *Wall Street Journal* could find nothing good in the kingdom. Its Islamic law, its veiling of women, its charitable giving institutions, its school system, its lack of democracy, and its support of the Palestinians were all severely condemned as barbaric, medieval, and anti-American. While some of the criticism pointed to real issues with which the Saudis are themselves wrestling, the harsh tone and sudden reversal of previously friendly attitudes stung as it became clear that Americans had forgotten, or perhaps never knew or cared, about the support Saudi Arabia had given them.

The bitterness this attitude caused was explained to me by the owner of a leading Saudi newspaper chain. The graduate of U.S. universities who spends much time at his second home in the United States, he described his shock that suddenly people who he had always thought of as friends now seemed to be suspicious of all Saudis. Even more significant was his description of the reaction of his 21-year-old son. Prior to September 11, the young man had been a student at a leading U.S. university where he had gone after graduating from a top U.S. preparatory school. He had always been a big fan of U.S. football and basketball, listened nonstop to American music, ate American junk food, played computer games, dated American girls, and paid no attention to politics or to the Israeli-Palestinian conflict. As my newspaper friend explained it, his son was for all practical purposes an American. Now, however, in the wake of the sudden reversal of American attitudes, he told me that the son has dropped out of the university and refuses to travel to America or even to meet with Americans in Saudi Arabia. Even more worrying to my friend is the fact that the son has become intensely interested in politics, regularly attends meetings of radical political and religious figures, and is now not only strongly anti-American, but also anti-Israeli.

This is only one example, but it is indicative of a broader feeling that is already having consequences for the United States. The giant Prince Sultan airbase has been a key element in the U.S. structure for constant surveillance of the Persian Gulf. In recent months, however, Saudi leaders have let it be known that once a war with Iraq is over, they will ask President Bush to withdraw all American armed forces from the kingdom. Indeed, many Saudis seem to think the best part of a new American was with Iraq will not be so much the elimination of Saddam's weapons of mass destruction, but the elimination of the American presence in Saudi Arabia. Thus, Osama bin Laden may yet see the dissolution of the Saudi-U.S. alliance he has long sought.

Like Saudi Arabia, Jordan and Egypt are also troubled. In meetings with Jordanian leaders, I was impressed with the frustration expressed at what they took to be Washington's misinterpretation of events in the region. Their views were shared and best expressed by Abdel Monem Said, the director of the Al-Ahram Center for Political and Strategic Studies in Cairo. Over a breakfast, he explained that Americans tend to see the problems of Iraq, Iran, fundamentalism, terror, and the Israeli-Palestinian conflict as discrete and to be solved individually. To Arabs, he said, these are all related. In particular, he went on, the problem is not Iraq nearly so much as it is the Palestinian question. Indeed, hitting Iraq will only exacerbate the situation in the Middle East, he said. In particular, it is likely not to dampen but to stimulate fundamentalism and violence between Arabs and Israelis. What you in America don't understand, he emphasized, is the deep sense of injustice virtually all Arabs feel. They ask: Why can Israel have atomic weapons and Arab countries cannot? Why can Israel ignore UN resolutions with impunity, but Saddam must be attacked immediately? Why can Israel get away even with sinking the American naval ship *Liberty* in the 1967 war and using Americans like Jonathan Pollard, who is now in prison, to spy on the United States itself, while Arab nationals residing in the United States are routinely rounded up for questioning about terrorist activities just because they are Arabs? Moreover, he said, Arabs don't see Saddam as nearly as great a threat as terror is. By going after Iraq, he noted, America is taking the easy way out by attacking a capital it can bomb. For half a century, he continued, the U.S. tie with moderate Arabs worked to contain communist expansion to hold back the waves of the Iranian revolution, and to end the threat of Saddam in the Gulf War of 1991. Now, he said, Arabs see the major force for instability in the region to be the United States itself.

That view was echoed on a broader basis by Malaysian Prime Minister Mahathir, who told the 116-member Non-Aligned Movement in February 2003 that the United States is no longer just fighting a war against terror. Rather, it is a war to dominate the world, he said. He emphasized American unconcern with the frustration in the Islamic world over the Israeli-Palestinian conflict and condemned the blatant double standards that infuriate Muslims, while arguing that current U.S.-led efforts are creating injustice and oppression of people of other ethnic origins and colors. This was the same Mahathir who had been feted at the White House less than a year previously for his staunch support of the United States on fighting terror.

SOUTH ASIA

The legacy of Pakistan's split from India in 1947 and the Cold War, combined with the advent of the War on Terror, have created a witches' brew in South Asia that makes it perhaps the most dangerous place in the world today. The bitter parting of India and Pakistan left millions dead, along with the running sore of the partition of Kashmir. Over the past fifty years, India and Pakistan have fought three wars and been constantly engaged in competitive and immensely expensive weapons development despite their mutual poverty. The United States became entwined in all this as a result of the Cold War.

Although India has always been a democracy, and Pakistan more often than not a military dictatorship, India, with its socialist economic system and suspicion of America's ties to its excolonial ruler, Britain, leaned toward the Soviet Union during the Cold War. The United States thus tended to lean toward Pakistan, which jumped with alacrity into U.S.-sponsored alliances of the 1950s like CENTO (the Central Treaty Organization) and SEATO (the Southeast Asian Treaty Organization). But the U.S. relationship with Pakistan was a hot and cold one. In the early days of the Cold War, it was hot as the U.S. looked for allies in Asia. Then, when China attacked India in 1962, there was a short period of India-U.S. warming as Washington provided some aid to India. But Pakistan soon became an ally of China, to which Nixon wished to make an opening in the late 1960s and early 1970s. The Pakistani leaders offered themselves as a channel to Beijing and so cemented a close tie to Washington. Indeed, it was so close that in the 1971 Indo-Pakistani War, the United States tilted toward authoritarian Pakistan and against democratic India. Thereafter, Washington seemed more or less to forget about the area until 1974, when India exploded its first nuclear device. Although it had trained Indian scientists and supplied critical nuclear material, the United States cut off supply of nuclear fuel to India after the explosion despite the fact that India promised not to weaponize its device. This only pushed India more tightly into the embrace of the Soviets, who gladly became India's supplier of heavy water.

Meanwhile, Pakistan had undertaken its own nuclear development program after its 1971 war with India. While Canada and Germany supplied critical equipment, the United States halted economic and military aid as an expression of opposition to what was not obviously a nuclear weapons program. By 1981, however, Pakistan had again become important to Washington as a result of the Soviet invasion of Afghanistan. To train, equip, and supply the Mujahedin, the United States needed a rear area, and Pakistan was perfect, being an Islamic country that harbored many of the same tribes that inhabited Afghanistan and spoke some of the same languages. The Reagan administration thus lifted the sanctions, despite arresting a smuggler attempting to ship two tons of zirconium to Pakistan, and renewed generous military and financial aid in return for help with the Mujahedin. In 1983, China reportedly supplied a bomb design to Pakistan; in response, Congress passed an amendment requiring economic sanctions unless the White House certified that Pakistan had not embarked on a nuclear weapons program. The White House so certified for the next five years, but finally imposed sanctions in 1990 when Pakistan, fearing war with India again, made cores for several nuclear weapons. The program continued, however, concluding in 1998 when both India and Pakistan conducted a series of nuclear test explosions. Again, Washington expressed its outrage.

In the wake of the collapse of the Soviet Union, and as a large number of Indian entrepreneurs came to strike it rich in Silicon Valley and returned to create new companies at home, U.S.-Indian relations began to warm. They got even warmer when the new Bush administration declared China a "strategic competitor" in 2001 and initiated greater military cooperation with India as a way of signaling to China that it was surrounded. Meanwhile, under the tutelage of Pakistan, the Taliban had taken control of Afghanistan, which the United States had abandoned and forgotten after the Soviet army exit in 1989. As the Taliban put women under the veil and out of jobs, schools, and even hospitals, and provided facilities and support for Osama bin Laden while imposing a truly medieval regime, the United States remained mute—until, that is, September 11.

Suddenly, we needed Pakistan again. Economic and military aid began to flow again, as President Musharraf pledged that in the war against terror he was "with" the United States. Actually, in this pledge, Musharraf proved himself a brave man. His own military and secret services were deeply penetrated by Islamic radicals and Taliban supporters, while public opinion in the country, particularly in the provinces bordering

Afghanistan, tended to be pro Osama. Given that Musharraf's is another military dictatorship, the possibility of assassination or a coup d'état was, and is, ever present. But if Musharraf was brave, he was also disingenuous. When Al Qaeda supporters in Pakistan seized *Wall Street Journal* report Danny Pearl and murdered him, Pakistan's internal security services were aware of and very possibly involved in the killing. Musharraf almost certainly knew this when he visited Washington in February 2002, yet he told the American public he believed Danny to be still alive. Maybe he had to in order to stay alive himself. In any case, the situation today is that while Musharraf remains president with U.S. backing, he does not control the western provinces or the so-called tribal areas of his own country. Nor does he seem to control some of his internal services that continue to support terrorist activity in Kashmir. This activity could easily lead to war with India, but the United States is telling the Indians to cool it because Washington needs Musharraf to back its policy in Afghanistan. Meanwhile, however, U.S. policy in Iraq and in Israel-Palestine is radicalizing Pakistan to such an extent that, as a leading Pakistani publisher told me, it is very possible that a Taliban-like group could kill off Musharraf and take over Pakistan with its nukes and ballistic missiles. If you think that sounds dangerous, it is.

NEW WORLD ORDER

The shape of the new world order is still somewhat amorphous, but increasingly uncomfortable. It is not exactly the United States against the world, as my Malaysian friend forecast. But tension between America and its old friends in South Korea, Europe, Japan, Southeast Asia, and Latin America are rising to dangerous levels. Relations with old opponents like Russia, India, and China have actually improved, but remain unpredictable. Indeed, the whole world order has become unpredictable and unstable. Is that, we need to ask ourselves, what we really want?

10

CITY ON A HILL

"No need of moon or stars by night or sun to shine by day. It was the new Jerusalem that would not pass away."

—The Holy City (Weatherly and Adams)

As I begin this last chapter, it seems very likely that U.S. troops, along with some British forces and perhaps a token representation of armed units from other members of the "coalition of the willing," will be occupying Iraq when this book appears. While that is probably better, at this point, than the alternative of allowing Sadam to defy and mock the UN Security Council while continuing to brutalize ordinary Iraqis, it seems to me that by trying to do the right thing, but in the worst possible way, we gave ourselves only bad options and created a lose-lose situation. For whether we go in soon, or, by reason of some last-minute change of Saddam's heart, delay, or don't go in at all, enormous damage has already been done. And even if the occupation goes by the book, and Iraq emerges as a model democracy in five years—a very long-odds scenario—the damage will have lasting consequences. This is particularly true if you look at Iraq and North Korea as part of a whole, rather than as discrete issues.

For one thing, by playing down the significance of North Korea's threats and withdrawal from the Non-Proliferation Treaty while moving heaven and earth to go to war with a so far nonnuclear Iraq, Washington sent a loud message that if you think you might be on America's bad side, you'd better go nuclear, quick. More fundamentally, by misunderstanding our own national interests and the basis of our power, we have already undermined it. The European Union, for example, is more than just a big market. It is the instrument that has laid to rest the ancient enmities and tribal warfare of Europe; that has created a generator and spreader of wealth able to be an equal partner with the United States; and that acts as a guarantor for the spread of democracy, peace, and stability in all of Europe, and now even in parts of Asia. This huge asset that the United States has historically promoted as being greatly in America's interest has been severely damaged internally by the divisions arising from the battle over how to handle Iraq, divisions that were exacerbated by U.S. policies. Beyond this, the relationship of the EU and most of the key European countries to the United States has been harmed. This is true even in those countries like Britain, where the leadership has backed America because the public-at-large had been overwhelmingly against U.S. policies. And don't be fooled by the "Old Europe-New Europe" rhetoric. New Europe is not going to send any troops or help foot any bills; and by dint of going along with Washington and estranging itself from Old Europe, it has probably damaged its own development prospects.

Take NATO as another example. Americans are wont to see NATO and the maintenance of U.S. troops in Europe as a kind of favor we do for the Europeans. In fact, however, with the demise of the Soviet Union, there is no military threat to Europe. On the other hand, the United States cannot project power into the Middle East or Africa without use of NATO bases and cooperation. The truth is that we need NATO perhaps more than the Europeans. Yet, already there is talk in Europe of possible termination or restriction of U.S. use of bases and air space. It is already clear that Saudi Arabia will be asking us to evacuate bases there in the near future, and it seems possible South Korea will request the same, perhaps followed by Japan. The great irony here is that American unilateralism appears to be eroding the very basis of the hegemony its apostles are trying to enlarge.

THE DREAM THAT MIGHT HAVE COME TRUE

It didn't, and doesn't, have to be that way. Another scenario was, and is, possible. It is not widely recognized that at the end of the Gulf War in

1991, neither the United States nor the UN put serious conditions on a cease fire. Indeed, when the Iraq army was fully routed, the coalition simply stopped fighting, and called for the Iraqi commanders to arrange a cease-fire. Operating with few instructions, commanding General Norman Schwarzkopf met on March 3, 1991 with Iraqi generals to arrange the terms of the cease-fire. No demands were made by the coalition for Saddam or any of his representatives to sign any document of surrender or of conditions calling for Iraqi disarmament, destruction of weapons of mass destruction, or protection of the Shia and Kurdish groups in Iraq that had been encouraged by the coalition to rise up against the Saddam regime. In effect, Saddam got a pass, and although Schwarzkopf did require that Iraq not fly fixed-wing aircraft near U.S. troops, no provisions were made to restrict helicopters. Thus, when the Shias and Kurds revolted, as urged by the coalition, they were butchered by Saddam's helicopters. Washington later blamed this on the need to respond to Saudi fears of the Shias, but top U.S. and Saudi officials, who were on the spot at the time, have told me that, in fact, the Saudis wanted to help the Shias. In any case, the United States eventually established the southern no-fly zone, but too late to rescue the Shias. Later, in April, the UN issued resolution 687 directing Saddam to destroy all weapons of mass destruction. Although Iraq's foreign minister responded with a letter accepting the directive, the moment for a decisive change had passed. It was now a cat-and-mouse game.

Suppose the United States and its allies (and they really were allies then) had imposed disarmament conditions on Iraq at the time of the cease-fire, requiring Saddam to sign a formal document with real conditions and enforcement mechanisms. We could have done what we are talking about doing now, with the full weight of world opinion backing us. Top U.S. experts who were in the area at the time have told me that such a requirement would definitely have meant the fall of Saddam. Instead, we allowed him to turn military disaster into political victory. We had most of the same leaders then that we have now: Cheney, Powell, Wolfowitz, Feith, and Haass were all there. Today, they argue that Congress and the UN only mandated them to eject Iraq from Kuwait, and that any advance to Baghdad would have torn the coalition asunder. While that may be true as far as it goes, it evades the point that there was no necessity to go to Baghdad, only a necessity to impose the conditions of the victor. You may remember that we feted these leaders, gave them ticker tape parades in Manhattan, and gave them accolades before Congress for their apparent victory over a third-world army. We should have been giving them a Bronx cheer, because they blew it, badly.

They blew it by not getting the weapons of mass destruction when they could have done so. They blew it again when they allowed Saddam to use his helicopters to gun down the rebel uprisings they had called for in the Kurdish and Shia areas of Iraq. They blew it out of a lack of post-war planning and out of ignorance of the true state of Iraq and, in fairness out of deference to our coalition allies who feared a vacuum in the region. They knew then that Saddam had used gas on his own people and that he was a brutal dictator. Certainly they hoped—and maybe even believed—that his officers would carry out a coup d'état, but they were ready to accept his survival because they thought he was defeated and would not be a threat again.

But put that all aside. It seemed right to many at the time. Instead, suppose the United States had ratified the final Kyoto agreement, which is very close to the original American proposals. Suppose the United States had signed onto the International Criminal Court or at least refrained from campaigning against it. Suppose we had signed onto the landmine treaty and the small arms treaty, not gutted the chemical weapons treaty, and supported the antigenocide agreements and the agreement on the status of women. Suppose the United States had been leading efforts to redefine and restructure NATO and its relationship to the EU along with the other outdated Cold War institutions, including the UN. Suppose that instead of saying, "Freedom itself has been attacked by a faceless coward" or, "They hate our values and our freedoms," we had had said something like "We have been attacked by religious fanatics who misunderstand our values and policies and who have hijacked Islam, just as Christianity was hijacked by the Crusaders, in an attempt to right imagined wrongs that have much to do with the difficulties of their own societies in modernizing, difficulties we are committed to helping them overcome." Suppose that instead of calling Ariel Sharon "a man of peace"—something no one in Israel, let alone the Arab nations, would call him—we had committed ourselves to action on the Abdullah peace plan. Suppose that, instead of saying "you're with us or against us," in the wake of September 11, the president had taken advantage of the great outpouring of sympathy for America and flown to Paris, Berlin, Moscow, Beijing, Cairo, Teheran, Seoul, Tokyo, and Islamabad and said, "Thank you."

Suppose he had called together the leaders of the world for a special conference to seek input and advice on how to deal with the terrorists and the sources of terrorism. Suppose the United States had not announced a new strategy of preemptive war with the objective of preventing the rise of any challenger to American hegemonic predominance.

In that context, suppose the United States had brought the matter of Iraq to the Security Council for a genuine debate instead of challenging the Council to make itself relevant. Would the international community have responded differently? Even if strong opposition remained, would there be more genuine support for the U.S. position? And in, ultimately, acting alone, would there have been less risk of doing so because it would have been seen as an exceptional act of unilateralism rather than the latest in a string of such acts? I believe our options now would be much better if we had been seen as a good international citizen rather than as a candidate for the rogue nation list.

What about the situation in Korea? Suppose instead of snubbing South Korean President Kim Dae-jung we had invited him to Washington and asked his advice on how to deal with the North. Suppose that instead of calling North Korea part of an "Axis of Evil," the president had maintained contact with North Korea's President Kim Jong-il, and assured him delivery of the promised electricity-generating equipment he so much needs. Suppose we had offered to negotiate a peace treaty to finally end the Korean War, and had offered diplomatic recognition to North Korea as we promised, and hadn't made such a big deal out of deploying a National Missile Defense to defend against "rogue nations like North Korea." Would we have a Korea crisis on our hands? Would the administration be in the ridiculous position of trying to explain why North Korea, which has nuclear weapons and long-range missiles and is gearing up to produce more of both, is less of a threat than Saddam. And again, would the North be so obviously frightened of us if we had not announced our preventive war strategy? I think the answer is no. We have contributed mightily to the development of the bad choices now confronting us.

* * *

At issue beyond the immediate crises is the very large question of what our national strategy should be, and behind that the even larger question of what kind of people and nation we really want to be. Let's begin with strategy. From the end of World War II until the end of the Cold War, the United States pursued two interlocking strategies—containment and economic globalization. The bargain America made with its allies was that they would get access to the huge American market and advanced American technology as well as American investment in return for embracing a system of geo-political partnership in which the United States was the senior but not always the dominant partner. As John Ikenberry has explained, "U.S. power didn't destabilize the world order because the United States bound itself to an understood and accepted system of common rules."[1] In other words, other countries identified their interests with U.S. interests because the United States "made its power safe." Writing in the *Atlantic* in October 2002, Benjamin Schwarz and Christopher Layne called this the "reassurance strategy."[2] What has generated the foreign sense of alienation, fear, and betrayal described in these pages is, first, a dramatic relative growth in U.S. power. The Oxford professor Timothy Garton Ash said it nicely when he wrote in the *New York Times*, "I love this country [the U.S.] . . . contrary to what many Europeans think, the problem with American power is not that it is American. The problem is simply the power. It would be dangerous even for an archangel to wield so much power . . . even democracy brings its own temptations when it exists in a hyperpower."[3] Garton Ash may be right, although the gap between the United States and the rest has not elicited his commentary in the past. It is noteworthy now, I believe, primarily because it has been accompanied by a fundamental shift in U.S. doctrine that increasingly makes American power "unsafe" in the eyes of the world.

The shift began at the end of the first Bush administration, when the study group under Cheney and headed by Wolfowitz first developed the draft paper (quickly leaked to the *New York Times*) that called for a strategy of preventing the rise of any challenging power.[4] Disavowed at the time as the unofficial musings of a few blue-sky thinkers, that doctrine has since become the official strategy of the United States as enunciated in the president's West Point speech, and in the National Security Strategy (NSS) document in September 2002. The United States no longer believes that containment works. The suicidal mentality of the adversary combined with the increasingly easy availability and transportability of weapons of mass destruction makes a no-first-strike strategy untenable. Thus, the new doctrine says, "We will not wait while dangers gather" or until the "mushroom cloud" rises. Instead we will strike preemptively and preventively wherever and whenever we sense unacceptable dangers gathering. This doctrine is presented in the guise and rhetoric of dealing with the instabilities caused by failed states and "rogue nations," and the NSS paper talks of cooperation among the major powers so as to allay their fears that it might also be aimed at them.[5]

But the second part of the doctrine undermines this reassuring tone by insisting that the United States will maintain such a power gap between itself and the rest that no country would even consider raising a challenge. This is the doctrine of absolute security through overwhelming military superiority. It is in many ways an apt doctrine for America. Only America has the human, institutional, natural, and technological resources to pull it off. It plays to the long-developed sense of American invulnerability as a birthright and to the habitual American trust in superior arms. It also reflects the sense Americans have of being exceptional and apart from the rest of humankind, a special, chosen people who can achieve immunity because they deserve immunity, and from whom the rest of the world need have no fear because Americans have been vouchsafed the "truth." And the truth has made them free and good. Thus the solipsistic Manichaeism so palpable in the president's rhetoric about "freedom's triumph over all its age-old foes."[6]

Make no mistake, this new doctrine is imperial, and it is heralded by a set of latter-day Rudyard Kiplings spawned by the *Wall Street Journal* and other right-wing publications that inaccurately label themselves "conservative" and call for America to "take up the white man's burden." A former *Wall Street Journal* editor, Max Boot, argues in *The Case for American*

Empire that the September 11 attacks were "the result of insufficient American involvement and ambition; the solution is to be more expansive in our goals and more assertive in our implementation."[7] Says Boot, "Afghanistan and other troubled lands today cry out for the sort of enlightened foreign administration once provided by self-confident Englishmen in jodhpurs and pith helmets."[8] The *Washington Post* columnist Sebastian Mallaby echoes this theme, saying that "the logic of neoimperialism is too compelling . . . to resist," and urges that orderly societies led by the United States "impose their own institutions on disorderly ones."[9] Not to be outdone, the *Atlantic Monthly* correspondent Robert Kaplan calls for bringing "prosperity to distant parts of the world under America's soft imperial influence."[10]

The argument is seductive on two counts. First, it is true that there are new asymmetric threats against which old deterrents may be inadequate. Second, to anyone living in a modern, secular, materialistic western ethos it seems obvious that American-administered order and economic development is preferable to chaos. Although its secularized proponents would deny it, this is the same thinking that McKinley invoked when, in deciding to add the Philippines to the American empire, he spoke of the need to "uplift them and Christianize them." Most neoimperialists would shrink from any association with "Christianizing," but substitute "Americanizing," and there isn't much difference.

The logic of the new doctrine is one of infinite expansion. In the era of globalization, the number of possible threats is very large, and the attempt to control one, such as Iraq, may only subject us to new dangers. We are already seeing this in Afghanistan. To counter the new threat it may thus be necessary to gain control over new territory or new entities. In the end, the only safety is in making every place an extension of yourself.

This would seem to be a daunting task. Traditional international relations theory holds that the rise of any imperial power will automatically generate counteralliances and cooperation among the other powers to offset the influence of the dominant power. As a result, the dominant power redoubles its efforts at countering the new alliance until eventually the empire becomes overstretched and collapses. But the neo-imperialists again believe America is exceptional—because it is a democracy and harbors no lust for territorial gain, and its imperium is attractive and userfriendly, one of soft, even seductive, power. There will be no counterbalancing activity because all will welcome the American way. Who would not want to be American if they could? Thus American women and men are to be sent to the far corners of the earth on a crusade to spread the American creed to a world hungering and thirsting for it.

It won't work. Let me count the reasons.

First, there is no such thing as absolute military security. Did our laser-guided bombs and nuclear missiles and satellite photos protect us from the September 11 hijackers' boxcutters and suicidal fanaticism? Are our sophisticated military capabilities cowing the North Koreans into submission? Is the proliferation of our overseas bases reducing our risks? The answer is no in every case, and the proliferation of bases may even be increasing our risks.

Second, even as nice as we Americans are, the rest of the world doesn't necessarily see us as we see ourselves, doesn't necessarily want to *be* like us even if it likes us, and is already moving to counterbalance our power. This movement can be seen most obviously in the maneuvering in the UN Security Council over Iraq, but it is also apparent in the EU's drive to achieve more equal status with the United States, in the renewed ties between Russia and China, and in many countries active efforts of to promote Linux over Microsoft's Windows as the main computer operating system. There is a fundamental human factor at work here that Americans find hard to understand but that, given our history, we should be the first to understand. Nations are very much like individuals. More than desire for material gain or fear or love, they are driven by a craving for dignity and respect, by the need to be recognized as valid and just as valuable as the next person or country. The Turkish novelist Orham Pamuk, when asked what leads an old man in Istanbul to condone the World Trade Tower attacks or a Pakistani youth to admire the Taliban, responded, "It is the feeling of impotence arising from degradation, the failure to be understood, and the inability of such people to make their voices heard."[11] Much as it may like and admire Americans (and, as I have said, it does), the rest of the world has its own traditions, ways, and values for which it wants respect.

Globalization does not change this fact. A Frenchman doesn't stop being French or turn his back on Descartes by eating a McDonald's hamburger, and a young Indonesian woman leaving a traditional village to work in a Nike shoe factory and live in its dormitory may cling the more tenaciously to, or even return to wearing, the Muslim head scarf as a way of holding onto her values in a strange world. We can't stamp this out, and we shouldn't try.

Third, an American crusade won't work because it will increasingly involve us in the kinds of alliances of convenience and ruthless actions that only complicate our lives in the long run even as they corrupt our own character and institutions.

Fourth, economic globalization and American profligacy have already undermined our economic sovereignty and made us more dependent than we know on those we would dominate. The charge of wanting to invade Iraq in order to control its oil, which sounds false to many American ears, has such credence abroad precisely because much of the world knows of American economic vulnerabilities and sees American military threats as intended to keep capital flowing to the American safe haven and to control the prices of vital resources so as to maintain "Bubba's" way of life. The U.S. economy is currently on an unsustainable track. Its growth is driven overwhelmingly by consumption that is based on ever-rising borrowing. As a nation, we consume increasingly more than we produce, and we are able to do so only by borrowing from abroad. Because of our status as the provider of the world's security and its major reserve currency, our dollar is strong, enabling us to enjoy a standard of living above what we actually earn. But the euro is beginning to provide an alternative reserve currency, and our international borrowing needs are rising to levels that increasingly make lenders nervous. How are we going to be the world's Caesar when we are shaking a tin cup, unless, of course, we just take what we need?

But that's the final reason why the American crusade won't work. Americans are not Romans or even Brits. America may do stupid and even bad things from time to time. But the American people don't regard body bags as symbols of their glorious valor, nor do they hanker to send their second sons or daughters into the colonial service. Having begun life in rebellion against empire, we never became really comfortable with the habit of empire and simply are not good imperialists. For one thing, we are too eager for people to like us.

What then is to be done? It's simple really, and something George W. Bush should be able to embrace in a heartbeat. In fact, Bush had it right the first time when he said during the campaign, "If we are a humble nation, they'll see that and respect it."[12] What we need is a return to real conservatism. The imperial project of the so-called neoconservatives is not conservatism at all but radicalism, egotism, and adventurism articulated in the stirring rhetoric of traditional patriotism. Real conservatives have never been messianic or doctrinaire. The very essence of conservatism, which the neoconservatives constantly preach, is limited government. Yet the imperial project they are proposing will greatly increase the role of government both at home and abroad. Already we have dramatically increased federal spending while beefing up our already overwhelming military machine and making the Department of Homeland Security the biggest domestic bureaucracy we have ever had. This is not conservatism. It is Big Government. Traditional conservatives have always been careful to balance the budget and to insist on each citizen's responsibility to perform civic duties. But the new imperialists are calling for tax cuts even as they raise spending. There is to be no draft and no sacrifice, and the president's only nod to civic duty came when he urged everyone to go shopping to help the economy.

This is neither conservatism nor liberalism but simple irresponsibility. Recall the words of the great conservative philosopher Edmund Burke, who said of Britain's power in an earlier era, "I dread our being too much dreaded." Power is a magnet for threats, and the reaction to them can spur radical projects. Governor Winthrop saw a "citty on a hill" as being attractive by dint of its virtue, not its power. And John Quincy Adams enjoined that we "not go abroad in search of monsters to slay." Those are all good conservative guides to consult on America's future strategy.

People often say that criticism of the United States is not to be taken too seriously, because it is normal for number one to be the butt of envy and complaint just as Rome and Britain were in their time. But this nonchalant injunction raises a serious question. Do we want to be like Rome or Britain? We say frequently that America must be the leader and that America is the "indispensable nation." But a Mexican friend asks, "Why? Why must America be in charge of everything? Who appointed you?" Of course, there is a long history behind all this, but his comment reminds us that there is an alternative strategy that would not call for abandoning America's commitments and responsibilities. The United States cannot and should not try to withdraw from deep engagement in global affairs. Let's remember that despite all its mistakes, the United States, according to the Pew polling data, is still considered a relatively safe hegemon. But it would be desirable, from all points of view, for the United States to be the call of last resort, rather than the call of first resort. Here are some thoughts on what such a strategy might entail.

At this point there is little choice but for the United States and whatever partners it can gather to overthrow Saddam and occupy Iraq. The cost of not doing so is now greater than that of doing so. But we should do all in our power to avoid a long American occupation. We could avoid becoming the occupier and help to heal recent wounds by reestablishing the significance of the UN and asking it to form a consortium of countries like Malaysia, Jordan, Switzerland, Canada, and others to oversee creation of a new Iraq. The U.S. would be a major participant and would pay a large part of the bill, but it would not be alone or in charge.

The future of the UN itself must also be addressed. Although flawed, the UN exists because, as Winston Churchill said of democracy, "it is the worst system except for all the rest." Rather than scrap it, we must revitalize and redesign it. India, Brazil, and perhaps Japan and Saudi Arabia should be added as permanent members of the Security Council. At the same time, Britain and France should be replaced by a single EU representative. At some time, conditions must be established for selection of rotating Security Council members, and the extent of veto power reviewed. It may seem utopian at the moment, but in the long run, a viable UN will make America more, rather than less, powerful.

Any action in Iraq should be coupled with a renewed effort at resolving the Israeli-Palestinian impasse. This should include making aid to Israel conditional on withdrawal from the West Bank and Gaza, a freeze on all settlement development, and closing of all settlements except those tentatively agreed on at Camp David and Taba. The outlines of the Taba nonagreement could be imposed with deployment of NATO troops on the West Bank and in Gaza to police it. In no way should any deal be conditioned on an end to all violence, a condition that simply gives veto power to the extremists on both sides.

With regard to North Korea, we should negotiate a new deal that both guarantees the security of the country from outside attack and assures it sufficient electricity and food; sign a peace treaty to conclude the Korean War and accord the North formal diplomatic recognition; and support South Korea's efforts at developing trade and investment with the North and at economic development. Internal economic development is far more likely to change the Kim regime than external threats. Of course, in return for all this North Korea must halt its nuclear weapons projects and make them subject to ongoing UN inspection and verification.

The term "adult supervision" has been used to describe America's relationship with Europe and Japan. Other observers, like Kagan, argue that these countries are living in an artificial paradise that enables them to indulge in empty posturing and selfish cosseting because they leave to America the burdens of dealing with the real world. There is truth in this, and the argument is used to denigrate the Europeans and Japanese as ungrateful and unwilling to do the things necessary to take care of themselves. What goes unsaid, as I have suggested, is that the United States prefers to keep them in a state of extended adolescence as a condition of its own dominance. Unfortunately, we buy this dominance at an increasing cost. Like adolescents, the other developed nations resent our supervision and become more and more rebellious. At the same time, the costs to us of protecting their oil lanes and their neighborhoods are high and growing.

So why not let them grow up into real adults or, as Ozawa would say, "normal countries"? Rather than object to an independent European Defense Force, why not welcome it and foster its development? We should relax restrictions on military technology flows to and from Europe, open Pentagon procurement to real European and Japanese participation, and encourage transnational consolidation of defense industries. The EU, of course, would have to agree to take complete responsibility for policing its own neighborhood in the case of future Kosovos or Bosnias. At the same time, we should consider revamping NATO to address more global issues. Why not let NATO patrol the oil routes and the Gulf? We would be part of it but not the only part. We could even lease a few carrier task forces to the Europeans. Beyond that, we could foster a truly common EU foreign and defense policy by declaring that we will deal only with the EU authorities on European defense and policy issues. This would end France's nostalgic pretensions to great power status, and a single EU authority would likely be more congenial to overall U.S. interests. At the same time, the EU would have to take on the responsibilities as well as the priveleges of the real power it so badly wishes to become.

In the Far East, once the North Korean situation is under control, the United States should reduce its troop deployments to a token force if the Koreans want them or remove them completely if they do not. The South Korean army should be placed under Korean command at all times, and SOFA agreements altered to assure that the Korean legal system is fully respected. The same is true in Japan. As for the National Missile Defense, it has already been shown not to prevent rogue states like North Korea from causing trouble. At the same time it does incite China to increase its military capacity, something not at all in our interest. So we should just stop deployment and save ourselves a lot of money. As with Europe, the United States should insist that Japan grow up and become a normal, adult country. This means first of all ending the Cold War by revising the U.S.-Japan security treaty such that it ends the fantasyland environment created by unilateral U.S. guarantees of Japan's security. A new arrangement should be mutual in terms both of responsibilities and decision-making power. Japan should be encouraged to end World War II by creating a formal commission to make a definitive statement on Japan's view of the causes, responsibilities for, and consequences of the war. This statement could be the basis for all textbooks and other commentary, and could also resolve contentions over visists to Yasukuni shrine. Moreover, Japan should be encouraged to do likewise and to make full apologies where apologies are due and generous restitution where restitution is due, such as for instance to the surviving "comfort women" (Korean and other women who were forced to serve as prostitutes to Japanese troops during the war).

Japan's constitution was written by Americans. It is unnatural and leads to dishonest distortions of Japan's political life domestically and internationally. The United States should encourage Japan to rethink it. As in Korea, U.S. troop levels should be drastically reduced. We should truly give Okinawa back to Japan. As for patrolling the western Pacific, the United States could propose a regional task force incorporating elements from the major countries in the area, including China.

The United States should make clear that it opposes any declaration of independence by Taiwan and would not defend Taiwan in the event of such a declaration. It should also make clear to mainland China that it would intervene in the event of an attack on Taiwan short of a Taiwanese declaration of independence, but at the same time it should refrain from further arms sales to and joint military activity with Taiwan. We should encourage further Taiwan-Beijing discussions aimed at achieving an internal modus vivendi. In our other dealings with China, we should take every opportunity to accord China the recognition and respect it craves.

For example, Russia is included in what was the G–7, and is now the G–8, group of the world's leading economic powers, whose leaders conduct periodic summit meetings to devise global economic strategies. China's economy is far larger than Russia's and its international currency reserves dwarf the Russian reserves. Why not include China? In fact, who not include China and India and make it a G–10?

The United States should immediately sign onto the Kyoto treaty, the landmine treaty, and the International Criminal Court. It should also review carefully its position on the other treaties discussed above and make a serious effort to sign if at all possible. We should also pay our dues to all international bodies of which we are members such as the UN. This should be coupled with a serious effort at reducing greenhouse gas emissions and reducing energy use. There is no reason why America can't adopt many of the measures already working in other industrialized countries. The Bush administration's proposed increase of more than a billion dollars in funding for hydrogen energy research is a step in the right direction. But if we can offer $30 billion for base rights in Turkey, it would seem logical to think in terms of similar sums to ensure that we don't have to depend on the energy suppliers who make these wars necessary. A Manhattan project for alternative energy is long overdue.

In view of the fact that we already spend more on defense than the next fifteen countries combined, it is likely that the very existence of this concentration of power adds to pressures for others to increase military spending. As we gradually shift burdens to others, so should we plan for a gradual reduction in defense spending. Japan has for years been trying to raise its spending at our behest to a target of 1 percent of GDP. Perhaps we could set a target of 2 to 2.5 percent of GDP toward which to descend over time. The savings could be transferred to aid, disease control, and support of other international efforts, moving us back toward the balances of 1948.

The procedure of American foreign policy badly needs to be reviewed. It is terribly damaging when one or two powerful congressional chairpersons can dictate U.S. policy, despite a lack of significant public support. Even more importantly, the question of who decides when America goes to war desperately needs to be clarified. Congress seems to be less and less involved. But America was not meant to be run by a Caesar. Doing all this would greatly reduce U.S. exposure and costs while improving our relations with many key areas of the world. It would allow us to turn our attention to the two crises, currently invisible over the horizon, that need to be dealt with now; if not, they will make the violence of the twentieth century look like kindergarten.

The first is globalization. Despite the hoopla about its wonders, it is clear that the "golden straitjacket" is not working, or at least not as the textbooks say it should. Countries like Mexico that are doing all the supposedly right things are falling behind. A conservative government should be against subsidies, and we need to stop subsidizing American cotton farmers so they can drive West African farmers out of business. The impact of China on other developing countries needs to be carefully analyzed, and appropriate polices devised to assure that countries like Mexico and Indonesia aren't the victims of China's development. It is clear that simply opening markets and waiting for free trade to solve problems frequently doesn't work. We need to give serious attention to the infrastructure and human capital and adjustment needs of the major developing areas. If economic development doesn't work, all the laser bombs and missile defenses in the world won't protect us, particularly because, while globalization may not automatically lead to development, it does let everybody see how others are living.

Even while we struggle to make globalization work, however, we need urgently to address more basic issues. In his recent State of the Union message, President Bush surprised everyone by announcing a $15 billion program to fight AIDS in Africa. It is a step in the right direction, but only a step. The devastation of AIDS in Africa has gotten some attention as infection rates have reached more than 40 percent in some countries, and the death count in sub-Saharan Africa has reached more than 2 million annually.[13] But even more ominous news has gotten little attention. Does anyone know that nearly everyone in West Africa has some form of malaria?[14] Or that tuberculosis is epidemic in much of the world, infecting more people than those who are suffering from AIDS?

What about issues like water, deforestation, desertification, soil depletion, and overpopulation? Is anyone at the National Security Council contemplating the possibility of war over water between our allies Turkey and Israel? Turkey's Ataturk Dam will soon control the flow of much of the water supply from its mountains to the countries to the south. According to the site manager, the flow of water to Syria and Iraq can be stopped for up to eight months.[15] Who is keeping track of the fact that by 2025 a third of the world's population will face water scarcity? Look at Pakistan, already one of the most dangerous countries on earth, with a congeries of ethnic groups increasingly influenced by Taliban-like elements and in possession of nuclear bombs and the ballistic missiles to deliver them. Nearly two-thirds of its land is dependent on intensive irrigation that is increasingly difficult to maintain because of extensive deforestation and rapid population growth. The country is heavily dependent on the Indus River, but so is India, which suffers from exactly the same problems on a larger scale. Already at the nuclear ready over Kashmir, what will these two countries do when the water runs out?

Deforestation has reduced Sierra Leone's primary rain forest from 60 percent of the country to 6 percent, while in China deforestation has led to increased flooding, topsoil erosion, and exhaustion of wells. As a result, arable land per capita has declined rapidly. Large-scale population movement is already a major problem in China, as people try to escape from the interior to the booming coastal areas.[16] Is anyone in Washington thinking about how to help China with this problem? The answer is made dramatically clear in our budget, which mandates an increase of more than $50 billion for the Pentagon while aid and development programs continue to languish at $16.8 billion.[17]

I know it's an alien concept for Americans, but sometimes smaller really is better and less really is more. A strategy of making our power safe for others, even of diminishing our relative power, of granting others the dignity of being treated like adults and of cooperating and sharing responsibility, will pay off in many ways. It will lower our profile and make us one among many targets rather than the only target. It will force others to understand our perspective by shouldering responsibilities more like ours. It will reduce envy and resentment by granting others greater equality. It will be much less costly because we won't have to control and pay for everything. It will mean sharing some power, but the Declaration of Independence was about liberty and the pursuit of happiness, not the pursuit of power, and the Constitution was about controlling and limiting power. America was not designed to be an empire.

If we are to adopt this unprecedented strategy of diminishing our geopolitical power, we must address one last thing—the creed. We are a well-intentioned people who have been blessed by fortune. We have an admirable democracy, but it is not the only possible democracy and not always the best possible democracy. We have a very successful economy, but so do others, and ours is not in all ways the best. We have a good system of justice with much to admire, but so do others, and ours is not always the best.

It has been a long journey of reading and experience that has brought me to this point. I always wanted to believe that America was purest and best in everything. So I can imagine that you, the reader, may be struggling with some of this. But the only way for America to be what I think is her ultimate, true self is to know and acknowledge the truth. And the truth will make her free and what she ought to be. In other words, we need to rethink American exceptionalism. Part of the shock of September 11 was the shattering of the myth that bad things happen only to other people. It was the shock of joining the world. It doesn't mean that we should be fatalistic, but in an age of globalization we need to recognize that others' problems are our problems too and that we don't have all the answers. Particularly, I would like to remind my fellow Christians of the words of Oliver Cromwell, who enjoined in a letter to the Church of Scotland: "in the bowels of Christ, please believe that you may be wrong."[18] As an elder of the Presbyterian Church, I want to emphasize that Christ was not about nations and power, and did not spread his gospel by force. When asked about taxes, he said, "render unto Caesar what is Caesar's and unto God what is God's." Christ saved the souls of individuals, one by one. The salvation of the churches of America has been the separation of Church and state. In view of the demise of the churches of Europe in the bear hug of the state, we Christians should avoid, rather than embrace, closer connections between Church and state here in America. Politicians who use God as a prop for their campaigns should remember that "God is not mocked." An America that stressed its tolerance rather than its might, its tradition of open inquiry rather than its way of life, and that asked for God's blessing on all the world's people and not just its own, would be the America the world desperately wants. It would be something else too. I'll never forget my first glimpse of the Italian town of Assisi, home of St. Francis. As I turned a curve in the road just before sunset, there it was, white and shimmering on the hill.

Epilogue

Shortly after I submitted the last chapter of this book to my publisher, at the end of February 2003, what I had anticipated came to pass. Following Secretary of State Colin Powell's February 6 presentation to the UN on Iraq's weapons of mass destruction programs, the Bush administration, with the support of Great Britain, pressed hard for a second Security Council resolution supporting an ultimatum to Iraqi President Saddam Hussein, demanding that he cease all nuclear, chemical, and biological weapons programs and open the country to UN inspection, and promising armed intervention if he remained defiant. France, with the support of Germany, Russia, and China, campaigned against an immediate ultimatum in favor of more time for the UN inspectors to search for illegal weapons. In the face of enormous pressure from the United States, French President Jacques Chirac eventually shortened his request for additional time to just one more month. But Washington remained adamant in pushing for a quick ultimatum.

For a couple of weeks the world was treated to the scene of the United States and France bidding against each other for votes in the Security Council from the likes of Angola and Pakistan. Support for the American position was surprisingly weak. This was dramatically demonstrated on March 3 when Turkey, long one of America's staunchest allies, declared that it would not allow U.S. forces to use Turkish territory for staging an invasion of Iraq. Other long-time friends such as Mexico and Canada expressed support for the French view. In response to the opposition of France and Germany, eight European prime ministers, including those of Italy, Spain, Poland, and Great Britain, signed a letter of support for the

U.S. position written and circulated to them by a *Wall Street Journal* editor. Nevertheless, when the vote in the Security Council finally came, the United States could not even garner a majority, let alone the two-thirds that it needed for passage.

Undaunted, President George W. Bush declared it "a moment of truth" for the UN, and then at a snap summit in the Azores with the Prime Ministers of Britain, Spain, and Portugal on March 17, he announced that "diplomatic efforts to disarm Saddam Hussein will end today." The following day he accused the Security Council of failing its responsibilities and issued a 48-hour ultimatum for Saddam to leave Iraq or face war "at a time of our choosing." Shortly afterward, Secretary Powell listed thirty members of the U.S.-led "coalition" but had to admit that one of the most visible, Spain, was not sending any troops. Then, on the evening of 19 March 2003, all the maneuvering became moot as the high-pitched wail of air-raid sirens blared over Baghdad. Shortly afterward at 10:16 P.M., President Bush walked before cameras in the Oval Office and announced to the world that U.S.-led military operations to disarm Iraq had begun. He warned that the war "might task the nation" and emphasized that fighting could take longer and be more difficult than some were predicting. Little noted but of later significance was the fact that hostilities had started not as part of the Pentagon's war plan but as an opportunistic strike at a gathering of Iraqi leaders thought to include Saddam Hussein. Early reports indicated that he had been killed or severely wounded, but this turned out not to be true.

In fact this was only the first of many miscalculations and surprises. The second was the speed with which the U.S.-led "Coalition of the Willing" brushed aside the Iraqi army. Contrary to the President's warning, the fighting was over more quickly and with less difficulty than anyone had predicted. The Iraqi army seemed to vaporize in the face of the Coalition forces, and the much-feared chemical and other weapons of mass destruction never came into play. By April 10, U.S. forces were in full control of Baghdad. Saddam's statue was toppled from its plinth amid cheering by jubilant Iraqis who kissed American soldiers and beat on Saddam's image with their shoes.

To the neoconservatives and others, it seemed that events were unfolding just as they had predicted. On May 1, the President announced that major combat was finished, and Prime Minister Blair warned those expressing doubts about finding banned weapons that they would "be eating some of their words." But then came the third and fourth surprises. As it turned out, things were not going at all as expected. The Iraqi cheering and kissing of U.S. soldiers was quickly followed by widespread looting of everything that was not bolted down, from nuclear waste to ancient art treasures. Even worse was the near-total collapse of Iraqi civil administration. The Bush administration had assumed it could knock out Saddam and the teachers, firemen, police, doctors, sanitation workers, and all the other key elements of a modern society would continue to operate more or less normally. They didn't. Going into the height of the sweltering Iraqi summer, there was no water, no electricity, no gasoline (in a country floating on oil)—and no one in charge. To add to the chaos, one of the first moves of the new ruling Coalition Authority was to disband the Iraqi army, thereby putting thousands of newly unemployed young men with weapons on the streets. Then the other shoe dropped. Using guerilla tactics, rocket-propelled grenades, and car bombs, irregular Iraqi forces launched a vicious war of attrition on Coalition forces, belying the President's claims about the end of combat, and killing or maiming on average seventy-five victims a week in a campaign that, at this writing, still continues. Even more confounding was the failure, despite the most intensive search efforts, to find the much-feared WMD whose putative threat had served as the main rationale of the war. How many times had the President, Vice President Cheney, and Prime Minister Blair warned against allowing the world's worst leaders to have the world's worst weapons? By fall, however, it was clear to almost everyone that Saddam had in fact not had such weapons. All doubts about this were laid to rest in late January when chief U.S. weapons inspector David Kay reported not only that he could find no weapons but also that Saddam had not had WMD for the past seven years. His programs were, in fact, in chaos, and he himself had been living in a fantasyland with top aides helping to maintain his illusions. Kay emphasized that U.S. intelligence had been inadequate and downright wrong.

The truth is that nothing went as the neoconservatives had predicted. On top of bad intelligence, their ideological and romantic assumptions led them to eschew the normal Pentagon and State Department planning for the postwar period. Indeed, it subsequently became clear that they had bypassed the normal channels from the beginning by establishing a special unit under Deputy Defense Secretary Paul Wolfowitz (and tied closely to the office of Vice President Cheney) that provided the White House with its own version of intelligence.

Unlike many critics of the administration's foreign policies, I did not oppose the invasion of Iraq. I had long felt that not going to Baghdad in 1992 was an historic mistake. Saddam was clearly one of history's great monsters, and his downfall would be no bad thing. Under the circumstances in spring 2003—a major buildup of forces in the Persian Gulf and a Security Council resolution calling for a full accounting of Iraq's weapons programs—the invasion seemed to me a lesser evil than pulling back and allowing Saddam to present himself as a victor over the United States and the UN.

Beyond this, however, I had a broader concern about America's role in the world and how the circumstances of the proposed invasion of Iraq would affect it. While it seemed to me desirable to get rid of Saddam, it seemed more desirable to do so in the company of allies and with the backing of the UN because that would share the burdens and risks while maintaining the moral high ground for the United States. Had I been President, I would have told the Security Council to tell me how long it wanted to inspect for weapons and that I would agree to whatever time period it desired, on the condition that the Council commit now to backing military action if its demands had not been met by the end of the designated period. But I was not President. So I accepted the invasion as the lesser of evils and hoped for the best. In particular, I hoped that once in control of Iraq, the United States would turn to NATO and the UN to police the territory and to direct its reconstruction. Of course, none of this happened, and we must now ask ourselves whether we are better or worse off as a result of our unilateral actions and whether unilateralism should continue to be our guiding star.

To answer that question, it is important to understand the real purposes of invading Iraq. It was not really about WMD. As Wolfowitz later admitted, WMD was only used as the excuse because that was the only issue on which the bureaucracies in Washington could agree and on which there was also some degree of allied agreement. The real objectives were much broader, even revolutionary. The first was simply to demonstrate American power and the willingness to use it. It had become an axiom of the neoconservatives that bad things were happening in the world because America was perceived as a paper tiger unwilling or unable to respond to attacks on its embassies, civil aircraft, and other exposed targets. Demonstrating that this was not true and that America had to be respected, it was believed, would chill hostile activity all by itself. Such a demonstration needed a target, and Saddam was perfect. Here was a leader everyone hated who was also in at least technical violation of several UN resolutions. Although he talked and acted tough, he was actually much weaker than he had been during the Gulf War of 1991–92. For ten years he had been under UN economic sanctions and had been subjected to no-fly zones in his own country and continuous U.S. and British aerial surveillance. Militarily he was easy pickings.

Knocking him out would have secondary advantages as well. It would result in the destruction of any WMD he might have and prevent him from passing them to others. America's bases in Saudi Arabia were increasingly a source of anti-American sentiment in this key oil-producing ally. By invading Iraq and installing a friendly government, the U.S. military could withdraw from Saudi Arabia and acquire new, more secure bases in Iraq, the country with the world's second largest oil reserves. It was also believed that knocking out Saddam would reduce support for Palestinian terrorism against Israel and thereby lead to a peaceful Israeli-Palestinian settlement while also removing any threat of the use of WMD against Israel. Finally, it was believed that establishment of a secular, democratic regime in Iraq would catalyze reform and movement toward democracy throughout the Arab world, thereby greatly reducing the threat posed by extremist Arabs. Best of all, the cost would be low because the Iraqis would cheer us on for removing the hated dictator, and such costs that might arise could be covered by the Iraqis themselves through the sale of their oil. In the wake of all these beneficial results, the UN and the rest of the world would ultimately come to embrace the U.S. policy. What could be easier and better?

There is more than a little to be said for the plus side of the ledger. Few lament the passing of Saddam, his sadistic sons, and the other fillers of mass graves. The removal of U.S. forces from Saudi Arabia to other bases in the region has taken place and is certainly a major plus for the Saudis as well as for us. Whether the demonstration of American power had anything to do with Iran's recent agreement with the EU to allow inspection of its nuclear facilities is difficult to say, but it certainly didn't stop the deal. The same could be said for Libya's agreement to give up its nuclear arms development programs. Moreover, the widely feared explosion on the "Arab Street" hasn't happened, and Saudi Arabia, Syria, and others appear to have become more cooperative in fighting Al Qaeda. The Saudis appear to be trying to effect some liberalizing reforms domestically as well. Pakistan, under the leadership of President Musharraf, has begun to back away from its role as general supplier of nuclear and missile technology to the developing world and is warming up toward long-time jousting partner India while attempting to gain control of Islamic extremists within its own government. Despite near-disastrous U.S. planning for the postwar situation, Iraq is slowly being reconstructed, and the Shia and Kurdish elements that form the overwhelming majority of Iraqis have been cooperating with the U.S. forces so far to create a new Iraqi regime. The Russians and French recently forgave old Iraqi debt at U.S. behest, and the Germans, Mexicans, and Canadians have been striving to get back into America's good graces despite, or perhaps because of, having been put in the U.S. icebox.

Alas, the ledger also has a debit side. By engaging in preventive war and adopting a formal and unilateral prevent-and-preempt security doctrine, the United States has given up the moral high ground, belied its own myth of exceptionalism, and made itself just another in a long line of hegemonic powers stretching back to ancient Egypt and Rome. It has also betrayed the trust of its own people, a corrosive act for any country calling itself a democracy. Does anyone believe the Congress and the American people would have supported the invasion if the President had told them there was no immediate threat from WMD but Saddam was a bad guy and anyhow we had to commit to about 5,000 dead and wounded American kids so we could demonstrate American power and catalyze democracy in the Middle East? The absence of WMD and the subsequent discovery that intelligence, if not manipulated, was certainly used selectively—and in some cases inaccurately—to make the case for immediate war has also created distrust abroad and been a boon for conspiracy theorists of all stripes. No one in the Middle East or South Asia, and few in other parts of the world, believes the CIA was unaware that there were no WMD. Everyone assumes that the Americans and their self-proclaimed gee-whiz technology can see and hear pretty much everything. Surely, it is assumed, they would know about the status of WMD.

So if there are no WMD, the conclusion of the vast majority of people around the world is that the war was really about America getting control of Iraq's oil. A more sophisticated group concludes that the war was about establishing clear American hegemony and preempting potential challenges from any other power or group of powers. The situation varies in different parts of the world, but the alienation from America that I felt so strongly while traveling in 2000/2001 and that led me to write this book, has only gotten worse. This is a disturbing development for anyone who continues to believe that America needs friends.

In more immediate terms, the United States finds itself committed to a much larger pacification and rebuilding effort in Iraq than it ever imagined. The unanticipated guerilla and terrorist war is taking a steady toll on U.S. soldiers and key Iraqi officials alike. So far, the American casualty count is over 10,000—and still climbing. With a majority of its battalions engaged, the U.S. Army is stretched tighter than a drum. Tours are being extended and reservists are increasingly being called up. The ability of the United States to engage in any other conflict that might arise is very much in question. The costs both of continuing military activity and of reconstruction are mounting rapidly. Already the United States has poured more than $150 billion into the Iraqi effort, and that may prove to be only the down payment. Iraqi oil production, which won't be increased for some time, is unlikely to pay much of the bill. As for contributions from our coalition partners and other countries, they've been a drop in the bucket. Aside from the British, the coalition is more of a label than an actuality. For example, the Spanish and Japanese governments have been accorded lavish praise by the Bush administration for their support. Yet the Spanish sent no troops, and the Japanese are finally getting 600 non-combatant soldiers into the field ten months after Bush declared an end to major combat. It is the United States, not the coalition governments, that is paying for most of the coalition troops in the field.

While the fall of Saddam is surely a good thing, the war in Iraq has distracted attention from Afghanistan and the hunt for Osama bin Laden. The only thing presently driving the Afghan economy is the resurgence of poppy cultivation that ultimately sends tons of opium base to the heroin factories of western Europe and the United States, under the direction of the warlords with whom the U.S. forces allied to topple the Taliban. The warlords have hardly been more respectful of women's or human rights than the Taliban and now appear in some cases actually to be allying with a resurgent Taliban to limit the writ of the nominal Afghan government more or less to Kabul. Meanwhile Osama and Al Qaeda have been regrouping just across the border in Pakistan, which is both an important ally of the United States and arguably the most dangerous country in the world. Although President Musharraf has put his country firmly in the U.S. camp for the time being, his control is tenuous. The Western Frontier area where Osama is hiding is for all practical purposes ungoverned by the central government. On top of that, a free election would surely bring to power extremist Islamists allied to Osama, and the internal security and intelligence services are heavily penetrated by Osama sympathizers. In December 2003, Musharraf narrowly escaped two assassination attempts. So the good news is that Musharraf's Pakistan is an ally trying its best to get extremists under control. The bad news is that Osama could very possibly gain control of Pakistan with its operational nuclear weapons and long-range ballistic missiles, and for the moment at least, we appear to be unable or unwilling to make the kind of push on Osama that we made on Saddam.

Just to make the picture more interesting, Saudi Arabia is another candidate for takeover by Osama. The reason for getting the American troops out was that their presence on the soil of Islam's most sacred country was generating increasing support of Al Qaeda and its program to overthrow the royal family. Saudi Arabia today is a country in ferment with the royal family's leaders aging and divided, and the powerful Wahabi Islamic sect increasingly in Osama's camp. Nothing can be ruled out here. Meanwhile, Al Qaeda appears still able to mount major terrorist actions anywhere in the world.

The absence of WMD has forced the Bush administration to find new rationales to justify its massive commitment to Iraq. At first it was argued that getting rid of Saddam was reason enough. But in the end the President has reverted to the democratization of the Middle East, beginning in Iraq but spreading from there to the rest of the Islamic world. Announcing his new rationale in stirring rhetoric, the President said that sixty years of accepting authoritarianism in the Middle East has not made us safer. Now the question is not only whether democratization can be achieved but whether, if it were achieved, it would actually make us safer. As to the first, the Shias constitute a majority of Iraqis. So far they have been cooperative with U.S. authorities, but they are insisting on direct elections of Iraqi bodies charged with creating a new regime. They will surely insist on direct elections of an ultimate government for the obvious reason that they will win. But this is just what the U.S. authorities cannot accept, because a Shia-dominated government would very likely be a cleric-dominated government. The Kurds have already indicated they want autonomy such that they would constitute a de facto state, and while they may moderate their demands a bit under U.S. pressure, it is hard to imagine them easily giving up the effective independence they enjoyed over the past ten years under the protection of the U.S. no-fly zone and sanctions against Saddam. So getting from here to there looks difficult.

The second question poses even greater difficulties. As noted above, a free election in Pakistan would almost surely return to power an anti-American government equipped with real WMD. While Saudi Arabia doesn't have WMD, a free election there would probably also yield a virulently anti-American and anti-Israeli regime. Egypt could well be in the same category. Moreover, in support of the war on terror, the United States has concluded alliances and established bases in a series of Central Asian countries, like Uzbekistan, that have some of the most despotic governments around. So when National Security Adviser Condoleezza Rice says it is condescending to think Muslim countries can't do democracy, she is no doubt correct, but one must wonder whether she really wants to be. The Bush administration has enunciated a major foreign policy objective it can't possibly desire to achieve. That everyone knows this except an American public kept in denial by high-flown rhetoric leaves the world cynical about U.S. motives.

This cynicism is only exacerbated by the U.S. approach to North Korea. Here is a country that clearly does have nuclear weapons and long-range ballistic missiles, and yet the United States has not called for preventive war—the reason, of course, being that any such war would devastate South Korea, whose capital of 20 million people lies within easy artillery range of the North. At the same time, however, by rejecting South Korea's "Sunshine Strategy" and taking a hard line of refusing talks with the North while calling for regime change, the administration has put itself in a very uncomfortable box from which it hopes the Chinese and maybe the Russians will extract it. As North Korea moves forward with the weaponization of its plutonium stockpile, Washington is relying on China to convene meetings with North Korea that include China, Russia, the United States, and Japan at which U.S. officials can talk to North Korean officials without admitting that they are doing an about-face from earlier refusals to talk to the North until it dismantled its nuclear program. That the Bush administration has in this instance been forced to embrace multilateralism only increases bitterness among those already wounded by U.S. unilateralism.

It is in this context that we need to look at some fundamental shifts in the structure of the global system. The most profound is the U.S. relationship with Europe, perhaps best symbolized by the President's state visit to London in November 2003. This trip to meet with our closest ally in the wake of victory in Iraq should have been an occasion for warm celebration. Instead it became an ordeal. Fear of anti-American demonstrations led to cancellation of the usual horse and carriage ride with the Queen to Buckingham Palace through the streets of London. Nor did the President who wants to democratize the Middle East address the Mother of Parliaments for fear of heckling. There were no press conferences.

This cold reception by our closest ally reflects the impact of the new American strategy toward Europe. The U.S.-European relationship has been the foundation of the global order since the end of World War II. The democratic, free-market principles shared by America and Europe are what defined and underpinned the free world and created the major international institutions. Most important, it was the U.S.-European alliance that won the Cold War. Throughout that period the United States promoted and encouraged the development of a more united Europe. The tone was set by President Kennedy at Independence Hall on July 4, 1962, when he said, "We don't regard a strong, united Europe as a rival, but as a partner." To prove it, he called for a united and independent European military force as well as for a "Declaration of Interdependence" between a united Europe and the United States. Today, the neoconservative disdain of Europe and the drive to invade Iraq at all cost have reversed that position. Washington now views a united Europe, and especially one with a military force independent of NATO, as a potential rival and has adopted a policy of divide and keep under hegemony.

Of course, the United States and Europe are not going to go to war, but neither will America be able to count on the old sense of shared values and objectives. The best evidence of that was the move by Britain's Tony Blair in late November 2003 to join with France and Germany in creating an independent European military planning unit. The irony of America's new hostility to Europe is that it may hasten the emergence of the united European rival that the Bush administration fears.

Nowhere is the truth of the aphorism "the more it changes, the more it remains the same" more amply demonstrated than in the case of the Israeli-Palestinian conflict. One reason given for knocking out Saddam was that the road to Jerusalem was said to lie through Baghdad. It is clear now that it didn't. In the immediate aftermath of the invasion, a much-ballyhooed Road Map for Peace was developed by the United States, the EU, Russia, and the UN. Because Washington insisted it would not deal with the Palestinians as long as Arafat was in charge, the Palestinians appointed a Prime Minister, Abu Mazen, to lead the government with Arafat as the ceremonial President. In response, Bush met with the new Prime Minister, as well as with Jordan's King Abdalluh and Israel's Prime Minister Sharon, and committed the United States to full support of a Palestinian state and of the Road Map as the way to get there. With Saddam gone and Bush looking actually committed, a ray of hope shone for a moment. But then the old dynamics reasserted themselves. Sharon refused to do anything until the Palestinians halted all violence. In particular, he refused to halt the Israeli security forces' program of targeted killings of suspected terrorist leaders. The Palestinians tried to persuade their various groups to observe a cease fire but succeeded only partially as Israeli settlements continued to expand inexorably. Important Palestinian factions refused to abjure violence until the Israelis began pulling back from the settlements. Bush refrained from putting any pressure on Sharon, and the Road Map quickly proved to be a dead end. Meanwhile, Israel continued building a security wall that will eventually enclose a bit less than half the current West Bank and effectively annex it to Israeli territory. Without a strong U.S. or NATO intervention, the situation continues to deteriorate. While it remains the same old game in many respects, there is one critical way in which things are different. The Bush administration had insisted that the road to Jerusalem lay through Baghdad and had committed to a major effort with the Road Map in the wake of the invasion of Iraq. That getting to Jerusalem is proving as difficult as before, and that Bush has obviously washed his hands of the matter without solving it, means that its continuation is leaching poison into most important U.S. relationships abroad. It is not too much to say that this single issue is becoming the Weapon of Mass Destruction to U.S. foreign policy.

In the Far East, China has been described by a senior Singapore government leader as a "new sun in the universe" that already shows signs of displacing the United States as the key power in the region. This became abundantly clear in October 2003 when President Bush made a visit to Australia, followed shortly afterward by Chinese President Hu Jintao. The contrast between the two visits could not have been starker. Bush was in a hurry and focused only on discussing the war on terror with Australian leaders. Although Australia is America's second closest ally after Great Britain, he was heckled when he addressed Parliament. He scheduled no public appearances and declined to answer questions from the press. Hu, on the other hand, toured the country, signed big trade deals, and amazingly for a Chinese leader, actually held an unscripted press conference. To longtime observers of the scene, it looked like America and China had traded places. One Australian commentator noted that "Bush came, but Hu conquered." The significance of all this was driven home to me during a recent visit to Australia, when several government and business leaders independently commented that they hoped Australia would never be asked to choose between America and China. No one in the rest of the Asia-Pacific region would put it that bluntly, but the sentiment is similar throughout the area. As one Indonesian leader said to me, "All American leaders want to talk about is help with the war on terror. They keep beating on us to stop money laundering. Don't they realize we can't even collect our own taxes? The Chinese don't harass us about human rights and terror. They talk business and free trade."

Indeed they do. In the past year, exports to China have accounted for the vast bulk of the increase in exports by every other country in the region, and even many like Brazil and Chile that are outside the region. Korea, Japan, Taiwan, Malaysia, and all the others owe their recent growth mostly to China. The Chinese are using diplomacy masterfully to assuage fears of competition with China and to become a facilitator and friend to all its neighbors, who are becoming increasingly addicted to dependence on China. Nowhere is this addiction stronger than in the United States, where China has become, along with Japan, the primary financier of the U.S. trade deficit and thus a main factor in enabling Americans to consume more than they produce. In these circumstances, it is difficult to imagine an American President pressuring China over human rights or anything else.

In the Western hemisphere, the January 1, 2004, celebration of the tenth anniversary of the launching of the North American Free Trade Agreement (NAFTA) should have been an occasion for mutual self-congratulation. Instead it only served to highlight the contrast between the goodwill and high hopes of ten years ago and the strains and fears of the present. For one thing, NAFTA, while more plus than minus, is not fulfilling the high hopes invested in it, largely because the United States is not honoring many of the commitments it made with regard to opening its markets and has been unwilling to address such issues as infrastructure, training, immigration, and social services. Indeed, in reaction to lack of support from both Mexico and Canada on the invasion of Iraq, the Bush administration has been in a mood to punish and ignore both. This seems to be changing in recent months, particularly with regard to Mexican immigration issues, which are important for the U.S. election. But the key point is that the old assumption of partnership, shared values, and objectives, particularly with Canada, has been negated and replaced by a more cynical understanding. This is true also in South America where U.S. hypocrisy regarding drugs and free trade continues to cause frustration and alienation.

Then there is the question of those two badly wounded multilateral institutions, the UN and the WTO. Until it belatedly recognized the need for UN help in persuading Ayatollah al-Sistani to work with U.S. officials to create an interim Iraqi government in June 2004, the Bush administration treated the UN like a hostile foreign power. As a result, the question of whether the UN can play any meaningful role in the future is very much on the table. Certainly, it could not today play the kind of role it played in 1999 in removing an oppressive regime in East Timor and launching the building of a new nation. Like Winston Churchill's democracy, the UN seems to be the worst system of world governance—except for all the rest. In Iraq, Washington has discovered that if you didn't have a UN, you would have to invent one.

Perhaps that is the point: The UN needs to be reinvented so that the missteps of the past three years are not repeated. But only the United

States could lead such an effort, and at this juncture that is an unlikely prospect. Thus the chances are good that the UN will go the way of the League of Nations, with the result that the risks and costs of policing the world will likely rise for the United States.

Equally unclear is the future of the WTO in the wake of the failure of negotiators to make any progress at the Cancun talks in the fall of 2003. After years of dealing primarily with issues of interest to developed countries, this round of talks was supposed to be dedicated to doing something for developing countries. At the heart of this effort is agriculture, and at the heart of the agricultural question is cotton. The talks collapsed at Cancun for a number of reasons, but one of the main ones was the refusal of the United States to offer any meaningful reduction of its cotton and other agricultural subsidies. In the wake of this failure, the United States has launched a unilateral effort to cut a series of so-called bilateral free trade agreements. But these typically are only doable with relatively small countries and wind up creating a hodgepodge of preferential trading arrangements not dissimilar to those that contributed to the disaster of the Great Depression of the 1930s.

Meanwhile, carbon dioxide continues to accumulate in the atmosphere; the glaciers and polar ice cap continue to melt; land mines continue to kill and maim hundreds of thousands of women and children each year; trade in small arms is flourishing; the flow of cocaine and heroin into the U.S. remains unabated despite more spraying of South American peasant crops and tougher surveillance of the air and sea lanes; AIDS continues to spread its devastation to Africa and now large parts of Asia; water tables continue to fall as populations rise; and the sale of SUVs in the U.S. auto market is hitting record highs. But, hey, we got Saddam, the NASDAQ is up over 50 percent from last year, and sales of SUVs are booming. In fact, the bigger they are, the more they sell. Who says this ain't a great country? Don't you know the foreigners are just jealous?

NOTES

CHAPTER 1

1. "A Dirty Business: Mr. Bush Has Put U.S. Credibility on the Line." *Guardian.* March 30, 2001, p. 21.

2. Colombani, Jean-Marie. "Nous sommes tous Américains." *Le Monde.* Paris, France, September 13, 2001.

3. All interviews in this book were conducted between April 2001 and October 2002, in the United States, Europe, Latin America, and Asia. Those not mentioned by name have requested to remain anonymous.

4. Constantine, Gus. "Taiwan Praised Bush Vow To Do 'Whatever It Takes.'" *Washington Times*, May 4, 2001. p. A1

5. "Swedish Host Blasts Wrong Policies on Environment," AP Canadian Press. June 14, 2001.

6. Pew Research Center for the People and the Press. *What the World Thinks in 2002: How Global Publics View: Their Lives, Their Countries, The World, America.* December 2002.

CHAPTER 2

1. Bacevich, Andrew J. *American Empire: The Realties and Consequences of U.S. Diplomacy.* Cambridge, MA: Harvard University Press, 2002, p.122.

2. Ibid., p.8.

3. Ibid., p.7.

4. Huntington, Samuel P. "The Lonely Superpower." *Foreign Affairs.* March/April 1999, p.38.

5. Speech by George W. Bush. "A Distinctly American Internationalism." Simi Valley, California, November 19, 1999; and Bacevich, p.201.

6. The Pew Research Center for the People & the Press, "What the World Thinks in 2002," p.70–71.

7. President Bush commencement speech at West Point Academy, June 1, 2002; www.whitehouse.gov/news/releases/2002/06/20020601-3.html.

8. The National Security Strategy of the United States of America. The White House, September 2002; http://usinfo.state.gov/topical/pol/terror/secstrat.htm#nssintro.

9. Armstrong, David. "Dick Cheney's Song of America: Drafting a Plan for Global Dominance." *Harper's.* October 1, 2002. Vol. 305, No. 1824, p. 76–82.

10. "Present at the Creation: A Survey of America's World Role." *The Economist*. June 29, 2002, p.5.

11. Kristol, Irving. "The Emerging American Empire." American Enterprise Institute, Washington, DC. August 18, 1997.

12. Kennedy, Paul. "The Eagle Has Landed." *Financial Times*. February 2, 2002, p.1.

13. Johnson, Chalmers. *Blowback: The Costs and Consequences of American Empire*. New York: Henry Holt and Co., 2000, p.36.

14. Wolffe, Richard. "Technology Brings Power with Few Constraints." *Financial Times*. February 18, 2002, p.4.

15. "Present at the Creation." *The Economist*. June 29, 2002.

16. Global Financial Profile Fact Sheet: Report of the High-Level Panel on Financing for Development; www.un.org/reports/financing/profile.htm; and Quick Facts: Market Capitalization, www.nyse.com/marketinfo/marketcapitalization.html.

17. "Present at the Creation." *The Economist*. June 29, 2002; and Owen, Geoffrey, "Entrepreneurship in UK biotechnology: the role of public policy." The Diebold Institute, 2001.

18. Barber, Benjamin R. *Jihad Vs. McWorld: How Globalism and Tribalism Are Reshaping the World*. New York: Ballantine Books, 1996, p.97–99, and Appendix B.

19. "The Acceptability of American Power." *The Economist*. June 29, 2002.

20. Sherman, Wendy R. "Listen to the South, and Talk to the North." *Washington Post*. December 24, 2002. p. A15.

21. Ozawa, Ichiro. *Blueprint for a New Japan*. Tokyo: Kodansha International Ltd., 1994. Published in Japan in June 1993.

22. Kristol.

23. Institute of International Education. "Matching Last Year's Increase as Highest Growth Since 1980." November 18, 2002; www.iie.org/Content/ContentGroups/Announcements/International_Student_Enrollment_in_U_S__Rose_6_4%25_In_2001 2002.htm.

24. Jayadev, Raj. "Silicon Valley Entrepreneurs Needed: 'Where Are You When the S. Asian Community Needs You?'" Pacific News Service, November 23, 2001.

25. Barber, p.69.

26. McDougall, Walter A. *Promised Land, Crusader State: The American Encounter with the World Since 1776*. New York: Houghton Mifflin, 1997.

27. McDougall, p. 112.

28. McDougall, p. 147.

29. Truman, Harry S. Address before Joint Session of Congress, March 12, 1947.

30. Higgs, Robert. "US Military Spending in the Cold War Era: Opportunity Costs, Foreign Crises, and Domestic Constraints." *Policy Analysis*, November 1998, Vol.114.

31. Neikirk, William, and David S. Cloud. "Clinton: Abuses put China 'on wrong side of history,' Beijing to limit arms sales." *Chicago Tribune*. October 30, 1997.

32. Harris, John F. "Jiang Earns Clinton's High Praise; At Trip's End, Optimism About China's Future." *Washington Post*. July 4, 1998, p.A1.

33. Gingrich, Newt. *To Renew America*. New York: Harper Collins, 1995.

34. Condoleeza Rice's speech before the Los Angeles World Affairs Council, January 15, 1999. www.lawac.org/speech/rice.html.

35. Friedman, Thomas L. "A Manifesto for the Fast World." *New York Times Magazine.* March 28, 1999, p.3.

36. Bacevich, p.127; and William J. Clinton, *National Strategy for a New Century,* Washington, DC: DIANE Publishing, 1998, p.8.

37. Second Presidential Debate, Wake Forest University, October 11, 2000.

38. Niebuhr, Reinhold. *Moral Man and Immoral Society: A Study of Ethics and Politics.* New York: Scribners, 1932, p.294.

39. Chesterton, G. K. *What I Saw in America.* New York: Dodd, Mead & Co., 1992, p.7.

40. Huntington, Samuel P. "The Erosion of American National Interests." *Foreign Affairs.* September/October 1997, Vol.76, No.5.

41. Lipset, Seymour Martin. *American Exceptionalism: A Double-Edged Sword.* New York/London: W. W. Norton, 1996, p.19.

42. National address by President George W. Bush, September 11, 2001.

43. Emerson, Ralph Waldo. *War.* Boston, MA: March 1838.

44. Turner, Frederick Jackson. *The Frontier in American History.* New York: Henry Holt, 1921, p.37.

45. "In Praise of the Unspeakable—Business People and Philanthropy." *The Economist.* July 20, 2002, p.28.

46. U.S. Department of Health and Human Services, National Center for Health Statistics Web site: www.cdc.gov/nchs/fastats/homicide.htm.

47. "America's tough crime policy is having unintended consequences." *The Economist.* August 10, 2002.

48. Allen, Steven Robert. "The United Police States of America." *Weekly Alibi.* March 9–15, 2000, www.alibi.com/alibi/2000-03-09/edit.html; and *The Punishing Decade: Prison and Jail Estimates at the Millennium.* Washington, DC: Justice Policy Institute. May 2000.

49. Current Population Survey Annual Demographic Survey, March Supplement. Table 1. "Age, Sex, Household Relationship, Race and Hispanic Origin—Poverty Status of People by Selected Characteristics in 1998." U.S. Census Bureau, revised Dec. 15, 1999.

50. Worth, Robert. "A Nation Challenged: Intelligence; Agents Wanted. Should Speak Pashto." *New York Times.* October 1, 2001, p.B7.

51. Marquis, Christopher. "More Say Yes to Foreign Service, but Not to Hardship Assignments." *New York Times.* July 22, 2002, p. A1.

52. Bonner, Raymond. "Pakistani Schools: Meager Fare for Hungry Minds." *New York Times.* March 31, 2002, p.3.

53. Dao, James. "Over US Protest, Asian Group Approves Family Planning Goals." *New York Times.* December 18, 2002, p.A7.

54. Wills, Gary. "Bully of the Free World." *Foreign Affairs.* March/April 1999, Vol.78, No.2.

55. Huntington.

56. Haass, Richard N. "Defining U.S. Foreign Policy in a Post–Post–Cold War World." Foreign Policy Association, The 2002 Arthur Ross Lecture. New York. April 22, 2002.

57. Nye, Joseph S. Jr. *Bound to Lead: The Changing Nature of American Power.* New York: Basic Books, 1991 (Reprint Edition).

58. Montesquieu, Charles Louis. *Considerations on the Causes of the Greatness of the Romans and Their Decline.* Trans. David Lowenthal. New York: The Free Press, 1965, Chapter 6—The Conduct the Romans Used to Subjugate All People.

59. J. R. (John Robert), Sir Seeley (1834–1895), British classicist, historian. *The Expansion of England,* Lecture 1 (1883); www.bartleby.com/66/58/48958.html.

60. Paterson, Thomas G. and Dennis Merrill. *Major Problems in American Foreign Relations,* Vol. 1: To 1920, 4th Ed. Lexington, MA: D.C. Heath and Co., 1989.

61. Prowse, Michael. "Greedy bosses, lying politicians and cheating teachers." *Financial Times.* June 15, 2002, p.2.

62. National Home Education Research Institute, "Facts on Home Schooling"; August 1999.

63. Friedman, p.40.

64. The Pew Research Center for the People & the Press.

65. APEC CEO Summit 2002 Report: Challenges for Development in an Era of Uncertaintly. APEC CEO Summit, Mexico, October 2002.

66. Hirsh, Michael. "Bush and the World." *Foreign Affairs.* September/October 2002, p.18.

CHAPTER 3

1. Chanda, Nayan. "Economic Survey: Rebuilding Asia." *Far Eastern Economic Review.* February 12, 1998.

2. Stiglitz, Joseph. *Globalization and Its Discontents.* New York: W.W. Norton, 2002, p.93.

3. Warde, Ibrahim. "Crony Capitalism: LTCM, A Hedge Fund Above Suspicion." *Le Monde Diplomatique.* November 1998; www.mondediplo.com/1998/11/05warde2.

4. Keto, Alex. "White House Watch: Bush Calls for Fast-Track Authority." Dow Jones News Service. May 7, 2001.

5. Toedtman, James. "Powell: Trade Is Vital in War on Terrorism." *Newsday.* February 2, 2002.

6. Thurow, Roger and Scott Kilman. "Hanging by a Thread: In U.S., Cotton Farmers Thrive; In Africa, They Fight to Survive–America's Subsidies Depress World Prices, Undermining Its Foreign-Policy Goals." Sowing Seeds of Frustration. *Wall Street Journal,* June 26, 2002, p.1.

7. "Production to Rise in 2003/04." International Cotton Advisory Committee. February 3, 2003.

8. Badiane, Ouemane, Dhaneshwar Ghura, Louis Goreux, and Paul Masson. *Cotton Sector Strategies in West and Central Africa.* World Bank Policy Research. July 2002.

9. Thurow, Roger, and Scott Kilman. p.1.

10. Hufbauer, Gary Clyde, and Ben Goodrich. "Time for a Grand Bargain in Steel?" *International Economic Policy Brief,* January 2002, Vol.2, No.1, Table 5.

11. Hufbauer, Gary Clyde and Ben Goodrich.

12. Howell, Thomas, William A. Noellert, Jesse G. Kreier, and Alan W. Wolff. *Steel and the State: Government Intervention and Steel's Structural Crisis.* Boulder, CO: Westview Press, 1988.

13. Statistics calculated from data collected by the International Iron and Steel Institute. May 2002.

14. "Table 1. Output per hour in manufacturing, 14 countries or areas, 1950–2001." U.S. Department of Labor, Bureau of Labor Statistics. September 2002; www.bls.gov/news.release/prod4.t01.htm.

15. For a more thorough account of the steel industry, I highly recommend Thomas R. Howell's book, *Steel and the State: Government Intervention and Steel's Structural Crisis*. See note No. 12.

16. Seeman, Roderick. *The Japan Lawletter*. April 1983; www.japanlaw.com/lawletter/april83/bed.htm.

17. May, Bernhard. "The Marshall Plan: Historical Lessons and Current Challenges in the Balkans," German Council on Foreign Relations; www.dgap.org/marshallplan.html, February 14, 2003.

18. "The History of American Technology: The Automobile Industry, 1940–1959." web.bryant.edu/~history/h364material/cars/cars_60.htm.

19. "Mexico-EU, Mexico Ranks Seven in World's Trade in 1998." EFE News Service. May 5, 1999.

20. World Data Profile. The World Bank Group, April 2002. devdata.worldbank.org.

21. "COFACE to Purchase CAN Credit Business Line in North America." *PR Line*. November 18, 2002.

22. Hutton, Will. *The World We're In*. London: Little, Brown, 2002. p.186.

23. Calculated from official U.S. government trade statistics.

24. Associated Press. "Policing the Net." CBS News. November 22, 2001.

25. Lavelle, Louis, with Frederick Jesperson and Michael Arndt. "Executive Pay." *Business Week*. April 15, 2002, p. 80.

26. Friedman, Tom. "Foreign Affairs: Big Mac I." *New York Times*. December 8, 1996.

27. "Inside a Chinese Sweatshop: A Life of Fines and Beating." *Business Week*. October 2, 2000, p.86.

28. Economy, Elizabeth. "Painting China Green: The Next Sino-American Tussle." *Foreign Affairs*. March 1, 1999, Vol.78, No.2, p.16.

29. Bonner, Raymond. "Indonesia's Forests Go Under the Axe for Flooring." *New York Times*. September 13, 2002, p.A3.

30. Cookson, Clive. "Fish Stocks Face Global Collapse." *Financial Times*. February 18, 2002.

31. "A Few Green Shoots: The World Summit in Johannesburg." *The Economist*. August 31, 2002, p.59.

32. Soloman, Jay. "How Mr. Bambang Markets Big Macs in Muslim Indonesia." *The Asian Wall Street Journal*. October 29, 2001.

33. Basu, Kaushik. "Globalization and Its Threat to Democracy." *The Straits Times*. May 3, 2002.

34. *Global Economic Prospects 2002: Making Trade Work for the World's Poor*. World Bank, November 2001.

35. Calculated from statistics gathered from the United Nations Statistics Division and the United Nations Conference on Trade and Development.

36. Millman, Joel. "A Good Job Spoiled: The Golf Exodus." *The Wall Street Journal*. July 24, 2002, p.A12.

CHAPTER 4

1. Bamberger, Robert. "Automobile and Light Truck Fuel Economy: Is CAFE Up to Standards?" CRS Report for Congress. Updated August 3, 2001.

2. Ibid.

3. Ibid.

4. Lancaster, John. "Debate on Fuel Economy Turns Emotional." *Washington Post.* March 10, 2002, p.A12; and "Hooray, down goes CAFE." *The Washington Times.* March 15, 2002, p. A20.

5. Japan Automobile Manufacturers Association. "Gasoline Prices in Japan Increase Slightly." *Japan Auto Trends.* June 2000, Vol.4, No.2.

6. International Energy Agency. "Energy Prices and Taxes Quarterly Statistics 2002."

7. Ibid.

8. National Highway Traffic Safety Administration, U.S. Department of Transportation.

9. International Energy Agency (IEA). "Electricity Information 2002."

10. Agency for Natural Resources and Energy (Japan). "Energy in Japan 2002." June 2001.

11. The Energy Conservation Center Japan. "World Primary Energy Consumption per GDP." Energy Conservation Databook 1999/2000.

12. Hu, Patricia S. "Estimates of 1996 U.S. Military Expenditures on Defending Oil Supplies from the Middle East: Literature Review." Oak Ridge National Laboratory. Revised August 1997.

13. Steckel, Richard H. "A History of the Standard of Living in the United States." EH.Net Encyclopedia, edited by Robert Whaples. July 22, 2002; www.eh.net/encyclopedia/steckel.standard.living.us.php.

14. Adams, Sean Patrick. "The U.S. Coal Industry in the Nineteenth Century." EH.Net Encyclopedia, edited by Robert Whaples. January 24, 2003.

15. U.S Environmental Protection Agency. "Imprint of the Past: The Ecological History of New Bedford Harbor." April 22, 2002. www.epa.gov/nbh/html/whaling.html.

16. Steckel.

17. Much of this account of the history of the oil industry is from David Yergin's Pulitzer prize-winning book, *The Prize: The Epic Quest for Oil, Money, and Power* (New York: Simon & Schuster, 1991). It is highly recommended for those who wish to read a thoroughly detailed account of the oil industry.

18. Yergin, p. 30.

19. Steckel.

20. Yergin, p. 208.

21. Ibid. , 178, 183.

22. Ibid. , pp. 379.

23. Ibid. , pp. 208–209.

24. Ibid. , p. 551.

25. Ibid. , p. 553.

26. *Historical Statistics of the United States: From Colonial Times to 1970.* Series M 138–142, in Part 1, p.593; Series M 178–187, in Part 1, p.596. U.S. Department of Commerce, Bureau of the Census, Washington, DC. 1975.

27. Yergin, p. 567.

28. Ibid., p. 567.

29. Ibid., p. 567.

30. Ibid., p. 568.

31. Ibid., p. 157–164.

32. Ibid., p. 425.

33. Ibid., p. 555.

34. Ibid., p. 601.

35. Ibid., pp. 616.

36. Ibid., p. 635.

37. Ibid., p. 428.

38. Ibid., p. 553.

39. Acheson, Dean. *Present at the Creation: My Years in the State Department.* New York: W. W. Norton, 1987. p. 568.

40. Yergin, p.718.

41. Nauman, Matt. "Sales, Demand Pick Up for Hybrid Cars." *San Jose Mercury News.* January 4, 2003.

42. Energy in Japan, MITI. June 2001.

43. Yergin, p.655.

44. Energy Information Agency (EIA) Country Analysis Brief, France; www.eia. doe.gov/emeu/cabs/france.html.

45. IEA. "Saving Oil and Reducing CO2 Emissions in Transport: Options and Strategies." OECD/IEA 2001, p.23.

46. Energy Information Administration. "World per Capita Primary Energy Consumption (BTU), 1980–2000"; www.eia.doe.gov/pub/international/iealf/tableelc.xls.

47. Yergin, p. 617.

48. Ibid., p. 660.

49. Ibid., p. 660.

50. Ibid., p. 660–661.

51. Ibid., p. 663.

52. Ibid., p. 695–696.

53. EIA. "World Primary Energy Consumption per Dollar of Gross Domestic Product, 1980–2000."

54. EIA. "Country Analysis Brief, Canada." December 2002.

55. Environmental Law Reporter. "The National Energy Plan: Hitless After the First Inning." 1977; Romm, Joseph, "Needed: A No-Regrets Energy Policy." *Bulletin of Atomic Scientists.* July/August 1991, Vol.47, No.6.

56. EIA. "World per Capita Primary Energy Consumption (BTU), 1980–2000."

57. EIA. "Annual Energy Review 1997." DOE/EIA–0384. July 1998. Table 5.22.

58. EIA. "Petroleum Overview 1949–2000." Annual Energy Review 2000, p.123.

59. Environmental Protection Agency (EPA). "U.S. Average Horsepower of a New Vehicle." Light-Duty Automotive Technology and Fuel Economy Trends through 1996. EPA/AA/TDSG/96-01.

60. EIA. "U.S. Retail Price of Electricity." Annual Energy Review 1997. DOE/EIA– 0384. July 1998. Table 8.13.

61. Association of Home Appliance Manufacturers. "Efficiency of an Average New Refrigerator in the U.S." *Refrigerators Energy and Consumption Trends.* July 14, 1997.

62. "Strategic Petroleum Reserve." U.S. Department of Energy, www.fe.doe.gov/spr.

63. Romm, 47:6.

64. Yergin, p.769.

65. Ibid., p.769.

66. Ibid., p.769.

67. Sullivan, Allanna. "Energy Options: It Wouldn't Be Easy, but U.S. Could Ease Reliance on Arab Oil–Natural Gas, Domestic Wells, Soviet Output Could Help if Price Gets High Enough—Don't Count on Windmills." *Wall Street Journal.* August 17, 1990, p.A1.

68. Yergin, p.772.

69. Yergin, p.773; and Romm.

70. Clark, Mark T. "The Trouble with Collective Security." *ORBIS.* March 22, 1995, Vol. 39 Issue 2, p. 237.

71. Romm.

72. Ibid.

73. Brown, Lester R., Gary Gardner, and Brian Halweil. "16 Impacts of Population Growth." *The Futurist.* February 1, 1999.

74. Moriz, Ernest J. "Energy Security." Congressional testimony by Federal Document Clearing House. June 15, 2000.

75. Schulman, Bruce J. "The Energy Crisis: America Has Mothballed Its Cardigan Sweater." *Los Angeles Times.* May 13, 2001.

76. Schneider, William. "America Keeps on Trucking." *National Journal.* March 23, 2002.

77. Ibid.

78. United Nations. "World Population Prospects, The 2000 Revision." Volume 1: Comprehensive Tables. New York, 2001.

79. Morse, Edward L. and James Richard. "The Battle for Energy Dominance." *Foreign Affairs.* March/April 2002.

80. Ibid.

81. Ibid.

82. Woolsey, R. James. "Spiking the Oil Weapon." *Wall Street Journal.* September 19, 2002, p.A16; and Morse, p.16.

83. Dickey, Christopher. "The Once and Future Petro Kings." *Newsweek.* April 8—15, 2002, p.40.

84. Schneider.

85. Hebert, H. Josef. "Senate Rejects Tough New Automobile Fuel Economy Standards." Associated Press. March 13, 2002.

86. Lovins, A. "Old Problems, New Solutions." *World Link.* July/August 2002.

87. Ibid.

88. Woolsey, p.A16.

89. Lacayo, Richard. "Buildings that Breathe: The Best of the New Architecture Uses Nature Instead of Fighting It." *Time.* August 26, 2002, Vol.160, No.9, p.A36.

90. "Fuel Cell Industry Is on the Verge of Commercial Ignition." *Manufacturing News.* July 16, 2002, p.9.

91. "War Proponents, Opponents Lobby to Influence FY-04 Budget." *Inside the Pentagon.* January 30, 2003, Vol.19, No.5.

CHAPTER 5

1. Dickey, Christopher and Adam Rogers, et al. "Smoke and Mirrors: The World Reacted in Outrage when President Bush Last Summer Spurned the Kyoto Treaty to Cut Emissions. His New Plan Won't Make Him Any Friends Either." *Newsweek International Atlantic Edition*. February 25, 2002.

2. Pianin, Eric. "U.S. Aims to Pull Out of Warming Treaty; 'No Interest' in Implementing Kyoto Pact, Whitman Says." *Washington Post*. March 28, 2001.

3. "President Bush Discusses Global Climate Change." June 11, 2001, www.whitehouse.gov/news/releases/2001/06/20010611-2.html.

4. Christie, Michael. "Outrage as U.S. Dumps Kyoto." *Daily Telegraph*. March 31, 2001.

5. "A Dirty Business." *The Guardian*. March 30, 2001.

6. Pianin, Eric. "EPA Chief lobbied on warming before Bush's emission shift; memo details Whitman's plea for presidential commitment." *Washington Post*. March 27, 2001, p. A7.

7. Christianson, p. 168–169; and Molina, Mario J. and F. S. Rowland. "Stratospheric Sink for Chlorofluoromethanes: Chlorine Atom–Catalysed Destruction of Ozone." *Nature*, 249. June 28, 1974, p. 810–812.

8. Christianson, Gale. *Greenhouse: The 200-Year Story of Global Warming*. New York: Penguin Books, 2000. p. 169.

9. Farman, J. C., B. G. Gardiner, and J. D. Shanklin. "Large Losses of Total Ozone in Antarctica Reveal Seasonal CO_2/NO_2 Interaction." *Nature*. 1985, Vol.315, p.207–210.

10. "Causes and Effects of Changes in Stratospheric Ozone: Update 1983." *National Academy Press*. Washington, DC. 1984.

11. Christianson, p.194.

12. Ibid., p.195.

13. Houlder, Vanessa, and Clive Cookson. "Goodbye Hole in the Sky." *Financial Times*. September 21–22, 2002.

14. For an account of the life and work of Fourier, See Chapter 1, "The Guillotine and the Bell Jar," in Christianson, op. cit., p. 3–12.

15. Christianson, p. 113.

16. Callendar, G. S. "The Artificial Production of Carbon Dioxide and Its Influence on Temperature." Quarterly Journal of the Royal Meteorological Society, 1938.

17. Ibid., p.155.

18. Ibid., p.167.

19. Gelbspan, Ross. *The Heat Is On: The Climate Crisis, the Cover-up, the Prescription*. Boston: Perseus Publishing, 1998, p. 136–139.

20. Sarewitz, Daniel, and Roger Pielke Jr. "Breaking the Global-Warming Gridlock." *Atlantic Monthly*. July 2000.

21. Schneider, Stephen. "Earth Systems Engineering and Management." *Nature*. January 18, 2001.

22. Christianson, p.171.

23. Kellogg, William, and Margaret Mead. *The Atmosphere: Endangered and Endangering*. Castle House Publications, 1977.

24. Gelbspan, p.139.

25. Christianson, p.216.

26. Ibid., p.218.

27. "International Environmental Conference Urges Tax on Fuels." *Reuters News*. July 1, 1988.

28. Christianson, p. 197.

29. Christianson, p. 196.

30. Commentary by Richard Lindzen. *Wall Street Journal*. June 11, 2001.

31. Houghton, J. T., G. J. Jenkins, and J. J. Ephraums, eds. *Scientific Assessment of Climate Change: Report of Working Group I*. London: Cambridge University Press, UK. 1990.

32. Christianson, p.176–177.

33. Ibid., p.180.

34. Ibid., p.178.

35. Charvolin, Florian. "1970: L'année clé pour la définition de l'environnement en France." *Revue d'Histoire du CNRS*. May 2001, No.4.

36. Seib, Gerald F. "He's Against Acid Rain; He's Also the Enemy, Say Many Environmentalists; He's John Sununu." *Wall Street Journal*. March 2, 1990.

37. Nelson, Daniel. "The Behind-the-Scenes Battles in the Lead-Up to 1992's Massive Environment Conference in Rio." *Guardian*. March 29, 1991.

38. Mathews, Jessica. "Gorilla in the Greenhouse." *Washington Post*. July 25, 1991.

39. Gutfeld, Rose. "Earth Summit Has Put Bush on the Spot: Issue Is Whether to Attend Meeting in Brazil." *Wall Street Journal*. April 7, 1992.

40. Weisskopt, Michael. "Germans Play Lead on Rio's Stage; With U.S. Sidelined, Europeans Take Initiative on Environment." *Washington Post*. June 13, 1992; and Devroy, Ann. "Bush Lashes Out at Critics; President Praises Results of Troubled Trip." *Washington Post*. June 14, 1992.

41. "A Greener Bush." *The Economist*. February 15, 2003.

42. Gore, Albert. *Earth in the Balance*. New York: Plume Books, 1993.

43. Combined News Services. "Gingrich Flashes His 'Green' Card, But Is Color Faded?" *Salt Lake Tribune*. February 17, 1995, p.A1.

44. Rep. Jim Hansen's letter to his Utah constituents. December 8, 1994.

45. Don Young's comment to the *Anchorage Daily News, The Spokesman Review*. December 18, 1996.

46. Don Young's comment to Alaska Public Radio in August 1996. *Salt Lake Tribune*. December 1, 1996.

47. Congressional Record, Government Press Releases by Federal Document Clearing House. January 31, 1996.

48. Gelbspan, pp. 1–3.

49. "Scientist Reports Cracking of Antarctic Ice Shelf." *Global Warming Network Online Today*. March 28, 1995.

50. Gelbspan, p. 15.

51. "IPCC Second Assesment Report: Climate Change 1995."

52. Szamosszegi, Andrew Z., Lawrence Chimerine, and Clyde V. Prestowitz Jr. *The Global Climate Debate: Keeping the Economy Warm and the Planet Cool*. Study by the Economic Strategy Institute and The Organization for Economic Cooperation and Development. September 1997. p. 14.

53. Gelbspan, p.4.

54. Christianson, p.256.

55. Watson, Traci. "Global Warming Treaty Hanging in Thin Air." *USA Today.* December 1, 1997, p.6A

56. Hall, Mimi. "Kyoto-bound Gore Accepts Political Risks in Making Trip." *USA Today.* December 2, 1997, p. 8A.

57. Christianson, pp.266–267.

58. Thoning, Margo. *Kyoto Protocol, Climate Change Policy and U.S. Economic Growth.* American Council for Capital Formation (ACCF), Center for Policy Research, Special Reports. October 1998.

CHAPTER 6

1. "The Problem of Landmine-History." Canadian Landmine Foundation. www.canadianlandmine.org/landmineProb_History.cfm.

2. Fehribach, Bob. "Using landmines offers no benefits to U.S. military." *Lansing State Journal.* January 14, 2003.

3. Wheat, Andrew. "Exporting Repression." *Multinational Monitor.* January 1995.

4. "Ban Landmines Campaign: International Campaign to Ban Landmines Condemns Clinton Administration Landmine Policy." Statement by International Campaign to Ban Landmines. September 1, 1996.

5. Dunne, Nancy. "Clinton to work for an end to land mines." *Financial Times.* May 17, 1996.

6. Turner, Craig. "Canada will Offer Treaty on Landmines by Next Year." *Los Angeles Times.* October 6, 1996.

7. Remarks by President Clinton on landmines, The White House. September 17, 1997.

8. Ibid.

9. Open letter to President Clinton, published in the *New York Times.* April 3, 1996.

10. Remarks by President Clinton on landmines, The White House. September 17, 1997.

11. Stewart, John S. "Survivors Protest Refusal to Sign Land-Mine Treaty." *Rocky Mountain News.* March 2, 1999.

12. Calmes, Jackie. "Land Mines Treaty Draws Skepticism." *Wall Street Journal.* August 2, 2001, p.A1.

13. "Veterans Urge Bush to Sign Land Mine Treaty." Associated Press. February 26, 2002.

14. Kellerhals, Merle D., Jr. "UN Small Arms Conference a Success, U.S. Official Says: Action plan focuses on illicit arms trafficking." August 20, 2001; http://usinfo.state.gov/topical/pol/arms/stories/01082001.htm.

15. Peck, Don. "The Gun Trade." *Atlantic Monthly.* December 2002, Vol.290, No.5.

16. Kellerhals; and "Small Arms in Failed States: A Deadly Combination." Center for Defense Information, 1999.

17. Laurance, Ed. *Small Arms Survey 2002.* New York: Oxford University Press, September 2002, p.206.

18. Bolton, John R., Undersecretary for Arms Control and International Security Plenary Address to the UN Conference on the Illicit Trade in Small Arms and Light Weapons. New York. July 9, 2001.

19. Ibid.

20. Linzer, Dafina. "Small Arms Conference Ends in Victory for U.S." Associated Press. July 21, 2001.

21. Raum, Tom. "Arms treaty expires today; Many mourn U.S. withdrawal from 1972 ABM agreement." The Associated Press. June 13, 2002.

22. Sergeyev, Marshal. "Russian Top Brass Develops Response in Case U.S. Drops out of ABM Treaty." *Daily News Bulletin*. December 26, 2000.

23. Raum.

24. "World: Americas U.S. Senate rejects test ban treaty." BBC News. October 14, 1999; http://news.bbc.co.uk/1/hi/world/americas/474220.stm.

25. Nitze, Paul H. "A Threat Mostly to Ourselves." *New York Times*. October 28, 1999, p.31, col.2.

26. "Analysis of Voter Attitudes Toward the Comprehensive Test Ban Treaty." Pollsters Mellman Group, Inc. and Wirthlin Worldwide. June 29, 1999.

27. Deutch, John, Henry Kissinger, and Brent Scowcroft. "Test-Ban Treaty: Let's Wait Awhile." *The Washington Post*. October 6, 1999.

28. Congressional Record–106th Congress. October 13, 1999, p.S12549.

29. "Report: U.S. used nerve gas against defectors in Vietnam." Associated Press Newswires. June 8, 1998.

30. Nalder, Eric. "An aging cache of nerve gas–U.S. plan to burn huge stores of outdated chemical munitions in Oregon has its risks." *The Seattle Times*. January 17, 1991, p. A1.

31. Daschle, Thomas. "S. EXEC. RES. 75, Resolution of Approval of U.S. Ratification of the Chemical Weapons Convention." Government Press Releases by Federal Document Clearing House. April 22, 1997.

32. Ibid.

33. Edwards, Rob. "War with tears." *New Scientist*. December 16, 2000, p.4.

34. "US gives up talks on germ warfare." *Yorkshire Post*. July 26, 2001, p. 12.

35. Higgins, G. Alexander. "US Rejects Anti-Germ Warfare Accord." Associated Press Online. July 25, 2001.

36. Brugger, Seth. "Chemical weapons convention chief removed at U.S. initiative." *Arms Control Today*. May 1, 2002.

37. "Toxic Diplomacy–US Unilateralism Claims Another Victim." *Guardian*. April 24, 2002, p. 17.

38. "Nothing Gained by America's Global Tantrum." *Canberra Times*. July 21, 1998, p. 9.

39. Schmitt, Michael N. "Into uncharted water: The international criminal court." *Naval War College Review*. January 1, 2000.

40. Neuffer, Elizabeth A. "US to Back Out of World Court Plan Envoy: Bush Team May 'Unsign' Treaty." *Boston Globe*. March 29, 2002, p. A22.

41. Gurdon, Hugo. "The U.S. Should Unsign Kyoto." *Wall Street Journal Europe*. October 11, 2002, p. A6.

42. Meyerstein, Ariel. "Security Council Grants US 12-month Immunity from International Court." July 23, 2002; www.crimesofwar.org/print/onnews/iccimunity-print.html.

43. "U.S. Military Spending, 1945–1996." Center for Defense Information, www.cdi.org/issues/milspend.html.

44. "2001–2002 Military Almanac."Center for Defense Information. www.cdi.org/products/almanac0102.pdf.

45. Leebaert, Derek. *The Fifty Year Wound: The True Price of America's Cold War Victory*. New York: Little Brown and Co., 2002, p. 251.

46. Mintz, John. "U.S. Acts to Thwart Missile Threat Against Airliners." *Washington Post*. January 15, 2003, p.A1.

47. Johnson, Chalmers. *Blowback: The Costs and Consequences of American Empire*. New York: Metropolitan Books, 2000, p.90.

48. Department of State Bureau of Verification and Compliance. "World Military Expenditures and Arms Transfers 1999–2000." October 2001; www.state.gov/r/pa/prs/ps/2003/17447.htm.

49. Stylinski, Andrzej. "Poland to Buy Lockheed Jets; U.S.-Backed Loan Aided Decision." Associated Press. December 28, 2002.

50. "Japan Tries to Rein in Runaway Cost of FSX Fighter." *Defense News*. July 24, 1995.

51. Tarnoff, Curt and Larry Nowels. "Foreign Aid: An Introductory Overview of U.S. Programs and Policy." Congressional Research Service Report. Updated April 6, 2001, p.23; and "Foreign Military Sales, Foreign Military Construction Sales and Military Assistance Facts." Defense Security Cooperation Agency Facts Book, September 26, 2002; www.dsca.osd.mil/programs/Comptroller/2001_FACTS/default.htm.

52. Ibid., p.12.

53. Ibid., p.18.

54. Bite, Vita. "UN System Funding: Congressional Issues." Congressional Research Service. January 8, 2003, p.5.

55. Recer, Paul. "Young Americans Flunk Geography, According to National Geographic Quiz Survey." Associated Press Newswire. November 21, 2002.

56. Wallerstein, Immanuel. "The Eagle Has Crash Landed." *Foreign Policy*. July/August 2002, p.60.

CHAPTER 7

1. Kornblut, Anne E. "In Seoul, Bush Tries to Assuage Those Wary of His Intent on North Korea." *Boston Globe*. February 20, 2002.

2. Turner, Frederick Jackson. *The Frontier in American History*. New York: Henry Holt, 1921.

3. Wilson, Woodrow. *War Messages*, 65th Congress, 1st Session, Senate Document No.5, Serial No.7264, Washington, DC, 1917; p.3–8, *passim*.

4. McDougall, Walter. *Promised Land, Crusader State: The American Encounter with the World Since 1776*. New York: Houghton Mifflin Co., 1997, p.163; and Thomas G. Patterson and Dennis Merrill, *Major Problems in American Foreign Relations*. New York: Houghton Mifflin Co., 1999, p.267–300.

5. McDougall, 169.

6. Yergin, Daniel. *Shattered Peace: The Origins of the Cold War*. New York: Houghton Mifflin Co., 1977, p.196–200.

7. McDougall, p.168; and Tony Smith, *America's Mission: The United States and the Worldwide Struggle for Democracy in the Twentieth Century*, Princeton: Princeton University Press, 1994, p.143.

8. McDougall, p.164.; and James P. Warburg, *Faith, Purpose, and Power: A Plea for a Positive Policy*. New York: Farrar, Straus and Co., 1950.

9. Kwitny, Jonathan. *Endless Enemies: The Making of an Unfriendly World*. New York: St. Martin's Press, 1984, p.273.

10. Ibid.

11. Mannion, Jim. "No reduction in US forces in Asia even if Korea reunites: Cohen." Agence France Press. April 6, 1997.

12. Kwitney, p.278–283.

13. Leebaert, Derek. *The Fifty Year Wound: The True Price of America's Cold War Victory*. New York: Little Brown and Co., 2002, p.329.

14. Ibid., p.328–329.

15. Ibid., p.330.

16. Sipress, Alan. "Indonesians Begin to See Conspiracy as Home Grown." *Washington Post*. January 14, 2003, p.A14.

17. Leebaert, p.158.

18. Kwitny, p.158.

19. Leebaert, p.407.

20. Ibid, p.408, Note 67.

21. Ibid, p.484.

22. Fisk, Robert. "Did Saddam's Army Test Poison Gas on Missing 5000?" *Independent*. December 13, 2002, p. 15.

23. *Financial Times*. February 23, 1983, cited in Mark Pythian's *Arming Iraq: How the US & Britain Secretly Built Saddam's War Machine*. Boston: Northeastern University Press, 1997.

24. Dobbs, Michael. "U.S. Had Key Role in Iraq Buildup." *Washington Post*. December 30, 2002, p.A1; *Financial Times* article February 23, 1983, cited in Pythian's (see previous note); and Bruce W. Jentleson, *With Friends Like These: Reagan, Bush, and Saddam, 1982–1990*. New York: W. W. Norton, 1994, p.52.

25. Dobbs, p.A1.

26. Windrem, Robert. "Rumsfeld Key Player in Iraq Policy Shift." NBC News. August 18, 2002; www.msnbc.com.

27. Mackay, Neil, and Felicity Arbuthnot. "How Did Iraq Get Its Weapons: We Sold Them." *Sunday Herald*. September 8, 2001, p. 1.

28. Auerbach, Stuart. "$1.5 Billion in U.S. Sales to Iraq: Technology Products Approved up to Day Before Invasion." *Washington Post*. March 11, 1991, p. A1; and Henery Weinstein and William C. Rempel, "Iraq Arms: Big Help from U.S. Technology was Sold with Approval—and Encouragement—from the Commerce Department but Often over Defense Officials' Objections." *Los Angeles Times*. February 13, 1991, p. 1.

29. Dobbs, p.A1.

30. Jentleson.

31. Senate Committee on Foreign Relations Hearings, 101st Congress, 1st Session, March 1, 1989, p.27–45.

32. Committee on Government Operations, House, "Strengthening Export Licensing System." July 2, 1991, Paragraph 10.

33. Dobbs, p.A1.

34. Auerbach.

35. "MUI Asks Indonesian Moslems to Pray for Iraqi People," LKBN Antara, February 11, 2003; and "Iran Judiciary Chief Says Stoning No Longer Handed Down," Agence France Presse, February 4, 2003.

CHAPTER 8

1. Harper, Jennifer. "Trouble for Ted Turner's CNN." *The Washington Times*, June 21, 2002.

2. Press release, "The Evangelical Lutheran Church in Jerusalem," Bishop Dr. Munib A. Younan. April 16, 2002.

3. "Friendly Fire: Why Palestine Divides Europe and America." *The Economist*. April 20, 2002, p.9.

4. Bennet, James. "Sharon Says Europe Is Biased in Favor of the Palestinians." *New York Times*. January 20, 2003, p.A6.

5. Toameh, Khaled Abu and *Jerusalem Post* staff. "Poll: 60% of Israelis Say They Are Fighting For Their Survival." *Jerusalem Post*. October 4, 2002.

6. Devi, Sharmila. "Intifada Inflicts Acute Pain on Israelis." *Financial Times*. October 24, 2002, p.9.

7. "West Bank Settlements Swallow All Before Them." *The Economist*. October 31, 2002.

8. Moore, Molly. "On Remote Hilltops, Israelis Broaden Settlements." *Washington Post*. December 8, 2002, p.A1.

9. Morris, Harvey. "Israel Faces 'Demographic Time Bomb.'" *Financial Times*. June 14, 2002, p.5.

10. Halpern, Orly. "An Education in Defiance." *Ha'aretz*. October 4, 2002.

11. Bishara, Marwan. "Israel's Pass Laws Will Wreck Peace Hopes; Apartheid in the Territories." *International Herald Tribune*. May 22, 2002, p.6.

12. "Question of the Violation of Human Rights in the Occupied Arab Territories, Including Palestine." UN Human Rights Commission. March 2001.

13. Gorenberg, Gershom. "The Thin Green Line." *Mother Jones*. September/October 2002, p. 50.

14. Christison, Kathleen. *Perceptions of Palestine: Their Influence on U.S. Middle East Policy.* Berkeley: University of California Press, 1999, p. 305; this book was of great help to me in writing this chapter, and provided an excellent analysis of U.S. policy in the Israeli-Palestinian dispute.

15. Christison, p.22.

16. "Truth from Palestine" by Ahad Ha'am, quoted in Tom Segev. *One Palestine, Complete: Jews and Arabs Under the British Mandate*. New York: Henry Holt and Company (An Owl Book) p. 104, 537; and Avineri, Shlomo, *The Making of Modern Zionism: Intellectual Origins of the Jewish State*. New York: Basic Books, 1981, p. 123.

17. Christison, p.31.

18. Speech to U.S. Senate, July 10, 1919.

19. Various estimates put the number of 1948 Palestinian refugees between 700,000 and 1 million; see Appendix 4 of the "General Progress Report and supplementary Report of the United Nations Conciliation Committee for Palestine, Covering the Period from 11 December 1949 to 23 October 1950" of October 23, 1950, which estimates the number at 711,000. (http://domino.un.org/unispal.nsf/); see also Abu-Lughod, Janet "The Demographic Transformation of Palestine," in Abu-Lughod, Ibrahim (ed.), *The Transformation of Palestine.* Evanston, IL: Northwestern University Press, 1971 (p. 139–161), where the estimate is 780,000.

20. Pear, Robert, with Richard L. Berke. "Pro-Israel Group Exerts Quiet Might as it Rallies Supporters in Congress." *New York Times.* July 7, 1987, p.A8.

21. Goldstein, Avram. "Christian Coalition Rallies for Israel in Comeback Bid." *Washington Post.* October 12, 2002, p.B1.

22. Findley, Paul. "Liberating America from Israel." Media Monitors Network. September 11, 2002.

23. Massing, Michael. "Deal Brakers." *American Prospect.* March 11, 2002.

24. Vlahos, Kelley Beaucar. "Pro-Israeli Lobby a Force to Be Reckoned With." FoxNews.com. May 28, 2002.

25. Engel, Matthew. "Meet the New Zionists." *Guardian.* October 28, 2002, p.2.

26. *Hardball.* MSNBC May 1, 2002.

27. Morris, Benny. "Camp David and After, an Interview with Ehud Barak." *New York Review of Books.* June 13, 2002.

28. Malley, Robert and Hussein Agha. "Camp David: The Tragedy of Errors." *New York Review of Books.* August 9, 2001.

29. Israeli-Palestinian Joint Statement. January 27, 2001.

30. Final Report of the Sharm El-Sheikh Fact Finding Committee (Mitchell Report), April 20, 2001.

31. Xinhua's China Economic Information Service. "Sino-U.S. Trade Imbalance Should Be Solved Through Development." December 23, 2002.

32. Mufson, Steven and Dana Milbank. "Taiwan to Get Variety of Arms; But U.S. Witholds Aegis Radar that China Strongly Opposed." *Washington Post.* April 24, 2001, p.A1.

33. Mufson, Steven. "President Pledges Defense of Taiwan; Policy Unchanged, White House Says." *Washington Post.* April 26, 2001, p.A1.

34. White, Theodore. *In Search of History.* New York: Harper Row, 1978.

35. Tuchman, Barbara. *Stillwell and the American Experience in China.* New York: Grove Press, 1971, p. 188.

36. White, p.134.

37. White, p.208.

CHAPTER 9

1. Fukuyama, Francis. *The End of History and the Last Man.* New York: Avon, 1993.

2. Friedman, Thomas. *The Lexus and the Olive Tree: Understanding Globalization.* New York: Farrar, Straus and Giroux, 2000, p. 99.

3. Population Action International Fact Sheet. "Why Population Matters to Natural Resources"; www.populationaction.org/resources/factsheets/factsheet_13.htm.

4. 1999 figures from "The EU's Relations with the United States of America"; Europa, www.europa.eu.int/comm/external_relations/us/intro/index.htm.

5. Pew Research Center for the People & the Press. "What the World Thinks in 2002"; http://people-press.org/reports/files/report165.pdf.

6. Daalder, Ivo and Philip Gordon. "Euro Trashing." *Washington Post*. May 29, 2002, p.A17.

7. Kagan, Robert. *Of Paradise and Power*. New York: Knopf, 2003, p. 3.

8. Moisi, Dominique. "Real Crisis over the Atlantic." *Foreign Affairs*. July/August 2001, p.152.

9. O'Sullivan, Jonathan. "Why the U.S. Should Beware of the E.U." *National Review*. August 6, 2001

10. Fukuyama. "The West May Be Cracking Europe and America." *International Herald Tribune*. August 9, 2002, p.4.

11. Mandel, Michael J. "The Rich Get Richer, and That's O.K." *Business Week*. August 26, 2002, p.88.

12. "Statistical Illusions." *The Economist*. November 8, 2001.

13. Barcellan, Roberto. "Gross Domestic Product 2001." Statistics in Focus: Economy and Finance; Theme 2–53/2002, November 11, 2002, Chart T5; and The Economic Report of the President, February 2003, p. 60.

14. The E.U.'s 1990–1999 trade balance registered an average annual deficit of $2.63 billion (at current price). See *Eurostat Yearbook 2002*.

15. Davenport-Hines, Richard. *The Pursuit of Oblivion: A Global History of Narcotics*. New York: W. W. Norton, 2002, p. 443.

16. Pew Research Center for the People & the Press. "What the World Thinks in 2002," p.53.

17. Quoted by Rifkin, David. "Europe in the Balance." *Policy Review*. June 1, 2001, pp. 41–53.

18. Reid, T. R. "EU Leaders Convene to Design Global Superpower." *Washington Post*. December 16, 2001, p.35.

19. Casey, Lee A. and David B. Rivkin. "The Alarmingly Undemocratic Drift of the European Union." *Policy Review*. June 1, 2001, p.41–53.

20. Ibid.

21. Burke, Al. "A Doubtful Referendum." Nordic News Network. January 1, 2001.

22. Smith, Dan. "Europe's Peace Building Hour." *Journal of International Affairs*. Spring 2002, p.41.

23. Speech by Prime Minister Tony Blair to the Polish Stock Exchange, October 6, 2000.

24. Sciolino, Elaine. "European Union Acts to Admit 10 Nations." *New York Times*. December 14, 2002, p.A7.

25. Solana, Javier. "The Transatlantic Rift." *Harvard International Review*. January 1, 2003, Vol.24, No.4, p.62.

26. Richburg, Keith. "Europe, U.S. Diverging on Key Policy Approaches." *Washington Post*. March 4, 2002, p.A13.

27. Wallace, William. "Europe, the Necessary Partner." *Foreign Affairs.* May/June, 2001, Vol.80, No.3, p.16–34.

28. Quoted in Wawro, Geoffrey. "U.S. Strategists Should Welcome the 'Euro Army.'" *Los Angeles Times.* December 31, 2000, p.M5.

29. Ibid.

30. Brzezinski, Zbigniew. "Living with a New Europe." *National Interest.* Summer 2000, p.18.

31. O'Sullivan, Jonathan. "The Curse of Euro-Nationalism." *National Review.* August 6, 2001, p.33–36.

32. Ibid.

33. Kagan, Robert. "Power and Weakness." *Policy Review.* June/July 2002, No.113.

34. Department of Defense, Directorate for Information Operations and Reports. "DOD Top 100 Companies and Category of Procurement—Fiscal Year 2002"; www.dior.whs.mil/peidhome/procstat/procstat.htm.

35. Latham, Andrew. "China in the Contemporary American Geopolitical Imagination." *Asian Affairs.* Fall 2001, Vol.28, No.3, p.140.

36. "Agreed Framework Between the United States of America and the Democratic People's Republic of Korea." Geneva, Switzerland, October 21, 1994, provision I.3.

37. Ibid., provision II.

38. Ibid., provision III.1.

39. Johnson, Chalmers. "The 1955 System and the American Connection: A Bibliographic Introduction." Japan Policy Research Institute. Working Paper No. 11, July 1995.

40. Schaller, Michael. "America's Favorite War Criminal: Kishi Nobusuke and the Transformation of U.S.-Japan Relations." Japan Policy Research Institute. Working Paper No. 11, July 1996.

41. Nakao, Annie. "Battle for History." *San Francisco Chronicle.* April 28, 2002, p.A3.

42. Pilling, David. "Japan Calls for Fewer U.S. Troops on Okinawa." *Financial Times.* February 3, 2003.

43. International Trade Administration, U.S. Foreign Trade Highlights; "Top 50 Deficit Countries in U.S. Trade in 2001." www.ita.doc.gov/td/industry/otea/usfth/aggregate/H01T13.html.

44. *What America's Users Spend on Illegal Drugs.* Executive Office of the President, Office of National Drug Control Policy, December 2001, p. 3, Table 1.

45. Davenport-Hines, Richard. *The Pursuit of Oblivion: A Global History of Narcotics.* New York: W. W. Norton, 2002, p. 15.

46. Ibid., p.428.

CHAPTER 10

1. Ikenberry, John G. "America's Imperial Ambition." *Foreign Affairs.* September/October 2002, p. 48.

2. Schwarz, Benjamin and Christopher Layne. "A Grand New Strategy." The Atlantic Monthly. January 2002, Vol. 289, No. 1 p. 36–42.

3. Ash, Timothy Garton. "The Peril of Too Much Power." *New York Times.* April 9, 2002, p. 25.

4. The National Security Strategy of the United States of America. September 2002, p.15.

5. Ibid., preface.

6. Bush, George W. "Securing Freedom's Triumph." *New York Times.* September 11, 2002, p. A33.

7. Boot, Max. "The Case for American Empire." *Weekly Standard.* October 15, 2001, p.27.

8. Ibid., pp.28–29.

9. Mallaby, Sebastian. "The Reluctant Imperialist: Terrorism, Failed States, and the Case for American Empire." *Foreign Affairs.* March/April 2002, pp. 2–3.

10. Kagan, Robert. *Warrior Politics: Why Leadership Demands a Pagan Ethos.* New York: Random House, 2002. Pp. 152–153.

11. "When Empires Strike Back." *Financial Times.* December 8, 2001.

12. Second Presidential Debate, Wake Forest University. October 11, 2000.

13. "HIV infections down in sub-Saharan Africa, up worldwide"; www.cnn.com/2000/ health/aids/11/28/hiv.africa.

14. Kaplan, Robert. "The Coming Anarchy." *Atlantic Monthly.* February 1994, p.48.

15. Ibid., p.68.

16. Kaplan, p.60.

17. Turnoff, Curt and Larry Nowels. *Foreign Aid: An Introductory Overview of U.S. Programs and Policy.* CRS Report to Congress. Updated April 6, 2001.

18. Letter to the General Assembly of the Church of Scotland. August 3, 1650.

Recommended Reading

Acheson, Dean. *Present at The Creation: My Years in the State Department.* New York: W.W. Norton, 1987.

Alagappa, Muthaiah (ed.). *Asian Security Order: Instrumental and Normative Features.* Stanford, CA: Stanford University Press, 2003.

Avineri, Shlomo. *The Making of Modern Zionism: Intellectual Origins of the Jewish State.* New York: Basic Books, 1981.

Bacevich, Andrew. *American Empire: The Realities and Consequences of U.S. Diplomacy.* Cambridge, MA: Harvard University Press, 2002.

Bandow, Doug. *Tripwire: Korea and U.S. Foreign Policy in a Changed World.* Washington, D.C.: Cato Institute, 1996.

Barber, Benjamin R. *Jihad vs. McWorld: How Globalism and Tribalism are Reshaping the World.* New York: Ballantine Books, 1996.

Bix, Herbert. *Hirohito and the Making of Modern Japan.* New York: Perennial, 2001.

Boniface, Pascal (ed.) *Les leçons du 11 septembre.* Paris: IRIS-PUF, 2001.

Boot, Max. *The Savage Wars of Peace.* New York: Basic Books, 2002.

Brackman, Arnold C. *The Other Nuremberg: The Untold Story of the Tokyo War Crimes Trials.* Tokyo: John Hawkins & Associates, Inc., 1987.

Carson, Rachel. *Silent Spring.* Boston: Mariner Books, 2002 (first published in 1962).

Chesterton, G.K. *What I Saw in America.* New York: Dodd, Mead & Co, 1992.

Christianson, Gale E. *Greenhouse: The 200-Year Story of Global Warming.* New York: Penguin Books, 2000. Originally printed by Walker Publishing Company, 1999.

Christison, Kathleen. *Perceptions of Palestine: Their Influence on U.S. Middle East Policy.* Berkeley, CA: University of California Press, 1999.

Clawson, Patrick L. and Rensselaer W. Lee III. *The Andean Cocaine Industry.* New York: St. Martin's Griffin, 1996.

Colombani, Jean-Marie. *Tous Américains? Le monde après le 11 septembre 2001.* Paris: Fayard, 2002.

Dasquié, Guillaume and Jean Guisnel. *L'effroyable mensonge–Thèse et foutaises sur les attentats du 11 septembre.* Paris: La Découverte, 2002.

Davenport-Hines, Richard. *The Pursuit of Oblivion: A Global History of Narcotics.* New York: W.W. Norton, 2002.

De Toqueville, Alexis. *Democracy in America.* New York: Vintage Books, 1990.

De Villiers, Marq. *Water: The Fate of Our Most Precious Resource.* New York: Houghton Mifflin, 2000. First published in Canada in 1999 by Stoddart Publishing Co. Limited.

Dickens, Charles. *American Notes: For General Circulation.* New York: Penguin USA, 2001 (Reissue).

Dinan, Desmond. *Ever Closer Union–An Introduction to the European Community.* Boulder, CO: Lynne Rienner Publishers, 1999.

Eisendrath, Craig, Melvin A. Goodman, and Gerald E. Marsh. *The Phantom Defense: America's Pursuit of the Star Wars Illusion.* Westport, CT: Praeger Publishers, 2001.

Friedman, Thomas L. *Longitudes and Attitudes: Exploring the World After September 11.* New York: Farrar, Straus, & Giroux, 2002.

Friedman, Thomas L. *The Lexus and the Olive Tree: Understanding Globalization.* New York: Anchor Books, 2000.

Fritsch-Bournazel, Renata. *L'Allemagne depuis 1945.* Paris: Hachette, 2002.

Fukuyama, Francis. *The End of History and the Last Man.* New York: Avon Books, 1993.

Gelbspan, Ross. *The Heat Is On: The Climate Crisis, the Cover-up, the Prescription.* Boston: Perseus Publishing, 1998.

Gingrich, Newt. *To Renew America.* New York: Harper, 1996.

Gore, Al. *Earth in the Balance: Ecology and the Human Spirit.* New York: Plume, 1993.

Graham, Bradley. *Hit to Kill: The New Battle Over Shielding America from Missile Attack.* New York: Public Affairs, 2001.

Haass, Richard. *The Reluctant Sheriff: The United States After the Cold War.* New York: Council on Foreign Relations, 1998.

Harding, Harry. *A Fragile Relationship: The United States and China since 1972.* Washington D.C.: The Brookings Institute, 1992.

Harrison, Selig S. *Korean Endgame: A Strategy for Reunification and U.S. Disengagement.* Princeton, NJ: Princeton University Press, 2002.

Harrison, Selig S. and Prestowitz, Clyde. *Asia After the Miracle.* Washington, D.C.: The Economic Strategy Institute, 1999.

Howell, Thomas, William A. Noellert, Jesse G. Kreier, and Alan W. Wolff. *Steel and the State: Government Intervention and Steel's Structural Crisis.* Boulder, CO: Westview Press, 1988.

Huntington, Samuel P. *The Clash of Civilizations and the Remaking of the World Order.* New York: Simon and Schuster, 1996.

Hutton, Will. *The World We're In.* London: Little, Brown, 2002.

Jentleson, Bruce W. *With Friends Like These: Reagan, Bush, and Saddam, 1982–1990.* New York: W.W. Norton, 1994.

Johnson, Chalmers. *Blowback: The Costs and Consequences Of American Empire.* New York: Metropolitan Books, 2000.

Kagan, Robert. *Of Paradise and Power: America and Europe in the New World Order.* New York: Knopf, 2003.

Kagan, Robert. *Warrior Politics: Why Leadership Demands a Pagan Ethos.* New York: Random House, 2002.

Kellogg, William and Margaret Mead. *The Atmosphere: Endangered and Endangering.* Castle House Publications, 1977.

Kissinger, Henry. *Does America Need a Foreign Policy? Toward a Diplomacy for the 21st Century.* New York: Simon & Schuster, 2001.

Kojima, Noboru. *Tokyo Saiban Vol.1 and Vol.2* [Tokyo war crimes trial]. Tokyo: Chuko shinsho, 1971.

Kupchan, Charles A. *The End of the American Era.* New York: Knopf, 2002.

Kwitny, Jonathan. *Endless Enemies: The Making of an Unfriendly World.* New York: St. Martin's Press, 1984.

Lampton, David M. *Same Bed, Different Dreams: Managing U.S.-China Relations 1989–2000.* Berkeley and Los Angeles, CA: University of California Press, 2001.

Laqueur, Walter and Barry Rubin. *The Israel-Arab Reader.* New York: Penguin Books, 1976.

Laurence, Ed. *Small Arms Survey 2002.* Oxford, England: Oxford University Press. September 2002.

Leebaert, Derek. *The Fifty-Year Wound: The True Price of America's Cold War Victory.* Boston, Mass.: Little, Brown and Co., 2002.

Lewis, Bernard. *The Middle East: A Brief History of the last 2000 years.* New York: Scribners, 1996.

Lipset, Seymour Martin. *American Exceptionalism: A Double-Edged Sword.* New York: W. W. Norton, 1996.

Lomborg, Bjørn. *The Skeptical Environmentalist: Measuring the Real State of the World.* Cambridge: Cambridge University Press, 2001.

Marsh, George Perkins. *Man and Nature.* Cambridge, MA: Harvard University Press, 1973.

McDougall, Walter. *Promised Land, Crusader State: The American Encounter with the World Since 1776.* New York: Houghton Mifflin, 1997.

Mead, Walter Russell. *Special Providence: American Foreign Policy and How it Changed the World.* New York: Knopf, 2001.

Meyssan, Thierry. *11 septembre 2001–L'effroyable imposture.* Paris: Carnot, 2002.

Mikuni, Akio and R. Taggart Murphy. *The Japan Policy Trap.* Washington, D.C.: The Brookings Institute, 2002.

Minear, Richard H. *Victors' Justice: The Tokyo War Crimes Trial.* Princeton: Princeton University Press, 1971.

Morita, Akio and Shintaro Ishihara. *The Japan That Can Say 'No.'* Jefferson Educational Foundation, Washington,D.C., 1990.

Murakami, Hiromi, Steven Clemons and Clyde Prestowitz, eds. *Japan and the United States Reconsidered: Evolution of Security and Economic Choices since 1960.* Washington, D.C.: Economic Strategy Institiute, 2002.

Niebuhr, Reinhold. *Moral Man and Immoral Society: A Study of Ethics and Politics.* New York: Scribners, 1932.

Nuttal, Simon. *European Political Cooperation.* Oxford: Clarendon Press, 1992.

Nye, Joseph S. Jr. *Bound to Lead: The Changing Nature of American Power.* New York: Basic Books, 1991.

Nye, Joseph S. Jr. *The Paradox of American Power.* Oxford: Oxford University Press, 2002.

Oberthür, Sebastian and Hermann E. Ott. *The Kyoto Protocol: International Climate Policy for the 21st Century.* Berlin: Springer, 1999.

Ohmae, Kenichi. *The Borderless World: Power and Strategy in the Interlinked Economy.* New York: HarperBusiness, 1999.

Ohnuma, Yasuaki. T*okyo saiban kara Sengo Sekinin no shisou he* [From Tokyo Trial to War responsibility]. Tokyo: Yushindo, 1985.

Oren, Michael B. *Six Days of War and the Making of the Modern Middle East*. New York: Oxford University Press, 2002.

Ozawa, Ichiro. *Blueprint for a New Japan*. Tokyo: Kodansha International Ltd, 1994.

Patterson, Thomas G. and Dennis Merrill. *Major Problems in American Foreign Relations*. New York: Houghton Mifflin, 1999.

Pells, Richard. *Not Like Us: How Europeans Have Loved, Hated, and Transformed American Culture Since World War II*. New York: Basic Books, 1997.

Phythian, Mark. *Arming Iraq: How The U.S. and Britain Secretly Built Saddam's War Machine*. Boston: Northeastern University Press, 1994.

Pyle, Kenneth B. *The Japanese Question: Power and Purpose in a New Era*. Washington D.C.: The American Enterprise Institute Press, 1992.

Revel, Jean-François. *L'obsession anti-américaine: Son fonctionnement, ses causes, ses inconséquences*. Paris: Plon, 2002.

Roger, Philippe. *L'ennemi américain: Généalogie de l'anti-américanisme français*. Paris: Seuil, 2002.

Schaller, Michael. *The American Occupation of Japan: The Origins of the Cold War in Asia*. Oxford: Oxford University Press, 1985.

Schonberger, Howard B. *Aftermath of War: Americans and the Remaking of Japan, 1945–1952*. Kent: The Kent State University Press, 1989.

Schoultz, Lars. *Beneath the United States: A History of U.S. Policy Toward Latin America*. Cambridge, Mass.: Harvard University Press, 2001.

Segev, Tom. *One Palestine, Complete: Jews and Arabs Under the British Mandate*. New York: Henry Holt (An Owl Book), 1999.

Servan-Schreiber, Jean-Jacques. *Le Défi Américain*. Paris, Denoël, 1967.

Shipler, David K. *Arab and Jew: Wounded Spirits in a Promised Land*. New York: Penguin, 1986.

Sigal, Leon V. *Disarming Strangers: Nuclear Diplomacy with North Korea*. Princeton: Princeton University Press, 1998.

Smith, Tony. *America's Mission: The United States and the Worldwide Struggle for Democracy in the Twentieth Century*. Princeton: Princeton University Press, 1994.

Stiglitz, Joseph. *Globalization and Its Discontents*. New York: W. W. Norton, 2002.

Suzuki, David and Holly Dressel. *Good News For A Change: Hope For a Troubled Planet*. Toronto: Stoddart Publishing Co., 2002.

Thoreau, Henry David. *The Maine Woods*. New York: Penguin USA, 1988.

Todd, Emmanuel. *Après l'empire–Essai sur la décomposition du système américain*. Paris: Gallimard, 2002.

The World Bank. *The East Asian Miracle: Economic Growth and Public Policy*. Oxford: Oxford University Press, 1993.

Tuchman, Barbara W. *Stilwell and the American Experience in China, 1911–45*. New York: Grove Press, 2001.

Turner, Frederick Jackson. *The Frontier in American History*. New York: Henry Holt, 1921.

Victor, David G. *The Collapse of the Kyoto Protocol and the Struggle to Slow Global Warming*. Princeton: Princeton University Press, 2001.

Vogel, Ezra F. (ed.). *Living with China: U.S.-China Relations in the Twenty-First Century*. New York: W. W. Norton, 1997.

Warburg, James P. *Faith, Purpose and Power: A Plea for a Positive Policy.* New York: Farrar, Straus, & Giroux, 1950.

White, Theodore. *In Search of History.* New York: Harper Row, 1978.

Woodard, Colin. *Ocean's End: Travels Through Endangered Seas.* New York: Basic Books, 2000.

Yergin, Daniel. *The Prize: The Epic Quest for Oil, Money & Power.* New York: Simon & Schuster, 1991.

Yergin, Daniel. *Shattered Peace: The Origins of the Cold War.* New York: Houghton Mifflin, 1977.

Zimmermann, Warren. *First Great Triumph.* New York: Farrar, Straus, & Giroux, 2002.

ACKNOWLEDGMENTS

I could not have written this book without the help of the hundreds of people who kindly met with me and shared their insights and opinions. The list is too long to mention each person here, but I wish to thank all who shared their time and thoughts in interviews and discussions.

A number of people worked long and tirelessly in researching and helping to organize the manuscript. In particular, I am deeply indebted to Ulrika "Riki" Swanson, who oversaw and coordinated the full research effort and intern army. I also want to thank Franck Journoud, who directed much of the European-related research, and Hiromi Murakami, who directed much of the Asia research; Sam McCoy, who put in many hours of study on the Middle East, along with Rachel Strein. Gladys Scott and Sonjai Harrison provided essential administrative support, and Lori Harmon always had the right contact information at the right time. Special thanks are also due to Monica "Queen" Bridgewater who kept the office humming in the face of extraordinary demands. To my indefatigable interns in the Pirate Cove: Ben Barden, Scott Friedman, Trisha Galowin, Sachiko Gause, Richard Khoe, Bory Kim, Bakur Kvashilava, Joshua Lagos, James Morrow, Melis Ozdogan, Hyo Eun Park, Tejal Patel, Eric Rahn, Kartik Ramachandran, Ryan Singer, Kevin Su, Ka-Ki Tse, James Tudor, and Stephanie Wolfinbarger . . . I also must express my gratitude.

Ambassador Chas Freeman of Projects International was of immense help in arranging interviews in China and the Middle East, and has long been a valued advisor, friend, and guide. Professor Chalmers Johnson has also been a mentor and friend, and I owe him a great intellectual debt. David Young and Arnie Nachmanoff of Oxford Analytica provided invaluable insights, assistance in meeting with key people, and both read and critiqued parts of the manuscript. My old colleague and friend Bob Perkins read the whole manuscript and provided valuable suggestions, as did Pat Malloy of the U.S. China Council. Jean Abi-Nader of the Arab American Institute was of immense help in arranging meetings for me in Jordan and on the West Bank. I am also grateful for the assistance of Roy Peled and David Levy, who helped me in making key contacts in Jerusalem and Tel Aviv. Stephen Cohen of the Center for Middle East Peace was of great assistance with his insights into Israel and the Israeli-Palestinian conflict. *New York Times* columnist Tom Friedman has been an important guide to the Middle East, as well as to globalization. I am deeply indebted to Selig Harrison for his assistance in arranging meetings in Korea and for providing invaluable background information on the Korean situation. I would also like to thank Professor Moon Chung-In of Yonsei University and Kim Chin-hyun for their help in Korea. Former Xerox CEO Paul Allaire and Xerox Vice President Mike Farren are long-time friends who have been very helpful in suggesting and helping to arrange meetings with leading European thinkers and policy makers. I also want to thank Etienne "Stevie" Davignon of Societe Generale de Belgique for his assistance in that regard. EU Ambassador to Washington Guenther Burghardt provided important insights and guided me to others with important views as well. Ambassadors Juan Jose Bremer of Mexico and Dato' Ghazzali Sheikh Abdul Khalid of Malaysia were immensely helpful in providing insights into their countries and also in arranging for meetings with key thinkers, business leaders, and policy makers. Swiss Ambassador to the UN Jenö Staehelin kindly arranged a dinner for me with his UN colleagues. President of Grupo Coraza Julio Millan helped me find and meet key people in Mexico as well as provided logistical support. In Malaysia, I also need to thank Dato' Mohamed Jawhar bin Hassan of the Center for Strategic and International Studies for his valuable insights and introductions to other thinkers. In Indonesia, my old friend Jusuf Wanandi of CSIS not only arranged my schedule, but also hosted a dinner/seminar with most of Indonesia's leading thinkers and key political leaders. I am also grateful to Khalid Shikaki of the Brookings Institute for his assistance in Palestine and to Minister Counselor Jean-Francois Boittin of the French Embassy in Washington for his advice and assistance with regard to Europe. Deputy Chief of Mission to the American mission to the EU Jim Foster kindly hosted a dinner in Brussels and assisted in numerous helpful ways. Bruce Stokes of the Council on Foreign Relations was most helpful in advising on public opinion abroad. Ira Shapiro provided his usual advice and read key parts of the manuscript. Bob Lees of Bearing Point and Steve Olson of the Pacific Basin Economic Council worked tirelessly to suggest people to see in Asia and made valuable suggestions regarding issues. Singapore Ambassador to Washington Heung Chee Chan was most helpful as a guide to Asian thinking as well as in arranging meetings in Southeast Asia. I am also grateful to Jacqueline Willis, chief of the Hong Kong mission to Washington, and Chris Jackson of the Hong Kong mission in Brussels for their insights and help. In China, Professor Yuan Ming and her colleague Fan Shiming of Beijing University were of invaluable assistance in arranging meetings and providing insights into developments in China. My old friend Fan Gang of China's National Economic Research Institute was his usual helpful self. At the Chinese embassy in Washington, Counselor Yue Xiaoyong was extremely helpful in supporting my efforts in China. My old friend and guide to Japan and *Sankei* newspaper editor-at-large Komori Yoshihisa, and his colleague Yamamoto Hideya, were very helpful in suggesting people to see in Japan and China. Also, Korean FTC Chairman Lee Nam-Kee, and his colleague Shin Ho-hyun, were extremely helpful, as was Winky So of the Hong Kong Mission's Economic and Trade office in Washington. I am grateful to Joerg Wolff of the Konrad Adenauer Foundation in Beijing for his support with meetings and dinners, and I would also like to thank Mr. and Mrs. Dean Ho for hosting dinner and helping with arrangements in Shanghai. I am grateful as well to Lu Zhongwei, President of the China Institute of International Relations who kindly hosted dinner with a number of researchers and writers on U.S.-China relations. I would like to thank Ken Hsu of Ford Motor Company in China who provided not only dinner but also many valuable insights. In addition, my longtime friend and Global Sources CEO Merle Hinrichs was his usual helpful self in Hong Kong; and I would like to thank Japanese Diet and Foreign Affairs and Defense Committee member Ohta Masahide for his suggestions and for hosting a very helpful dinner in Tokyo. And, finally, I'd like to thank John Larkin, bureau chief of the Far Eastern Economic Review, Seoul. Bill Krist of the Woodrow Wilson Center provided valuable assistance on environmental issues.

I was blessed by having a great editor in Bill Frucht, who is creative, persistent, and sympathetic, and who has become a good friend. I must also thank my writing mentor, Phoebe Hoss, from whom I have learned so much.

While all these people gave generously of their time and of their views and information, the responsibility for the book and its statements is entirely my own.

Last, but far from least, I must thank my muse, advisor, critic, editor, researcher, tea brewer, constant companion, best friend, and wife Carol Ann Prestowitz.

INDEX

Abortion, 38, 40, 236
Acheson, Dean, 96, 223, 228
Acid rain, 122, 123, 129
Adams, John Quincy, 31, 277
Advanced Research Projects Agency (ARPA), 72
Afghanistan, 266, 274, 290
  and drugs, 259
  Soviet war in, 12, 103, 145, 163, 186–187, 259,
    265
  Taliban of, 7, 12, 81, 156, 187, 190, 265
  and terrorism, 240
  U.S. support for Mujahedin in, 12, 103, 106, 181,
    186–187, 259, 265
  U.S. war in, 7, 26, 81, 190, 231, 242, 254, 266
Agriculture
  overseas, 59–61, 79, 282
  U.S., 12, 59–62, 73, 282
AIDS, 45, 48, 79, 168, 229, 282
Airline industry, 62, 90, 91
Al-Omari, Abdul Aziz, 3
Al Qaeda, 10, 13, 290, 292
  in Afghanistan, 7
  birth of, 187
  and Iraq, 190
  and Palestinians, 194
  and September 11 attacks, 3, 5, 194
  supporters in Pakistan, 266
Alba, Luis Alfonso de, 151
Albright, Madeleine, 241
Algerian terrorists, 36
Allende, Salvador, 181
Amaya, Naohiro, 97
America. *See* United States
American Association for the Advancement of
  Science, 127
American exceptionalism, 31, 32, 34, 284
American Israel Public Affairs Committee (AIPAC),
  211
American Notes, 114
American Servicemembers Protection Act, 159
Americanism, 35–38
Angell, Norman, 80
Annan, Kofi, 159

Anti-Ballistic Missile (ABM) Treaty, 2, 7, 22, 35,
  144, 151–152, 162, 244
Arafat, Yasir, 13, 194, 196, 199, 200, 201, 202,
  203–204, 205, 206, 207, 211, 212–213,
  214–216, 217, 218, 295
Arbenz, Jacobo, 181
Argentina, 45, 57, 256
Armey, Richard, 212
Arrhenius, Svente, 118
Asia
  economic miracle of, 52–53
  perceptions of United States in, 244–245, 261
  U.S. relations with, 244–256
  See also specific Asian countries
Asia Pacific Economic Cooperation (APEC) forum,
  24–25, 48, 51, 53
Asian Monetary Fund (proposed), 56
Atlantic Monthly 272, 274
Atta, Mohammed, 3
Aum terrorists, 36
Australia, 79, 113, 126, 131, 133, 139, 140, 183, 296
Automobiles, 68, 73, 87, 89, 90, 91, 118
  and fuel economy, 81–84, 91, 97, 98, 99, 100,
    103, 105, 107, 108, 109, 128
"Axis of Evil," 3, 9, 39, 41, 163, 246, 247, 271
Axworthy, Lloyd, 147

Baker, James, 102
Baldrige, Malcolm, 67
Balfour, Lord, 208
Balfour Declaration, 208, 209
Bali, 182, 184
Bangladesh, 45
Barak, Ehud, 200, 204, 205, 212–213, 214, 215,
  216–217
Barber, Benjamin, 43
Barbosa, Rubens, 51, 79, 257
Basle Accord, 74
Basu, Kaushik, 77
Baywatch, 42, 43
Begin, Menachem, 198–199
Belgium, 67, 82, 84, 95
Benedick, Richard E., 117

329

Bennet, James, 197–198
Berlin
   1948 crisis over, 44
   fall of wall of, 44, 101, 227
Berlin Mandate, 130
Bidaya, Thanong, 53
Bilderberg Meeting (2002), 46–47, 230
Bildt, Carl, 238
bin Hassan, Dato' Mohamed Jawhar, 195
bin Laden, Osama, 49, 266
   and Gulf War, 103
   and Saudi Arabia, 187, 190, 262
   and September 11 attacks, 3, 187, 245, 253
   and Soviet invasion of Afghanistan, 103, 187
   and Taliban, 265
   U.S. effort to catch, 81, 256, 291–292
   U.S. funding of, 12
Biological weapons. See Chemical and biological
   weapons
Bissell, George, 85
Blair, Tony, 236, 238, 239, 286–287. 295
Blix, Hans, 6
Bolton, John, 150, 152, 154, 156, 159, 160–161
"Bomber gap," 162
Boot, Max, 24, 273–274
Borah, William, 174
Bosnia, 279
   ethnic strife in, 238–239
   and European Union, 241
   UN peacekeeping in, 160
Boyce, Ralph L., 39
Brazil
   cutting of mahogany forests in, 77
   economy of, 257
   exports of, 12, 258, 296
   and globalization, 79
   loans to, 12, 57
   and UN, 278
   and U.S. arms, 165
Bretton Woods agreement, 69–70
Brinkhorst, Laurens Jan, 127
Broecker, Wallace S., 119
Brown, Jerry, 127
Brzezinski, Zbigniew, 241
Burke, Edmund, 277
Bush, George, Sr.
   and 1992 Earth Summit, 77, 111, 128
   and chemical weapons, 154
   and energy, 102
   and environment, 126, 127
   and Iraq, 102, 189
   and Israel, 209, 210
   and nuclear testing, 152
   and Taiwan, 221
   trip to Tokyo in mid–1980s of, 29
Bush, George W., 176, 296
   and ABM Treaty, 151
   and agriculture, 60
   and AIDS, 282
   Berlin visit of, 44

   election of, 35
   as emperor, 25, 30, 35
   and energy, 104, 109
   and European Union, 241
   and global warming, 12, 77, 112, 113, 139
   and idealism, 173
   and International Criminal Court, 159
   and Iraq, 190, 285–287
   and Israel, 193–194, 195, 196, 198, 203, 205,
      207, 212, 213
   and Kyoto Treaty, 139–140
   and landmines, 148
   and Latin America, 257–258
   and Middle East, 14
   on need for consumption, 43
   and North Korea, 5, 180, 271
   and October 2002 conference, 25
   and preemption doctrine, 22, 23, 254, 273
   and Saudi Arabia, 262
   says United States not an empire, 21–22
   and September 11 attacks, 3, 35, 36, 41, 271
   and South Korea, 171
   and steel, 62
   and Taiwan, 11, 220, 225, 253
   as threat to world peace, 1–2
   and Trade Promotion Authority, 58–59
   and U.S. humility, 276
Business Week, 234
Byrd, Robert, 133

Calderon, Nissim, 202, 206
Callendar, George, 118–119
Cambodia, 145, 146
Canada, 285, 290
   and environment, 126, 131, 133, 139, 140
   and International Criminal Court, 157
   and landmines, 147
   opinion on U.S. customs and ideas in, 45, 46
   and Pakistan, 40, 264
   religion in, 37
   and synthetic oil, 100
   U.S. trade with, 69, 296
Canning, George, 42
Carnegie, Andrew, 38
Carson, Rachel, 114
Carter, Jimmy
   and Afghanistan, 186
   and energy, 98–99, 102
   and Israel, 198
The Case for American Empire, 273
Central Treaty Organization (CENTO), 264
Chavez, Hugo, 260
Chemical and biological weapons, 149
   and Iraq (See Iraq (and weapons of massdestruction))
   treaties, 144, 154–156, 270
Cheney, Dick, 23, 24, 269, 272, 287–288
Chenoweth, Helen, 129
Chesterton, G. K., 35
Chiang Kai-shek, Generalissimo, 178, 221, 222,
   223, 224

Chiang Kai-shek, Madame, 221, 222, 223, 224
Chile, 157, 181, 258, 260, 296
China, 285, 293–294, 296–297
    abortion in, 40
    and Chiang Kai-shek, 221, 222, 223
    and Clinton, 34, 220
    and Cold War, 176
    deforestation in, 283
    economy of, 26, 27, 69, 169, 219, 225, 227, 248, 252, 256, 281
    and environment, 77, 126, 131
    and European Union, 232
    factories in, 76, 79, 258
    foreign investment in, 79–80, 256
    increase in living standards in, 78
    and India and Pakistan, 264, 265
    and Indonesia, 182
    industrialization of, 103, 282
    and International Criminal Court, 158
    and Korean War, 177, 178
    and Microsoft, 40
    military spending of, 243, 254
    and missionaries, 221
    and nuclear weapons, 153, 254
    and oil, 105, 106
    opinion toward United States in, 254–255
    revolution of, 222, 223
    as rising power, 48, 229, 253–254, 255
    and Russia, 275
    and Soviet Union, 178–179, 252
    as "strategic competitor" of United States, 2, 11, 35, 152, 253, 256, 265
    and Taiwan, 219–221, 223–225, 253, 254, 255, 280
    Tienanmen Square incident in, 252
    and UN, 279
    U.S. diplomatic representation in, 40, 168, 169
    U.S. military surveillance of, 253, 254
    U.S. relations with, 6, 10–12, 152, 178–179, 219–221, 223, 224, 225, 245, 252–253, 254, 255–256, 266, 280–281
    U.S. trade and investment with, 12, 172, 219, 256
    and U.S. missile defense, 152, 163, 254, 280
    and war against Japan, 178
    and World War II, 88, 221, 222
    and WTO, 258
Ching-kuo, 224
Chirac, Jacques, 4, 236, 285
Christian Coalition, 211
Chun Doo-hwan, 179
Churchill, Winston, 92, 175, 278, 297
CIA (Central Intelligence Agency)
    and Afghanistan, 187, 259
    and Bali, 184
    and Indonesia, 182
    and Iran, 180–181, 185
    and Iraq, 188, 270
    and Japan, 250
    and Noriega, 259
Civil War, U.S., 144, 172, 173
Cliff, Jimmy, 127

Climate Change Action Plan, 128
Clinton, Bill
    and 1997–1998 financial crisis, 54, 55
    and China, 34, 220, 252
    and environment, 103, 128
    and globalization, 34
    and International Criminal Court, 159
    and Israel-Palestine, 200, 204, 205, 212, 213, 214, 215, 216
    and landmines, 146, 148
    and North Korea, 179, 180, 247
Coal, 85, 96, 97, 98, 99, 104, 124, 139
Coca-Cola, 30
Cohen, William, 157, 180, 241, 248
Cold War (new), 2, 232, 244
Cold War (old), 32–33, 34, 44, 62, 147, 168, 179, 228, 244, 261, 266
    discussed, 175–177
    end of, 6, 42, 52, 74, 162, 166, 167, 168, 169, 225, 227, 228, 229, 245, 252, 272
    and Europe, 238
    and NATO, 230
    and South Asia, 264
    U.S. military spending during, 161
Colombia, 256, 259
Common Foreign and Security Policy (CFSP), 239, 241
Comprehensive Nuclear Test Ban Treaty (CTBT), 144, 152–154
Conference of the Parties (COP), 130, 131
Connally, John, 71
Containment doctrine, 33, 176, 272, 273
Convention Against Torture, 156
Convention on Elimination of All Forms of Discrimination Against Women, 156
Convention on Genocide, 156
Cotton, 59–62
Council of the Americas, 59
The Coward's War: Landmines in Cambodia, 146
Cromwell, Oliver, 284
Cuba, 32, 173, 226
Czech Republic, 241

D'Arcy, William Knox, 92
Davignon, Etienne, 8, 231
Davies, John Patton, 178
Death penalty, 38, 44, 237
Defense, U.S. See United States (military might, force, spending, and programs overseas of)
Deforestation, 282, 283
del Valle, Rodolfo, 129–130
Deller, Nicole, 144
Denmark, 108
Deregulation, 11, 52, 74, 75, 79, 258
D'Estaing, Giscard, 238
Diallo, Mody, 61
Diana, Princess, 147
Dickens, Charles, 114
Dobriansky, Paula, 140
Dodge Plan, 68

Dollar standard, 70–72
Dominican Republic, 181
Double standards. *See* United States (double standards of)
Drake, "Colonel" E. L., 86
Drug trafficking, 258–260
Dulles, John Foster, 67, 223

Earth in the Balance, 128
Earth Summit (Rio), 77, 111, 121, 123, 124, 125, 126, 127–128, 130
The East Asian Miracle: Economic Growth and Public Policy, 80
East Timor, 149, 183
The Economist, 66, 195
Edison, Thomas, 87, 118
Egypt, 290, 293
  opinion toward United States in, 45, 46, 262, 263
  and Six-Day War, 94, 198
  and Suez Canal, 93–94
  U.S. aid to, 168
  U.S. relations with, 261
  and U.S. weapons, 164
  wheat production in, 229
Eisenhower, Dwight D., 68, 90, 94, 96
Eizenstadt, Stuart, 135–136, 137, 140
"Electronic Herd," 52, 53, 55
Emerson, Ralph Waldo, 21, 35, 36
Emissions trading, 134, 135, 136, 138, 139, 140
The End of History, 33
Energy
  conservation, 96–100, 102, 104, 106–109, 281
  use, 6, 83–89, 90, 91, 100–101, 102, 103, 104, 105, 107
Environment
  concern over, 45, 103, 106, 111–142 (*See also* Earth Summit [Rio]; Global warming; Greenhouse gases; Kyoto Treaty; Ozone hole)
  and globalization, 76–77
  and Reagan and Bush administrations, 123–124
  United States as leader on, 113–114
Environmental Protection Agency, 114
Erekat, Saab, 204–205, 215
Europe
  and changing global relationships, 230–244, 266, 294–295
  and Cold War, 238
  conflict with U.S. economy of, 233–235
  economic achievement of, 232–233, 235–236
  future of, 237–238, 239–240
  and religion, 236, 237
  unification of currencies of, 234
  U.S. ambivalence and negativity toward, 241–243
  U.S. investment in, 230
  and values, 236–237
  See also European Union; North Atlantic Treaty Organization; specific European countries
European Commission, 238
European Common Market, 62

European Community (EC), 126, 127, 129
European Union (EU), 62
  accomplishments of, 233, 268
  Acquis Communitaire of, 232
  bringing less developed countries into, 78
  development of, 229, 233
  economy of, 235
  and energy, 83, 108, 125
  and environment, 129, 130, 131, 133, 135, 136, 138, 139, 140
  foreign policy of, 239–240
  GDP of, 26
  and global warming, 112
  imports to, 63
  and International Criminal Court, 160
  and Internet, 235–236
  and Iraq, 268
  and NATO, 241, 243, 270
  and policing in Europe, 279
  proposed security capacity of, 241, 242
  and Spain and Portugal, 258
  and terrorism, 240
  and Turkey, 237
  and UN, 279
  and United States, 232, 244, 268, 275, 279
  and Yugoslavia, 238–239
Evans, Lane, 146

Farman, Joseph, 116
Fascism, 41, 122–123, 173, 227, 237
Feith, Doug, 231, 269
Financial crisis of 1997–1998, 2, 29, 52, 53–58, 75, 78, 183
Findley, Paul, 211
Fisher, Joshka, 123
Fonda, Jane, 127
Ford, Gerald, 98, 183
Ford, Henry, 118
Foreign Affairs, 232
Fourier, Jean-Baptiste-Joseph, 118
Fox, Vicente, 25, 257
France, 27, 36, 285, 290, 295
  and energy, 97–98, 124, 125, 131
  and environment, 122, 129, 132
  GDP of, 84
  and gold, 71
  and International Criminal Court, 160
  and landmines, 146
  and North Korea, 247
  and nuclear weapons, 152, 153, 245
  opinion toward United States in, 45, 237
  and Suez Canal, 93–94
  and UN, 191, 278
  and World War I, 173
Franklin, Ben, 21
Free trade, 53
  as growth factor, 69
  U.S. advocacy of, 11, 33, 52, 54, 58–59, 62, 65, 68, 75, 143, 258
  See also specific agreements

Friedman, Thomas
  on globalization, 34, 42, 52, 75, 228
  and real problems, 48
  on United States as enforcer, 43
Fukuyama, Francis, 33, 74, 227, 228, 232

G–8, 281
Galvin, Robert, 68
Gansler, Jacques, 163
Garcia, Maria Consuelo, 76
Garcia, Paz, 167
Garton Ash, Timothy, 272
Gates, Bill, 20
Gayoom, Maumoon Abdul, 111
General Agreement on Tariffs and Trade (GATT),
  68, 73, 75, 229
Geneva Convention, 198
Geneva Declaration, 131
Geneva Protocol, 154
Genocide, 156, 173, 189, 270
George, Walter, 223
Gephardt, Richard, 194
Germany, 85, 92, 285, 290, 295
  economy of, 26
  and environment, 122, 129, 131
  factories in, 124–125
  GDP of, 84
  and global warming, 112
  Greens in, 112, 123, 129
  imperial, 41
  and International Criminal Court, 157
  and Iraq, 112, 231
  opinion toward United States in, 45
  and Pakistan, 264
  and steel, 62, 64
  and World War I, 88, 173
  and World War II, 88, 174
  See also Berlin
Gifford, Kathie Lee, 76
Gingrich, Newt, 34, 128, 164
Glaspie, April, 189
Global Climate Coalition, 132
Global Compact, 77
Global warming, 117
  disagreement over, 6, 12–13, 112–113
  and greenhouse gases, 118–122
  and industry, 124
  IPCC on, 130–131, 140–141
  and Kyoto Treaty, 2, 3, 12, 77, 112–113, 136,
    137, 138, 139
  and Maldives, 111
  Sununu on, 124
  and Treaty of Rio, 13
Globalization, 65, 67, 255, 284
  and 1997–1998 financial crisis, 2, 58
  as Americanization, 6, 34, 42, 75, 275–276
  crisis of, 282
  criticism and protest of, 2, 61, 75–80, 123
  defined, 52
  and democracy, 228

  and doctrine of integration, 41
  and dollar standard, 72
  and economic inequality, 229
  and the environment, 76–77
  and Europe, 235, 236
  as good for non-Americans, 69
  and home schooling, 43
  and September 11 attacks, 230
  and threats, 274
  touting of, 52, 59
  undermining of nation state by, 43
  and unions, 76
  United States in driver's seat of, 72, 272
  unstoppability of, 80
  and U.S. and European economies,
    230, 234
  and U.S. dependency, 276
  and U.S. trade deficit, 67
Gold, 71
Gorbachev, Mikhail, 44, 152
Gore, Al, 128, 136, 139
Great Britain, 41, 294, 296
  and automobiles, 82
  becomes broke, 175
  and Bretton Woods, 69
  and China, 178
  as empire, 27, 42, 277
  and energy and environment, 124, 125, 126, 129,
    131, 132
  income in, 87
  and International Criminal Court, 158, 160
  and Iran, 184, 185
  and Iraq, 267, 268, 285–286, 289, 291
  and nuclear weapons, 245
  and oil, 92, 93
  opinion toward United States in, 45, 46
  and Palestine, 208–209
  and September 11 attacks, 242
  and steel, 62
  and Suez Canal, 93–94
  terrorism in, 36
  and UN, 278
  and U.S. weapons, 164
  and World War I, 88, 173
  and World War II, 88
Great Depression, 58, 69, 114
The Great Illusion, 80
Great Society programs, 71
Greece, 164, 175, 181
Green, Marshall, 182
Greenhouse gases, 111, 118–122, 125, 127, 131,
  133, 135, 136, 137, 281
Greens, 112, 123, 129
Greenspan, Alan, 58
Grinberg, Lev, 201
Guam, 173
Guardian (London), 2, 113
Guatemala, 181
Gulf War (1991), 34, 102, 103, 154, 187, 189,
  209–210, 227, 263, 268–270, 289

Gun regulation, 44
Gurria, Angel, 256, 257

Ha'am, Ahad, 208
Ha'aretz, 205
Haas, Richard, 24, 41, 269
Hagel, Chuck, 133
The Hague, November 2000 meeting in, 136,
    138–139
Halevi, Yossi Klein, 200
Hamas, 196, 203, 204, 206–207, 210
Hansen, James, 120, 121
Hansen, Jim, 129
Harrison, Sonjai, 3
Hawaii, 219
Hay, John, 173
Helms, Jesse, 153, 159, 160–161, 224, 241
Herzl, Theodore, 207
Hess, Moses, 207
Hester, Ed, 61
Hezbollah, 207
Hilsman, Roger, 250
Hirsh, Michael, 48
Hitler, Adolf, 88, 174, 189
Ho Chi Minh, 181
Hofstader, Richard, 35–36
Holocaust, 156, 174, 209
Homeland Security, Department of, 277
Honduras, 167
Hong Kong
    1997 IMF/World Bank meeting in, 55
    and 1997–1998 financial crisis, 55–56, 58
    economic miracle in, 52
    foreign factories in, 69
Hood, Ken, 59, 60
Hu Jintao, 296
Human Rights Watch, 146
Hungary, 241
Huntington, Samuel, 40, 169
Hussein, King, 261
Hussein, Saddam, 1, 2, 5, 6, 49, 187, 285–289,
    291–293, 295
    and Gulf War, 227, 263, 269, 270
    and Iran war, 101, 186, 188
    and Kurds and Shiites, 189
    and Kuwait, 102, 189
    and terrorists, 190
    U.S. diplomatic relations with, 188, 189
    U.S. effort to remove, 8, 242, 263, 267
    and weapons of mass destruction, 103, 190–191,
        262, 269, 278
Hussein, Sharif, 208

Ickes, Harold, 91
Ikenberry, John, 272
Inderfurth, Karl F., 147
India
    and AIDS, 79
    and Coca-Cola, 30
    and Cold War, 264

economy of, 69, 103
and environment, 126
and European Union, 232
and G–8, 281
and nuclear weapons, 47, 229, 264, 265
and oil, 105, 106
and Pakistan, 47, 264, 265, 266, 283
and Silicon Valley, 30, 265
and UN, 278
U.S. relations with, 264, 265, 266
and U.S. pop culture, 45
and water, 283
Indochina, 88
    See also Vietnam War; specific countries
Indonesia
    1994 meeting in, 53
    and 1997–1998 financial crisis, 54, 55, 56, 58, 183
    and China, 282
    and Coca-Cola, 30
    conditional loans to, 12
    cutting of tropical rain forests in, 77
    and Iraq, 278
    McDonald's in, 77
    Nike in, 275
    opinion toward United States in, 45
    recent U.S. military ties with, 183–184
    and Suharto, 181–183
    U.S. diplomatic representation in, 39, 40
Intellectual property protection, 73–74, 78
Intergovernmental Panel on Climate Change
    (IPCC), 121, 122, 130, 131, 132, 136, 140
International Atomic Energy Agency (IAEA), 246
International Campaign to Ban Landmines (ICBL),
    146
International Convention on the Rights of the
    Child, 156
International Criminal Court (ICC), 47, 144,
    156–160, 231, 232, 270, 281
International Monetary Fund (IMF), 11, 52, 230
    and 1997–1998 financial crisis, 29, 54, 55, 56,
        58, 75
    control of, 234
    creation of, 68, 70, 174
    and Indonesia, 182, 183
    and Latin America, 256, 257
    roles following Bretton Woods, 70
Internet, 27
    origins of, 72
    privacy, 236
Interstate Highway Act, 90
Iran, 263, 289
    and CTBT, 153
    faltering of rule of ayatollahs in, 191
    and Hezbollah, 207
    and Iraq, 101, 102, 186, 188, 189, 190, 270
    oil in, 93, 95, 101, 102, 184–185
    overthrow of Mossadegh in, 181, 184–185
    as part of "Axis of Evil," 163
    revolution of, 263
    U.S. support for Shah in, 185

Iraq, 1, 2, 6, 274, 285-292
and CTBT, 153
economic sanctions against, 190
and Gulf War (1991), 34, 189, 227, 269–270
impending U.S. war with (2003), 6, 16, 105, 109, 163, 170, 190–191, 207, 231, 240, 242, 244, 246, 254, 261, 262, 263, 266, 267, 268, 271, 275, 276, 278
inability of Americans to locate, 169
and International Criminal Court, 158
and Iran, 101, 102, 186, 188, 189, 190
and Kurds and Shiites in, 188, 269, 270
and Kuwait, 102, 189
and NATO, 8
no-fly zones in, 269
oil in, 93, 101, 103, 276
rebuilding of, 281
as rogue nation, 6
and terrorism, 187–188
U.S. aid to and diplomatic relations with, 188, 189
and water, 282
and weapons of mass destruction, 4–5, 8, 101, 103, 155, 188, 189, 190, 191, 231, 269, 270, 286–292
Irish Republican Army, 36
Ishihara, Shintaro, 251
Islamic Jihad, 196, 203, 204, 207
Israel, 6, 293, 295
American views of, 194
attacks on Palestinians of, 13, 194, 195, 197, 203, 204, 205, 217–218, 289
and Camp David, 199, 200, 205, 212–216, 217, 278
economy of, 197–198
and enmity toward United States overseas, 193, 225, 240, 261, 263, 266
establishment and roots of, 93, 200, 207–209
European criticism of, 237, 243
flouting of UN resolutions by, 191, 195, 198, 263
and International Criminal Court, 158
lobby of, 211–212, 218
missile attack on airliner of, 163
nuclear weapons of, 195, 245, 263
and occupied territories, 13, 191, 193, 194, 196, 197, 198–200, 201, 202, 206, 207, 209–210, 211, 214, 216, 278
and Oslo peace process, 198, 199–200, 201, 210, 214, 227
and preservation of Jewish state, 200–202
reprisals by, 193, 195, 197, 204, 212
significance of, for United States, 13, 193–218
sinking of Liberty by, 263
Six-Day War of, 94, 96, 198, 209
and Suez Canal, 93
suicide bombers in, 13, 193, 194, 196, 197, 200, 203, 204, 212
and Taba talks, 199, 200, 216–217, 278
U.S. aid to, 168, 197, 198, 210, 212, 278
U.S. embassy in, 203
and U.S. media, 194, 195, 196, 226
and U.S. weapons, 164, 195

and water, 282
Yom Kippur war of, 94, 261
Italy, 84, 146, 285

Jackson, Andrew, 31, 172
Japan, 291, 294, 296–297
and 1997–1998 financial crisis, 54, 56
and automobiles, 82, 97, 249
banks of, 74, 80, 249
broken politics of, 229
bullet trains of, 83
and China, 178, 222, 252
constitution of, 280
defense spending of, 251, 281
and Dodge Plan, 68
economic miracle in, 52
economy of, 131–132, 233, 248–250
and energy conservation, 96–97, 98, 99
and energy use, 83, 91, 95, 100, 105, 108
and environment, 126, 131, 133, 136, 137, 139, 140
exports of, 68–69, 73, 74, 249, 251
freedom in, compared to United States, 37
GDP of, 26, 84
and global warming, 112, 113
government debt of, 197, 250
and Gulf War, 102
imports to, 63–64, 249
and lawyers, 143
Liberal Democratic Party (LDP) in, 249–250, 251
and Matthew Perry, 172–173
"miracle" of, 66, 67
and North Korea, 247
and nuclear weapons, 45
and oil, 186
opinion toward United States in, 45, 251, 252
post–World War II recovery of, 70
remilitarization of, 48
as satellite of United States, 28–29, 228–229, 251, 279
and steel, 62, 64, 65, 249
terrorists in, 36
and UN, 278
U.S. commercial agreements and trade with, 5, 11, 12, 67, 68, 251
U.S. disagreements with, 266
U.S. troops in, 48, 250, 251–252, 268, 280
and U.S. weapons, 164, 165
and World War II, 41, 88, 222, 250, 251, 280
Japan-U.S. Security Treaty, 169, 280
Jefferson, Thomas, 20, 21, 31, 172
Jerusalem Post, 197
Jiang Zemin, 4, 25
Jihad, 43, 103, 106
See also Islamic Jihad
Joffe, Josef, 238
Johnson, Lyndon, 4
Johnson, U. Alexis, 250
Joint Combined Exchange Training (JCET), 167–168
Jones, James Earl, 126

Jordan
  anti–United States sentiment in, 15–16, 45, 262–263
  and Palestinians, 207, 209
  and Six-Day War, 198
  U.S. relations with, 261, 295
  and Iraq, 278

Kagan, Robert, 231, 240, 242, 279
Kaplan, Robert, 274
Kase, Hideaki, 251
Kawaguchi, Yoriko, 251
Kay, David, 287
Keeling, Charles, 119, 121, 128
Kellogg, William, 119, 120
Kelly, James, 247
Kennan, George, 175
Kennedy, John F.
  and Berlin, 44
  and Europe, 232, 241, 294
  and "missile gap," 162
Kennedy, Ted, 224
Kerry, John, 107
Keynes, John Maynard, 70, 71
Khomeini, Ayatollah, 95, 185
Khrushchev, Nikita, 62
Kim Dae-jung, 9, 171, 179, 180, 246, 271
Kim Jong-il, 5, 271, 278
Kinkel, Klaus, 135
Kiplings, Rudyard, 273
Kissinger, Henry, 95, 153, 157, 158, 178, 183, 237, 239
Kitty Hawk, U.S.S., 26
Kobayashi, Yoshinori, 251
Koizumi, Junichiro, 25
Korean War, 9–10, 161, 177–178, 179, 180, 223, 246, 271, 278
Kosovo, 43, 239, 279
Kristol, Irving, 24, 29
Kuwait
  Iraq invasion of, 102, 189, 269
  oil in, 93
Kyoto Treaty, 125, 128, 132, 133–138, 141, 281
  U.S. rejection of, 2, 3, 12, 16, 77, 112–113, 139–140, 142, 231, 270

Lafayette, Marquis de, 20
Lamy, Pascal, 65
Landmine treaty, 3, 144–149, 151, 270, 281
Latin America, 256–263
  See also specific Latin American countries
Lawrence, T. E., 208
Layne, Christopher, 272
Le Monde, 4, 195
League of Nations, 32, 174, 208
Leahy, Patrick, 146, 147
Lebanon, 45, 181, 207, 209, 261
Lee Hoi Chang, 28
L'Enfant, Pierre, 19
Libya, 158, 290
Like Minded Group, 157

Lincoln, Abraham, 20
Lindzen, Richard, 121
Lodge, Henry Cabot, 174
Long Term Capital Management (LTCM), 57–58
Lott, Trent, 82, 153, 220
Lovins, Amory, 107–108
Loy, Frank, 138, 139, 140
Luce, Henry B., 221, 222, 223
Luxembourg, 238

MacArthur, Douglas, 177–178
MacLaine, Shirley, 127
MAD (mutual assured destruction), 154, 162
Mahathir Mohamed, 55, 56, 57, 58, 263
Mahley, Donald, 155
The Maine Woods, 114
Malaysia, 296
  and 1997–1998 financial crisis, 54, 55, 56, 58
  anti–United States sentiment in, 14
  conditional loans to, 12
  economic miracle in, 52
  and environment, 126
  foreign factories in, 69
  and Iraq, 278
  and oil, 100
  and steel, 63
Maldive Islands, 111–112
Mali, 59, 60–61
Mallaby, Sebastian, 274
Malley, Robert, 214
Man and Nature, 114
Manifest Destiny, 31
Mao Zedong, 221, 222, 223
Marcos, Ferdinand, 33
Marsh, George Perkins, 114
Marshall Plan, 68, 176
May, Ernest, 21
McCarthy, Joe, 223
McCarthyism, 178
McConnell, Mitch, 194
McGowan, John, 119
McKinley, William, 32, 173, 274
McMahon, Henry, 208
McRae, Norman, 66, 67
Meacher, Michael, 112, 135
Mead, Margaret, 120
Melville, Herman, 19, 31
Mexico, 285, 290
  and China, 79
  and drugs, 259, 260
  economic troubles in, 54, 258
  factories in, 76, 78–79, 258
  and globalization, 282
  and Mexican-American War, 31, 173
  and NAFTA, 12, 69, 78–79, 258
  October 2002 APEC conference in, 24–25, 48
  and oil, 100, 258
  and steel, 63
  unemployment and falling wages in, 256, 258
  U.S. trade with, 12, 69, 258, 297

Microsoft, 27, 40, 275
Middle East. *See* specific Middle Eastern countries
Mikulski, Barbara, 105
Miles, Ed, 148
Military, U.S. *See* United States (military might, force, spending, and programs overseas of)
Miller, Zell, 105
Milosevic, Slobodan, 239
Mine Ban Treaty. *See* Landmine treaty
Missile defense, U.S. (NMD), 2, 7, 11, 35, 151, 152, 154, 162–163, 244, 254, 271, 280
"Missile gap," 162
Mitchell, Colin "Mad Mitch," 145
Mitchell, George, 217
Mitterand, Francois, 146
Moisi, Dominque, 232
Monina, Mario J. [AU: Monina or Molina? *See* pages], 115, 116
Montesquieu, 42
Monti, Mario, 234
Montreal Protocol, 117, 121, 125, 133
Moore, Molly, 199
Morita, Akio, 251
Mossadegh, Mohammed, 181, 184
Movies and television, 72
Murphy, Richard, 189
Musharraf, 265–266, 290, 292

NASA, 116
Nasser, Gamal Abdel, 93
National Academy of Sciences, 116, 119
National Cotton Council, 59
National Labor Committee, 76
National Missile Defense (NMD). *See* Missile defense, U.S. (NMD)
The National Review, 232, 242
Native Americans, 13, 31, 127, 172
NATO. *See* North Atlantic Treaty Organization (NATO)
Nature, 115, 116
Nazism, 41
Neoconservatism, 277, 286–288
Netherlands, 66–67, 84, 122, 235
New Scientist, 155
New world order, 266
New York Times, 24, 40, 48, 197–198, 272, 273
New Zealand, 79, 131, 133, 183
Ngo Dinh Diem, 181
Nicaragua, 106
Niebuhr, Reinhold, 35
Nigeria, 45, 48–49, 100
Nike, 76
Nitze, Paul, 153
Nixon, Richard
  and chemical and biological weapons, 154, 155
  and China, 11, 178, 223, 252, 264
  and energy, 98
  and Environmental Protection Agency, 114
  and gold, 71
  and Suharto, 183

Noboru, Seiichiro, 155
Noriega, Manuel, 259
North American Free Trade Agreement (NAFTA), 229, 297
  and Mexico, 12, 69, 78, 258
  U.S. support for, 12
North Atlantic Treaty Organization (NATO), 169, 218
  and Afghanistan, 231
  and Cold War, 230
  creation of, 176
  and European Union, 241, 243, 270
  and Iraq, 8, 288
  and Israel, 278
  and Kosovo, 239
  and Poland, 165
  revamping of, 279
  and Russia, 152
  and September 11 attacks, 7
  and United States, 231, 268, 294
North Korea, 6, 251
  and Europe, 239
  and Kim Dae Jung, 179, 180
  and Korean War, 177, 178, 278
  and landmines, 147
  and nuclear weapons, 9, 163, 179–180, 246, 247, 267, 271–279, 293–294
  as part of "Axis of Evil," 9, 163, 246, 247, 271
  as threat, 169–170
  U.S. effort to destabilize, 10
  U.S. tensions with, 171, 246–247, 271, 275, 278, 279
Norway, 150
Nuclear power, 96, 97, 98, 99, 100, 108, 124, 131
Nuclear weapons, 149
  of China, 254
  as defense against United States, 267–268
  and double standards, 245, 263
  and India and Pakistan, 47, 229, 264–265, 266, 283
  and Iraq, 189, 190
  of Israel, 195
  and North Korea, 9, 163, 179–180, 246, 247, 267, 271–279
  of Russia, 151, 152
  of Soviet Union, 176
  of United States, 24, 151, 152, 154, 247
  U.S. concern over, 45
  See also Comprehensive Nuclear Test Ban Treaty (CTBT)
Nuremberg trials, 23

Of Paradise and Power, 231
Office of Global Communications, 169
Ohmae, Kenichi, 52
Oil
  age of, begins in United States, 85–87
  consideration of alternatives to, 95–101 (*See also* Energy (conservation))
  demand in future for, 105
  development of, in Middle East, 92–93
  and Europe, 242

Oil *(continued)*
  and George W. Bush, 139, 289, 291
  and Iraq-Iran war, 101
  lobbyists, 90
  and Mexico, 100, 258
  shocks and crises over, 81, 93–95, 96, 185
  synthetic, 96, 98, 99, 100
  U.S. imports and dependence on, 6, 82, 83, 91–92,
    94, 100, 101, 102, 104, 105–106, 242, 258, 276
  whale, 85
  in world wars, 87–88, 91, 92
  See also specific countries
Omunu, Victor, 48
Operation Anaconda, 81, 82
Operation Desert Storm, 102, 189
Organization for Economic Cooperation and
    Development, 56, 92
Organization of Petroleum Exporting Countries
    (OPEC), 87, 94, 95, 101, 125, 126, 185
Oslo peace process, 198, 199–200, 201, 206, 207,
    210, 212, 214, 227
O'sullivan, John, 232, 242
Ottawa Conference on landmines, 146–147, 148
Ozawa, Ichiro, 28, 29, 279
Ozone hole, 114–117, 121, 124, 125

Paemen, Hugo, 8
Pahlevi, Reza, 185
  See also Shah of Iran
Pakistan, 61, 285, 290, 292–293
  and Cold War, 264
  and India, 47, 264, 265, 266, 283
  Islamic Madrassas in, 40
  and nuclear weapons, 47, 229, 264–265, 266, 283
  opinion toward United States in, 45, 46
  and Pearl kidnapping, 266
  radicalizing of, 266
  and resistance to Soviets in Afghanistan, 186, 187
  and Taliban, 265, 283
  textile exports of, 79
  U.S. diplomatic representation in, 40
  U.S. relations with, 264–266
  and water, 283
  wheat production in, 229
Palestine, 7, 295
  and Balfour Declaration, 208–209
  emigration of European Jews into, 208, 209
  as land promised to Jews, 198
  proposed state of, 193–194, 200, 201, 207, 212,
    213, 216
  proposed two-state solution, 209
  and U.S. media, 226
  See also Palestinians
Palestine Liberation Organization (PLO), 194, 203,
    205, 206, 207, 210
Palestinian Authority (PA), 196, 203, 206, 207
Palestinians
  and Camp David, 199, 200, 204, 205, 212–216,
    217, 218
  complex politics of, 206–207

  economic and social conditions of, 204, 205–206
  Israeli attacks on and battles with, 13, 194, 195,
    197, 203, 204, 205, 209, 217–218
  and Israeli occupation, 13, 191, 196, 197, 198–200,
    201, 202, 206, 207, 209, 210, 212, 214
  and location of U.S. embassy in Israel, 203
  and Oslo peace process, 198, 199–200, 201, 206,
    207, 210, 214, 227
  refugees, 200, 205, 209, 212, 216
  Saudi support of, 261
  and Taba talks, 199, 200, 216–217
  and Temple Mount, 217–218
  terrorists, 13, 193, 194, 196, 197, 200, 203, 204,
    207, 209, 211, 212, 289
  and United States, 13, 194
Pamuk, Orham, 275
Panama, 259
Panitchpakdi, Supachai, 51–52, 54
Park Chung-hee, 179
Patten, Chris, 238, 240
Pearl, Danny, 266
Perry, Matthew, 172
Perry, William, 166
Persian empire, 27
Persson, Goeran, 13
Peru, 259, 260
Pew Research Center for the People and the Press,
    15, 44
Philippines, 182, 274
  and 1997–1998 financial crisis, 54
  and agriculture, 79
  becomes U.S. colony, 32
  dictator in, 181
  and Spanish-American War, 173
Physicians for Human Rights, 146
Pinochet, Augusto, 181
Pinsker, Leo, 207
Plaza Accord, 74
Poland, 63, 160, 164–165, 241, 243–244, 285
Polk, James, 173
Pollard, Jonathan, 263
Poos, Jacques, 238
Portugal, 183, 258, 286
Powell, Colin, 285–286
  and CTBT, 153
  and free trade, 59, 61
  and Iraq, 4, 5, 8, 191, 269
  on United States as bully on the block, 7, 23
  and U.S. defense strategy, 23
Preemption doctrine. *See* United States (preemption
    doctrine of)
Preez, Jean Du, 151
Prescott, John, 139
Present at the Creation, 96
Prevention of Genocide Act, 189
Privatization, 11, 52, 74, 75, 79, 258
Project Independence, 98
Prowse, Michael, 42
Puerto Rico, 173
Putin, Vladimir, 3

Qatar, 158
Quandt, William, 211

Rabin, Yitzhak, 199, 201, 210
Rachmadi, Bambang, 77
Raheek, 202
Railroads. *See* Trains and railroads
Rand, Ayn, 58
Rea, Lord, 156
Reagan, Ronald, 17, 228
  and Berlin wall, 44
  and environment, 116, 123
  and "Evil Empire," 41, 227
  and Iraq, 188, 189
  and Star Wars, 162
The Reluctant Sheriff, 24
Revelle, Roger, 119
Revolutionary War, 172
Reyes, Camillo, 151
Rice, Condoleezza, 3, 34, 293
Rio. *See* Earth Summit (Rio)
Robertson, Pat, 211
Rockefeller, John D., 87
Rockefeller, Nelson, 98
Rodgers, John, 173
Rogue nations
  according to United States, 3, 5, 152, 163, 245, 254, 271, 273
  United States as one, 1–2, 5, 6, 105, 231, 271
Roh Moo Hyun, 28, 245–246
Rohrabacher, Dana, 132–133
Roman empire, 27, 42, 234, 277, 290
Romania, 160
Roosevelt, Franklin, 32, 59, 114
Roosevelt, Theodore, 114
Ross, Dennis, 213, 217
Rowland, F. Sherwood, 115, 116
Rumsfeld, Donald, 188, 190
Rusk, Dean, 223
Russia, 27, 285, 290, 293–294
  and ABM Treaty, 151–152
  and chemical weapons, 155
  and China, 275
  and CTBT, 153
  economy of, 26, 57, 281
  and environment, 131, 139, 140
  and European Union, 239
  and euros, 234
  and G–8, 281
  and NATO, 243
  oil in, 104
  opinion toward United States in, 45
  rising living standards in, 201
  and UN, 279
  U.S. diplomatic representation in, 40, 169
  U.S. relations with, 244, 252, 254, 266
  and World War I, 173
Rwanda, 156

Sadat, Anwar, 94, 95
Said, Abdel Monem, 263
Sangare, Mody, 59, 60
Saud, King Ibn, 93
Saudi Arabia, 290, 293
  energy reserves of, 84, 87, 93, 94, 100, 102, 104, 105–106, 107, 184, 261
  and Gulf War, 103, 269, 270
  relationship with United States of, 105–106, 187, 261–262
  and resistance to Soviets in Afghanistan, 187
  and UN, 278
  U.S. diplomatic representation in, 40, 169
  U.S. troops in, 187, 189, 229, 240, 262, 268, 289
  and U.S. weapons, 164
  and Yom Kippur war, 94
Savir, Uri, 206
School of the Americas, 167
Schreiber, Jean Jacques Servan, 67
Schroder, Gerhard, 112, 231
Schwarz, Benjamin, 272
Schwarzkopf, Norman, 102, 269
Schweizer, Louis, 235
Science, 119
Sciolino, Elaine, 239
Scotland, 122
Scowcroft, Brent, 153
Seattle, Washington, anti-globalization protest, 75–76
September 11, 2001, terrorist attacks, 35, 77, 79, 104, 187, 252, 271, 275
  and Europe, 241–242
  failure to predict, 16
  and fight against evil, 41
  foreign sympathy with United States over, 3–4, 17, 142, 253, 271
  and Indonesia, 183
  and Iraq, 190
  and Israel, 14
  Max Boot on, 274
  and missile defense, 152, 163
  and NATO, 8
  occurrence of, 3, 5
  and Office of Global Communications, 169
  and Pakistan, 265
  and Palestinian terrorists, 194
  patriotism following, 36
  and Saudi Arabia, 106, 261, 262
  and shifts of global relationships, 230
  shock of, 284
  and U.S. enemies, 170
  and U.S. military spending, 109
  and U.S. security, 275
Sergeyev, Igor, 151
Service, John, 178, 222, 223
Shah of Iran, 33, 95, 181, 185, 186, 188
Shah of Persia, 92
Shamir, Yitzhak, 188, 210
Sharon, Ariel, 193, 195, 196, 198, 203, 204, 205, 206, 207, 212, 213, 270, 295
  walk on Temple Mount of, 217–218

Shelton, Henry, 153
Sheng, Andrew, 42
Shikaki, Khalid, 207
Shultz, George, 188, 189
Sierra Club, 126
Sierra Leone, 43, 149, 283
Silent Spring, 114
Silicon Valley, 30
Silva, Luis Inacio da, 79
Singapore
  economic development of, 52, 260
  foreign factories in, 69
  provident fund of, 80
Sinks, 134, 135, 136, 138, 139, 140
Small arms trade ban, 144, 149–151, 270
Smith, John, 31
Smith, Tony, 177
Solana, Javier, 239, 240
Somalia, 149
Soong, T. V., 221
Soros, George, 55, 79
South Africa, 150
South Asia, 264–266, 290
  See also specific South Asian countries
South Korea, 6, 169, 271, 278, 293, 296
  and 1997–1998 financial crisis, 54, 55, 56–57, 58, 78
  and China, 248
  criticism of United States in, 9–10, 28, 180, 247–248
  death of two teenage girls in (2002), 28
  democracy in, 229
  economic assistance to North of, 180
  economic miracle in, 9, 52
  estrangement between United States and, 245–246, 247, 266
  foreign factories in, 69
  and George W. Bush, 171
  and John Rodgers, 173
  and Korean War, 177, 178, 179
  Kwangju Massacre in, 179
  and landmines, 146, 147, 148
  religion in, 248
  as satellite of United States, 28, 29, 228–229
  Status of Forces Agreement with United States of, 9, 28
  and steel, 63
  "Sunshine Policy" of, 171, 179, 246, 247
  takeovers and coups in, 179
  U.S. trade with, 11, 179
  U.S. troops in, 48, 170, 180, 246, 247, 248, 268, 280
  and U.S. policy toward the North, 247
  and U.S. weapons, 164, 165
Southeast Asian Treaty Organization (SEATO), 264
Soviet Union, 41, 96
  and 1948 Berlin crisis, 44
  and Afghanistan, 11, 103, 145, 186–187, 259, 265
  atomic test of, 176
  and chemical and biological weapons, 154, 155
  and China, 178–179, 225, 252
  and Cold War, 175, 176, 264
  collapse of, 11, 23, 169, 187, 227, 228, 229, 238, 265, 268
  and India, 264
  and Iran, 184, 185
  and Korean War, 177
  military of, 161, 162
  and natural gas, 97
  and nuclear testing, 152
  weakened, 34
Spain, 258, 285–286, 291
Spanish-American War, 32, 173, 176
Special Operations Forces (SOF), U.S., 167–168
Stalin, Joseph, 175
Star Wars, 162
  See also Missile defense, U.S. (NMD)
Steel, 12–13, 62–65, 87, 249
Stilwell, Joseph, 222
Stock market, U.S., 27, 74
Strategic Defense Initiative (SDI), 162, 163
Suburbs, 89–91
Suess, Hans, 119
Suez Canal, 93–94
Suharto, 182, 183
Sukarno, 182
Sukarnoputri, Megawati, 184
Summers, Larry, 21
Sununu, John, 123–124, 127
Sutherland, Peter, 8, 230, 232, 244
SUVs, 81–82, 84, 100, 107
Swarthmore College, 5, 6
Sweden, 112, 122, 146, 235
Switzerland, 66, 123, 278
Synghman Rhee, 179
Syria, 94, 198, 282, 290

Taiwan, 11, 181, 266, 296
  Chiang Kai-shek flees to, 223
  and China, 178, 219–220, 221, 223–225, 253, 255, 280
  democracy in, 225
  economic development of, 52, 260
  and enmity toward United States overseas, 225
  foreign factories in, 69
  and independence, 280
  and Korean War, 178
  lobby of, 221
  significance of, for United States, 193
  United States recognizes, later dumps, 223–224
  and U.S. media, 226
  and U.S. weapons, 164, 220, 221, 224, 254, 280
Taiwan Relations Act of 1979, 224
Talbott, Strobe, 21
Taliban, 7, 11, 81, 156, 187, 190, 265, 275, 283, 291–292
Terrorism
  in Bali, 181–182, 184
  and European Union, 240

and globalization, 61
and Iraq, 187–188, 190
in Kashmir, 266
and missiles, 163
as perceived threat to regional security, 48
war on, 6, 10, 16, 61, 170, 181, 263, 264, 265, 266
See also Algerian terrorists; Aum terrorists; Hamas;
    Irish Republican Army; Islamic Jihad; Israel
    (suicide bombers in); Jihad; Palestinians
    (terrorists); September 11, 2001, terrorist attacks
Texas Railroad Commission, 87, 91, 92, 93, 94, 105
Textiles, 73, 76, 79
Thailand, 51, 52
    and 1997–1998 financial crisis, 53–54, 55, 58,
        183
    dictator in, 181
    economic miracle in, 52, 53
    and landmines, 146
Thomas, Lee M., 117
Thoreau, Henry David, 114
Three Mile Island nuclear accident, 99
Time, 221, 222, 223
Tinbergen, Jan, 51
Tobacco, 73
Tocqueville, Alexis de, 37
Tojo, General Hideki, 251
Tolba, Mostafa, 125
Trade Promotion Authority, 58–59
Trains and railroads, 83, 87, 90, 91, 99
Trans-Atlantic Policy Network, 231
Traore, Bakary, 61
Treaty of Rio, 13
Treaty of Westphalia, 23
Truman, Harry
    and Cold War, 32–33, 175–176
    and Korean War, 177, 178
Turkey
    communist insurrection in, 175
    and European Union, 237
    and Iraq, 270, 285
    opinion toward United States in, 45
    U.S. bases in, 281
    and U.S. weapons, 164
    and water, 282
Turner, Frederick Jackson, 37
Turner, Ted, 127

Ukraine, 239
Ulmer, Alfred C., Jr., 250
United Kingdom (U.K.), 82, 85
    and energy conservation, 108
    GDP of, 84
    See also Great Britain
United Nations Environment Program (UNEP),
    116, 120–121
United Nations (UN), 127, 161, 270, 285–286,
    297–298
    and atomic energy, 174–175
    becomes more workable body, 169
    Charter, 23

and chemical and biological weapons, 154, 155
creation of, 174
and CTBT, 152, 153
and European Union, 240, 278
Framework Convention on Climate Change, 127
and genocide, 156
Human Rights Commission, 206
and Indonesia, 182
Intergovernmental Negotiating Committee (INC),
    125
and International Criminal Court, 47, 157, 158,
    160
and Iran-Iraq war, 101
and Iraq, 5, 190, 191, 231, 240, 242, 267, 269,
    271, 275, 278
and Israel, 191, 195, 198, 209, 210, 216
and landmines, 146, 147
overhaul of, 278
and Palestine, 205, 206, 209, 210
peacekeeping, 160, 183
Population Fund, 40
Security Council Resolution 687, 190, 269
Security Council Resolution 1441, 5, 191
and small arms, 149–151
U.S. debt to, 168, 229, 281
United States
    alienation from and criticism of, overseas, 1–3, 5–6,
        8–10, 14–17, 44–49, 61, 126, 137, 140, 144,
        151, 160, 177, 180, 185, 191, 193, 195, 218,
        225, 231, 232, 240, 244–245, 247–248, 257,
        260, 261, 262–263, 272–273, 277, 279, 283
    anti-imperialist tradition of, 20–21
    arms exports of, 164–166, 168
    backing of dictators of, 33
    as bully on the block, 7, 23
    crime and imprisonment in, 38, 237
    doctrine of integration of, 41–42
    double standards of, 191, 195, 245, 257, 263
    early riches of, 84–87
    economic dominance of, 26–27
    economic inequality in, 38–39, 74
    as empire, 25–35, 36, 39, 42, 283
    equal opportunity in, 36–38, 39
    as export market of choice, 63–64, 73
    founding ideas of, 35–38
    good will toward, 15, 44
    military might, force, spending, and programs
        overseas of, 26, 33–34, 72, 109, 161–168,
        169–170, 175, 228, 243, 245, 275, 277, 281, 283
    and nation building, 35, 68
    need for real conservatism in, 276–277
    against "other," 40–41, 169, 176
    overseas nonmilitary spending of, 168
    pensions and health care in, 63, 64
    pop culture in, 45, 72
    preemption doctrine of, 22–24, 47, 190, 231,
        254, 271, 273–276
    procedure of foreign policy of, 281–282
    protectionism of, 12–13, 62, 63, 64, 65, 69, 73
    religion in, 37–38, 236

United States (continued)
  as "reluctant superpower," 21
  as rogue nation, 1–2, 5, 6, 105, 231
  self-righteousness of, 14, 15, 39, 46–47, 49, 58, 105
  trade deficits of, 11, 67, 69, 70, 71, 72, 83, 104, 106, 235, 256
  and treaties, 143–161, 231, 270, 281
  unilateralism of, 2–3, 6, 7–9, 11, 14, 16, 31, 34, 47, 62, 71, 172, 176, 268, 271, 272
  wars and interventions of, 171–191
  See also other specific topics
United Steel Workers, 64
U.S. Commerce Department, 188
U.S. Defense Department, 147, 188
U.S. Defense Intelligence Agency, 188
U.S. Department of Health and Human Services, 40
U.S. Information Agency, 169
U.S. State Department, 168, 187, 188
U.S. Treasury Department, 29, 52, 57, 74

Vedrine, Hubert, 42
Venezuela, 184, 257, 260
Versailles Peace Conference, 208–209
Vienna Convention, 116
Vietnam Memorial, 20
Vietnam Veterans of America Foundation, 146, 149
Vietnam War
  author's defense of, 6
  and domino theory, 181
  Gulf of Tonkin incidents in, 181
  and landmines, 145, 148
  and media, 226
  payment for, 71
  soldiers going home from, 39
  and Thailand, 52, 54
  U.S. misperceptions about, 16
Villepin, Dominique de, 5
Virgin Islands, 173
Volkswagen, 68

Wal-Mart, 76
Wall Street Journal, 59, 102, 234, 261, 266, 273, 274, 286
Wallace, William, 240
Wallerstein, Immanuel, 170
War of 1812, 172
Warburg, James, 177
Warsaw Pact, 227
Washington, D.C., city and monuments of, 19–20
Washington, George, 20, 21, 31, 172
"Washington Consensus," 52, 75, 229, 257
Washington Post, 1, 81, 82, 199, 274
Water, 282–283
Watergate scandal, 98
Watt, James, 123
Weapons of mass destruction
  and Iraq, 4–5, 101, 103, 155, 188, 189, 190, 191, 231, 269, 270, 285–293

and preemption doctrine, 273
  small arms as, 149
  See also Chemical and biological weapons; Nuclear weapons
Webster, William, 189
Welch, Jack, 233–234
White, Theodore, 221, 222–223
Whitman, Christine Todd, 112, 113
Williams, Jody, 146, 148
Wills, Gary, 40
Wilson, Woodrow, 32, 34, 43, 143, 173, 174, 208–209
Winthrop, John, 1, 16, 31, 33, 277
Wirth, Tim, 131
Wolf, Martin, 231, 232, 235, 240
Wolfowitz, Paul, 23, 269, 272, 288
Women's Commission for Refugee Women and Children, 146
Woolsey, James, 105
World Bank, 52, 55, 61, 230
  control of, 234
  creation of, 68, 70, 174
  East Asian Miracle of, 80
World Economic Forum, 230
World Resources Institute, 126
World Trade Center. See September 11, 2001, terrorist attacks
World Trade Organization (WTO), 8, 51, 219, 230, 297–298
  and AIDS, 79
  and China, 258
  creation of, 229
  first major meeting of, 75
World War I, 32, 68, 80, 87–88, 92, 144, 154
  and Palestine, 208
  U.S. entry into, 173
World War II, 24, 62, 95, 123, 186, 249
  and Bretton Woods, 69
  and China, 221, 222
  and European power, 238, 240
  and Japan, 41, 88, 222, 250, 251, 280
  as just war, 174
  and landmines, 144, 145
  nation building after, 67–68
  and oil, 88, 93
  and Palestine, 209
  Pearl Harbor attack in, 88
  United States after, 8, 32, 169, 175, 176, 272
  U.S. policy in, 32

Yeltsin, Boris, 155
Yemen, 158
Young, Don, 129
Yugoslavia, 156, 238–239

Zaga, Mayer, 79
Zaire, 181
Zinser, Aguilar, 160
Zonsheine, David, 206

Contents

INTRODUCTION   4

Where to go	5	Things not to miss	12
When to go	10	Itineraries	20

BASICS   22

Getting there	23	Festivals and events	34
Getting around	25	Sports and outdoor activities	36
Accommodation	29	Culture and etiquette	36
Food and drink	30	Travel essentials	38
The media	34		

THE GUIDE   44

1	Amsterdam	44	4 The north and the Frisian Islands	192
2	Noord-Holland	100	5 The eastern Netherlands	232
3	Zuid-Holland and Utrecht	142	6 The south and Zeeland	272

CONTEXTS   320

History	321	Books	347
Art	337	Dutch	350

SMALL PRINT & INDEX   356